Penguin Random House

Senior Editor Alastair Laing
Senior Art Editor Sara Robin
Managing Editor Esther Ripley
Managing Art Editor Alison Donovan
Editors Sharon Amos, Emma Callery
Designers Tina Vaughan, Kathy Gammon, Vanessa Hamilton, Vicky Read
Illustrator Andy Crisp
Photographer Peter Anderson
Production Editor Ben Marcus
Creative Technical Support Sonia Charbonnier
Production Controller Man Fai Lau
Picture Researcher Jenny Faithfull
Publisher Mary-Clare Jerram
Art Director Peter Luff

US Editors Shannon Beatty, Christine Heilman, Lori Hand
US Consultants Marc Schmidt, Megan Schmidt
US Publisher Mike Sanders

This American Edition, 2017
First American Edition, 2010
Published in the United States by DK Publishing,
345 Hudson Street, New York, New York 10014

A catalog record for this book is available from the Library of Congress.

ISBN 978-1-4654-5699-1

DK books are available at special discounts when purchased in bulk
for sales promotions, premiums, fund-raising, or educational use.
For details, contact: DK Publishing Special Markets, 345 Hudson
Street, New York, New York 10014
SpecialSales@dk.com

Printed and bound in China

IMPORTANT NOTICE
Neither the authors nor the publishers take any responsibility for any
injury or damage resulting from the use of techniques shown or described
in this book. The reader is advised to seek appropriate expert advice
before undertaking electrical work. For all construction work the reader
is advised to wear protective clothing and follow instructions carefully
throughout. Advice on natural remedies in this book is not intended
as a substitute for medical advice and use of them is entirely at the
reader's own risk.

All images © Dorling Kindersley Limited
For further information see: www.dkimages.com

DICK & JAMES STRAWBRIDGE

SELF-SUFFICIENCY
FOR THE 21st CENTURY

Contents

Authors' introduction

We are lucky enough to live on a small farm in a beautiful part of Cornwall in our own valley and half a mile from the sea. Our move to Newhouse Farm was documented in the BBC TV series *It's Not Easy Being Green*, but it was not inspired by television; it was a family decision that was the culmination of years of experimenting and dreaming about the good life.

We have always had an interest in self-sufficiency. Some of Dick's earliest memories are of helping his father in the garden, or collecting mushrooms with his mother; quality time that produced the tasty vegetables he remembers from his childhood. James has always been involved with nature and the garden, going for walks, collecting berries, or digging over the gardens of the many houses we've lived in. Now we both write and work in television. There is still a mortgage to pay, so we have to spend time away from Newhouse Farm, but returning is always calming and makes us smile; it reminds us why we have our small farm.

This book is aimed at everyone who has a desire to be a bit more self-sufficient or to live life more sustainably. There is absolutely no reason not to start today. It doesn't matter where you are living—there is something in this book for you. You can reduce your energy bills, make cheese in any kitchen, grow herbs and tomatoes on any windowsill, and learn more about sustainable living and apply it to your situation. This book is a collection of the information that we have been amassing for years. We don't expect you to jump in and do it all at once, but no matter what stage in your life you are at, we are sure there will be something in here for you.

Don't forget to have fun—if you're not smiling, you're doing it wrong!

Dick & James

SAFETY WARNINGS

While we want you to feel empowered to try many of the things included in this book, we don't want you to take risks, cut corners, or get out of your depth. We use a wide range of sharp implements and power tools in our projects. Make sure you familiarize yourself with them at the outset and feel competent to use them before you start work. Also read through the advice and cautions included here.

Renewable energy options

We've focused on what is possible on a range of sites and showed you the nuts and bolts of our own solutions, but before you consider putting any of this into practice on your property, find out if state or local permits or zoning approvals are needed. Seek advice from and work with a licensed electrician and your energy supplier at all times.

Biofuels and anaerobic digestion

We've shown how we made our reactor and a digester from an assortment of oddments to prove that you don't need expensive custom-built gear. However, we're able to fall back on years of engineering experience. If you have any doubts about your own competence, get some expert help. When dealing with chemicals, heat, and gas, you can't be too careful.

Animal husbandry

Some advice about hygiene: if you have a young family, insist on scrupulous hand-washing after children come into contact with livestock to reduce the risk of *E. coli* infection. Lambing time is especially risky for pregnant women, as contact with newborn lambs or any of the by-products of the birth carries a risk of infection that can cause miscarriage. Partners attending lambing ewes should wear protective clothing and gloves and wash thoroughly to remove potential contamination.

Dairy products

Keep everything you use and your kitchen environment scrupulously clean while you make dairy products. And if you are pregnant, avoid using unpasteurized milk, as products may harbor listeria or campylobacter bacteria.

Making natural remedies

It's always best to seek proper medical advice before you self-treat with home remedies, especially if you are suffering from recurring symptoms or have a serious or long-standing illness. When using tinctures, try small amounts first; also test our salves and creams on a small area of skin before using them to check for allergic reactions. Be especially cautious if you are pregnant or breastfeeding, as some herbs are contraindicated during these times.

NEW WAY TO SELF-SUFFICIENCY

What are the basics for life?

We're lucky that life in the 21st century is easier than it has ever been at any other time in history, but convenience can come at a price, and many people now want to get back to basics. So, what are the basics for life? Food and shelter is the simplest answer, but we are looking for a good quality of life, too, and for that we need comfortable shelter, quality food, and a good amount of pleasure.

Turning dreams into reality

Most people have a dream where their life is very different from how they live now. There are so many things that we would like to do, but time and/or money tends to be the main stumbling block. So work is partly the problem and partly the solution. Should we live to work or work to live? A few of us are able to say that our work is fun, fulfilling, and we would choose to do it even if we weren't being paid. However, the vast majority of us have yet to find a way of living our dream. So what's stopping us?

We've always been struck by John Seymour's idea that he was writing for "dreamers and realists," and we're keen to help dreamers turn their dreams into reality—hopefully sooner rather than later.

Living the dream

Rushing around in our modern world, it's tempting to put convenience before quality. But we have very firm views on what we call "quality" food, and living on our smallholding at Newhouse Farm, growing our own fruit and vegetables, and rearing our own meat, we put this ahead of convenience every time.

Everyone here cooks, and we're lucky that we're all quite good at it. Time spent in our large farmhouse kitchen preparing meals is very sociable; we look in the fridge, see what needs harvesting outside, and then create a menu. There's nothing quite like fresh, quality (there's that word again) produce, enjoyed just after it's been picked and prepared. It may be old-fashioned, but we also still sit down around the table for lunch and supper, which allows everyone to catch up and talk.

Even without the produce of a small farm at your fingertips, quality food is achievable. As you will see in this book, everyone can grow something that they can eat.

Rediscovering local food

Modern transportation systems keep the supermarkets stocked with an abundance of foods, and it's easy

1   2   3   4

to forget what is seasonal and local. Consumers have demanded variety at a reasonable price and the supermarkets have responded; or have supermarkets led and we have followed? Either way, it now seems acceptable for food to travel halfway around the world and then be stored and distributed in the supermarket chain before we get a chance to eat it.

When we buy food, our first choice is local, seasonal, organic produce. If what we need doesn't fit all these criteria, we go for local and seasonal, or seasonal and organic. We have been known to deviate from our principles, but let's not forget Douglas Bader's words: "Rules are for the obedience of fools and the guidance of wise men."

Gimme shelter

Our homes come in many shapes and sizes, and offer comfortable shelter, but we question the definition of "comfort." We've been "ecovating" our old farmhouse for years, aiming for a home that's warm and cozy, and generates very few bills, so that as we grow old we won't have to worry about the escalating cost of water and energy. We believe that to be truly comfortable you need to know you can live within your means, even in an uncertain future.

There are many ways to achieve this. The simplest is to concentrate on reducing the amount of fuel and water you use, and then to find ways of providing the utilities you need. This approach is valid for any home; in fact, we would go further and say it's essential for every home.

The pleasure principle

The final requirement for a good quality of life is enjoyment. We're all different, and we find happiness, peace, harmony—call it what you will—in our individual ways. We've tried many aspects of sustainable living; some we've really enjoyed, others we haven't. Our philosophy is that you should try as many different things as you can and then continue to do those that suit you.

It's important to remember, too, that you don't have to wait until you've bought your ideal property to embark on a more sustainable lifestyle. Start now! The experiences you gain and the fun you have may be the catalyst you need to fulfill your dream of a better life.

1. Collecting rainwater *and deploying it where it's needed makes the best use of this natural resource.* **2. The farmhouse** *in winter is warm and well insulated, and the energy is sourced in a variety of sustainable ways.* **3. Seasonal crops,** *such as strawberries, harvested when they are ripe, taste a hundred times better than early forced crops.* **4. We have fun** *mixing clay for an earth oven.* **5. Local produce** *has a low carbon footprint and helps generate income for small farms like ours.* **6. Wind turbines** *are a dependable source of energy if you live in an exposed area.* **7. Learning new skills** *like basketry is fun and creative.* **8. Home baking** *is one job we really enjoy on cold winter days, when the smell of fresh bread lifts the spirits.*

Self-sufficiency vs. sustainability

A sustainable lifestyle takes planning, preparation, and practice, but to be truly self-sufficient and live off the land means an even bigger commitment. There may be many reasons why you can't fully adopt the good life immediately, but there's nothing to prevent you from pursuing part of that dream right now, regardless or where you live or the size of your property.

ESSENTIAL CONSIDERATIONS

How much time do you have to spend working?
Time spent sitting behind a desk to pay the bills is time that you're not on your land enjoying your chosen lifestyle. However, you have to go into things with your eyes open and accept that to provide sufficient funding for, say, a small hobby farm or an even larger property, it may be necessary to postpone your full commitment to the paradise you have planned.

Where should you live?
Many of us need to be near a workplace, perhaps in an urban setting, for part of our life. If you have no choice where to live, it's important to make the best use of your environment to try out all those things you want to do later. If you're taking the plunge and moving to the country, it's easier and cheaper to find a farm in a remote place away from the modern world, but that also limits your opportunities for paid employment, and usually means you have a very small choice of facilities close by. We liked the idea of being part of a community and felt we needed some of the trappings of 21st-century living, such as good rail and road links, broadband, and cell phone coverage.

How much support do you need to fulfill your dream?
On a farm, there's always more to do than you have time for. Nature is always keen to reclaim any land, so there's an ongoing struggle, which depends on the size of your chosen battlefield. In a rural community you will find lots of local expertise, but that can cost money if you want more than a bit of advice. It's important to assess how fit you are and what you are capable of. One thing's for sure: you'll get in shape in a hurry.

What do we mean by self-sufficiency?
For us, self-sufficiency is a way of life where you endeavor to produce all you need from the resources that are available to you. In the past, such a lifestyle was essential for subsistence farmers; the communication infrastructures we take for granted didn't exist and people had to live on what they could obtain within a few miles of their homes. Communities formed where natural resources were concentrated and people traded their skills and produce to ensure everyone had all they needed to live. It was often a matter of trying to survive rather than having a good quality of life. In many countries this is still the case, but in the developed world today we don't need to do everything ourselves or within the local community. That has some positive benefits, but reaching outside the community, especially across the continents, can have a serious impact on the planet.

What do we mean by a sustainable lifestyle?
Living a sustainable lifestyle means using no more than our fair share of the planet's resources to meet our needs. In the future we can expect energy and food to increase in price as resources become scarcer, and consequently, a degree of self-sufficiency will become essential. Self-sufficiency automatically leads to a sustainable lifestyle, as you try to produce everything you need, but sustainability is achievable without being entirely self-sufficient, if you make sure you are acting as a conscientious consumer.

A better way of doing things
Until a couple of years ago, all books on living sustainably would start by having to justify the need to do it; now, few people outside the US won't acknowledge that we're living beyond the planet's means. The eco-warrior's mantra of "Reduce, Reuse, Recycle" is the best way we can all contribute. Put simply, we have to cut down on the resources that we're using, and stop throwing so much away.

Whether you live on a farm or in an urban loft, you can make your lifestyle more sustainable. Reducing what you use in all aspects of your life also makes sense financially—from saving energy in the home to minimizing unused food that's thrown away, and mending old clothes instead of discarding them. Identifying areas where you can cut down will help you to realize what really is important and what you simply won't miss. Sign up to your local Freecycle website and use it to dispose of items you don't need and acquire things that still have a useful life in them, rather than buying new.

1. Friends and family *help to make light work of a construction job.* **2. Smoke from our woodburner** *floats above the cold air in the valley on a fall morning.* **3. Hard physical work** *is part of our lifestyle, but keeps us fit and feels better than going to the gym.* **4. The good life** *is not all hard work; bubbly elderflower champagne is one of the pleasures.* **5. Onions** *and our intrepid mouse hunter enjoy the warmth of our hoop house.*

How much land do you need?

When we first started out, we were in rented army accommodations with small plots, so we know what it's like to have very little land. We then moved to our own row house, a semi-detached house, and finally onto a small farm with space. We may have been the neighbors from hell, but we tried everything we could think of on each of our properties, from keeping bees to building smokers.

Make the most of what you have

We all wish we had more land, whatever our property size. We'd love space for livestock, woodlands, and even for some natural meadows, but we know that our first priority is to make full use of what we've got. You can have a really productive plot, even in a tiny urban garden, and if you're out at work all day, this may be as much as you can handle in your spare time.

Living in a "normal" house can mean space is an issue if you want to be self-sufficient; but it should not be a major problem if you are aspiring to a sustainable lifestyle. Suburban living doesn't have to be about immaculate lawns and washing the car every weekend—you can be very productive on an average urban or suburban plot: your veggie patch, cloches, greenhouse, hoop house, beehive, and chickens can go a long way to help you achieve a degree of self-sufficiency. In fact, your garden may even make you the envy of your friends and neighbors.

If you live in a city where good public transportation means you don't need a car, you can reduce your demand on finite fuel reserves. There are probably also stores where you can buy local, environmentally sound produce and products. Taking all this into account, you may end up with a lower-impact lifestyle than those with a similar-sized rural property.

Where to acquire more land

If you are using your available space to the fullest, and you have time and energy to take on more land, the next problem is how to get hold of some. The odds are that your local land is expensive, or you may find your ideal plot has been sold, but persevere. Most landowners are not keen to sell, so see if you can rent a fallow or unproductive area from a farmer, and after years—yes, years—of softening him up with boxes of produce, he may give in and decide to sell.

Community gardens

In the UK, we're fortunate to have a formal "allotment" program under which local government has a duty

1

2

3

4

to provide land for residents to grow their own fruit and vegetables. The origins of allotments can be traced back over centuries, but the system as we know it came into being in the late 19th century, when philanthropic Victorians wanted to provide poor people with the chance to grow their own produce, and to stop them from getting drunk in their leisure time.

In the United States, shared land for cultivation usually comes in the form of community gardens, which are on the increase. They tend to be in urban areas, often on reclaimed wasteland, where they provide a valuable space for city-dwellers to grow their own food. Generally run by volunteers, they are also a great way of bringing people together.

Economically hard-hit cities are increasingly making unused land available for community gardens. These programs take a lot of effort to get off the ground and organize, but if there is one near you, it is well worth joining.

Be aware that many community gardens have waiting lists, and when you eventually get a plot, you should expect restrictions on planting trees, erecting fencing, digging a pond, or using the plot for business purposes.

Another way to get your hands dirty is to volunteer on an urban farm, where you can help alleviate hunger in your community while practicing your gardening skills. Or you may be able to find a CSA (community-supported agriculture) work share where you trade a few hours of work every week for discounted produce.

Landshare programs

Landsharing may seem altruistic, but it is practical and many people are happy to allow others to cultivate some of their land. A handful of states have organizations that connect landowners with would-be farmers. Alternatively, there is a very good chance that someone will know who in your area could use a helping hand; for example, an elderly person

who can no longer cope with a large garden and would appreciate a box of veggies in return for use of a plot, or a farmer with some fallow land.

With any luck you'll end up with the extra growing space you need, while landowners benefit from a productively cultivated plot and some produce to sample in the bargain.

1. **Community garden** *plots are in short supply in some areas, but it is still worth joining some waiting lists.*
2. **A productive urban garden** *can be as beautiful as it is bountiful with some flowering fruit and vegetables.*
3. **Large areas of farmland** *may be unavailable or impractical to buy, but you may be able to rent some fallow land from a local farmer.* 4. **If you want cattle** *you will need a few acres of good pasture, and possibly space for a shed for them in winter.* 5. **Fruit trees** *that have been grafted onto dwarf rooting stocks are ideal for growing in pots in a small courtyard garden.* 6. **Before you buy livestock,** *make sure that your property is correctly zoned for the type and number of animals you plan to keep.*

5

6

The cycle of the seasons

We moved to rural Cornwall to live closer to nature, and every day we learn more about the seasons and the nuances of living in our valley. No matter where you live, there is a real opportunity to make the most of each season, to appreciate the variety of local produce available, to observe different wildlife, and to enjoy the changing weather, come rain or shine.

Enjoying seasonal food

With fresh strawberries in summer, warming squash soups over winter, and a turkey at Christmas, we really enjoy the fruits of our labor. Each one offers a real treat and marks the passing of the seasons.

It's equally frustrating, though, to realize that it's May and oysters are out of season until September (the wild ones, not the farmed variety). Or that it's September and yet again we have failed to get our fly rods out and missed the wild trout.

Nothing compares to the taste of local produce in season. Although we're not fully self-sufficient—some things, such as flour, rice, and sugar cane, we can't or won't produce ourselves—we eat extremely well. We grow our food, rear it, harvest it, kill it, forage for it, hunt it, prepare it, cook it—and enjoy every mouthful.

Getting back to nature

We get in touch with our roots in many different ways—we know that sounds a bit "new age," but it is a fair description. Most involve being up close and personal with nature. In fall, for example, there's nothing more impressive than watching a murmuration of starlings gathering before dusk on a clear evening. Seeing wildlife at different times of year outside your front door is very special, so don't miss out. Go for walks or enjoy some feathered company while you work on your plot.

Adjusting to the climate

We live in a changing world and the seasons appear to be changing, too. They still follow one another, but climate change seems to be playing havoc. We get hail in June, floods in July, and long periods of sunshine in January. Nature is responding too—birds nest before their food sources are available, and plants flower early and are then killed by frost.

We've tried to choose the best time of year for certain projects in this book based on our experience, but year after year we are having to adjust to adapt to changes in our Cornish microclimate, as well as globally.

Even though it feels small, Britain has significant natural variations in climate. It is drier in the east than in the west, much colder in the north than in the south, windy at the coast and on mountains, where it is also colder. Valleys have frost pockets and mountains create rain shadows.

Our experience and advice from Cornwall is definitely not "one size fits all." It takes years to learn about the conditions specific to a given geographical location, and you will need to adjust your dates and activities to suit the microclimate in the area you call home.

The seasons at Newhouse Farm

No matter what time of year it is, and whatever the weather, we always find something to enjoy in our valley.

Winter We tend to rely on our stored harvest in winter and supplement outdoor veggies with crops from the greenhouse, geodesic dome, and hoop house. We put the chickens in the hoop house to feed on the pests and leftover soft fruit. We plant trees in unfrozen soil and leave the potatoes to sprout in the potting shed. We maintain our tools, practice indoor crafts, plan projects or study, experiment and research.

Spring At the spring equinox, when the sun is higher, we prepare the vegetable beds and harden off plants we sowed earlier under cover. They can be transplanted when the risk of frost has passed. We also incubate eggs, and hatch and raise chicks, ducklings, and goslings.

Summer The vegetable beds are in full production, giving us time off "to smell the roses" and go to the nearby seaside. We buy five-week-old turkeys to fatten for Christmas and spend time preserving and storing—late summer is filled with making jams, chutneys, and cider.

Fall This is when we harvest crops and clear the land. As turkeys and geese fatten up, we kill and process our pigs to ensure the freezer is full and that new salamis and air-dried hams are hanging for next year.

1. **In early summer** *the runner beans are in flower and squashes are scrambling over the raised beds.* 2. **Late summer** *is a bountiful time when we can sell some of our produce.* 3. **Winter stores** *of apples provide delicious treats months after the harvest.* 4. **Fattening up the turkeys** *in summer and fall reminds us of the pleasures yet to come.* 5. **In late winter** *it's too cold to plant seed outside, but we can sprout potatoes indoors for an early crop.* 6. **Spring** *is a busy time, as we hatch eggs and rear goslings, ducks, and chicks.*

Urban opportunities

In the US, roughly 80 percent of the population lives in urban areas, and whether you see city life as a necessary stage before moving to your rural idyll or you're a confirmed city-dweller, you'll be amazed how easy it is to reduce your carbon footprint. A few small steps—from growing your own salads to reducing the amount of garbage you set out at the curb—can make a big difference.

Make the most of city life

It may come as a surprise, but a sustainable lifestyle can be easier to achieve in an urban setting than in the country. Mass transit systems mean you don't need a car, while densely packed housing tends to be very energy-efficient.

A car uses lots of energy, from the embodied energy used to manufacture it, to the fuel to run it, so using buses and trains is one of the greenest things you can do.

In urban dwellings such as row houses and condominiums, your neighbors' homes serve as a direct form of insulation to reduce heating bills, and smaller spaces require less energy to heat them in the first place.

Energy and waste in the city

Add to your home's energy advantage by insulating your attic and hanging thick curtains to keep heat in. Reduce electricity bills by choosing energy-efficient appliances when it's time to replace a dryer or freezer, and replace light bulbs with energy-saving types. You may also be able to switch to a green energy supplier.

Trying renewables

If you are aspiring to the rural idyll, an urban house or apartment is a long way from your destination, but that doesn't mean that it can't be "en route" to your final dream home. It may be easier to be sustainable in an urban setting where the infrastructure, if selectively used, can reduce the amount of energy needed to support a person or family. That said, it's nearly impossible to be self-sufficient in an urban setting, although there are many things you can do and learn while living in the city.

Saving energy should be your priority, but there may also be scope to try out a couple of renewable options. If you live in a house, check out your roof. If it has a south-facing slope, consider installing a solar thermal system to heat water. Of all the renewables this would be our top priority; it can pay for itself very quickly and even in winter it will capture enough solar energy to preheat your water.

1

2

3

4

Household waste

Composting prevents waste from going into landfills and produces the perfect soil improver for raised beds and containers. In a small garden or on a patio, the most compact option is a worm bin; it produces great compost, plus a potent liquid fertilizer (see page 127). A bokashi tub (see page 104) will compost cooked food and dairy waste. For other items, check out the recycling facilities offered by your municipality so that only the bare minimum goes into the landfill each week.

Save water

Reducing the amount of water you use makes environmental sense and can save you money. Aerated faucets, dual-flush toilets, and water-saving showers, dishwashers, and washing machines all cut water consumption.

If you have a patio or garden, connect a rain barrel to a gutter on the house to catch rainwater. Use it to water the garden and indoor plants.

Growing your own

In a city, outdoor space is always at a premium. You may only have a balcony or windowsill, but however small the area, use it to capacity. FIll window boxes, both outside and inside, with herbs, salad leaves, cherry tomatoes, or chili peppers.

If you don't have anywhere to grow your own, look for community gardens where neighbors grow food on spare local land; you may have to put your name on a waiting list. Or volunteer on a CSA (community supported agriculture) farm.

If you can't grow your own at all, you can still shop seasonally at farmers' markets and buy produce with few associated food miles.

City foraging

Gathering wild foods is easier than you think. Look for fencerow berries along train tracks and bicycle paths or in public parks. Nettle is common in open areas; pick it to brew beer (see page 255).

In the kitchen

Try being a bit more self-sufficient in the kitchen too. How about baking your own bread (see pages 232–235), and making chutney with the green tomatoes left on your patio plants (see pages 236–237)? Churning your own butter or making cheese is fun (see pages 226–229) and gives you a real sense of achievement.

1. Making preserves *to stock the pantry is something we can all do, wherever we live.* **2. Start off plants** *in trays on a sunny windowsill before planting out in pots or raised beds.* **3. Hanging baskets** *are ideal for growing strawberries. Suspend them with copper wire to deter slugs and snails; the wire gives the pests a mild electric shock.* **4. A worm bin** *transforms kitchen waste into compost, takes up minimal space, and you can even grow a zucchini on top.* **5. Grow herbs** *in pots on a patio or on a windowsill.* **6. Use a garden irrigation system** *to water plants in containers.* **7. Small solar PV panels** *may provide useful energy around the garden.* **8. Tomatoes** *can be grown in large pots and baskets.*

5   6   7   8

The urban yard

There are lots of different ways to maximize your use of space, however tiny your plot. Think vertically: grow climbing beans up walls, tie in a grapevine along a trellis, and train fruit trees as space-saving espaliers. Tuck a worm bin into a corner and catch rainwater in a rain barrel. Don't forget wildlife, even in the city. Plant nectar-rich flowers in among vegetables to attract pollinating insects and keep a bird feeder well stocked to encourage birds into your yard that will munch their way through insect pests. If you want to keep livestock, you don't need much space for a couple of chickens in a movable ark, and you'll have the satisfaction of eating your own eggs for breakfast.

Espalier apple trees (2) *take up very little space, and training increases the harvest.*

KEY TO YARD

1	**Tool and potting shed** *(pp.130–131)*
2	**Espalier fruit trees** *(pp.154–155)*
3	**Small lean-to greenhouse** *(pp.112–115)*
4	**Solar panel for irrigation** *(pp.110–111)*
5	**Wall pots for edibles** *(pp.124–125)*
6	**Bee B&B** *(p.123)*
7	**Herb and vegetable bed** *(pp.140–147)*
8	**Cold frame for protection** *(pp.116–117)*
9	**Raised bed for vegetables** *(p.126)*
10	**Climbing plants, such as beans**
11	**Potato bag**
12	**Loft insulation** *(pp.42–43)*
13	**Solar thermal collectors** *(pp.62–63)*
14	**Edibles in windowboxes** *(pp.124–125)*
15	**Bokashi bin** *(p.104)*
16	**Recycling bins** *(pp.92–93)*
17	**Solar dryer** *(pp.244–245)*
18	**Rain barrel** *(p.78)*
19	**Seating area**
20	**Herbs in pots** *(pp.156–157)*
21	**Flowers to attract pollinating insects**
22	**Trellis for climbing plants**
23	**Hanging baskets for edibles** *(pp.124–125)*
24	**Worm bin** *(p.127)*
25	**Compost bins** *(pp.104–106)*
26	**Bed for salads** *(p.143)*
27	**Fig tree for fruit and shade** *(p.151)*
28	**Salad and vegetable bed** *(pp.140–147)*
29	**Small wildlife pond** *(p.123)*
30	**Grapevine** *(p.149)*
31	**Chicken run for fresh eggs** *(pp.188–195)*
32	**Bird feeder close to water supply** *(p.122)*

A solar dryer (17) *uses the sun's energy to preserve foods, such as tomatoes and apple slices, by drying out all the moisture.*

A bee B&B (6) *provides shelter for solitary bees, which are vital for pollinating plants and ensuring a crop.*

A bokashi bin (15) *converts cooked food and dairy scraps into compost—with no unpleasant smells.*

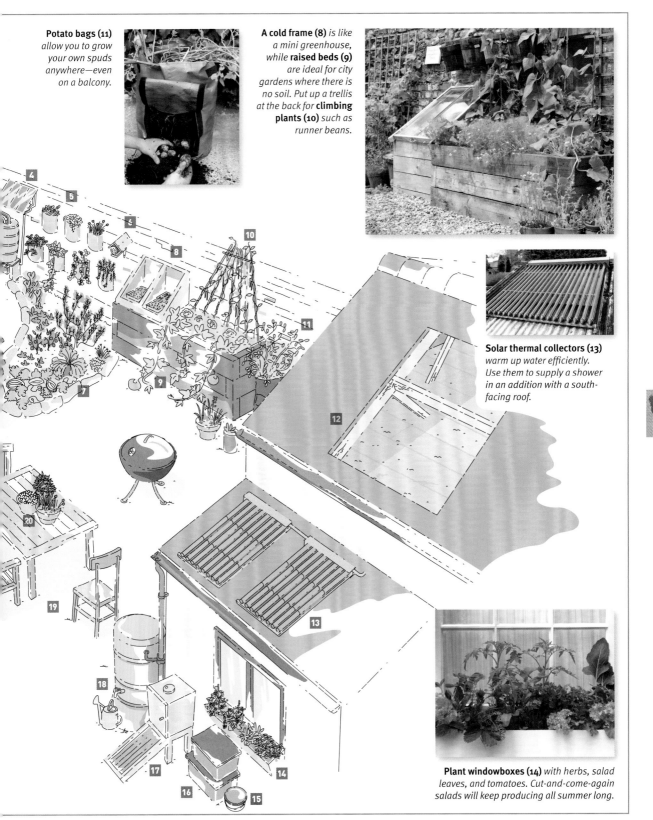

Potato bags (11) *allow you to grow your own spuds anywhere—even on a balcony.*

A cold frame (8) *is like a mini greenhouse, while* **raised beds (9)** *are ideal for city gardens where there is no soil. Put up a trellis at the back for* **climbing plants (10)** *such as runner beans.*

Solar thermal collectors (13) *warm up water efficiently. Use them to supply a shower in an addition with a south-facing roof.*

Plant windowboxes (14) *with herbs, salad leaves, and tomatoes. Cut-and-come-again salads will keep producing all summer long.*

23

Suburban expansion

Yards in the suburbs tend to be larger than city plots, offering greater opportunities to become self-sufficient. In fact, we believe that a well-designed suburban garden can be more productive than a larger plot that's difficult to manage efficiently. A house and garden with hens, fruit trees, a hoop house, and some renewable technologies can provide you with almost everything you need.

Becoming energy-efficient

Wherever you live, your top priority should be to reduce the amount of energy you use. In the suburbs you may be able to take this a step further with "microgeneration technologies," which generate power from the sun, wind, and other renewable sources on a domestic scale. Combine these with energy-saving ideas and there is absolutely no reason why you shouldn't become completely self-sufficient in electricity.

Assessing the possibilities

To find out if your site is suitable for microgeneration of electricity, start by assessing the possibilities offered by your roof (see renewable energy options, pages 58–59).

One practical option could be solar photovoltaic panels (see pages 60–61), which make electricity from sunshine. However, the panels must be positioned on a south-facing roof to operate efficiently.

Heating your home

Using woodburning stoves to heat part or all of your house is feasible in an area where pollution control regulations are not too restrictive (see pages 82–83). Regulations do vary, so you'll need to check with your municipality first. Solar thermal panels use the sun's energy to heat water (see pages 62–63). Like photovoltaic panels, they should be installed on a south-facing roof.

Saving and collecting water

Dual-flush toilets, aerated showers, and low-water-usage washing machines are all essential if you want to reduce water consumption, and a rain barrel is a must for any urban and suburban garden.

You can also expand the ways in which you collect rainwater and how you use it. For example, you could install a rainwater harvesting system, storing runoff from the roof in an underground tank (see pages 76–79). You could then use this water to supply toilets, showers, and other household appliances.

Converting your garage

We have never actually kept our car in the garage: the space is far too valuable. Like many people, we use it as a workshop and a store. For more information about equipping a workshop, see pages 52–53.

It is also possible to turn a corner of your garage or any outbuilding into a biodiesel plant to produce fuel from waste vegetable oil—we find making fuel for our car very empowering (see pages 84–87).

A shed can become more than storage space for tools. Add a lean-to and turn it into a smokehouse for curing foods, or a storeroom for air-dried hams, pumpkins, and homemade beer and wine.

Making the most of your garden

If you have space for either a greenhouse or a small hoop house, you can greatly extend your growing season. They not only protect young plants from frost, enabling you to start crops earlier in the year, but they can also allow you to grow salads and herbs over winter.

Improve the productivity of your greenhouse or hoop house by installing a heat sink (see pages 118–119) to keep it frost free in winter.

In larger yards you'll have room to plant some fruit and nut trees (see pages 150–153). Trees take little tending and, when established, can produce large crops.

Attracting friendly wildlife

Extra space in a suburban yard means more room for wildlife too (see pages 120–123). Dig a shallow pond to encourage frogs—they eat slugs—and attract bees, which pollinate fruit and veggies, with a patch of wildflowers and bee-friendly plants like lavender. A beehive, sited away from busy paths and seating areas, is also possible (see pages 212–213).

Expanding your flock

Hens are easy to keep where regulations allow (see pages 188–195). Keep your flock out of the garden while your crops are growing, but let them roam freely in fall and winter when the garden is at its least productive.

To keep ducks in a suburban yard, you'll need a pond or pool for them, and you'll be unpopular with the neighbors if you keep geese or roosters—they're too noisy.

1. Biodegradable seed pots *are easy to make from recycled cardboard tubes.* **2. Chickens** *are simple to keep if you have a large yard.* **3. Raised beds** *provide productive spaces for growing rows.* **4. Start your crops early** *by sowing seed in a greenhouse.*

The suburban yard

The backyard of a typical suburban house can be turned into an extremely productive plot, with a good-sized vegetable patch, greenhouse, and fruit trees, and plenty of room to house a flock of chickens and to try your hand at keeping bees. There's also space to experiment with making your own biodiesel to fuel your car, and to install a combination of renewable energy systems to reduce your electricity bills.

Compost bins (2) *are best placed in a shady, secluded spot close to the kitchen garden.*

KEY TO YARD

1 **Beds for crop rotation** (pp.108–109)
2 **Compost bins** (pp.104–106)
3 **Willow trees** (pp.278–279)
4 **Compact fruit trees** (pp.150–155)
5 **Beehives** (pp.212–213)
6 **Hoop house for early crops** (p.115)
7 **Trained fruit trees** (pp.150–155)
8 **Shed and smokehouse** (p.130, p.248)
9 **Smoker for smoked food** (pp.250–251)
10 **Bed of medicinal plants** (pp.264–265)
11 **Herb spiral** (pp.158–159)
12 **Chicken pen** (pp.188–195)
13 **Roof-mounted wind turbine** (pp.64–67)
14 **Birdhouse and wildlife area** (pp.120–123)
15 **Woodstore** (p.82)
16 **Windowboxes for herbs** (pp.124–125)
17 **Solar photovoltaic panels** (pp.60–61)
18 **Solar thermal panel** (pp.62–63)
19 **Rainwater storage tank** (pp.78–79)
20 **Biodiesel reactor** (pp.84–87)
21 **Straw-bale extension** (pp.50–51)
22 **Air-source heat pump**
23 **Bokashi bin for meat and dairy** (p.104)
24 **Household recycling bins** (pp.92–93)
25 **Rain barrel to collect rainwater** (p.78)
26 **Pots of herbs and salads** (pp.124–125)
27 **Greenhouse plus heat sink** (pp.118–119)
28 **Worm bin for kitchen waste** (p.127)
29 **Automated irrigation system** (p.110)
30 **Wildlife pond** (p.123)
31 **Earth oven** (pp.252–253)
32 **Pumpkin patch** (p.141)
33 **Mushroom logs** (pp.160–161)
34 **Wildflower garden** (pp.120–122)
35 **Living willow hut** (pp.278–279)
36 **Solar dryer** (pp.244–245)
37 **Seating area**

A wildlife pond (30) *attracts frogs and toads, your allies in the war on slugs.*

A large greenhouse (27) *has space for sensitive plants, from melons to tomatillos, as well as room to start off seedlings under cover.*

Plan vegetable beds (1) *carefully to crop over a long season.*

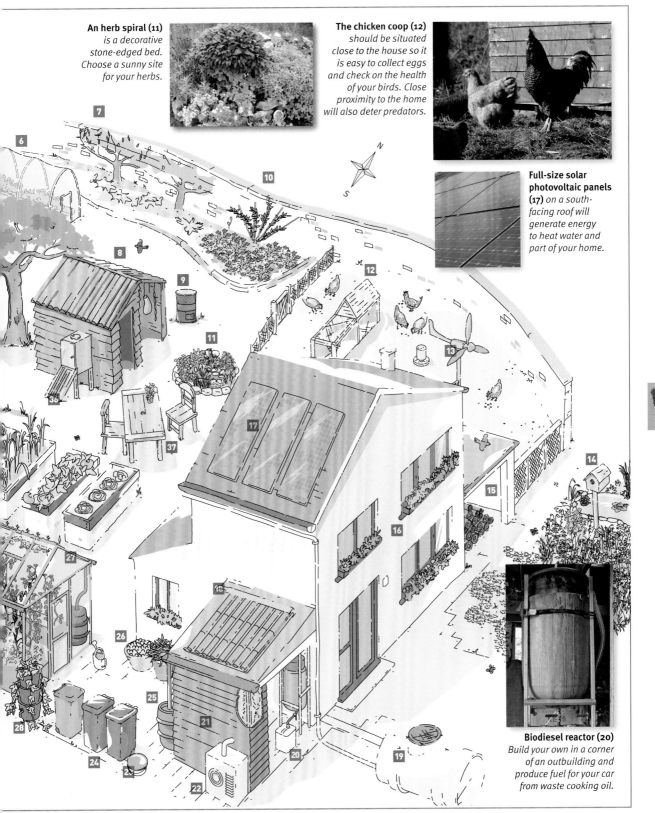

An herb spiral (11) *is a decorative stone-edged bed. Choose a sunny site for your herbs.*

The chicken coop (12) *should be situated close to the house so it is easy to collect eggs and check on the health of your birds. Close proximity to the home will also deter predators.*

Full-size solar photovoltaic panels (17) *on a south-facing roof will generate energy to heat water and part of your home.*

Biodiesel reactor (20) *Build your own in a corner of an outbuilding and produce fuel for your car from waste cooking oil.*

Rural adventure

If you're planning to make the move to a farm, do it with your eyes open. The possibilities are enormous, from growing most of your own food to selling your electricity back to the grid. You'll find that every day brings different challenges, and stamina and a sense of humor come in handy. Life on a small farm is hard work but rewarding, and enormous fun.

Making the most of the land
When you're looking for a property, the physical features of the land will determine what you can do with it. The orientation of the lot determines what you can grow, and whenever we look at a potential site, we automatically check to see how much of the land faces south and is therefore sunny and warm with lots of potential. A south-facing slope is ideal for planting grapevines, for example. If there's a stream running through the property, then using water power to generate electricity will be an option (see pages 68–73). Other beneficial features to look for are woodland to manage for fuel and fencing, and a field to graze sheep or cattle.

The human factor
If you have enough space, time, money, and motivation, you can achieve anything on a small farm, from growing most of your own fruit and vegetables, to rearing your own bacon. Even now, years after we bought our farm, we still talk about using the potential of our land and we're still excited about it.

Earning enough money to live on means you must plan projects carefully, but you have to be flexible. Priorities are overridden on a daily basis—all it takes is the rain to get in where it shouldn't, or an animal that looks unwell—but the work makes us smile. It's satisfying and we're here because we want to be.

Watch out for red tape
There are a number of restrictions that may dampen your enthusiasm, from paying fees for building permits to getting planning permission for erecting a wind turbine. Some towns and counties have an enlightened approach to environmentally friendly projects, but expect complications if you live in a historically significant building, or if your property adjoins residential subdivisions or protected natural areas such as wetlands or nature preserves.

Maximizing energy production
Even in a suburban backyard, it is possible to generate enough electricity to power a home, but on a small farm you may even be in a position to sell some power back to the grid. Analyze your property to work out which options to go for. Take wind speed readings, measure water flow if you have a stream, and note south-facing roofs on barns and outbuildings as well as the house (see pages 56–73).

We were keen to experiment with water power, so six months after we moved in, our waterwheel was up and running, generating enough electricity to light our home.

Heating
Solar thermal panels for hot water are one of the best investments you can make. In winter, boost their effect by using a wood-fired back boiler to heat up the water to a more comfortable temperature (see pages 62–63 and 82–83).

Woodburning stoves are the sensible option in a rural area, especially if your property has woodland that you can coppice for a free supply of carbon-neutral fuel (see pages 182–183).

Dealing with waste water
Most rural properties rely on a septic system to process waste water. You can take this a step further and install a reed bed system to purify gray water (see pages 80–81). The ultimate in human waste management has to be a compost toilet (see page 77). You will save lots of water used to flush a conventional toilet, and the waste decomposes into a useful compost to be used on fruit and nut trees—but not the lettuce!

Increasing your livestock
You need a few acres to keep cattle and sheep, but goats can be kept in smaller spaces—we once had a pair in a large backyard. Pigs need space and can earn their keep by clearing and manuring uncultivated land (see pages 200–209).

Growing fodder for animals
Once you have a few chickens, goats, and a pig or two, it's easy to run up a sizable feed bill. Reduce it by growing animal fodder crops (see pages 176–179). As well as corn, kale, and fodder beets, try sunflowers. Feed pigs the leaves and stems, and you can enjoy the seeds.

1. **Install a waterwheel** *if you have a fast-running stream on your land.*
2. **Pigs rototill the ground** *for you as well as making bacon.* 3. **Keep hens** *and you'll have a ready source of fresh eggs.*
4. **A woodburning stove** *supplies free heat if you have woodland.* 5. **Large veg beds** *and fruit trees can cut food bills.*

The small farm

With more space to play with, you can keep a wider range of animals and grow the crops to feed them. Growing crops under cover on a large scale, combined with successional sowing and crop-storage systems, will let you grow and eat your own food nearly all year round. And you'll have scope for different renewable technologies.

Ducks (5) *such as these Indian Runners should have access to a large pond.*

KEY TO FARM

1 **Bamboo for garden canes** *(p.178)*
2 **Ram pump to supply water tank** *(pp.74–75)*
3 **Grapevines, tea, and hops** *(p.149, p.179)*
4 **Spring plus dual-powered pump** *(p.79)*
5 **Duck enclosure with pond** *(pp.198–199)*
6 **Netted strawberries** *(p.150)*
7 **Compost bins** *(pp.104–106)*
8 **Water tank to feed hoop house** *(pp.114–115)*
9 **Cold frame** *(pp.116–117)*
10 **Greenhouse with heat sink** *(pp.118–119)*
11 **Fruit cages** *(p.152)*
12 **Beds for crop rotation** *(pp.108–109)*
13 **Pig enclosure** *(pp.200–203)*
14 **Waterwheel and aqueduct** *(pp.72–73)*
15 **Fodder crops** *(pp.176–179)*
16 **Turkey enclosure** *(pp.196–197)*
17 **Woodland** *(pp.182–183)*
18 **Beehives** *(pp.212–213)*
19 **Mushroom logs** *(pp.160–161)*
20 **Goose enclosure** *(pp.198–199)*
21 **Fruit and nut orchard** *(pp.150–155)*
22 **Grid-linked wind turbine** *(pp.64–67)*
23 **Geodesic dome** *(p.114)*
24 **Medicinal garden and wildlife area** *(p.265)*
25 **Sheep and cattle area** *(pp.204–211)*
26 **Pollarded willows** *(pp.278–279)*
27 **Chicken enclosure** *(pp.188–195)*
28 **Solar dryer and raised bed** *(p.244, p.126)*
29 **Woodstore** *(p.82)*
30 **Recycling bins and worm bin** *(pp.92–93, p.127)*
31 **Herb spiral** *(pp.158–159)*
32 **Earth oven and smoker** *(p.252, p.250)*
33 **Reed bed system** *(pp.80–81)*
34 **Rainwater storage tank** *(pp.78–79)*
35 **Solar thermal panels on roof** *(pp.62–63)*
36 **Ground-source heat pump**
37 **Grid-linked solar PV panels** *(pp.60–61)*
38 **Workshop and hay shed** *(pp.52–53, p.180)*
39 **Biodiesel reactor in outbuilding** *(pp.84–87)*
40 **Compost toilet** *(p.77)*
41 **Root cellar** *(p.181)*

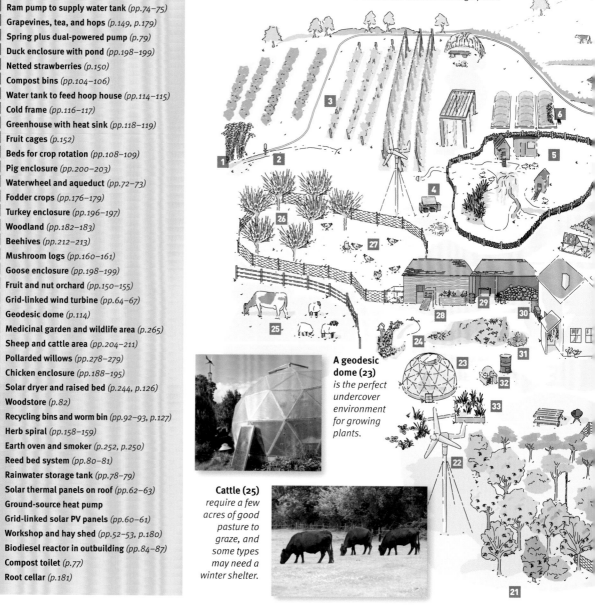

A geodesic dome (23) *is the perfect undercover environment for growing plants.*

Cattle (25) *require a few acres of good pasture to graze, and some types may need a winter shelter.*

A hoop house (8) *extends the growing season so that you can pick salad leaves in winter and start off artichoke seedlings ready to plant out for an early crop.*

N
S

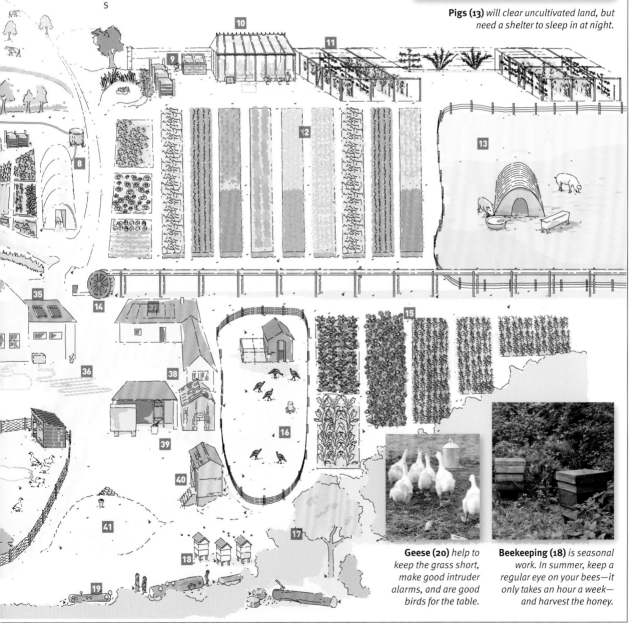

Pigs (13) *will clear uncultivated land, but need a shelter to sleep in at night.*

Geese (20) *help to keep the grass short, make good intruder alarms, and are good birds for the table.*

Beekeeping (18) *is seasonal work. In summer, keep a regular eye on your bees—it only takes an hour a week— and harvest the honey.*

31

IN THE HOUSE No matter what sort of home you live in—be it large or small, townhouse or farmhouse—you'll find that it's possible to reduce your energy usage and save a lot of money in the process. Whether you plan to build your dream home or simply want to renovate an existing property, this chapter will help you understand how your home actually works and suggest possible ways to make it more energy-efficient. We'll also fire your imagination with some more radical options for green builds...

Taking stock

Most homes were designed before the idea of sustainable living was taken seriously, and only the newest homes built over the last few years are designed to truly conserve energy. However, new or old, you can make your house more environmentally friendly and save lots of cash by reducing your use of gas, electricity, and water, and making a few simple changes to your lifestyle.

TAKE AN ENERGY AUDIT

Assess your energy consumption and bills by taking an audit of different areas in your house, using this checklist. Then read this chapter and see where savings can be made.

EXTERNAL AND BUILDING INFRASTRUCTURE
- Lights
- Faucets
- Roof and attic
- Windows and doors
- Chimneys
- Gutters and rainwater
- South-facing walls, roof, and windows

LIVING, DINING, AND BEDROOMS
- Energy usage
- Standby usage
- Lights
- Windows and curtains
- Doors
- Radiators/heat registers

BATHROOM
- Energy usage
- Standby usage
- Lights
- Windows and curtains
- Doors
- Faucets
- Toilets
- Showers
- Bathtub
- Hot water
- Gray water
- Radiators/heat registers

KITCHEN
- Appliance energy usage
- Standby usage
- Lights
- Windows and curtains
- Doors
- Faucets
- Refrigerator and freezer
- Exhaust fan
- Hot water
- Gray water
- Radiators/heat registers

Making the most of your house

If you are about to build a new property, be sure the performance of the structure is super-efficient. For the rest of us, it's a matter of getting the best from the house we have. Our farmhouse is hundreds of years old and was made from materials that were available at the time, but it was built to last and in places our walls are over 4 ft (1.2 m) thick, so it has some amazing insulation properties.

Your most important, and free, source of energy is the sun, so it's worth checking where it rises and sets, and for how long it falls on windows, walls, and patio doors, as well as the garden. You will then know where to install solar panels and thermal systems, or make windows larger to capture more of this free heat (see pages 60–63).

Reducing your consumption

Your best starting point is to get out all your utility bills to see where you are hemorrhaging cash. Draw up a simple chart, noting the cost of each monthly bill for heating, electricity, water, and transportation, as well as the unit price. This will then highlight how much money you are paying, and areas where savings can be made. Reducing your consumption is always the first step, before you start any big "green" projects.

The following ideas will instantly reduce bills and energy consumption.

Heating Turn it down one degree and reduce your bill by ten percent. Pull the curtains at night and replace bottom sweeps on doors. Turn the heat down for a period before you go to bed; a well-insulated house will stay warm. Install reflectors behind old radiators so that they heat the room, not the walls. Make them by sticking foil to pieces of cardboard.

Electricity Use low-energy bulbs and turn lights off when not in use. Turn the computer, TV, and other equipment off completely—never leave them on standby, which costs as much as leaving a couple of light bulbs on all night. Switch to a green electricity plan that will supply your needs from renewable sources.

Household tasks Only use your washing machine and dishwasher when you have a full load, and dry clothes outside for free. Use pressure cookers—they're fast, very energy-efficient, and economical.

Water Take showers not baths, but don't use shower booster pumps that use lots of water. Install a water saver in the toilet tank (see page 77).

Lifestyle Take the bus, bicycle, or walk whenever possible. When shopping, think about the miles your purchases have traveled and what they are made from. Look for local, seasonal, organic products, or those labeled "fair trade," which help to protect workers in poorer countries.

1. Sunlight *entering your windows can be harnessed and used to heat areas of the house.* **2. Solar PV panels** *installed on south-facing roofs can heat the water in your home.* **3. Hang laundry outside** *to dry—it's free and makes clothes smell really fresh.* **4. Don't leave faucets running** *when washing; fill the sink instead.* **5. Locally produced goods** *reduce transportation costs and pollution and help support small businesses.*

Conserving energy at home

We have become dependent on a huge range of appliances in our homes, from essential items like refrigerators and washing machines to laptops and sound systems, and they all need electricity. In addition, most of us use lots of energy to keep our homes warm in winter. But adopting energy-saving strategies makes financial and ecological sense, whatever your house size or lifestyle.

Don't waste heat

Heating or cooling your home takes a lot of energy, so obviously it pays to install an efficient system. However, even more fundamental is to ensure that your system doesn't waste the heat you are using.

One way of reducing waste is to draftproof your house. You wouldn't have the heating on in your home when the windows are open, and it makes equally little sense to let all the heat escape through lots of gaps. Minimize this loss by weather-stripping doors and windows (there are even systems to reduce the wind rattling through old sash windows).

You also don't need to pay for new windows to have a warmer home; thick curtains that you can close every evening are really effective at keeping the heat in.

Remember, too, that not all of the house needs to be heated to the same temperature. Thermostatic valves on radiators or zoned central heating will save energy in bedrooms or rooms that are seldom in use.

Energy-efficient appliances

If you want to save money on your electricity bill, make sure you buy an energy-efficient product when you replace any of your household appliances. Be sure to look at the manufacturer's label (see box opposite) to check a product's energy efficiency. It often pays to spend more for an efficient appliance, such as a freezer or refrigerator, that over its working lifetime will generate significant energy savings, without compromising performance.

Comparing running costs

To calculate the running costs of an appliance, multiply its consumption (given in kWh on the label) by the price you pay for electricity, and then multiply again by the number of hours you use the appliance.

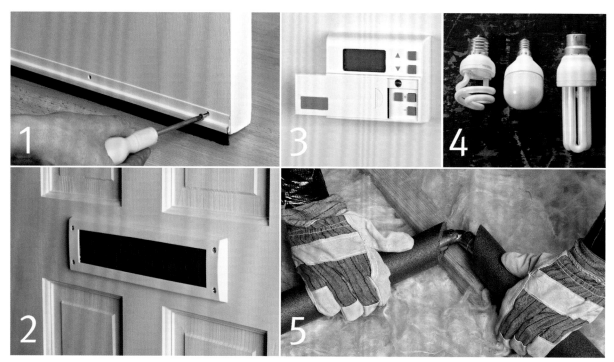

1. **Add door sweeps** to all external doors to keep your home warm.   2. **Draft-proof a letterbox** with brush strips.
3. **Programmable thermostats** and zoned central heating allow you to heat rooms to different temperatures and save energy costs.   4. **Low-energy light bulbs** are available in options to suit all fixtures.   5. **Insulate pipes** in a cold attic to reduce heat loss.

A plug-in monitor is handy when working this out. Then when you go shopping for a new washing machine, for example, you can make a proper comparison.

▪ **The manufacturer's energy label** on a new appliance shows how much electricity it uses under standard operating conditions. It is measured in kWh per year for refrigerators and freezers or kWh per cycle for washing machines and dishwashers.

▪ **Laundry and dishwasher labels** also have ratings for washing, spin, and/or drying performance.

Choose low-energy light bulbs

At Newhouse Farm the light bulbs in our lighting circuit are powered by the waterwheel (see pages 72–73), but that doesn't mean we aren't careful about conserving our own energy. We were amazed by the difference it made when we switched to using low-energy light bulbs rather than old-fashioned incandescent ones.

Many modern homes are equipped with halogen lights mounted on the ceilings, mainly because they look good—but they give off significant amounts of heat, like incandescent bulbs. And any light bulb that emits heat is wasting lots of energy doing this, rather than creating light.

There are now low-energy compact fluorescent lamps (CFLs) that fit into any light socket; some of these are even compatible with dimmer switches. Replacing just one 100W incandescent bulb with a CFL that provides the same light for just 20W will reduce the energy usage of that light fixture by 80 percent.

LED savings

Light-emitting diodes (LEDs) are the most energy-efficient option of all. An LED uses about 4W to produce as much light as a 50W halogen bulb and can last for up to 25 years. Check out the numbers:

▪ 10 lights with halogen bulbs in a kitchen use 50W each. If they're on for three hours in the morning and five in the evening, they're using electricity for 8 hours every day.

▪ 500W for 8 hours is 4 kWh of electricity a day. A kWh is a kilowatt hour, or 1,000 watts for an hour.

▪ If you are paying 12¢ per kWh, you are spending 48¢ per day, or about $175 per year, to light the kitchen.

▪ Replacing the halogen bulbs with LEDs at approximately 4W each reduces energy consumption to 40W for 8 hours, or 0.32 kWh per day.

▪ That means you will pay roughly 4¢ per day, or $14.60 per year.

Replacing your halogen light bulbs with LEDs will therefore save you more than $150 per year—and that's just in the kitchen!

ENERGY LABELS

Energy labels rate products in terms of energy efficiency. They show how much electricity is used under standard operating conditions. Labels should be shown on all refrigeration and laundry appliances, dishwashers, electric ovens, and light-bulb packaging.

In Australia, *energy labels feature a star rating for quick assessment and also show annual energy consumption based on average usage.*

In the US, *the Energy Star label means that a product has met, or even exceeded, the government's stringent energy-efficiency requirements.*

In the EU, *energy labels are used to rate products from A* (the most efficient/least energy used), down to G (the least efficient/most energy used).*

QUICK FIXES

These ideas don't cost much to implement, but will make a sizable difference to your bills.

▪ Install **thermostatic radiator valves** or zoned thermostats for central heating.
▪ Change **incandescent bulbs** to low-energy bulbs, CFLs, or LEDs.
▪ Buy a **wireless electricity monitor** to keep track of how much energy you are using. This will provide an exact reading and show you where savings can be made.

▪ **Insulating** your hot-water tank, and the pipes around it, will pay for itself in a couple of months—and the savings will continue long after that.
▪ If your water heater is more than 15 years old, replacing it with a **new efficient water heater** can generate significant energy savings for you. Consider a demand (tankless or instantaneous) water heater, which heats water as it's needed, reducing standby energy losses associated with storage water heaters.

Using passive solar gain

The sun is a fantastic source of free heat that can be harnessed very simply to warm our homes, using a technique called "passive solar gain." We refer to it as passive because there are no moving parts, switches, motors, or control systems; we let nature do all the work. The idea is to collect and store heat when the sun is shining, and to radiate it back after the sun has gone down.

Collecting the heat

The sun's heat energy passes easily through glass and warms the room beyond, which means windows make ideal solar collectors. For maximum capture of solar energy, a house needs large south-facing windows. In a new build this is easy to achieve by siting the house accordingly. Even if it can't be oriented precisely north– south, you can still harness a good percentage of the sun's energy (see box below).

If you want to adapt an existing house, there are several options. You can install bigger windows on south-facing walls, or replace the glass in existing windows (see box opposite), and consider laying a stone floor in south-facing rooms. A black floor is the most efficient at absorbing and storing heat, but any solid floor can act as the main heat sink—the material that stores warmth.

Warm air rises because it is less dense. By using this effect—thermo-siphoning—and installing a system of vents, you can move air warmed by the sun around your house. The most efficient way to do this is with a heat

Capturing the sun's heat

Using solar energy is a constant balancing act between capturing enough heat during the day and preventing it from escaping at night, while ensuring the house doesn't overheat in summer.

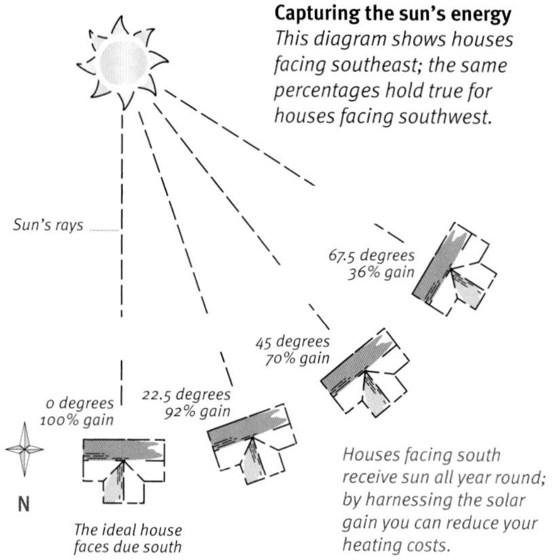

Capturing the sun's energy
This diagram shows houses facing southeast; the same percentages hold true for houses facing southwest.

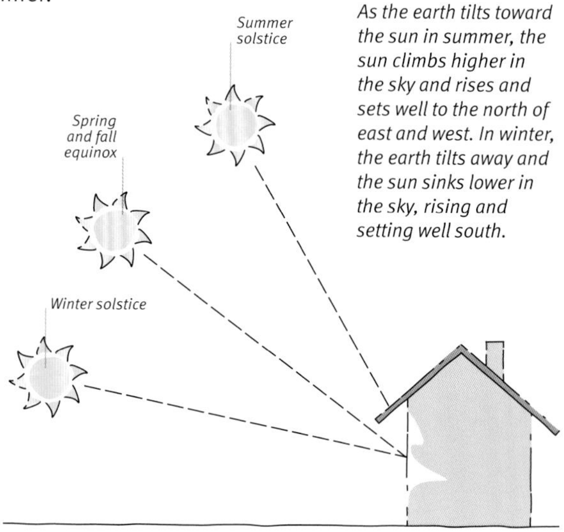

Sun's rays

67.5 degrees
36% gain

45 degrees
70% gain

22.5 degrees
92% gain

0 degrees
100% gain

N

The ideal house faces due south

Houses facing south receive sun all year round; by harnessing the solar gain you can reduce your heating costs.

Summer solstice

Spring and fall equinox

Winter solstice

Seasonal variation
As the earth tilts toward the sun in summer, the sun climbs higher in the sky and rises and sets well to the north of east and west. In winter, the earth tilts away and the sun sinks lower in the sky, rising and setting well south.

The ideal position for passive solar gain

A house that faces due south will be most efficient at capturing the sun's energy, but even if your house is 45° off south you will still be able to harness 70 percent of the possible solar gain.

Keeping cool in summer

A roof overhang shades windows in summer but doesn't affect heat gain in winter when the sun is lower in the sky. Deciduous trees similarly allow light through in winter and block out summer sun.

recovery ventilation (HRV) system (see pages 42–45), though it's not strictly passive as it uses a pump.

Optimize your windows

The type of glass in your windows determines how efficiently you can capture solar energy, and it is assessed in two ways:

■ **Solar control** refers to how much of the sun's energy passes through the glass and into the room. The solar heat gain coefficient (SHGC) compares the total amount of energy that passes through the glass to the amount of solar energy actually striking the glass. An SHGC of 0.86 means that 86 percent of the solar energy hitting the window enters the room. The lower the SHGC, the less energy entering the house.

■ **Thermal control** refers to the insulating value of glass. It measures the rate at which heat is lost from a warm room to the cool air outside. Up to 60 percent of heat loss in a well-insulated home is through the windows, but thermal control can be improved by coating the surface of the glass with a microscopic layer of metal or metallic oxide. This is known as a "low-emissivity coating" (see box below). The disadvantage is that the coating reduces the SHGC of the glass, so that less energy is absorbed in the first place.

Connect a sunroom *to an HRV system to pump air warmed by the sun around the house during the day. Create a heat sink with a dark stone floor, and it will move the stored heat in the evening, too.*

Storing the heat

The materials for a heat sink range from concrete or masonry walls and floors to tanks of water (see page 118). In the average room, the heat sink will be the floor. Walls are a less likely option, unless your house has solid stone walls or eco-walls designed to store heat (see page 48). A material's capacity to store heat is known as its "thermal mass"; the more heat your heat sink stores, the bigger its thermal mass.

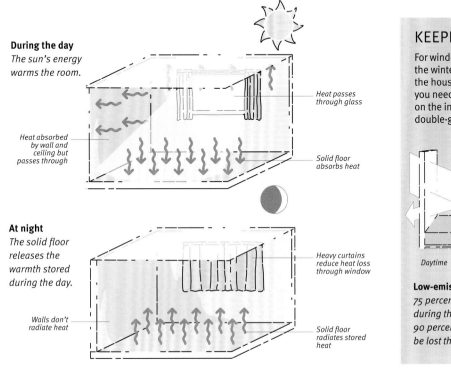

During the day
The sun's energy warms the room.

Heat absorbed by wall and ceiling but passes through

Heat passes through glass

Solid floor absorbs heat

At night
The solid floor releases the warmth stored during the day.

Walls don't radiate heat

Heavy curtains reduce heat loss through window

Solid floor radiates stored heat

KEEPING HEAT IN

For windows that capture heat in the winter and retain heat inside the house as the air outside cools, you need a low-emissivity coating on the inside pane of glass in a double-glazed unit.

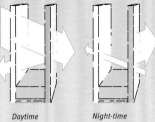

Daytime   *Night-time*

Low-emissivity coating *allows 66–75 percent of heat energy to enter during the day, then reflects back 90 percent of the heat that would be lost through the glass at night.*

Improving home infrastructure

Our houses vary hugely in design, size, and the materials they are made from. In the UK some of the housing stock is ancient and, in many cases, the buildings are a long way from being efficient to run and heat. That said, they have stood the test of time, and it is usually much greener to slightly modify an older building than to sink lots of energy into a new build.

Improving thermal properties

Harnessing the potential of your home so you can live as sustainably as possible means using what you have to the best of your ability.

Not surprisingly, the first thing to do is reduce the amount of energy it takes to run your home. Improving its thermal properties is the logical solution to reducing your energy consumption. There are two main areas involved: insulating, with the minimum amount of thermal bridging; and improved airtightness—drafts mean lost heat.

Thermal bridging

The purpose of insulation is to slow down the movement of heat; the higher the conductivity of a material, the more quickly heat can move through it. Insulation materials are rated by their resistance to heat transfer, the R value. The higher the R value, the lower the heat transfer.

When different materials with different thermal conductivities make up a wall or ceiling, the heat will flow through the different materials at different rates. Areas that have poor insulation or where the materials allow lots of heat to flow through them are called "thermal bridges."

An attic hatch tends to be a thermal bridge. Walls and, more specifically, the seams between walls and the ceiling, need to be carefully thought about, to ensure that they are airtight.

If you decide you need to add more insulation, you must fix all the thermal bridges and drafts or your investment will be wasted.

Remember that the first layer of insulation is the most effective. The law of diminishing returns dictates that each additional layer of insulation is less effective than the previous layer.

Superinsulation

It is now possible to insulate a property so that you should not need any heating in it at any time of the year. All the heat you require can be produced by other sources in the house. For example, humans produce about 100 watts of heat per day. Even your cat and dog give off heat—and how about the surplus heat given off every time you boil an egg? If you want to go down the path of superinsulation, heating predominantly by intrinsic heat sources (that is, waste heat

INSULATION MATERIALS

It is fair to say that any insulation is good insulation. However, there is a big difference in the raw materials used to make it, and this difference is reflected in the price, with eco-friendly options at the top of the scale.

If you can afford the more expensive, environmentally friendly insulation, that's great. But if you are put off by the price, we would encourage you to get whatever you can afford and install it as soon as you can. Any insulation is better than no insulation. Of all the eco-projects you can possibly undertake at home, insulating provides the best return and will save you the most energy.

Insulation options
Recycled materials that can be turned into insulation include plastic bottles spun into fleece, recycled denim, newspaper waste, and sheep's wool that is too coarse for knitting and weaving. Wool is naturally fire-resistant (no chemical treatment necessary), won't go moldy, and is completely safe to handle—no masks or gloves needed—making it much more suitable for DIY.

Insulation for every situation *From left: expanded foam for pipework, a blanket for a hot water tank, a large roll of sheep's-wool attic insulation, recycled plastic insulation, and foil reflectors for radiators.*

generated by appliances and the body heat of the occupants), with very small amounts of backup heat, you must address every area where you can possibly be losing heat. Solutions include:

▨ Very thick insulation under floors, on walls, and under roofs.

▨ Detailed insulation where walls meet roofs, foundations, and walls.

▨ Airtight construction, especially around doors and windows.

▨ A heat recovery system to provide fresh air (see page 44).

▨ No large windows.

Adding superinsulation to an older house may involve building new exterior walls to allow more space for insulation. You must install a vapor barrier to prevent condensation and possible mold and mildew. A vapor barrier should be no farther out than a third of the R value of the insulated portion of the wall. This way, the vapor barrier will not usually fall below the dew point, and condensation will be minimized. Alternatively, an interior retrofit will preserve the external look of the building, but room sizes will suffer.

Airtightness

It's surprising how drafty the majority of older homes are. Unless houses have been built to exacting standards and tested, there is a very good chance the airtightness will be less than desirable. The "build tight—ventilate right" concept has been promoted since the 1980s and there are standards set for new builds that specify maximum air permeability to prevent uncontrolled air leakage. See the box for how to assess your home, and likely areas that will need draftproofing.

Assessing airtightness

Reducing air permeability is a cost-effective way of improving energy efficiency. You can hire a specialty company to run a controlled building air-permeability test to measure the performance of your home, but you probably have a good idea where the problem areas are. Fortunately, they can easily be resolved with simple, inexpensive forms of draftproofing. Here are the main weak spots in a house.

Air leakage not only wastes energy, it allows warm, moist air to flow into cooler areas, resulting in condensation.

Draftproof crucial areas
Use brush strips and foam-backed tape to seal windows and doors. Make sure holes are filled where pipes and cables pass through the walls.

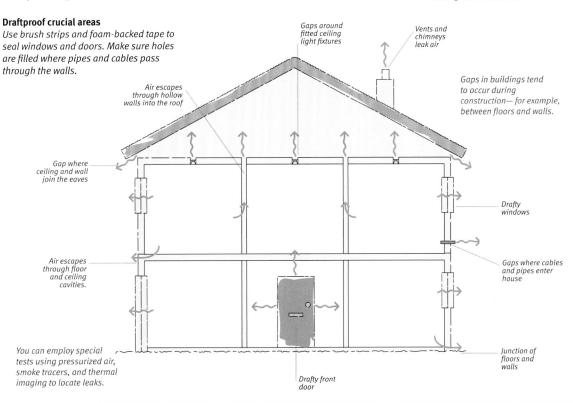

Gaps around fitted ceiling light fixtures

Vents and chimneys leak air

Gaps in buildings tend to occur during construction— for example, between floors and walls.

Air escapes through hollow walls into the roof

Gap where ceiling and wall join the eaves

Drafty windows

Air escapes through floor and ceiling cavities.

Gaps where cables and pipes enter house

You can employ special tests using pressurized air, smoke tracers, and thermal imaging to locate leaks.

Junction of floors and walls

Drafty front door

The principles of heat recovery

The idea behind the heat recovery ventilation (HRV) system is very simple. Your house has warm areas, warm wet areas, and cooler areas. All you have to do is get rid of the moisture and take some of the heat from the warm parts and pass it to the cold parts. You may not find it as warm as central heating, but the temperature should be comfortable.

A heat recovery unit *installed in an attic. The pipes running to and from the unit are insulated to prevent heat loss.*

How it works

A system of ducts connects the extractor vents from the warm areas to a heat recovery unit. A roof vent draws in fresh air, which is warmed and forced through another set of pipes to supply warmed fresh air to the cooler areas. Meanwhile, the stale air is vented to the outside. Heat recovery is very efficient: well over 90 percent of the heat should be kept in the house.

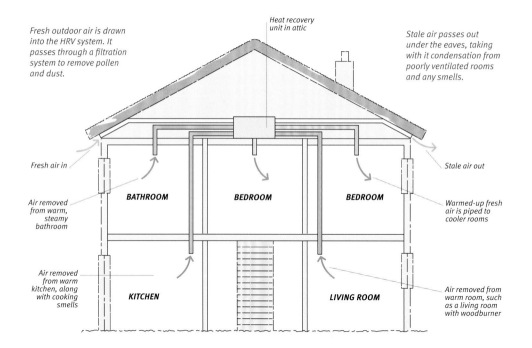

Fresh outdoor air is drawn into the HRV system. It passes through a filtration system to remove pollen and dust.

Heat recovery unit in attic

Stale air passes out under the eaves, taking with it condensation from poorly ventilated rooms and any smells.

Fresh air in

Stale air out

Air removed from warm, steamy bathroom

BATHROOM

BEDROOM

BEDROOM

Warmed-up fresh air is piped to cooler rooms

Air removed from warm kitchen, along with cooking smells

KITCHEN

LIVING ROOM

Air removed from warm room, such as a living room with woodburner

How warm is warm?
Hundreds of years ago, the people who lived in our farmhouse would not have expected it to be warm, but this is the 21st century and we want to be comfortable. There's an ongoing battle at Newhouse Farm as to the exact technical definition of "comfortable."

MOVING HEAT AROUND THE HOUSE

At Newhouse Farm we have four woodburners downstairs. Extraction vents and pipes distribute their heat upstairs to the bedrooms. But a system can work using other heat sources; for example, using the warmth generated in a busy kitchen to warm a living room.

Traditional homes

Living in a historic building has its pluses and minuses. Newhouse Farm has lots of character, and we are very aware of being custodians of our heritage, but we are also restricted as far as how much we can disrupt the fabric of the building. The historical preservation orders on the building mean we need permission to make changes, which affects how we can improve the building's thermal properties.

Airtightness vs. breathing

Airtightness as a way of conserving energy appears contrary to an old building's need to "breathe" to stay dry. And when we arrived at Newhouse Farm, moisture was certainly an issue. Somehow an earlier owner had managed to install double-glazed windows, so the rattling sash windows you would expect in an old building—and that would have provided some ventilation—were nearly all missing. (We are gradually replacing the PVC windows with wooden, double-glazed ones, with special sash seals to reduce the drafts.)

So our method of letting the house breathe, without losing heat, was to install a whole-house ventilation and heat recovery system, which has been a triumph (see box opposite). The air-flow system stops moisture from building up, while the heat recovery unit minimizes heat loss and actually distributes heat from warm rooms to cooler areas of the building.

Accepting what you've got

With an old building, it is necessary to just accept it for what it is. Stone and slate have been used as building materials for centuries, and trying to calculate their R value can be meaningless. A thick rubble wall will have very good insulation value provided it is solid. However, all old

Traditional buildings *around the globe were built from local materials, which means their environmental impact is low.* **1. Wooden shingles** *on a house in New England.* **2. Stone cottages** *in a Cotswolds village, UK.* **3. Timber framing** *in Alsace, France.* **4. Wooden** *colonial houses in the Philippines.*

SETTING RENOVATION PRIORITIES

Anyone renovating a home faces a lot of decisions. Here's how we prioritize.

Draw up a list of jobs and rate them as urgent or important. Arrange them using this diagram, to work out which jobs are both urgent and important—a leaky roof falls into this category. Do those jobs now to the best of your ability. Then tackle important tasks before they become urgent. If you let them drag on until they're in the top corner, you spend your time firefighting rather than working to a plan.

	IMPORTANT	
	DO WELL ENOUGH TO SATISFY YOU NOW	DO NOW TO THE BEST OF YOUR ABILITY
	DON'T WORRY AND DON'T FEEL GUILTY ABOUT IGNORING	MAKE A PLAN AND DO PROPERLY WHEN YOU CAN
		URGENT

45

rubble-stone walls have cavities and it is by no means certain what material is inside the core. Even if you were permitted to improve the performance of the walls on the outside, you would undoubtedly change the character of the building. As the rooms of many older, more modest buildings are so small, it is not really viable to insulate on the inside. Sometimes it is best to accept that older buildings were not meant to be so warm you can walk around in your underwear.

Green buildings

If you decide to build a sustainable home, we think the only limitations you have are your imagination, money, and local planners. Each of these will be an issue, so you may as well reconcile yourself to that fact.

As the earth's resources become scarcer, it is important to reassess the ways that we use energy and materials. Environmental impact and, very importantly, running costs will soon be critical factors in designing new buildings.

We can learn from traditional methods. Do we have to build from materials that have been shipped halfway around the world, using large amounts of energy in the process? Or could we take the trouble to find locally produced materials that could do the job as well, if not better? Here are some ideas:

■ **Use wood** from trees grown locally, or at least sustainably.

■ **Source natural materials** that do not rely on high-energy processing. For example, try sheep's-wool insulation.

■ **Avoid wood preservatives** and certain paints to remove the need for additives made from toxic chemicals.

■ **Specify durable lumber** that does not need decorating at all—rather than repainting every few years.

■ **Consider a green roof** (see box opposite). It is insulating, attractive, and reduces your carbon footprint.

We are wary of statistics, but it is obvious that learning to build and live sustainably is becoming more of an issue, and it has been shown that buildings consume some 40 percent of the world's total energy and about 16 percent of the water.

Designing for efficiency

In new construction, the cost of extra insulation and the wall framing needed to contain it can be offset by removing the need for a dedicated central heating system, for example.

But there is a more fundamental calculation required. Whole-life costs also need to be taken into account. If you have a choice of two similar-sized properties and one has bills that will consume about 5–10 percent of your net income (this will obviously fluctuate from year to year due to supply problems, natural disasters, or geopolitical events), and the other has negligible bills, which one would you rather live in? We have an aversion to giving lots of our hard-earned cash to the utility companies, so that question is a no-brainer!

Think about shapes

We've become very used to houses being boxes. Why? The obvious reason is they're easy to build. But for an object to have the smallest surface area—which will minimize heat loss—it should be spherical.

1. The first environmentally friendly housing development *in the UK—Beddington Zero Energy Development (BedZED). Homes are made from reclaimed or natural materials.* **2. Earth shelters** *in New Mexico are made from rammed earth and car tires (see pages 48–49).* **3. A zero-carbon house** *in Kent, UK, needs no fossil fuels for heating. Its vault shape gives it high thermal mass.*

SEDUM ROOFS

Green roofs have been standard practice in many countries for thousands of years. Their insulating properties are used in the cold climates of Scandinavia to help retain heat and in African countries to keep buildings cool.

What you should know

Sedum roofs are a mixture of flowering dwarf succulent plants grown on matting for easy installation. They are low-maintenance, not no-maintenance, and should be checked at least once a year in spring, when you can give them a dose of fertilizer. The orientation of your roof will affect the plants' growth rate—they need four hours of sun per day—and if you have a south-facing roof they might need an irrigation system. Consider these points before installing a green roof:

■ Your existing roof should be sound and watertight, with no gutters leading onto it.
■ Running water will erode the sedum matting and standing water will kill the plants.
■ The roof surface must be smooth to avoid creating air pockets under the sedum matting.
■ The building will have to be strong enough to support the weight—a sedum roof can weigh more than 88 lb per sq yd (40 kg per sq m). You may find that your roof will need reinforcing.
■ The roof will be a lot heavier after snow or rain and any subsequent flexing of the building could cause windows to break.
■ Consult an architect or structural engineer if in any doubt.

A sedum roof *can be installed on a flat or sloping roof, but the incline should ideally be less than 25°. You'll need access to the roof from time to time to weed it and water if necessary in dry spells.*

We are not suggesting everyone try living in an igloo, but maybe boxes are not the way ahead? There are lots of creative architects out there—it's all a matter of deciding what you are prepared to live in.

Materials are now available to enable you to build any shape of property you want. It's slightly more problematic to design a custom kitchen, but that's a minor issue. If you are truly starting with a blank piece of paper, you can get as close to nature as you want. But even if you are only considering building an energy-efficient addition, you can still explore all sorts of less popular materials—straw bales, (see pages 50–51), car tires, or an earth shelter (see pages 48–49).

Then you can turn your attention to the interior of your home. One area where there is a readily available, eco-friendly choice is paint.

Eco-friendly decorating

Conventional paints can release compounds into the air that are known to harm human health and the environment. There is an alternative. Eco-paints do not contain toxic chemicals such as benzene, toluene, formaldehyde, and mercury. They are completely free from volatile organic compounds (VOCs)—the solvents that carry the pigment and then evaporate as the paint dries, and can cause headaches, sore throats, and eye irritation.

Another advantage is that they are "breathable" and allow moisture to evaporate from walls. Combined with a natural breathable drywall on the walls, this can reduce condensation and high humidity levels.

It may feel odd buying "organic" paints, but they have real benefits. Even the production process has a smaller carbon footprint.

Organic eco-paints *use natural pigments for color and natural solvents such as citrus oil to carry the pigment. Other eco-paint formulations use casein, which is a milk protein, and come in powder form so you just add water and stir.*

Building an earth shelter

Earth shelters are buildings that use soil piled against the external walls to provide an effective thermal mass that will conserve heat when it is cold and keep the temperature cool in warm summers. This is a sustainable form of construction that relies on well-designed passive solar systems (see pages 40–41) and often uses renewable materials for the fabric of the building.

Could you live in one?

Let's tackle the perceived problems with living in an earth shelter right up front. The question on many people's lips is: are they damp and cold? It's a fair question: some below-ground designs could be damp, like a basement. The answer is to put in a damp-proof course and drainage, and the sun's energy will keep the shelter warm. Passive solar gain can be used to heat all the rooms with the help of a Heat Recovery Ventilation (HRV) system (see page 44).

Construction types

In its most basic form an earth shelter could be a cave in a hillside. But we're not suggesting going back in time and living like cavemen; building practice has evolved so that designs now incorporate many forms of modern sustainable architecture in an efficient, earth-covered shell. Like any new building, earth shelters need planning permission. And if you aren't an experienced builder, you will need help with construction.

The earthship

In this design, the majority of the living space is below ground, with a bank of windows along one wall

Off-grid earthship

This is our favorite style of earth shelter. It has to be built into a south-facing hill or slope, so that the northern side of the house is highly insulated by the natural shape of the earth and the south side acts as a great source of solar energy (vice versa if you were in the southern hemisphere). Many designs are completely off-grid; that is, self-sufficient in electricity and water.

TIRE WALLS

Old tires are easy to come by and make solid walls with great load-bearing qualities. They are weather-proof and fire resistant.

■ **Shovel dirt** into the tire one scoop at a time. Pack in the soil by hitting it with a sledgehammer. Keep adding more soil, working evenly around the tire. Do this in situ, as you build the wall.

■ **Stagger the tires** like bricks. Fill the gaps between them with soil.

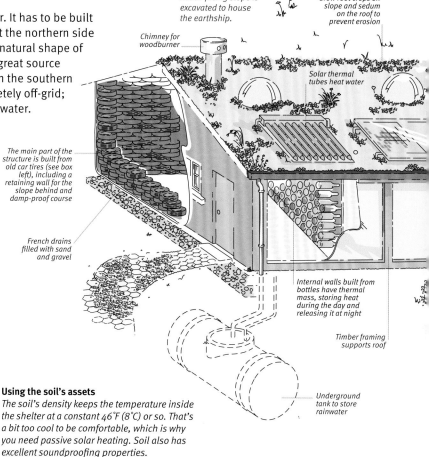

South-facing slope is excavated to house the earthship.

Chimney for woodburner

Grow root crops on slope and sedum on the roof to prevent erosion

Solar thermal tubes heat water

The main part of the structure is built from old car tires (see box left), including a retaining wall for the slope behind and damp-proof course

French drains filled with sand and gravel

Internal walls built from bottles have thermal mass, storing heat during the day and releasing it at night

Timber framing supports roof

Underground tank to store rainwater

Using the soil's assets
The soil's density keeps the temperature inside the shelter at a constant 46°F (8°C) or so. That's a bit too cool to be comfortable, which is why you need passive solar heating. Soil also has excellent soundproofing properties.

(see below). Its soil roof means you don't lose any growing space on your plot: planting your roof can even help prevent erosion.

Earth berming

Earth berming involves piling soil against a building's external walls and sloping it away from the house.

You can't simply add earth berms to a conventional house. Typically, you'd need a specially built, heavy-duty wood-framed structure or stonework, stacked with thick layers of soil. Imagine a giant molehill with a cavity of rooms within it. The roof can either be covered completely with earth or heavily insulated with your chosen material, from sheep's wool to stone wool to composite insulation. With this type of earth shelter there is less risk of damp, compared to building below ground level, and there is little digging apart from foundations. Nor are you confined to a specific landscape.

Going underground

An underground home is a major project, usually for people living in very hot climates. It involves excavating a central courtyard area, often called an atrium, to supply adequate ventilation and light to the rooms leading off it. Unless the ground is really hard, internal structural supports will be a crucial element of the construction.

DESIGN FACTORS

■ **The topography** of the land will decide what you build. An earthship must have a south-facing slope; earth berms and underground homes are suitable for flat sites.

■ **Find the natural water table**. If you dig down below it, not only will you have damp problems, you may end up with flooding.

■ **The soil** around the shelter should ideally contain plenty of sand and gravel for drainage. It's a good idea to install French drains, effectively ditches filled with gravel and sometimes pipes, to channel water away from the foundations.

■ **With the huge weight** of soil resting on the building, it's crucial that the initial structure be strong enough to support it.

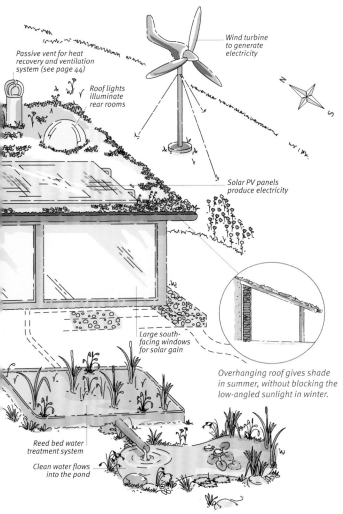

Passive vent for heat recovery and ventilation system (see page 44)

Roof lights illuminate rear rooms

Wind turbine to generate electricity

Solar PV panels produce electricity

Large south-facing windows for solar gain

Overhanging roof gives shade in summer, without blocking the low-angled sunlight in winter.

Reed bed water treatment system

Clean water flows into the pond

By working with the landscape *to build an earthship, you end up with a structure that blends comfortably into the surrounding area, as well as one that has a smaller ecological footprint.*

Earth berms *can be incorporated into more familiar houses. These traditional Icelandic homes have stone foundations, timber framing, and a covering of thick sod for insulation, and can be built on level ground.*

49

Building with straw bales

Straw bales are among the most ecologically sound building materials available, and using them for construction is a highly sustainable option. They have great load-bearing strength, are nonflammable, have effective insulation properties, and they look good too. As well as these benefits, the building process is simple, satisfying, and forgiving, as well as being creative and fun.

Why build with straw?

Building structures with straw bales is empowering because you can create your own structure even if you are inexperienced or unfamiliar with many conventional building techniques. Bales are also cost-effective per unit when compared to bricks and mortar, and ecologically sound—the buildings can be composted at the end of their life, which can be over 100 years.

Of course, there are disadvantages. Splashback from rain bouncing up from the surrounding ground onto the base of the walls may cause damp problems, but can be avoided by raising the first straw bales above ground level. High humidity can also be a serious issue in wet regions and

in exposed sites, where straw bales benefit from an outer skin of wooden siding to protect the walls from wind-driven rain and water damage. However, we feel the positive factors far outweigh the negative points.

Materials

Straw is made from the dead plant stems of grain crops like wheat, barley, rye, or oats. Bales are fairly easy to find, and are often available at farm stores or garden centers. They should be dry when you buy them and must be kept under cover if there is a risk of rain. The bales should be well compressed, too; if it is difficult to get your fingers under the string around them, then it is tight enough. Due to their density and the lack of

air in them, bales are nonflammable when built, but it's still wise to make the storage area a fire-free zone.

Performance

The thermal insulation properties of straw bales are excellent; indeed, they are better than many current building codes require. So straw bales could keep your new home or addition nice and cozy and working efficiently, but only if you make sure you insulate the floors and any gaps in the walls too. They also have superb sound-proofing qualities.

Principles of building

Straw bales can be used to build anything from two-story houses and barns to small house additions. Straw bale building is divided loosely into two methods, which aren't mutually incompatible.

◾ **For load-bearing walls** that can withstand the weight of the roof, bales are placed on top of each other like giant building blocks. They are pinned together with coppiced hazel, and windows and doors are placed inside wooden structural box frames. The flexibility of this style makes it fun to try curved and circular walls.

◾ **Infill** involves first building wooden frames for the walls and the roof to provide structural support. The wall spaces are then filled in with bales. The benefit of this method is that you can store the bales beneath the roof out of the rain while you are working. Infill is the best option for creating large open spaces such as warehouses or industrial units, but requires good carpentry skills.

DESIGN FACTORS

◾ **Aim to make the walls** the length of a number of whole bales with no areas smaller than half the length of a bale, especially by windows and doors.
◾ **Position doors and windows** at least one bale length away from load-bearing corners.
◾ **Build the foundations** so they are the width of the walls.
◾ **Avoid using metal pins** in the walls as they may encourage condensation from the warm, moisture-laden air inside the house.
◾ **Use a breathable** lime wash or lime-based paint to finish your building and help protect it against the weather.

1. **Load-bearing walls** *have excellent lateral strength to protect them from wind damage and even earthquakes.*
2. **Wooden wall frames** *are expensive but provide greater stability for windows and doors than load-bearing walls.*

The structure of a straw bale wall

Before starting to build with straw bales, you need to create a solid and stable base that distributes weight evenly over the ground beneath. The base does not need the same degree of solidity as foundations for bricks and mortar, as straw weighs about 60 percent less. We recommend self-draining foundations made of rubble, stone, or tires, which could then be reused if the building is dismantled.

Working with bales

It is good practice to "dress" a bale before positioning it. Tighten the strings if they are loose and make the ends squarer with a claw hammer, dragging it along either side of the string. Then pull and tease the straw until the end looks square. If you need to customize bales to the right length, restring both halves of a bale before cutting the original strings. Use a baling needle, which is a giant needle with two holes at one end for the two strings to be threaded through the bale. To curve a bale, simply place one end on a log and jump on top of it until you have your desired curve; but make sure that the string stays in place.

A wooden frame *built with bale-sized spaces between the uprights is the perfect support.*

Walls built from bales *are remarkably straightforward structures. Wooden pins and lime plaster continue the use of natural materials.*

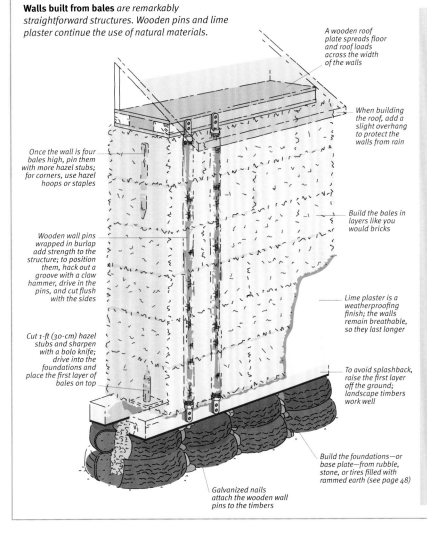

A wooden roof plate spreads floor and roof loads across the width of the walls

When building the roof, add a slight overhang to protect the walls from rain

Once the wall is four bales high, pin them with more hazel stubs; for corners, use hazel hoops or staples

Wooden wall pins wrapped in burlap add strength to the structure; to position them, hack out a groove with a claw hammer, drive in the pins, and cut flush with the sides

Cut 1-ft (30-cm) hazel stubs and sharpen with a bolo knife; drive into the foundations and place the first layer of bales on top

Build the bales in layers like you would bricks

Lime plaster is a weatherproofing finish; the walls remain breathable, so they last longer

To avoid splashback, raise the first layer off the ground; landscape timbers work well

Build the foundations—or base plate—from rubble, stone, or tires filled with rammed earth (see page 48)

Galvanized nails attach the wooden wall pins to the timbers

LIME PLASTER

Lime plaster is one part quicklime powder to three parts damp sand (or 1:2 for the first coat, so it is stickier) and is best made two months in advance of using. Mix with a shovel and wear goggles. It gets very warm, so mix it regularly.

■ **Before applying,** trim the walls, ironing out unwanted bumps.

■ **Apply a thin coat** by hand, wearing thick gloves, and rub it in well. Leave for 1–2 days to dry.

■ **Wet the walls** with a mister and apply two more coats, preferably mixed with chopped straw. Rework over cracks, misting and squishing it firmly into any gaps. Protect from direct sunlight, heavy rain, and frost until it has dried.

Lime plaster *can be colored with pigments or painted after it dries.*

Setting up a workshop

A workshop can save you money. You'll be able to make things instead of buying them and repair objects yourself, rather than taking them to a shop to be fixed at great expense. As well as standard hand tools, we think every workshop needs a cordless power drill, an angle grinder, a collection of hammers, and some welding equipment. We also recommend setting up a charging station for cordless power-tool batteries, with clearly labeled areas for "charged" and "charging". This extra bit of organization means you can always find a fully charged battery when you need one.

You can't have too many outlets: the more you have, the quicker you get a job done

Keep an eye wash kit to wash out grit or dust

Wear a sparkproof leather apron to stop clothing from catching fire when welding

KEY TO WORKSHOP

1. Dustpan and brush
2. Overalls
3. Leather apron
4. Paper towels
5. Selection of wall fixings
6. Outlets
7. Eye wash kit and Steri-strips
8. Nails
9. First-aid kit
10. Screws
11. Pens/pencils
12. Window for natural light
13. Voltmeter
14. Big battery charger
15. Power-tool chargers
16. Power tools
17. Cutting disks
18. Goggles
19. Radio
20. Vertical bench drill
21. Portable workbench
22. Trash can
23. Plumbing parts
24. Lathe
25. Bench metal grinder
26. Painting/decorating equipment
27. Drill bits and screws
28. Charged batteries
29. Ammo boxes for hand tools
30. Strong vise
31. Compressor
32. Drawers for small items
33. Welding mask
34. Welder
35. Wire brush

Keep the workshop floor clean with the wire brush and dustpan and brush

A compressor is useful for inflating tires, blowing dust out of old engines, and putting in rivets

The main workbench *is the heart of a workshop. We try to keep it as clear as possible so we always have space to work, though it helps to have pens, pencils, and a tape measure within reach.*

Generous floor space *gives you room to work under cover.*

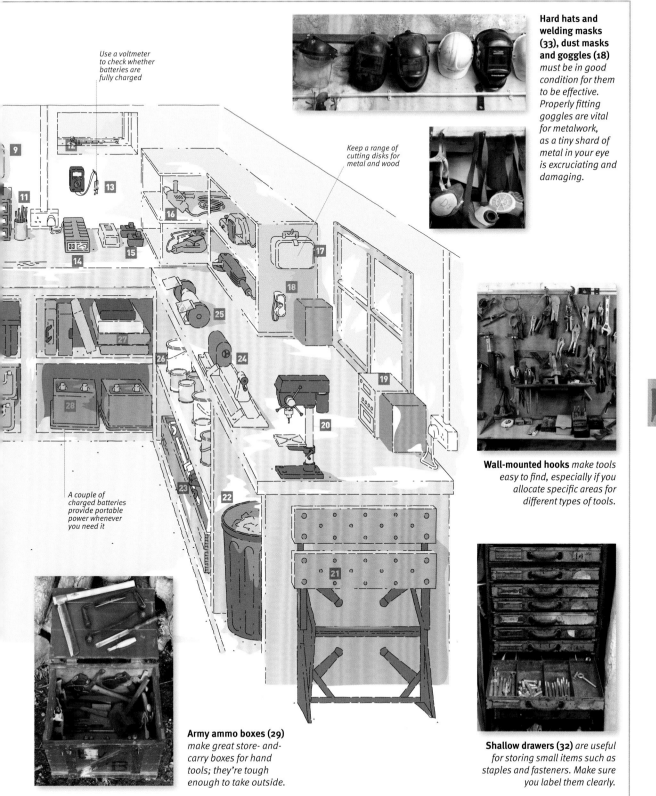

Hard hats and welding masks (33), dust masks and goggles (18) *must be in good condition for them to be effective. Properly fitting goggles are vital for metalwork, as a tiny shard of metal in your eye is excruciating and damaging.*

Use a voltmeter to check whether batteries are fully charged

Keep a range of cutting disks for metal and wood

A couple of charged batteries provide portable power whenever you need it

Wall-mounted hooks *make tools easy to find, especially if you allocate specific areas for different types of tools.*

Army ammo boxes (29) *make great store- and-carry boxes for hand tools; they're tough enough to take outside.*

Shallow drawers (32) *are useful for storing small items such as staples and fasteners. Make sure you label them clearly.*

9, 11, 12, 13, 14, 15, 16, 17, 18, 19, 20, 21, 22, 23, 24, 25, 26, 27, 28

ENERGY AND WASTE Having reduced the amount of energy you are using, why not start generating your own? Any investment you make now will help future-proof you against price hikes that you have no control over—and all the hard-earned cash that used to go to the utility companies will be yours to spend on the good life. Even the most technophobic will discover that there is something very empowering about not being reliant upon others for your energy, water, and waste-disposal needs.

Understanding electricity

Before you decide what renewable energy systems you're going to install, it's definitely worth getting an overview of the basic science governing electricity. So here's the techie part—this is not an excuse to skip ahead! Take a crack at reading these pages. They'll help you figure out what your needs are and what renewable options are possible on your property.

KEY TERMS

■ **Amps** The flow of electrons forming an electric current is measured in amperes or "amps."
■ **Conductors** Materials such as metals, where atoms have loosely bound electrons and thus little resistance, make good conductors.
■ **Insulators** Materials, such as rubber, that do not readily conduct electricity because their electrons are not easily displaced.
■ **Power** A measurement of how much energy you are using each second, measured in watts.
■ **Volts** The "potential difference" between two points on a conductor.

Generating power

You can use renewable technologies to generate electricity in one of two ways. One option is to generate alternating current (AC) electricity mechanically by moving magnets past wires (see below)—this is what a wind turbine or the axle of a water wheel does. Another method that we use on a domestic scale absorbs energy from the sun into solar photovoltaic (PV) panels, generating direct current (DC) electricity. The energy can be used immediately, for example, to light your home or run a pump, or can be stored in batteries.

Storing energy

In a battery, a chemical reaction occurs and then electrons travel through a wire from one terminal to the other, and the result is direct current (DC) electricity (see below). Batteries are particularly useful for off-grid systems as they are fairly cheap and power can be stored and used when needed. If you wish to store electricity that you have generated in a battery bank, use deep-cycle batteries—the sort used in motor homes, boats, or to power electric fences. They are designed to deliver less current for a longer

THE ESSENCE OF ELECTRICITY

At the center of every atom is a nucleus, which is divided into even smaller particles called protons and neutrons. Around the nucleus, electrons orbit.

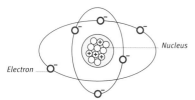

Electron   *Nucleus*

The protons within the nucleus have a positive charge and the orbiting electrons are negative. When there is a balance between the two, the atom is neutral.

Usually atoms have fixed numbers of electrons, which cannot be moved away from the atom. But if there is an excess of free electrons on some atoms in one site (for example, in one of the silicon-based layers of a solar panel), and a deficiency of electrons on other atoms in a neighboring site (such as the adjoining layer of the solar cell), and there is a route between them, then the electrons will start to move from one location to the other. This flow of electrons is called current. The "potential difference" between the two sites is known as voltage and the electricity generated is measured in volts.

Direct current (DC) electricity

When a battery is connected to a circuit, some of the material in the battery starts to dissolve and some of the atoms lose electrons. This means there is a deficiency of electrons at one of the terminals. This potential difference sets the electrons in motion and the

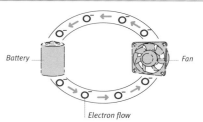

Battery   *Fan*

Electron flow

Direct current *can be used for small appliances that are often associated with camping, such as a 12V hotpot or a fan.*

current flowing. The current that a battery produces is called direct current, or DC—this is easy to remember because DC electricity travels from one battery terminal *directly* to the other terminal.

Alternating current (AC) electricity

AC is the standard household electricity supply, so it's good to be able to produce it at home to either sell back to the grid or feed into the existing electrical circuits in your house.

period of time. Once flat, they are intended to be recharged. They cost about the same as car batteries, but the latter are not suitable for most renewable applications as they aren't meant to be fully discharged then recharged once they are flat.

AC/DC conversions

You might imagine that one form of power would work for everything, but there are good reasons for having the capability to switch from AC to DC and vice versa. Rectifiers and inverters are devices that enable such conversions.

Rectifiers change an AC supply into DC. We use a rectifier to charge up a set of batteries using the AC current produced by our spinning water wheel. We can then store the energy that the wheel generates in batteries that can be drawn upon in the evening when we use the most indoor lighting.

Inverters work the other way from rectifiers, converting DC to AC, and are pretty well essential if you want to continue to enjoy a 21st-century lifestyle while making full use of green technology.

There are a number of inverters available with significant differences in quality. It has to be said that some inverters can cause lights to flicker and have been known to destroy complex electronic equipment such as computers.

So it's worth opting for the more expensive, most useful version. This is the pure sine wave inverter, which ensures the electricity you produce matches the electricity distributed in the regional grid.

When choosing an inverter, know what sort of appliances you want to power from it. Ask the installer and, if in doubt, check the details with your electrician.

1. Our grid-linked wind turbine *allows us to sell any excess electricity we create back to the power company.* **2. Energy created** *by these solar PV panels is stored in deep-cycle batteries for such things as pumping water from our spring.*

To understand AC, it helps if you think back to your school days, as you may remember a diagram of a magnet with lines of flux linking the two poles (see right). These lines of flux illustrate the invisible power in a magnet. Now imagine moving a magnet near a coil of copper wire. The magnetic field passing through the wire will cause the electrons to move inside the coil and so generate a current. The stronger the magnets, the more lines of flux cut the copper coil, and the more electricity you generate. You can make more electricity either by moving the magnets past the coil faster or by bringing them closer to the wire.

Mount a set of magnets on a rotating disk and you have a system that makes AC (see right). All you have to do to create electricity is to put in energy to

cause the magnets to spin. In this way you could harness the power running in a stream or the energy contained in a breeze blowing over an exposed hill.

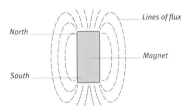

Lines of flux *between the north and south ends of a magnet are invisible.*

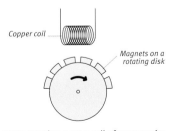

Magnets *rotating past a coil of copper wire generate alternating current (AC).*

GRID LINKING

Consult a licensed electrician to ensure you are set up correctly so that you can be linked to the grid. All systems must have a safety mode that switches them off if the grid connection fails. It's easy to imagine what would happen if you were merrily feeding electricity into the grid while a repair crew was working on a problem, assuming that the power was safely shut off. Also, renewable energy systems must synchronize to the grid. If they are not in sync, the combined effect will produce dirty AC.

Renewable energy options

Before you start harnessing the elements to heat and light your home, it is worth considering your motivation, as this will determine what systems are best for you. You also need to assess your site, as you may not have suitable resources. Finally, you should decide how self-reliant you want to be. Do you want to remain connected to your local infrastructure as a safety blanket?

Why do you want to use renewable energy?

If you simply wish to reduce your impact on the planet and money is not an issue, then all you need to ensure is that the energy it takes to set up your renewable energy technology, known as the "embodied energy," will be less than the energy you save during its lifetime.

However, for the majority of us, financial savings tend to be just as important as environmental savings—so the systems you choose must make financial sense now and for the future, as well as helping the planet. When doing the math, you may be concerned about the length of the payback time, but remember that your investment can also future-proof you against energy price hikes and possible shortages. So add peace of mind into your calculations.

There is also the advantage that well-chosen renewable energy systems will add to the value of your property, making them a better investment than many interior refurbishments.

What are your resources?

Your opportunities depend on the specifics of your property. Carry out a site survey and ask yourself some key questions before hiring a certified installer to put in an expensive system. For example:

▢ Do you have **south-facing roofs** or surfaces on which to place solar thermal systems or solar PV panels?

▢ Do you get **winter sun**?

▢ Can you **use the wind**? To decide this you will need to know: Where are the prevailing winds? What is the average wind speed? And will your municipality give you permission to erect a wind turbine?

▢ Do you have **water source**? If so, how far will you have to move the water? Is there sufficient flow/drop to turn water energy into electricity? (See pages 68–73.) You will almost certainly need a permit from your state's department of natural resources.

When you are considering what is possible on your property, you should also think about what you would really *like* to do. If you have always wanted a wind turbine or a water wheel and either or both will work on your site, then go for it. Better that than take the "kid in a candy store" approach and overdo it. You need to prioritize because ultimately cost will dictate what you can achieve.

How self-reliant should you be?

There are some big advantages to using a regional grid as a buffer for your renewable projects. You have something to fall back on if any of your systems fail and you can sell any surplus to the grid. There is also something comfortingly mainstream and normal about still being connected to the outside world.

That said, grid connection does mean you won't have a truly independent system, and unless you are disciplined and use no more than you produce, you will still be facing regular bills and price hikes when energy costs increase.

1. The water wheel *at Newhouse Farm generates enough electricity to light our house.* **2. The grid-linked turbine** *is positioned as high as possible to take advantage of the wind.*

Our renewable energy systems

Here at Newhouse Farm we decided to remain connected to the grid, but not to be fully dependent upon it, so we have some systems that are grid-linked and others that are standalone.

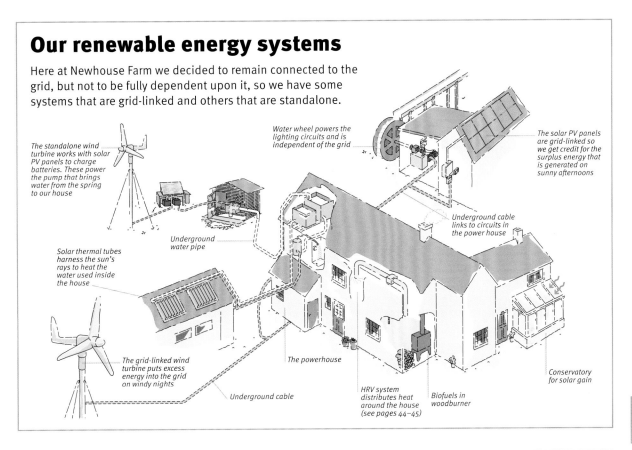

The standalone wind turbine works with solar PV panels to charge batteries. These power the pump that brings water from the spring to our house

Water wheel powers the lighting circuits and is independent of the grid

The solar PV panels are grid-linked so we get credit for the surplus energy that is generated on sunny afternoons

Solar thermal tubes harness the sun's rays to heat the water used inside the house

Underground water pipe

Underground cable links to circuits in the power house

The grid-linked wind turbine puts excess energy into the grid on windy nights

The powerhouse

Underground cable

HRV system distributes heat around the house (see pages 44–45)

Biofuels in woodburner

Conservatory for solar gain

If you wish to break free and go off-grid, you won't be able to use the infrastructure that currently exists for electricity, gas, or water as a backup to your own systems. You will be taking full responsibility for your own energy and water supplies, and although that is a heady prospect, the reliability of the systems you are putting in place will become a key issue. Start by addressing a series of "what ifs?". What if…

- it's not sunny for days/weeks?
- it's not windy for days/weeks?
- it's neither sunny nor windy for days/weeks?
- the water flow from your source reduces during the summer?
- you have to take a system out of service for planned maintenance?
- something malfunctions in a system and you need to fix it?
- your stored/harvested water is not replenished for a day/week/month?

A huge storage capacity for excess energy may seem like the answer, but providing lots of storage that you may only use occasionally is a very expensive option. Instead, focus on what you consider to be essential and then be prepared to compromise if nature temporarily leaves you a bit short. For example, you may consider that it's essential to flush the toilet but baths are a luxury. So if your rain-water tank starts to get low, you will choose to limit baths and use the shower instead.

There are plenty of other examples that demonstrate that limiting your energy usage is not necessarily a hardship. How about limiting the amount of time the television is on each day; or heating water on the woodburner rather than switching on an electric hotpot? You can also give up the clothes dryer and use a clothesline instead.

CALCULATE YOUR ENERGY USAGE

Before you invest in a renewable energy system, you need to figure out how much energy you use so you can calculate how much you need to make. To find out the amount of energy an appliance uses, multiply its power by the number of hours it is turned on, or use a plug-in energy monitor. The standard unit to measure this is kilowatt-hours (kWh)—one kilowatt is 1,000 watts—and it is the unit of electricity you get billed for.

- A 2-kW heater that is run for 1 hour will use 2 kWh of energy.
- A 100-W light running for 5 hours will use 0.5 kWh.
- A 3-kW electric oven run for 3 hours will use 9 kWh.

If your ambitions lie in the realm of living off the grid, using only home-generated power, it's important to first reduce the amount of energy you are using (see pages 36–39).

Using solar PV panels

Whenever the sun shines, it offers us a powerful source of energy in the form of photons that can be converted instantly to direct current (DC) electricity by photovoltaic (PV) cells. These can be used for all sorts of jobs, from powering low-voltage water pumps to charging a cell phone. Solar panels can be installed on most roofs and are often the best value systems for linking to the grid.

Improved efficiency

In the past, solar panels were considered to be expensive and inefficient, but recent technology breakthroughs have increased their efficiency to as high as 80 percent and reduced the price per kilowatt of power. The increased efficiency means a small area of roof can provide enough power to be useful for an average home.

The life of a solar PV system is impressive, as there are no moving parts to convert the solar energy into electricity, and the glass is self-cleaning. Our system is guaranteed to supply at least 80 percent of the 3kW peak (see box opposite) for the next 25 years. Indeed, some of the earliest PV panels are still making electricity after 40 years of service.

How solar panels work

Each solar panel is a remarkable lattice of layers of silicon-based cells. When the sun's photons hit a layer of silicon that has free outer electrons around the atoms, these move to the layer beneath, which comprises atoms with electrons missing. The resulting flow causes a small current, but because there are many cells linked together, the whole panel produces a usable voltage of DC electricity. This current is then changed to AC through an inverter if it is being grid-linked (see opposite), or remains as DC current if it is going straight into a battery.

Power capability

As a rough guide, a south-facing solar panel installation with a 3kW peak capability should provide enough energy over the year to meet the estimated average household demand of 3,300kW.

Solar PV systems are specified as having a "peak power capability," because they depend on how much sun shines on the panels. Surprisingly, the systems do still make electricity on overcast days, though obviously less than on sunny days. However, it

SITE CHECKLIST

▨ How much **electricity** do you use in your house? Can you reduce it?
▨ Do you have a **south-facing roof**?
▨ Does your roof get **winter sun**?
▨ If you are hoping to install panels on the roof of your house, have you **checked with your municipality** to see what permits are needed?
▨ Are there any **grants or tax incentives** available?
▨ Size does matter—**how much space** do you have for your panels?
▨ What is the **peak output** in kW of the system you're considering (see opposite)? How long is the **predicted payback**?
▨ Have you considered a **combined system** for operating a small off-grid energy solution?

1. Solar PV panels *on the roof of our barn.*
2. Adjustable ground-mounted panels *enable you to track the sun during the day and are an alternative if you don't have a suitable roof.*
3. A small panel *powers the fan in our greenhouse heat sink (see pages 118–119).*

is also worth mentioning that your specific microclimate is key when making any decisions about power capability. After all, a solar panel simply might not be the right option if you live in a shady valley.

Standalone systems

Solar PV panels are extremely useful for charging batteries and are ideal for powering a standalone system that is remote from the household supply, such as a pump for a watering system. For a standalone system, it is important to be sure that your solar panel can provide enough energy to power what you intend to use it for. If you are using your pump for two hours a day, work out how much power you will use (see right) and install enough panels to supply it. As long as your panels are a suitable size and you have sufficient batteries, you should seldom have an occasion when there is not enough power to work the pump because you will

have enough stored energy for these "just-in-case" situations.

We use solar PV panels to run the pump that we use near a spring to provide water for the farmhouse. It wouldn't be acceptable for us to run out of water just because there has been no sunshine, so we opted for a dual wind/sun system in addition to the charging batteries. The wind turbine acts as a backup over the winter when there is less sunshine, and in summer, when there is more sun, the solar panels take over.

There are times (and these are surprisingly frequent) when nature provides us with so much energy that the batteries are full and risk being damaged if they continue to be charged. To overcome this, we have connected a charge controller to the PV panel. It monitors the battery voltage and when the battery is full, the charge controller simply turns off the panels by disconnecting them from the battery.

FIGURING OUT HOW MANY BATTERIES TO USE

The amount of energy that a battery can supply is specified in ampere hours (Ah). So a 12-volt battery that is specified as 100Ah can theoretically deliver 1 amp for 100 hours or 100 amps for 1 hour. Multiplying the volts and amps gives you the power (watts) the battery will emit. For this battery, then, it is possible to have:

- 12 volts x 1 amp = 12 watts for 100 hours OR
- 12 volts x 100 amps = 1200 watts for 1 hour.

Back in the real world, these numbers don't quite add up, as you can't expect to get more than 80 percent capacity from your battery. Also, the smaller deep-cycle batteries aren't designed to deliver lots of current, so you shouldn't really drain more than about 10–15 amps (that's a device of about 120–180 watts). The pump at our spring needs 60 watts to function, so we divide 60 watts by 12 volts, which gives us 5 amps. As we use our pump for 2 hours a day, a fully charged battery will therefore last us about 8 days.

Important elements of a PV system

The position of your panels makes a big difference in how much energy is obtainable. South-facing is ideal; as the angle of incidence of the sun varies by season and time of day, the optimal pitch is 40 from vertical.

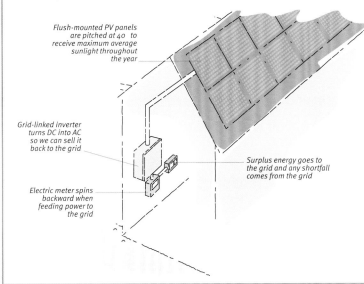

Flush-mounted PV panels are pitched at 40 to receive maximum average sunlight throughout the year

Grid-linked inverter turns DC into AC so we can sell it back to the grid

Electric meter spins backward when feeding power to the grid

Surplus energy goes to the grid and any shortfall comes from the grid

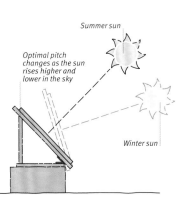

Summer sun

Optimal pitch changes as the sun rises higher and lower in the sky

Winter sun

Adjusting pitch
Optimal pitch is the angle from the vertical that PV panels should be positioned to receive maximum sunlight at solar noon. This changes according to season and where you are in the world. Here in Cornwall, our optimal pitch in June is 64° but only 16° in December, and we adjust our ground PVs accordingly. Roof-ground mounts and pole mounts allow you to adjust roof PVs, but they are more expensive and difficult to install.

Using solar thermal systems

Solar thermal generation is one of the simplest means of harnessing the sun's energy. It works by the direct transfer of energy; no power is generated, which means there's no messing around with electricity. Solar thermal systems rely solely on the power of the sun to warm water and neatly provide you with plenty of pollution-free hot water for your home—as long as the sun shines.

How it works

Solar thermal units, or solar collectors, are the most widely used type of solar power. In its simplest form, a unit comprises a black heat-absorbing plate, bonded to a series of pipes that allow water to flow through them, which is housed in an insulated box with a glass cover to protect the unit from cooling winds. Sunshine passes through the glass and heats up the plate, and the resulting heat is transferred to the water flowing through the pipes, which is then pumped to wherever it is to be used.

Key elements

The solar collector This is the key part of the system, as it captures the solar energy. There are several different types that vary in price and efficiency, ranging from a plastic system (the cheapest and least efficient), to a copper system, and finally to heat pipes inside evacuated tubes (the best and usually most expensive). Evacuated tubes are double-walled glass tubes with a vacuum between the layers to stop heat from escaping. They have black-painted copper fins attached to a heat pipe inside them, which transfers heat up to a manifold, or "junction," where cold water passes over it and is instantly heated up to a higher temperature. Once you decide which type of solar collector you wish to purchase, remember that in this context size really does matter, as you want to capture as much solar energy as possible.

Solar hot water tanks These are usually double insulated, so when you heat water it is still warm enough for a shower the next morning. There is a sensor at the top of the tank that allows you to confirm the temperature of the water.

Solar water feed This feed is positioned at the bottom of the tank, so when it's sunny you get lots of free hot water, but when you have to use a regular water heater, you only heat the top portion rather than the whole tank.

The controller This is the brains of the outfit and it makes the simple decision that if the collector is hotter than the tank, it turns the pump on to circulate the hot water until the whole tank has heated up; if the collector is cool it turns the pump off.

Our thermal setup

At Newhouse Farm our home is a historic house, so we had to install our solar thermal system on an outbuilding. To overcome the losses we expected because the water would travel a great distance from outside to the hot water tank, we installed a slightly bigger system than was theoretically required and made sure the pipes were heavily insulated.

System efficiency

Our system averages out to the equivalent of running an electric water heater for 3–4 hours per day in the summer and about 30 minutes per day in the winter. It was a revelation to discover that we still get enough solar energy to help heat our water even in the middle of the winter.

Header tank

Hot water to faucets and shower

Immersion heater as backup

Controller

Solar hot water feed

Solar collector

Pump

Cold water feed

Secondary hot water feed from woodburner back boiler (see pages 82–84)

SITE CHECKLIST

▓ How much do you **currently pay** to heat your water?

▓ Do you have a **south-facing** house roof or outbuilding?

▓ What will you need to do in order to obtain the proper **building permit** for a solar installation from your municipality?

▓ If you are not granted **permission for a roof-mounted system**, would ground-mounted be an option?

▓ Are there any **grants or tax incentives** available?

▓ Have you researched different manufacturers and checked what they quote as the **peak kWh performance** per m²? Compare this to other companies to find an efficient system at the right price.

1. When we first *moved to the farm, there was no plumbing, so we used a camping solar shower. This is a black plastic water carrier that is filled with water and left in full sunlight; within a couple of hours it is hot enough to provide a luxurious shower.* **2. Our solar collectors** *comprise evacuated tubes with heat pipes connected to the manifold at the top, through which water flows and is heated.*

DIY solar shower

It is possible to make your own garden solar shower for next to nothing using a recycled radiator, a large black plastic garbage can, and a variety of leftover materials. An ideal location for the shower would be a large garden shed with a south-facing roof for mounting the collector to receive maximum sunlight. When you are ready to start using your shower, fill the reservoir with enough water so that it comes above the level of the top pipe from the collector, then leave it to heat up. Empty the reservoir after each use to prevent the water from turning into an unhealthy bacterial soup; refill using a garden hose.

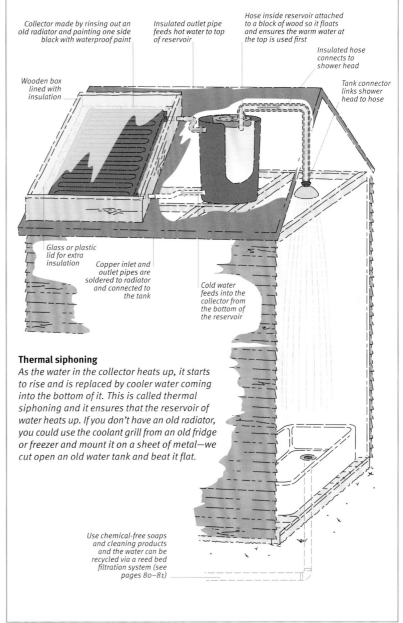

Collector made by rinsing out an old radiator and painting one side black with waterproof paint

Insulated outlet pipe feeds hot water to top of reservoir

Hose inside reservoir attached to a block of wood so it floats and ensures the warm water at the top is used first

Insulated hose connects to shower head

Wooden box lined with insulation

Tank connector links shower head to hose

Glass or plastic lid for extra insulation

Copper inlet and outlet pipes are soldered to radiator and connected to the tank

Cold water feeds into the collector from the bottom of the reservoir

Thermal siphoning
As the water in the collector heats up, it starts to rise and is replaced by cooler water coming into the bottom of it. This is called thermal siphoning and it ensures that the reservoir of water heats up. If you don't have an old radiator, you could use the coolant grill from an old fridge or freezer and mount it on a sheet of metal—we cut open an old water tank and beat it flat.

Use chemical-free soaps and cleaning products and the water can be recycled via a reed bed filtration system (see pages 80–81)

Harnessing wind energy

Wind power ultimately derives from the action of the sun warming the earth and creating weather patterns. Here in the UK we benefit from strong winds, mainly caused by depressions coming in from the Atlantic. A wind turbine uses that wind to create electricity: the wind turns the blades, which rotate a series of magnets past coils of copper wire, which generate electricity.

Wind on your plot

Jutting out into the Atlantic Ocean, Cornwall is a windy place, and here at Newhouse Farm we harness this free energy with a grid-linked turbine that provides electricity for the house, and a standalone turbine that we use to charge batteries in order to power a pump for the spring. The term "stand-alone" simply means that this turbine isn't connected to the grid.

The standalone turbine works as part of a dual-system with a solar PV panel (see pages 60–61), which illustrates the first thing to bear in mind when considering a wind energy option: wind is not classified as "firm power" as it does not always blow. This means it has to be part of a mix of generation capabilities, or you have to store the energy you harvest in batteries for times of low or no wind (see pages 56–57).

There are two other important things about wind that you should know if you are considering installing a wind turbine:

Wind speed matters—a lot. The power you can get from a wind turbine is proportional to the cube of the wind speed (i.e., speed x speed x speed). You can get information about average wind speeds in your area by doing an internet search and then use these figures to see if it is worth your while to install a wind turbine. Even if you don't have a lot of wind, with the right kind of turbine it's still possible to generate electricity.

Local wind turbulence is another crucial factor. The key to a good output from the turbine is to have "smooth" wind (known as "laminar") with no turbulence (see box, below). A wind turbine will never be efficient in turbulent air since it will be constantly trying to change direction. In addition, the rotor speed will fluctuate, which will reduce the power output of the turbine and increase wear and tear.

With a bit of preparation you will be in a good position to make that most crucial decision of where to locate the turbine. Get it right and whenever the wind blows you'll be

COMING TO GRIPS WITH TURBULENCE

Turbulence is caused by obstacles on or near the ground, which change the wind from a smooth flow from one direction into vortices. These cause the wind to rapidly change speed and direction, which is not a good thing for a wind turbine (see the illustration, below left). As a result, a turbine on the coast will probably get "better air" compared to one in the middle of a city, where there are many more obstacles causing turbulence. But local deviations in the strength and laminar quality of the wind can be huge, even out in the countryside where you'd think air flowed freely. The illustration below, right, shows how obstacles can affect turbulence. As a general rule, to avoid turbulence, plan for a turbine to be 20–30 ft (6–9 m) higher than any obstacle within 330 ft (100 m). If in doubt, higher is always better.

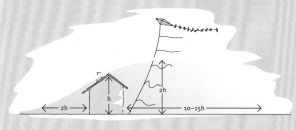

The turbulence caused by an obstacle begins twice its height before reaching the obstacle and carries on for 10–15 times the height after the obstacle, peaking at twice its height.

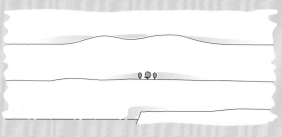

The gray areas above show where turbulence is created when the wind blows over hills (long areas of turbulence) and over a cliff, where the turbulence is relatively short.

1. The standalone turbine *stores the energy it creates in a battery.*
2. Our two turbines *are situated on opposite sides of a small valley for optimum wind power.* **3. The grid-linked turbine** *is atop a sturdy tower that has steel guys to help keep it in place on particularly windy days.*

rubbing your hands with glee at all that free power. Get it wrong and you will not only get very disappointing results, but you will waste a lot of time, money, and effort.

How to buy

It was not so long ago that commercially bought wind turbines were very expensive and if you wanted a lot of power for your dollar, then the only real way forward was to build your own. Growing environmental awareness, cheaper foreign imports, and increased competition have created a huge market for wind generation products, which means it's much more economical than it once was to buy an off-the-shelf system and have it installed. On the other hand, building your own is hugely rewarding and a lot of fun, and by the same token it is relatively easy to source the individual components of the turbine (see pages 66–67).

A quick internet search will reveal most of the commercial turbines available. The market is constantly changing, so to make a good buy you need to check all the claims made by manufacturers, especially those about their rated power. Manufacturers will claim different power outputs based on different wind speeds so they are difficult to compare. For example, a turbine rated 500W at 8m/s is almost the same as one that claims 1900W at 12.5m/s. The best thing to do is to ask for the power curves based on how you will use the turbine—for example, to charge a 24V battery. Power curves show the power supplied by the turbine at different wind speeds. This will then allow you to compare like with like.

Roof-mounted systems

There are systems that mount onto the side or the roof of your house. For people in urban and suburban locations, this may be your only option and, if so, it is still possible to obtain reasonable performance using one of these systems. This isn't the way we'd go, however, and you need to be aware of a few issues relating to roof-mounted installations:

▦ **Turbulence** can have a negative effect. Just imagine the turbulence around a huge obstacle like a house—a roof-mounted turbine is located in this zone of turbulence.
▦ **Wind turbines create noise** and if a turbine is mounted directly to your house, the sound may be very noticeable and could become a source of irritation, not only for you but also for your neighbors.

SITE CHECKLIST

▦ Do you understand **how the wind blows** on your property?
▦ Have you found out the **average wind speed** for your area?
▦ Have you established the **direction of the prevailing wind**?
▦ Have you identified **topographical features** that will create turbulence and figured out how they might be overcome?
▦ Have you obtained **planning permission**? Virtually all wind turbines need this, and the following factors need to be investigated before planning permission is granted: proximity to power lines, airports, roads, and railroads; shadow flicker; noise; electromagnetic interference; siting and the landscape; ecology, archaeology and historic buildings; disturbance during construction.

Components of a wind turbine

If you are to harness the wind, you will require all of the items that are discussed on these pages. If you are intending to build your own turbine, most parts can be bought on the internet at very reasonable prices. This allows you to customize the turbine for your own needs—for example, if your location isn't very windy you may need bigger blades.

Blades

Betz's law says that, even with the best-designed blade in the world, you can only ever harness 59 percent of the wind's energy. So, if you can harness only some of the energy, it is important that you have good blades that are as big as possible. Designing turbine blades is a little complicated, and the choices vary from the cheaper blades with a constant angle of attack and width (rather planklike) to the complex ones that vary in width and look twisted. The better the blade, the more efficient your turbine. It will also be less noisy, especially in high winds, and it will be easier to start the blades spinning.

Electrical generator

It may not seem like it when you look at a wind turbine, but the blades rotate relatively slowly with only a couple of hundred rpm, even in high winds. Because of this low rpm, there is really only one type of electrical generator to use: a permanent magnet alternator (PMA), which can start generating useful power at as little as 50 rpm and can have an efficiency of 90 percent. A few points worth noting:

■ **Buy a multiphase alternator**. These produce continuous power and have much-reduced "cogging." Too much cogging can make it hard to start turning the blades.

■ **Efficiency**. Check out the power curves of any PMA that you are considering using.

■ **Rectifiers**. If you intend to use the turbine to charge batteries, you will need to change from AC to DC (see box opposite). Some manufacturers of PMAs and wind turbines have rectifiers built in, while with others you have to buy or make your own at extra cost.

High-speed protection

It is essential that all wind turbines have an emergency shutdown device to protect them from damage in high winds. If a turbine over-spins, due to either heavy weather or malfunction, there is a risk of mechanical damage and, if a blade breaks off, it can travel a long way and potentially injure someone.

Furling systems

The term "furling system" is used to describe a system that turns the rotor of the turbine away from the direction of the wind, either horizontally or vertically, to prevent damage. Furling not only protects the turbine from over-spinning, but will also reduce excess loading on the tower and its supports. Check out these designs:

■ **Variable-pitch blades.** This is the best system, but the most complex. The blades automatically adjust their pitch depending on the wind speed.

■ **Tail furling.** The turbine and tail are mounted to the side of the yaw bearing and the tail is hinged onto the turbine body.

■ **Tilt-back furling.** The turbine is hinged so it can tilt backward.

■ **Blade flexing.** The blades bend back and twist during high winds.

The parts of a wind turbine aren't numerous, but there are choices to be made for the blades, inverter, and generator. Tail furling (1), flaxing blades (2), cheap/noisy blades like planks (3), well-designed efficient blades (4), electrical generators (5), electrical generator with integrated blades (6), pure sine inverter (7), charge controller (8), cheap quasi-sine inverter (9), switchover switch (10), and homemade monitoring capability (11).

Shutdown systems

These are systems that can be used to manually shut down the turbine for maintenance or weather protection.

■ **Electrical shutdown**. This is the most popular method of shutdown. Another advantage of using a PMA is that if the AC outputs are shorted, the PMA becomes very difficult to turn and so stops the blades from turning. Be sure there is a change-over switch installed to prevent damage to the PMA.

■ **Mechanical shutdown** forces the turbine out of the wind or applies a brake to stop the blades from turning.

Tower

There are two main types of tower:

■ **The tilt-up tower** can be assembled on the ground and then raised into the vertical position. It also has the advantage that it can be tilted for maintenance. However, this type of tower usually requires guys to keep it steady and will therefore take up a larger area.

■ **The fixed tower** is assembled in place, usually using a crane, and the turbine is attached to it later. This type of tower can be freestanding and relatively trouble free, but for maintenance, you have to climb the tower or remove it to the ground.

Whichever system you go for, it must be extremely strong. A 1-in (2.5-cm) steel pipe may feel strong if you have 3 ft (1 m) of it, but it is very easy to bend 33 ft (10 m) of steel pipe. Some people recommend that you should spend at least as much on the tower as you do on the turbine, and we'd be inclined to agree with them.

Electrical setup

There are two main types of electrical installations that apply to wind turbines.

■ **Direct grid tie**. These systems are usually only an option on larger turbines. There are two main components: the turbine and a grid-tie inverter. These systems can be linked to the electricity grid in the same way as the solar PV system.

■ **Battery storage**, which stores the electricity produced by the turbine in batteries until it is needed. If necessary, it can then be converted to 120V AC to run equipment by a suitable inverter. Batteries have the advantage that the electricity can be stored and then used, even if the wind stops blowing. Most installations use lead-acid batteries, which is why the voltage of most systems is in multiples of 12V. If you can find them, forklift or submarine batteries also work well. If you intend to store energy in batteries, you will have to ensure the battery bank is close to the turbine.

BATTERY STORAGE SETUP

Turbines are usually optimized to match the voltage of the battery bank that you will be using, such as 12V or 24V. The turbine usually produces AC electricity, which must be converted before it can be used to charge batteries. Lead acid batteries will always "hold" the voltage generated by the turbine to their own voltage until they are fully charged. When the voltage increases dramatically, it could easily "boil" the batteries (which will ruin them and creates an explosion hazard). To prevent this from happening, use a charge controller and dump load. Heating elements are the best dump loads. Do not use light bulbs or motors as they have a large start-up current, which could damage the charge controller.

The elements of battery storage

■ **The rectifier** converts AC electricity to DC, which can then be used to charge batteries.

■ **The battery bank** holds the electricity generated by the turbine.

■ **The charge controller** monitors the charge state of the batteries, and when they are full, diverts the incoming electricity into a dump load.

■ **The dump load** takes the excess electricity and so must be able to cope with the maximum amount of power produced by the turbine.

■ **An inverter** converts DC power from the batteries to AC and will be needed if you want to generate household electricity at 120V AC.

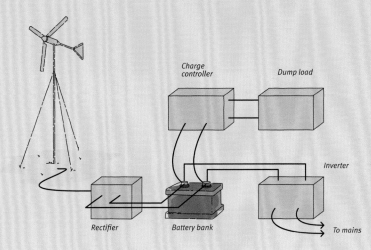

Charge controller

Dump load

Inverter

Rectifier

Battery bank

To mains

Harnessing water energy

Anyone who has carried watering cans back and forth to their crops knows that they are heavy, and therein lies a blessing and a curse. As water flows downhill, it has lots of energy that can be harnessed, but to transport it to a convenient location, such as a water tank, takes a fair bit of effort, and additional energy, which we have to provide.

Water power

The most efficient way of harnessing the energy in moving water is to use a water turbine, which converts water power into rotational power at its shaft. This is then converted to electrical power by a generator.

Waterwheels are covered on pages 72–73, and here we are looking at a hydroelectric system. This is a series of interconnected components, with water flowing in one end, and electricity coming out of the other (see opposite page).

Getting started

Before you can begin planning your system, or estimating how much power it will produce, you will need to make a few essential measurements:
■ **The flow**, which determines how much water is available to use.
■ **The head** is the vertical distance between where you plan to start

capturing the water and where you intend to use it.

These are the two most important facts you need to know about your site. To measure them, see pages 70–71. You simply cannot move forward without these measurements, as they determine everything about your hydroelectric system, including the pipeline size, turbine type, rotational speed, and generator size. Even costs are impossible to estimate without flow and head measurements, as you need them to calculate the potential power output generated by your hydroelectric system.

When you have measurements, do an online search for domestic water turbine companies to find those that can either build and install the whole thing for you, or, if you have some engineering experience, supply the components for you to make one yourself.

The turbine

This important piece of equipment is the heart of the hydroelectric system. Its efficiency determines how much electricity is generated. There are two main types:
■ **Reaction turbines** run immersed in water and are used in low-head/high-flow systems. They include Francis, propeller, and Kaplan.
■ **Impulse turbines** operate in air and are driven by one or more high-velocity jets of water. They're typically used with high-head systems and use nozzles to produce the high-velocity jets. Examples of these turbines include Pelton and Turgo.

There are many types of turbines, and making the right selection requires considerable expertise. A Pelton design, for example, works best with a high head, whereas a crossflow design works better with a low head but high flow.

SITE CHECKLIST
■ **Have you received** permission for your water power system from your local zoning authority and your state's department of natural resources, and purchased any necessary licenses or permits?
■ **Have you measured** the flow and head (see pages 70–71)?
■ **Have you discussed** your system calculations with potential installers to see if you have satisfied the minimum requirements?

1. This Pelton turbine *is an example of an impulse-type turbine driven by high-velocity water jets.* **2. Even small streams** *may be able to create enough power to run a turbine.*

A hydroelectric system

The major components of a hydroelectric system are a water diversion, a pipeline for creating pressure in the water, a turbine and generator for generating electricity, a tailrace for exiting water, and transmission wires. You need to divert water from a stream by building the diversion, where water enters the pipeline that feeds your turbine.

An expert must match *the turbine design to your flow and head. This will ensure that the turbine works efficiently and generates the maximum amount of power.*

Water diversion
At the start of the system you need to build a water diversion. This is a deep pool of water that creates a smooth flow and removes dirt and debris before it reaches the pipeline.

The pipeline
Water is transported to your turbine via a pipeline that forces the water into a limited space and creates pressure as gravity takes it downhill. Its diameter, length, and route affect the overall efficiency.

The turbine and generator
Your system's efficiency depends on the turbine's design, especially the water entry and exit points. Controls ensure that the generator constantly spins at the correct speed. Both the turbine and generator must include an emergency shutdown.

The tailrace
This directs water back to the water course. If part of the tailrace is a sealed pipe below the turbine, it can increase the head.

The open stream dissipates energy as it travels downstream

The pipeline focuses all the water power at the bottom of the pipe where the turbine is connected.

Deep pool of water creates a smooth, air-free inlet to the pipe

The water diversion is located at the highest point of a hydro system; build a dam for the water to pool into before being directed into a pipeline

Transmission lines

The electrical equipment must be installed in a powerhouse for safety and protection

The turbine is located at the bottom of the slope

The generator is located next to the turbine

The tailrace directs water away from the turbine and back to the water course

Avoid using *all your water, as plants, fish, birds, and other wildlife rely on the stream for survival.*

Taking measurements for head and flow

Before you set up your hydro system, measure the flow and head of your water, as these measurements will help you to assess the viability of the system. Flow is expressed as volume (liters or cubic feet) per second or minute. Stream levels change through the seasons, so it is sensible to measure the speed of water flow at different times of the year. Greater flow means greater power. The head is measured as a vertical distance in meters or feet. The higher the head, the greater the pressure—and the available power.

MEASURING THE FLOW

Method 1: Measuring how long it takes to fill a container

▓ **Build a temporary dam** with a single outlet pipe. Place a container of known volume at the end of the pipe. Use a stopwatch to time how long it takes to fill.

▓ **Divide** the container volume by the seconds. For example:
Container = 15-liter [4-gallon] bucket
Time to fill = 3 seconds
Flow = 15 liters / 3 seconds

Temporary dam forces the water through a single outlet pipe

The time it takes to fill the bucket is the "flow"

Small stream method
This is an ideal way to calculate the flow of very small streams.

Method 2: Measuring with a float

▓ **Measure the average depth of the stream**. Lay a plank across the stream and measure the stream depth at 12-in (30-cm) intervals. To work out the average depth, add all the measurements together and divide by the number of measurements you have made.

▓ **Calculate the cross-sectional area** of the stream. Multiply the average depth you just worked out by the width of the stream. For example, if the average depth is 8 in (0.2 m) and the width is 60 in (1.5 m) then the cross-sectional area is 3.23 sq ft (0.3 sq m).

▓ **Measure the speed** of the stream by marking off a 5-yd (5-m) length of the stream that includes the point where you measured the cross-section. Place a weighted float that can be seen clearly in the stream, a good distance upstream from your measurement area, and then use a stopwatch to time how long it takes to cover the length of your measured section. The stream speed will probably vary across its width, so record the times for different locations and calculate an average. To work out the speed, divide the distance traveled by the time it took. For example, if it took 10 seconds for the float to travel 5 m:
Speed = 5/10, or 0.5 m per second (equivalent to 18 in per second).

▓ **Calculate the flow** by multiplying the speed by cross-sectional area.
Flow = 0.5 m per sec x 0.3 sq m
= 0.15 cubic m per second.
This is equivalent to 150 liters (40 gallons) per second.

▓ **Account for friction**. Because a stream bed creates friction with the moving water, the bottom of the stream moves a little slower than the top. This means the actual flow is less than our calculation, but by multiplying the result by 0.83, we get a more accurate rate: Flow = 0.15 x 0.83 = 0.1245 cubic m per second. This is equivalent to 124 liters (33 gallons) per second.

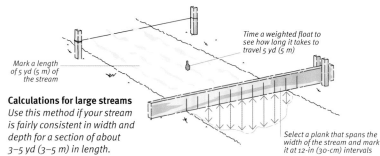

Calculations for large streams
Use this method if your stream is fairly consistent in width and depth for a section of about 3–5 yd (3–5 m) in length.

Mark a length of 5 yd (5 m) of the stream

Time a weighted float to see how long it takes to travel 5 yd (5 m)

Select a plank that spans the width of the stream and mark it at 12-in (30-cm) intervals

MEASURING THE HEAD

Method 1: Using horizontal planks and vertical poles
▨ **Measure 3 ft (1 m)** from the intake point and hold a measuring pole vertically at that point. Place a horizontal plank from the intake point to the vertical pole.
▨ **Measure the height** on the vertical pole from the horizontal plank to the ground and note it.
▨ **Repeat to the bottom** of the hill, ensuring that the horizontal plank in each setup starts from where you took the last measurement.

▨ **Add up** all the measurements taken from the vertical pole. The result is the "head."

Find a friend
This job is easier with two people. One holds a horizontal plank with a level on it; the other holds a vertical measuring pole or long ruler.

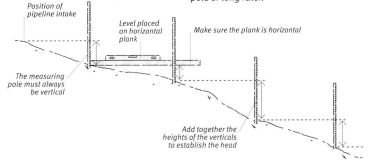

Position of pipeline intake

Level placed on horizontal plank

Make sure the plank is horizontal

The measuring pole must always be vertical

Add together the heights of the verticals to establish the head

Method 2: Measuring pressure
If you measure the pressure in a hose, you can calculate the elevation change of your system. This method relies on the fact that each vertical foot of a head creates 0.433 pounds per square inch (psi) of water pressure (10 vertical feet would create 4.33 psi).
▨ **Run the hose** (or hoses) from your proposed intake site to your proposed turbine location.
▨ **Attach an accurate pressure meter** to the bottom end of the hose and completely fill the hose with water. Read the gauge on the meter. If the pressure were to read 4.33 psi, the head would be exactly 10 ft; if it reads 6.49 psi, the head would be 15 ft.

Fill the hose with water from a watering can

Pipeline intake

A pressure meter attached to the end of the hose gives an accurate reading of pressure in pounds per square inch

Make sure there are no high spots in the hose that could trap air

Using a garden hose
If the distance is short enough, you can use one or more garden hoses to measure the head.

HOW MUCH POWER IS AVAILABLE?

Now you can roughly estimate the power output from your system. Note, however, these figures don't account for the inevitable losses from your system, so actual power output will be considerably less.

Theoretical power (W) = flow (liters/sec) x head (meters) x gravity (9.81 m/s²)

If, for example, a stream has a flow of 150 liters per second and a head of 10 meters, the maximum theoretical power is:

Theoretical power = 150 x 10 x 9.81 watts
= 14,715 watts (14.7 kW)

What's great about this figure is that you can see just how much electrical power your hydroelectric system could theoretically make.

14.7 kW for one hour = 14.7 kWh.
In a day, this totals 14.7 x 24 = 352.8 kWh.
In a year, this totals 128,772 kWh.

Assuming an average house uses 3,300 kWh, the stream in our example could theoretically generate enough power for more than 40 houses.

Accounting for loss of power
The friction of the water moving through the pipeline and turbine, and the energy loss in the drive system, generator, and transmission lines, account for some loss of power from your hydroelectric system. **For example,** a home-sized system generating direct AC power may operate at about 60–70 percent "water-to-wire" efficiency, measured between turbine input and generator output.

Building a waterwheel

Waterwheels are a long-established way of harnessing water power. In fact, industry was powered by watermills for hundreds of years. The principle is simple: the wheel comprises a series of angled buckets, and as the flow of water enters each bucket, it pushes the wheel around before pouring out again, and this turning of the wheel can be converted into electrical power.

The waterwheel system

As with water turbines, a waterwheel system must make the most of the quantity of water flowing and the drop it falls through, or "head" (see pages 70–71). Having said that, it is still possible to operate a waterwheel system on a stream without any head, using an undershot wheel design (see box opposite).

■ **The water source** (the flow) can be a lake, river, stream, man-made mill race or, as in our case, a spring-fed stream that is diverted along an aqueduct. The diversion or sluice is usually the main civil works to be undertaken. Get permission from your local zoning authority and your state's department of natural resources before diverting any water.

■ **Aim to have the largest wheel possible** to create the maximum drop. The distance from the center of the shaft to the inside edge of the buckets determines the torque. So the longer the distance, the more power it creates. It is also worth considering making the wheel wider to fully utilize the flow of water rather than making the buckets deeper.

■ **To harness the power** from the rotating shaft, you can use a direct belt drive, as used to drive machinery; a gear box to increase the shaft speed so it is possible to drive a generator; or a system of cogs and chains or pulleys and belts, which can achieve the same increases in shaft speed as a gear box.

Our waterwheel system

We use our waterwheel to provide the power for all the lights at Newhouse Farm. Our wheel is only 13 ft (4 m) in diameter and has very little flow, so the power it produces is limited to between about 40W under normal conditions and 250W when the stream is flooding.

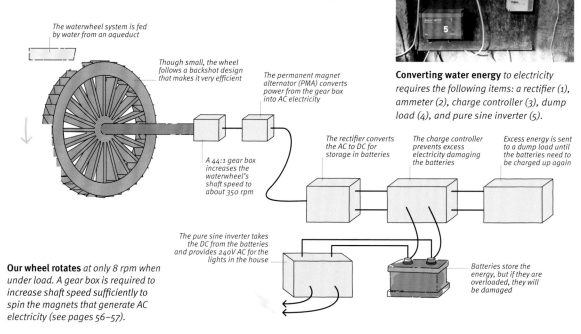

The waterwheel system is fed by water from an aqueduct

Though small, the wheel follows a backshot design that makes it very efficient

The permanent magnet alternator (PMA) converts power from the gear box into AC electricity

A 44:1 gear box increases the waterwheel's shaft speed to about 350 rpm

Converting water energy *to electricity requires the following items: a rectifier (1), ammeter (2), charge controller (3), dump load (4), and pure sine inverter (5).*

The rectifier converts the AC to DC for storage in batteries

The charge controller prevents excess electricity damaging the batteries

Excess energy is sent to a dump load until the batteries need to be charged up again

The pure sine inverter takes the DC from the batteries and provides 240V AC for the lights in the house

Batteries store the energy, but if they are overloaded, they will be damaged

Our wheel rotates *at only 8 rpm when under load. A gear box is required to increase shaft speed sufficiently to spin the magnets that generate AC electricity (see pages 56–57).*

Maximizing efficiency

It sounds a bit trite, but the one fact you need to remember is that the angle of the bucket should be 114 . You might assume that such an exact figure has a long and complex mathematical derivation, but actually, it has been arrived at empirically over hundreds of years, as engineers experimented with waterwheel design. Having unveiled the great secret of waterwheels, it must be said that there are still many more decisions to make, and the efficiency of your system will ultimately depend on optimizing the use of the water you have at your disposal. For example, the type of wheel you choose or indeed are able to install, depending on your site, can mean the difference between 90 and 20 percent efficiency.

What to do with the power

We store our energy in batteries (see box opposite), so that we can use more than 40W for those periods when we need lights—mainly early morning and evening. If we are generating at 40W for the full 24-hour period, that means we can use 160W for a 6-hour period, which is equivalent to about 16 low-energy bulbs—more than enough for our lighting needs at Newhouse Farm!

As you can see from the details of our waterwheel system, we don't produce a great deal of electricity. But if you have sufficient power, it may be worth thinking about grid-linking your output power and selling the excess back to the grid. To achieve this you would need to include a grid-linked inverter in your system.

1. If you need to include an aqueduct, *it must be as level as possible so you don't lose the energy stored in the water until it is being used to turn your wheel.*
2. The waterwheel *is a remarkably simple design, but it isn't always as efficient as it could be (see box, right).*
3. The gear box *is crucial for getting the permanent magnet alternator (PMA) spinning and efficiently generating electricity.*

WHEEL TYPES

Your major decision is what sort of wheel to build or install. This depends on the available water flow and head, the possible route for the aqueduct, and the site for your wheel.

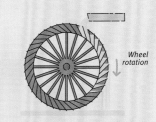

Wheel rotation

A backshot wheel *is the most efficient and can convert nearly 90 percent of the water energy into useful power.*

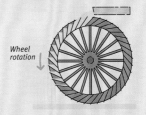

Wheel rotation

Overshot wheels *can achieve up to about 70 percent efficiency when converting water energy into power.*

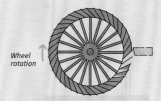

Wheel rotation

Breastshot wheels *only achieve up to 50 percent efficiency. They are useful when there is not much head.*

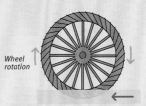

Wheel rotation

Undershot wheels *are very inefficient (up to 20 percent) and are used when there is no head. They are basically paddles on a wheel that are driven by the water flowing under the wheel.*

Using a hydraulic ram pump

A ram pump is an ingenious device that uses the water's own pressure to move it to where you need it most—and no electricity supply is necessary. With a bit of plumbing know-how, you can put one together yourself. We've installed a ram pump in our stream, to pump water uphill to a bulk container behind our hoop house, where we use it to water the plants.

What is a ram pump?

A hydraulic ram, or ram pump, is a water pump—powered by water. When water is flowing down a pipe and is suddenly stopped, the energy in all that moving water is reduced to zero with a thump. This is sometimes called the "hammer" effect. A ram pump utilizes the effect to force a portion of the water that powers the pump upward, to a point higher than the original water source.

The mechanics

A ram pump is cheap to build, easy to maintain, and very reliable. It has only two moving parts: a spring- or weight-loaded waste valve—or "clacker" valve—and a delivery check valve.

Water flowing into the waste valve eventually forces it to close. Then the hammer effect opens the delivery check valve. This pushes some water into the delivery pipe. Because this water is being forced uphill, the flow slows down. When the flow reverses, the delivery check valve closes and the whole cycle repeats itself.

A pressure vessel cushions the shock when the waste valve closes and improves efficiency.

You also need a delivery pipe to take water to your storage tank, and a drive pipe to bring water from the water source. The pump should run indefinitely unless air gets into the drive pipe or the valves get blocked.

HOW A RAM PUMP WORKS

To power the pump, the water source has to be running water that is higher than the pump. The higher the "head," the higher the water can be pumped—up to 10 times higher than the head. Site the pump so that it has a decent head of at least 6 ft 6 in (2 m).

The flow rate of the source water also affects how much water can be pumped and how fast. A ram pump can be used to supply a household or an entire village with minimal maintenance.

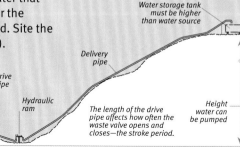

Water storage tank must be higher than water source

Delivery pipe

Drive pipe

Hydraulic ram

Source of running water

Head of water above ram pump

The length of the drive pipe affects how often the waste valve opens and closes—the stroke period.

Height water can be pumped

RAM PUMP COMPONENTS

■ Water flows from the drive pipe into the inlet (1) and out of the open waste valve (2). The delivery check valve (3) is closed.
■ The water picks up speed and kinetic energy, and forces the waste valve to close.
■ The "hammer" effect raises the pressure and forces open the delivery check valve.

■ A pressure vessel (4) containing air reduces hydraulic pressure shock when the waste valve closes, prolonging the life of the pump. The pump will work without it, but less efficiently, as the vessel also creates a more constant flow rate.
■ Water flows through the faucet (5) into the attached delivery pipe and is forced uphill.

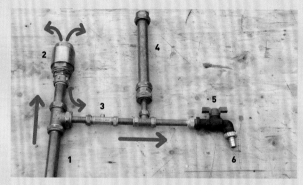

A ram pump *works on an endless cycle of opening and closing valves, powered solely by the pressure of water.*

PROJECT Make and install a ram pump

Building the pump entails joining different widths of copper pipe. The simplest way is to use reducers and make compression joints. To carry the water to and from the pump we used polyethylene piping. The choice of materials and pipe sizes is flexible, depending on what size valves and joints you have.

YOU WILL NEED

- Copper piping
- 2 brass T-joints
- Brass one-way valve
- Brass spring-loaded one-way valve
- Delivery check valve
- Brass end cap
- Adjustable wrenches
- Filter and mesh cage
- Pliers
- Faucet
- Polyethylene piping

ASSEMBLING THE RAM PUMP

1. Make a compression joint. Slide the end nut over the end of the pipe. Slide the olive onto the end of the pipe. Push the pipe into the connector. Hand-tighten the nut onto the connector. **2. Tighten compression joints** using two adjustable wrenches, twisting connector and nut in opposite directions. **3. Use the same technique** to connect the pressure vessel—a length of 1-in (28-mm) copper pipe sealed with the end cap. **4. Connect** the delivery check valve the same way.

ATTACHING THE PUMP TO THE WATER SUPPLY

5. Attach a filter to the drive pipe to stop debris from clogging the system. Make sure it is submerged—we tie ours to a post under the water. **6. Add** an additional coarse mesh basket to stop larger debris from sticking to the filter. **7. Run the drive pipe** from the water source to the pump. **8. Connect the drive pipe** to the pump. Water should flow freely through the waste valve. **9. Fix the ram pump upright**. We built a frame from spare lumber and lashed the pump to it.

10. Unscrew the waste valve to adjust the spring. **11. Cut the spring down** using pliers if it won't close, or add a stronger spring if it won't open. **12. Connect** the delivery hose. **13. Push in** the "clacker" element of the valve with a finger, to charge the ram and start normal operation.

Conserving water

We take a plentiful supply of clean water for granted in the developed world, but in recent years droughts and a less-than-efficient capture and distribution infrastructure have led to watering bans in some areas. Combined with rising water rates, this has made us aware that drinking water should be valued and used more sparingly. Here are some ideas for conserving this precious resource.

Using less water

Treating water so it's safe to drink when it comes out of the faucet takes time and energy. Water is heavy, too, so moving it around is significant. To get an idea, fill an upstairs bathtub from an outside faucet using buckets. Now imagine the "work" or energy needed to move water to your bathroom from the nearest water treatment station.

So before you even think about harnessing your own water supply or using rainwater, try to reduce waste. Simple ways include:

■ **Take showers,** not baths, but do not use shower pumps, which can use nearly as much water as a bath.

■ **Dual-flush toilets** Devices can be fitted to older toilet handles so the tank flushes only when the handle is held down. With this, you can use as much or as little water as you wish. Or why not put a water saver in the tank (see box below)?

■ **Aerated faucets** and shower heads add air to the water to give the effect of using more water.

■ **Dishwashers and washing machines** should be run on **full load** and **economy** settings. An efficient machine may cost you more initially, but it will save throughout its life, especially when water and electricity prices inevitably increase.

Reusing gray water

Waste water from all sources—other than the toilets—is known as gray water (sewage is sometimes referred to as black water). Many gray water recycling systems collect and treat waste water from showers, baths, and bathroom sinks rather than the more contaminated water from washing machines, kitchen sinks, and dishwashers. It can be reused where you do not need drinking-water quality—for flushing toilets and watering gardens, for example.

Before deciding to install a gray water recycling system, you should compare how much you are likely to generate (which depends on the number of baths and showers taken) with your demand for reclaimed water (which depends on the number of toilet flushes or volume required for the garden). Only then can you calculate the potential savings.

Treating gray water

You can't simply collect gray water in a tank for reuse. It doesn't take a lot of imagination to picture what happens if waste water containing dead skin, hair, and so on is left to stand for a period of time. Treatment of the water is essential, and can be based on either physical or biological filters, or a combination of both. You will also need somewhere for a storage tank of an appropriate size. The systems are expensive and they need energy to power them.

TOILET WATER SAVER

You can buy a ready-made water saver, but it's just as easy to make your own from a plastic bottle. Put it in the tank underneath the large float. When the toilet is flushed, the water that is sitting in the saver isn't used in the flush, saving that much water.

To make a water saver cut the top off a 1-quart (1-liter) plastic bottle. Add pebbles to the base to weigh it down. Stand it upright in the toilet tank.

Your own water source

If there is a spring, stream, or even an old well on your property, you can be far less reliant on municipal water.

Before you look at water treatment systems, decide what you will use the water for. If you plan to use it only to flush the toilets, you won't need to do much to it—simple filtration will remove debris. If you plan to drink it, you'll need a purification system.

Filtration

There are a number of ways to filter water, each with varying degrees of effectiveness, and different costs, but all with the same general purpose of improving the hygienic and aesthetic qualities of the water.

Activated carbon filters have been around for a long time and work by absorbing and removing unwanted compounds. They have a very large surface area of highly porous material that attracts and holds chemical pollutants. They are used primarily to improve taste and odor.

Water distillation involves heating the water to the boiling point and condensing the steam. An obvious drawback to this system is that it requires a large amount of energy. Generally, the distilled water is very high quality, but tastes flat as there

Compost toilet

A typical compost toilet has two chambers, and while one is in use, the other is composting the contents. When the second chamber is nearly full, you can use the compost from the first compartment. For composting to work, urine must be separated from solids. There are absolutely no bad odors, and a clever fly trap takes care of pests.

Instead of flushing *sprinkle half a cup of sawdust down the toilet and—very important—close the lid.*

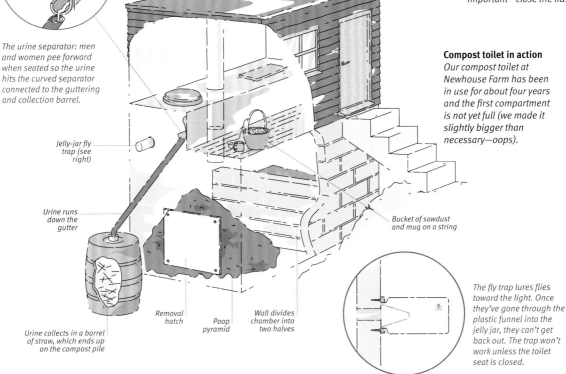

Air vent

The urine separator: men and women pee forward when seated so the urine hits the curved separator connected to the guttering and collection barrel.

Jelly-jar fly trap (see right)

Urine runs down the gutter

Urine collects in a barrel of straw, which ends up on the compost pile

Removal hatch

Poop pyramid

Wall divides chamber into two halves

Bucket of sawdust and mug on a string

Compost toilet in action
Our compost toilet at Newhouse Farm has been in use for about four years and the first compartment is not yet full (we made it slightly bigger than necessary—oops).

The fly trap lures flies toward the light. Once they've gone through the plastic funnel into the jelly jar, they can't get back out. The trap won't work unless the toilet seat is closed.

is less oxygen dissolved in it. You can make a solar still to distill water, using the sun as an energy source.

■ **Sand-based water filters** have been used for more than 100 years to treat waste water. They can be employed on a large scale to treat a water supply for a whole community, or they can be scaled down to suit an individual household (see pages 80–81). Most require a constant flow of water to work correctly.

■ **Reverse-osmosis filters** force water under pressure through a semi-permeable membrane. They allow water through but filter particles such as bacteria, toxins, and salts.

■ **Ultraviolet (UV) filters** kill the majority of bacteria and viruses in the water that passes through them. However, they won't remove chemical pollutants. For a UV filter to work

effectively, the water must be filtered first to remove any solid particles, so there is nothing for bacteria and viruses to hide behind and avoid being zapped.

In a typical system, UV radiation from a lamp passes through a special quartz-glass sleeve and into the untreated water, which flows in a thin film over the lamp. The glass sleeve keeps the lamp at an ideal working temperature of 104°F (40°C).

UV treatment does not remove organisms from the water; it merely inactivates them. The intensity of the lamp decreases over time, and it needs to be replaced regularly. UV treatment is an effective technique, but the disinfection only occurs inside the filter unit, which means that any bacteria introduced afterward can be an issue.

Water from wells and springs

One of the reasons we moved to Newhouse Farm was that it had a spring. We realize not everyone is fortunate enough to have such an accessible water source, but you may be able to find water by drilling down to the water table, or if you have an older property, you may have an old well that has been capped.

We have our spring water tested regularly by our local environmental health department, just in case it becomes contaminated somewhere along the line. We use the water for everything except the cold water faucet in the kitchen, which is municipal water, and we also have a municipal water backup system.

Harvesting rainwater

In the UK there is no real shortage of water; in fact, the rain tends to be a regular topic of conversation. We measured the surface area of the roof on our house, researched the average rainfall, and calculated that about 54,700 gallons (207,000 liters) of water fall on our roof every year—never mind the outbuildings! When we realized that even our little shed received more than 1,000 gallons (4,000 liters), the logic was obvious. Even if you don't want to invest in a whole system (see box opposite), at least install a couple of rain barrels.

Unfortunately, rain doesn't fall regularly throughout the year. If you want to use rainwater, you will have to store it. A big underground tank is expensive, but installing a system that isn't big enough to meet your needs is a false economy and means you will end up using city water as a backup more often.

On average we use 40 gallons (153 liters) of water per person per day in the UK (in the US it is about 129 gallons or 489 liters), which is shocking when you consider we only drink about 2 quarts (liters) each.

1. Pump water *directly from a stream for a domestic water supply if you don't have a well or spring.* **2. Battery-powered pump** *draws water from the stream to irrigate the greenhouse.* **3. Rain barrels** *are the simplest way to collect rainwater from sheds and greenhouse roofs for your garden.*

Rainwater harvesting system

Before designing a system, decide how much water you need to store. Check your water meter to see how much you use in a day and calculate what size tank to install.

Filtering rainwater

A vortex rainwater fine filter installed in the underground piping removes debris and diverts 90 percent of clean water to the storage tank. It consists of a stainless steel fine-mesh filter in a polypropylene housing and needs regular cleaning.

Rainwater is best used *for supplying household appliances rather than for drinking water. It would need more complex filtration and purification systems to make it safe to drink.*

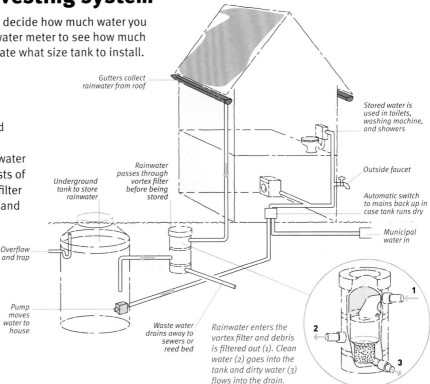

Gutters collect rainwater from roof

Stored water is used in toilets, washing machine, and showers

Outside faucet

Rainwater passes through vortex filter before being stored

Underground tank to store rainwater

Automatic switch to mains back up in case tank runs dry

Municipal water in

Overflow and trap

Pump moves water to house

Waste water drains away to sewers or reed bed

Rainwater enters the vortex filter and debris is filtered out (1). Clean water (2) goes into the tank and dirty water (3) flows into the drain.

PUMPING FROM WELLS AND SPRINGS

In a shallow well or spring, you can use a pump that floats on the water surface. But if you don't know the level of the water or don't have easy access to it—for example, in a bore hole or a deep well—use a submersible pump.

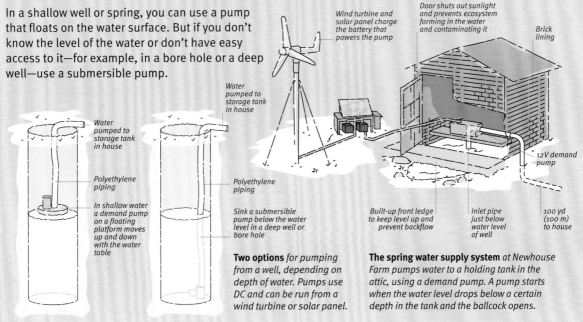

Wind turbine and solar panel charge the battery that powers the pump

Door shuts out sunlight and prevents ecosystem forming in the water and contaminating it

Brick lining

Water pumped to storage tank in house

Water pumped to storage tank in house

Polyethylene piping

Polyethylene piping

In shallow water a demand pump on a floating platform moves up and down with the water table

Sink a submersible pump below the water level in a deep well or bore hole

Built-up front ledge to keep level up and prevent backflow

Inlet pipe just below water level of well

12V demand pump

100 yd (100 m) to house

Two options *for pumping from a well, depending on depth of water. Pumps use DC and can be run from a wind turbine or solar panel.*

The spring water supply system *at Newhouse Farm pumps water to a holding tank in the attic, using a demand pump. A pump starts when the water level drops below a certain depth in the tank and the ballcock opens.*

Using sand filters and reed beds

If you are lucky enough to have a spring on your land that you can use for drinking water, you will need to filter and then purify it first using a sand filter. How about building your own sand filter? Then you will need to deal with the waste water and sewage your household produces. This is where reed beds come in—they're environmentally friendly, as well as being truly functional.

Using a sand filter

Sand filters require no energy or chemicals to filter water, and need very little maintenance. They filter out small particles, and remove more than 90 percent of bacteria, making them an excellent primary filter, but it's a good idea to use an ultraviolet filter afterward (see page 78). Sand filters are generally used in tandem with a water storage tank, as they produce a constant flow of water.

Before setting up a sand filter and drinking well or spring water, ask your local environmental health department to test the water to see if it will be a suitable treatment. If analysis shows traces of metal and chemical pollutants, you may want to use a reverse-osmosis filter, too.

You also need to get appropriate approval and permits from your environmental agency and your local zoning board.

Using a reed bed

A vertical flow reed bed is a sealed, gravel-filled trench with reeds growing in it (see box opposite). The common reed (*Phragmites australis*) oxygenates the water, which helps to create the right environment for colonies of bacteria to break down unwanted organic matter and pollutants. The reeds also make the bed attractive to wildlife.

Before you build a reed bed, get approval from your environmental agency and your local zoning board. Then install a settlement chamber to separate the solids from the liquid effluent. An existing septic tank is fine, or you can a make a new, similar, chamber. You will also need to deal with the solid sludge that separates out, just as you do with a septic tank.

The downside to reed beds is that they use up lots of land space and they do take quite a long time to produce clean water.

Final treatment stage

If you are intending to drink the water or give it to your livestock, or if it is issuing into a stream, we recommend a two-stage water treatment system: a vertical flow bed (see box opposite) for the initial treatment, and then a horizontal flow bed for the final stage of treatment.

The horizontal flow bed is a lined shallow bed that produces an oxygen-depleted environment to enable bacteria in the reeds' root zone to break down nitrates. The water runs through the bed from one end like a stream and you can plant it with wetland plants like blue flag iris (*Iris versicolor*) and marsh-marigold (*Caltha palustris*). The purified water is clean enough to run into a fish pond or dry well.

1. Reed bed filters *are based on wetland ecosystems that naturally purify water flowing through them. They can be used as a finishing treatment in sewage plants or on a domestic scale if you have space.*
2. The common reed (Phragmites australis) *grows to about 6½ ft (2 m) high, and in wetlands, forms an important habitat for insects and birds. Buy plants from specialty suppliers or grow from seed, but don't take them from wetland areas.*

How a sand filter works

Raw untreated water, known as the "supernatant," passes through the filter from the top to the bottom of the tank, under pressure from the water above the sand. This process takes up to two hours, and, generally, the smaller the grains of sand, the more effective the filter.

Filtering the water
Algae grows on top of the sand and forms a sticky net that strains out large particles. Small bits of unwanted organic matter form a green slimy layer in the top ¾ in (2 cm) of sand, which is eaten by protozoans and bacteria.

Cleaning the filter
Drain and clean the filter every 3 months. Take off the top ¾ in (2 cm) of sand; rinse it clean and return it to the filter.

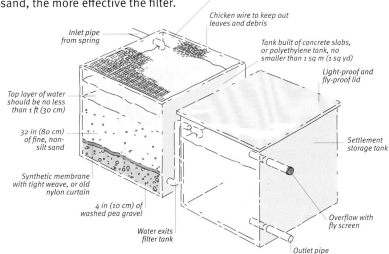

Internal sides of the tank should be rough, so the water cannot run quickly down the sides and has to pass through the sand

Chicken wire to keep out leaves and debris

Inlet pipe from spring

Tank built of concrete slabs, or polyethylene tank, no smaller than 1 sq m (1 sq yd)

Light-proof and fly-proof lid

Top layer of water should be no less than 1 ft (30 cm)

32 in (80 cm) of fine, non-silt sand

Settlement storage tank

Synthetic membrane with tight weave, or old nylon curtain

4 in (10 cm) of washed pea gravel

Water exits filter tank

Overflow with fly screen

Outlet pipe

How a vertical flow reed bed works

Vertical flow beds work by gravity and need a fall of more than 6½ ft (2 m). The effluent flows onto the surface of the bed and percolates slowly through the different layers into an outlet pipe, which leads to a horizontal flow bed. There is no standing water so there should be no unpleasant smells.

Digesting the waste
Waste water flows through layers of sand, reed roots, gravel, and stones, and is cleaned by millions of bacteria, algae, fungi, and microorganisms that digest the waste, including sewage.

Getting the size right
Design your reed bed to allow 1 sq yd (1 sq m) per person in the household, and allow for about 25 gallons (100 liters) flow per person per day.

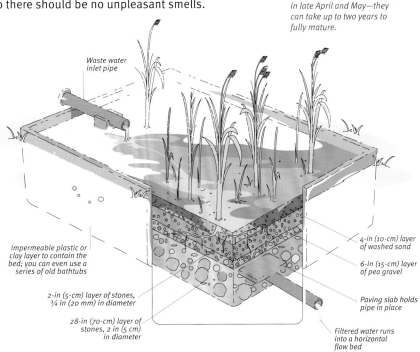

Plant 4 reeds per sq yd (sq m) in late April and May—they can take up to two years to fully mature.

Waste water inlet pipe

Impermeable plastic or clay layer to contain the bed; you can even use a series of old bathtubs

2-in (5-cm) layer of stones, ¾ in (20 mm) in diameter

28-in (70-cm) layer of stones, 2 in (5 cm) in diameter

4-in (10-cm) layer of washed sand

6-in (15-cm) layer of pea gravel

Paving slab holds pipe in place

Filtered water runs into a horizontal flow bed

81

Using biofuels

The simplest definition of biofuels is any fuel that is obtained from a renewable biological resource. This distinguishes them from fossil fuels, which where laid down millions of years ago and are considered nonrenewable. Some examples of biofuels are wood (in its many forms), elephant grass, ethanol, methanol, biodiesel, and even animal waste.

Wood

As a fuel source, wood is sometimes described as "biomass," which means vegetable mass that is used as a source of energy. Biomass is subdivided into woody biomass and nonwoody biomass, which includes materials like animal waste, high-energy crops (sugar cane, rapeseed oil, and corn), and biodegradable by-products from food processing.

The most common type for domestic use is woody biomass, which can fuel a range of appliances, from open fires to ultra-modern pellet-burning boilers and room heaters. By far the best wood is free wood, though it usually takes considerable effort to cut it to size and season it. However, even if you buy wood for fuel, it is usually significantly cheaper than oil or gas, and, if it is sourced locally, there's the additional environmental benefit in the lower transportation miles, emissions, and pollution.

Apart from the sun's rays, open fires are probably the oldest form of heating known to humans. Everyone knows that an open fire forms a mesmerizing focal point, but it is extremely inefficient, with only about a fifth of the heat generated from the fire being radiated into the room, while the remainder goes to waste up the chimney.

Wood burners

Unlike fires, modern wood burners can be about 80 percent efficient, which means the vast majority of the available heat warms the room. In real terms, putting three logs on a wood burner for the evening will provide you with about the same amount of heat as 12 logs on an open fire. As if that isn't enough reason to invest in a wood burner, the high temperature and complete burning that takes place means less residue collects in your chimney, so it needs sweeping less frequently.

Commercial wood burners are usually made from cast iron or steel, but ceramic ones are also available.

CHOPPING WOOD

You can use either an ax or a hydraulic log splitter to split rounds, but in our minds, there is no competition. Our hydraulic log splitter has been a great buy as it makes short work of splitting logs and is much safer than wielding an ax. Before investing in a hydraulic log splitter, you need to think about a few factors, such as:

■ **Power/size** Ours has a seven-ton push, which is enough for us.

■ **Vertical or horizontal design** Our log splitter operates horizontally, which suits us perfectly as we will never split logs too big to lift onto it.

■ **Safety first** You must wear goggles at all times.

When chopping kindling it's useful to have a large block of wood set at a convenient height, a sharp ax, and a sharpening stone on hand. A couple of productive hours of chopping will supply a few months' worth of kindling. We also save all our little offcuts of wood for kindling in a dry area of the pole barn.

Never hold the wood you intend to chop; instead, hold it steady using another offcut while you cut into it with an ax.

A hydraulic log splitter is relatively expensive, but in the long run it will save you money, time—and your back.

1. If you have felled trees *on your property, split them and leave them to season for a couple of years before burning.* **2. Elephant grass** *looks like a crop of corn and yields 4–7 tons of biomass per acre.* **3. An ecofan** *on a log burner circulates the warm air.*

A well-designed burner is extremely efficient, preheating the air that is drawn in prior to combustion so that the flow of gases will ensure that as complete combustion as possible takes place. If you want to make one yourself, there are plans on the internet that show how to make a wood burner or sawdust burner out of old gas cylinders.

If you are to use wood as a fuel, it needs to be well seasoned (ideally left for a minimum of two years after cutting in a dry, ventilated store) and it must be free of preservatives, paint, or galvanized nails, as these can all emit harmful gases when burned. At Newhouse Farm all our heating is provided by four wood burners. The heat is then transferred around the house using a heat recovery ventilation system (see pages 42–45), and we only have to empty our ash about once a week.

It is also possible to fuel your central heating with wood by installing a back-boiler attached to certain higher-output wood burners, or by installing one of the new technology wood-pellet- or chip-burning boilers. If using a log-fired wood burner with a back-boiler, take into account that the burner will not heat the room it is in to the same degree as it would normally because the heat is being diverted around the pipes and radiators instead. Also be prepared to feed your burner large quantities of wood to make it function properly.

Wood pellet boilers

There has been a recent increase in the popularity of domestic and small industrial wood pellet boilers. The wood pellets are generally the by-products of sawmills, though an increase in demand has led to new plants that produce the pellets commercially. Despite the fact that this processing takes energy, pellets are nearly carbon neutral and much less detrimental to the environment than a fossil fuel-powered system.

Modern domestic boiler systems can achieve efficiencies of nearly 90 percent because they are computer controlled for best results. For wood pellets to compete with fossil fuels in terms of convenience, automatic methods of delivering pellets to the burner have been developed. This greatly increases the time between refills.

Wood chip boilers

Wood chip boilers can be as flexible as wood pellet boilers. Indeed, it is probably easier to source local chips than pellets, but therein lies some of the issue; fuel quality may vary, depending upon your source.

Elephant grass

Growing elephant grass (*Miscanthus*) for fuel is relatively new. These crops are essentially biological solar panels and batteries as they capture sunlight and store it in a form that can be readily harvested and used as fuel. Companies will plant for you with special equipment, and after a year of fairly careful weed control and a bit of fertilizer, the grass should be established. In a couple of years, it grows up to 10 ft (3 m) tall annually. Sell your crop to power stations, or commercial combined heat and power (CHP) systems are available.

Biodiesel

Biodiesel is the biofuel equivalent to conventional fossil diesel, and it can be made from vegetable oils or, less frequently, animal fats. Biodiesel is not raw vegetable oil, but an ester created by reacting vegetable oil with an alcohol. The scientific name for this is "transesterification"—the reaction of a triglyceride (fat/oil) with an alcohol to form esters and glycerol. At Newhouse Farm we make our biodiesel from (WVO), which is vegetable oil that has been used for cooking.

Pros and cons

There are many benefits to using biodiesel instead of conventional diesel as a fuel.

■ **Biodiesel is nearly carbon neutral,** and although energy is required to make it, when the vegetable crop was growing it was absorbing CO_2 and when the fuel is combusted, roughly the same amount of CO_2 is released.

■ **Biodegradable as sugar,** biodiesel is also less toxic than table salt.

■ **Biodiesel reduces emissions** of tailpipe particulate matter, hydrocarbon, and carbon monoxide from most modern, four-stroke compression ignition engines.

■ **Biodiesel has a very low concentration of sulfur.** Sulfur in other fuels can lead to production of sulfur dioxide and, as a result, acid rain. The amount in biodiesel is significantly lower than in traditional diesel and is comparable to ultra-low-sulfur diesel (ULSD).

All this makes it sound like the new "wonder fuel," but there are a few disadvantages to using biodiesel:

■ **It starts to coagulate** at a higher temperature than fossil diesel, which can be a problem if the fuel is used in cold climates.

■ **On some older diesel engines** it has been known to dissolve the rubber seals within the fuel system and engine—not a good thing!

■ **It is a great source of food** for microbes—add some water and they will have all they need to multiply and become a problem, resulting in blocked filters.

The all-important reactor

If you're serious about making your own biodiesel, you will need to build yourself a reactor. This is less scary and complicated than it sounds, but does require a certain amount of engineering know-how and isn't something we can comprehensively cover in this book. What you don't need is a whole lot of special equipment; we built ours from a recycled water tank housed in a galvanized metal frame. The maze of pipework beneath is explained overleaf on page 86.

Starting the process

Before you begin making biodiesel, it is essential that you first clean and dry your WVO (see box opposite). Then you can move on to the science. Biodiesel is produced from the reaction of triglycerides (vegetable

1. Our reactor is made from an old copper water tank topped with a metal trash can lid. **2. Biodiesel and glycerol** are mixed together when first reacted. They are then left to stand so they separate. **3. The heavy glycerol** is very dark compared to the brighter biodiesel. The difference in color makes it easy to see when all the glycerol has been drained off.

oil) with methanol. Unfortunately, if you just mix the two together, nothing will happen, so you need a catalyst. In this case, an alkali is needed and those most commonly used are sodium or potassium hydroxide.

To aid the delivery of the solid catalyst into the biodiesel reaction, it is first dissolved in the methanol. The amount of methanol needed is about 20 percent of the volume of oil used. For example, if you were using 50 gallons of oil, then you would need 10 gallons of methanol.

There is a standard amount of catalyst needed for the biodiesel reaction—many people agree that it is 3 g per liter of oil, although some use 5 g without any problems. If WVO is being used, then a titration (chemical analysis) must be carried out to determine the amount of extra catalyst required to neutralize the acidity of the oil. The acidity is caused by cooking food, which produces free fatty acids (FFAs).

If there are FFAs present, they will react with the catalyst before the biodiesel reaction is complete, which results in a very poor yield of biodiesel and it will be contaminated with unreacted oil. Therefore, you need to add extra catalyst, so that after reacting with the FFAs there is still enough left to make biodiesel.

Carry out a titration

A titration must be carried out on WVO to test for the amount of FFAs present. A titration does not take a lot of time, but it can look a little complicated on paper. The basic idea is to react a small sample of the WVO (which will be acidic as it contains FFAs) with a measured amount of sodium hydroxide (which is a base). When the acid is neutralized, you can assume that all the FFAs have been used up.

Titrations are carried out on a very small scale using accurately

SOURCING, CLEANING, AND DRYING WVOS

Local restaurants, school and work cafeterias, and catering companies are your best bet for sourcing waste vegetable oils, or WVOs. People are usually happy to give you the oil, as it saves them time and money disposing of it, but some do demand a small charge as more of us cotton on to biodiesel.

Any bits of food must be filtered out and water removed by heating the oil. It is very important that all of the ingredients used in the production of biodiesel are as water-free as possible (if you are using new vegetable oil, it is already dry) or you will end up with soap.

Pour the WVO through some muslin into a storage barrel to filter out any large pieces of food in the oil.

Allow the oil to settle so that smaller pieces of food sink to the bottom of the barrel.

Draw off the oil from a tap set about a third of the way up the barrel, and remove the cleaner oil above the food contaminants.

Dry the oil in your reactor. It is of paramount importance that the oil contains no water. Heat the oil to about 140°F (60°C) and then pump it around the system so there is an opportunity for the water molecules to escape. This drying process takes up to 4 hours.

measured amounts of chemicals. Steps 1 to 6 on page 87 explain how to prepare and carry out a titration. We know that all the FFAs have been used up when the pH rises to about 8.5, which is also the point at which phenolphthalein indicator solution changes from colorless to purple. This is also the point when you stop adding drops of sodium hydroxide.

It is essential that you note how many drops you have used. Each drop from the pipette contains 0.0455 ml or, to put it another way, there are 22 drops in 1 ml. Repeat steps 5 and 6 on page 87 three times and take an average of the result. If one result is totally different from the others, you have probably made a mistake, so ignore it and do another one. And that's it. You can then scale up these numbers to figure out how

many extra grams of catalyst are required per liter of WVO.

For example, say the titrating solution required 2.5 ml to use up the FFAs, then an extra 2.5 g of catalyst should be used for each liter of WVO. In the example on page 87, we used 1 ml of WVO (which is $1/1000$ of a liter) and a solution that contained $1/1000$ g of sodium hydroxide per liter. Therefore if 2.5 ml of solution is needed for 1 ml of oil, then 2,500 ml would be needed for 1 liter of oil and 2,500 ml of solution would contain 2.5 g of sodium hydroxide. Phew!

Once you know the correct amount of sodium hydroxide to add to the methanol for an efficient biodiesel reaction, mix carefully, shaking all the time, and pour into a large plastic container. Then attach to the reactor with a hose, checking for leaks.

Use a reactor to effect a separation

The oil is heated to about 122°F (50°C) and then the methanol/catalyst solution is added. Place the lid on the tank so that any methanol that evaporates from the reactor will condense on it and drip back into the tank. After everything has mixed for about an hour, turn off the reactor and let its contents settle (see box below).

Once the reaction is complete, you are left with a mixture of biodiesel and glycerol. Luckily, the glycerol is heavier than biodiesel and will therefore separate out naturally and sink to the bottom. When the glycerol has settled, drain it off.

Wash the biodiesel

The biodiesel at this stage is by no means ready to use. It will still contain some methanol, sodium hydroxide, soap, and glycerol. These impurities could easily damage parts of a diesel engine and must be removed. Luckily they are all soluble in water, so they can be "washed" out, which we do with a process called "bubble washing" using a fish tank aerator.

Add water to the reaction vessel (we use a hose attached to a funnel so the water goes straight to the bottom) in a ratio of about 1 part water to every 2 parts biodiesel.

Lower the fish tank aerator into the bottom of the tank and switch it on to the lowest setting that creates bubbles. Each bubble carries a small amount of water through the biodiesel and when it bursts at the surface, the water drop sinks back through the biodiesel and dissolves the impurities. **Allow the biodiesel to wash** for 2–4 hours. Turn off the air pump and leave to settle for a further hour. Then drain off the water (use the hose to watch for the color change again). Each wash takes two hours and then the water is drained off. It should take four or five washes until the water comes out clear.

Once the biodiesel has been washed it will be slightly cloudy because it has been saturated in water. Dry it as you did the original WVO (see box on page 85) and avoid breathing in the fumes.

The final product

The biodiesel should now be ready to use. It should be a clear, amber-colored, pH-neutral nectar. Although it is theoretically possible to get about a 98 percent yield, realistically you can expect 80 percent plus.

USING THE REACTOR

Our reactor comprises a water tank, immersion heater, and a set of pipes and valves. Be careful to prevent methanol fumes escaping from the top of the tank. It's best to try to seal the lid and vent the tank to the outside. When making biodiesel, you use a reactor as follows:

■ **Slowly open** valve 4 and the methanol/catalyst is sucked in and mixed with the oil.
■ **When** the methanol/catalyst tank is empty, close valve 4.
■ **Let reaction mix** for 1 hour. Turn off pump and close valve 1.
■ **Some of the mixture** will remain in the pump and pipe. Use valve 2 to drain this off and pour it into the top of the tank (you may want to put a bit into a glass jar so you can watch it).
■ **Close all the valves** and leave everything to separate for about 6 hours.
■ **Drain the glycerol** once it has separated out by opening valve 1 and 2. Attach a piece of clear hose below valve 2 so you can watch for the color change between the glycerol and biodiesel, which shows that the glycerol has drained off.

NB: Oil must always cover the immersion heater element when it is switched on.

If an emulsion forms when washing

■ **Stop** the washing and drain the water, leaving the emulsion/biodiesel in the tank.
■ **Close valve 2** and open valves 1, 3, and 5.
■ **Switch on** the immersion heater and pump and leave to heat up to 122°F (50°C).
■ **Turn off the heater and pump** and close the valves (drain off the pipes and put the mixture back into the tank).
■ **As the mixture cools**, the emulsion should break and the water will separate out. Adding a little vinegar to the first wash may help prevent emulsions from forming.

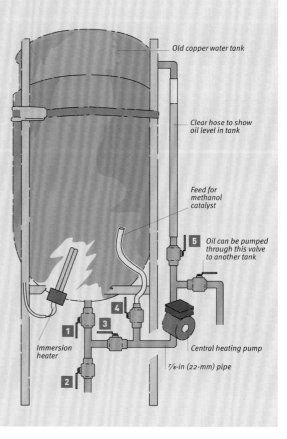

Old copper water tank

Clear hose to show oil level in tank

Feed for methanol catalyst

5 Oil can be pumped through this valve to another tank

Immersion heater

Central heating pump

⅞-in (22-mm) pipe

PROJECT **Make biodiesel**

Observe all safety procedures when handling these chemicals. Always wear suitable gloves and goggles and read the labels. Wash all equipment and rinse with deionized water before use. Read through the instructions before you start and make sure that you understand them and have everything ready.

YOU WILL NEED
- Sodium hydroxide (anhydrous)
- Propan-2-ol (isopropyl alcohol)
- Phenolphthalein indicator solution
- Deionized or distilled water
- 2-ml graduated syringe
- Graduated pipettes
- Beakers and conical flask
- Gloves
- Scales (accurate to 0.1 g)

1. Mix the sodium hydroxide solution by measuring out 1 liter of distilled water and dissolving 10 g of sodium hydroxide into it. Measure out 100 ml of the solution and add 900 ml of distilled water. Stir and pour this solution into an airtight bottle and label it.   **2. Measure** 10 ml of propan-2-ol and add it to a conical flask.   **3. Using a syringe,** measure 1 ml of the waste vegetable oil.   **4. Put it into the conical flask.** Swirl the contents vigorously until the oil dissolves, and then add a couple of drops of the phenolphthalein solution and mix. You must be accurate with your measuring and keep records.

5. To carry out the titration, use a separate pipette to draw up 3 ml of the sodium hydroxide solution and add it to the flask drop by drop while swirling continuously. Each drop will cause the liquid to turn pink temporarily, and then it returns to pale yellow.   **6. When it turns pink** and stays pink for 20–30 seconds, stop adding drops. Repeat steps 2 to 6 three times and do the calculations described under "Carry out a titration" on page 85, so you know how much extra sodium hydroxide is needed.   **7. Measure the sodium hydroxide** catalyst and mix it up carefully with the methanol in a large container.

8. Attach the catalyst container to the reactor with a clear hose. Heat the WVO in the reactor to 122°F (50°C), add the catalyst/methanol mixture, and turn the immersion heater off, but keep the pump running. Follow the process for opening and closing valves described opposite.   **9. As the catalyst mixes** with the oil and the reaction takes place, the oil turns cloudy.   **10. Once the glycerol has separated out,** the biodiesel is ready to be washed (see opposite).   **11. Wash the biodiesel.** Repeat the washing until the water comes out clear. Dry the biodiesel again as described in the box on page 85.

Using an anaerobic digester

An anaerobic digester can take any type of organic matter, from food waste to manure and sewage, and convert it into a soil fertilizer and biogas, which can be used as an alternative energy source. It's ideal for farms and municipal waste-processing plants, and can be used on a small farm if you produce enough waste to run the digester.

What is anaerobic digestion?

Anaerobic digestion is the process whereby naturally occurring bacteria break down organic waste material in an oxygen-free environment. These anaerobic bacteria are part of nature's waste management and are found in soils and deep waters, as well as in landfill sites. Anaerobic digestion converts organic waste into a residue, which can then be used as a fertilizer, and a biogas that can be used as a renewable energy source.

Producing biogas

Most people throw away about a third of the food they buy, and if we add to that the waste from commercial catering and food processing, as well as farm manure and crop waste, it creates an awful lot of material that could be turned into biogas.

This organic waste often ends up in landfill sites, where it generates harmful methane as it decomposes—methane is 24 times more damaging than carbon dioxide as a greenhouse gas. But you can recycle your waste in a system known as a digester. This creates a controllable supply of biogas, which is a mixture of 40 percent carbon dioxide and 60 percent methane, plus other trace elements, and can be harnessed as a renewable energy source. Although anaerobic digestion also releases carbon dioxide, the carbon was absorbed by plants recently and so forms part of a complete carbon cycle. The released gas does not contribute to global warming in the same way as carbon released from fossil fuels, which has been trapped underground for millions of years.

Types of digesters

There are commercial anaerobic digesters, designed for farms, which have the capacity to produce 100KW to 1MW of electricity. For a smaller plot, we have created a DIY digester (see box opposite), or you can use an anaerobic lagoon (see box below) to make biogas in a large balloon.

1. The contents of a compost bin *heat up, and naturally occurring anaerobic bacteria break down the organic material.*
2. The residue *or digestate from anaerobic digestion goes back onto the land to improve soil fertility.*

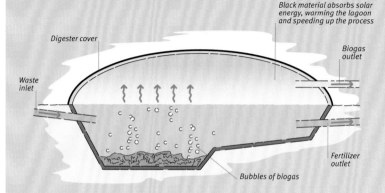

ANAEROBIC LAGOON

Like the digester, this anaerobic lagoon creates biogas from your waste organic material, and you can buy the materials to make one from specialty suppliers. You add organic matter to a large closed balloon with no air in it—biogas plus air is an explosive combination—and when anaerobic digestion takes place, the biogas balloon inflates. Heat enhances the reaction.

Black material absorbs solar energy, warming the lagoon and speeding up the process

Digester cover

Biogas outlet

Waste inlet

Fertilizer outlet

Bubbles of biogas

Size matters
The volume of the lagoon must be right for the amount of waste you are adding. Ask a specialist to advise you.

DIY digester

We used an old muck spreader for the anaerobic digester in the system that we designed for a farmer friend. He uses it to manage the waste produced on his farm, and the biogas is used to power an oil press to make biodiesel, while the fertilizer goes back onto the fields.

Use biogas to power a generator to produce electricity. Or go for a combination of heat and power, running a generator and feeding heat back to speed up the digesting process. Collecting solar energy from black radiators is another way of generating the heat needed. You can also simply burn the biogas for heat, or use it instead of gasoline to power machinery. In countries such as India and China it is very common to build domestic digesters to power gas stoves.

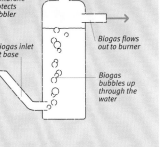

The digestate is an excellent fertilizer and can be applied with a muck spreader.

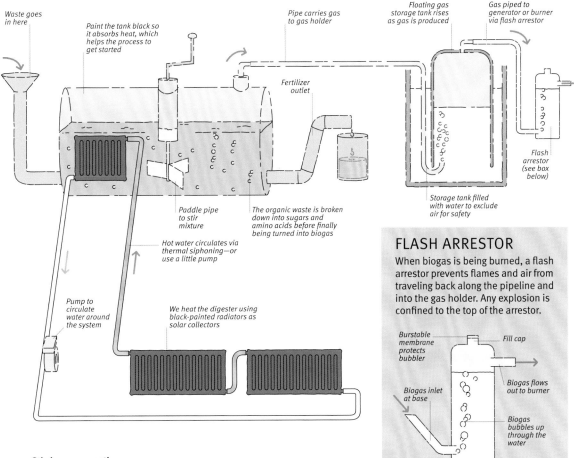

Waste goes in here

Paint the tank black so it absorbs heat, which helps the process to get started

Pipe carries gas to gas holder

Floating gas storage tank rises as gas is produced

Gas piped to generator or burner via flash arrestor

Fertilizer outlet

Flash arrestor (see box below)

Storage tank filled with water to exclude air for safety

Paddle pipe to stir mixture

The organic waste is broken down into sugars and amino acids before finally being turned into biogas

Hot water circulates via thermal siphoning—or use a little pump

Pump to circulate water around the system

We heat the digester using black-painted radiators as solar collectors

FLASH ARRESTOR

When biogas is being burned, a flash arrestor prevents flames and air from traveling back along the pipeline and into the gas holder. Any explosion is confined to the top of the arrestor.

Burstable membrane protects bubbler

Fill cap

Biogas inlet at base

Biogas flows out to burner

Biogas bubbles up through the water

Cut a hole in the top of the cap and place a burstable membrane to limit damage.

Stirring up a reaction
The process can slow down if waste is allowed to separate into layers. Stirring the mixture speeds things up—it can take up to a month to produce biogas. The gas is explosive when in contact with air, so sinking the paddle pipe below the level of the liquid in the digester ensures that no air is introduced.

Reusing and recycling

We are committed to recycling at Newhouse Farm and have got sorting waste down to a fine art. But before we send anything off to be recycled—from old cabling and cardboard boxes to plastic bottles—we try to go one step further and find an alternative use for it around the house or in the garden. After all, one person's waste is another person's treasure.

The waste problem

Waste has evolved as a result of rapid economic development, but its disposal is not an entirely new problem. Court records show that in Stratford-upon-Avon in the mid-16th century, Shakespeare's dad was fined for "depositing filth in a public street." Later, mass industrialization led to an increase in waste, and in the 1800s dustmen were introduced to collect ash from coal fires.

To reduce our waste, we limit the amount we bring into our home in the first place by cutting down on packaging and disposable items, and only buying what we really need. We also aim to lengthen the life of items and reuse good materials to keep them out of the landfill.

When we look at a piece of rubbish, we see its whole life cycle. First, there is the cost and embodied energy it has taken to make the object. Then there's its useful life span. If it has been designed for only one use, this is followed by the serious question of, what next? We then look for ways to use it so it doesn't go into the trash.

Reusing different materials

Reusing is a creative, money-saving, and environmentally friendly activity. We reuse all sorts of different materials around Newhouse Farm— it's not only a lot of fun but also an incredibly satisfying process.

Household and office garbage

■ **Paper** can be recycled, but we first use scraps for writing notes, or stick a piece of paper over a used envelope as a label. You can even buy a gadget that turns paper into a "brick" for burning.

■ **Ink cartridges** in printers are easily refilled.

■ **Rechargeable batteries** can be reused repeatedly, keeping toxic chemicals from going into a landfill.

■ **Glass jars** are excellent for storing your own preserves, dried food, seeds, and chutneys. Clean them thoroughly and keep the right lid next to the right jar.

Building materials

■ **Reusing old lumber** is hard work. De-nailing, sanding, and planing it can take time and effort, but the satisfaction of turning what could be termed garbage into furniture, or using it as a building material, makes the effort worthwhile. Plus, old lumber is much cheaper than new wood and you can use the offcuts as kindling in a wood burner. Beware of creosote coatings on reclaimed lumber and avoid painted wood, as it takes much more work to prepare. Wooden pallets can be dismantled and turned into anything from a shed to a compost bin (see page 106).

1. **Reclaimed beams** *from an old building made a strong frame for our raised bed (see page 126).* **2. Rocks** *grubbed up by our pigs were used to build an herb spiral (see page 159).* **3. An oil drum** *is easily turned into a cold smoker (see pages 250–251).*

PROJECT **Reuse materials around the home**

Some plastic bags can't be recycled, so rather than just throw them away, we reuse them as pillow stuffing. We also enjoy making our own scented candles from those irritating leftover ends. You'll need a packet of wicks from a candlemaking supplier.

YOU WILL NEED
FOR THE PILLOWS:
- Plastic bags
- Scissors
- Pillow cover

FOR THE CANDLES:
- Old candle ends
- Double boiler
- Silicone or paper cupcake cups
- Candle wicks

STUFFING A PILLOW

1. Cut plastic into long, thin strips. You can mix different types of plastic bags and packaging, but make sure you clean them before you start. **2. Stuff the strips** into a pillow cover. Pack it full as the strips will flatten down with use.
3. The finished pillow with eco-friendly stuffing. Shredded plastic makes great stuffing for pet beds, too.

HOMEMADE CANDLES

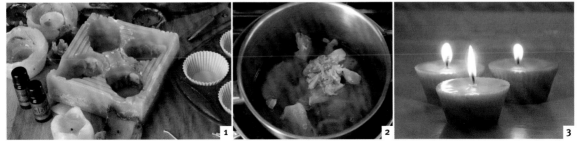

1. Break up used candles. Keep colors separate to avoid murky-colored new candles. **2. Heat the wax** in a double boiler. Fish out any old wicks as the wax melts. Take off heat and stir in a few drops of essential oil. Put a wick in a mold—we used muffin cups—and pour in a little wax. Leave it to set, to hold the wick fast; refrigerate to speed things up. Then add more wax in different colored layers. Leave to set between layers. **3. Remove the molds** when the wax cools.

■ **Copper and plumbing parts** are valuable commodities. We have used them for all sorts of projects, from building a ram pump (see pages 74–75) to constructing a solar shower (see page 63). If you don't reuse your copper, make sure you get a good price for it at a scrap yard.

■ **Old cables and electrical components** are slightly harder to reuse if you are not an experienced electrician, but replacing and wiring a plug is relatively simple. It's also worth stripping out the lengths of copper inside cables and using it to suspend slug-proof hanging baskets (see pages 20–21).

■ **Ferrous or scrap iron** is another great material for reusing in all sorts of projects. We keep a small metal store so that if we need to fix a wheelbarrow or build a spit roast, there is always metal available for us to weld together.

In the garden
■ **Glass** that is still in a window frame is great for building cloches or making cold frames in the garden (see pages 116–17). Once glass breaks, it's harder to reuse, but we have made a heat sink in the greenhouse from broken glass, maximizing its thermal properties (see pages 118–19). Handle glass with care.

■ **Old gutters** make perfect trays for sowing pea seeds (see page 142).

■ **Plastic bottles** can be transformed into mini cloches (see box below), or, if you've got lots of them, you can make an ingenious recycled downspout to feed a rain barrel. Sort the bottles into similar sizes and cut off the bottoms. Link them together with some wire, so that one fits inside another, and hang them upside down. Attach them to a gutter and place a rain barrel underneath.

■ **Egg cartons** can be composted, but we first use ours to grow seedlings (see page 134).

■ **Rubber tires** can be reused as towers for growing potatoes. Fill the base tire with potting soil and add sprouted potatoes. When shoots appear, stack another tire on top and fill with more soil. Add two or three more tires for the perfect pot.

Recycling explained

We will only consider recycling an item after we've first reused it around the house and garden, because the energy taken to recycle materials is still significant.

We were fortunate enough to follow our recycling bags to the local processing center, which proved a real eye-opener. Once the truck arrived on site, our bags were part of an extremely well-choreographed sorting operation. They were emptied onto a conveyor belt and plastic bags were separated by hand before the first of the clever machines did its bit.

A rotating belt with a very powerful electromagnet sucked steel cans about 1 ft (30 cm) off the conveyor and sent them into a huge cage. Then the main belt passed an area where

an electromagnetic vortex flung aluminum cans into yet another cage. Pallets of crushed aluminum cans are so valuable they are kept under lock and key. And recycling aluminum can save up to 95 percent of the energy needed to make it from raw materials.

The plastic bottles made their way to another huge pile and were fed onto yet another conveyor belt to be sorted by hand to extract anything that was not recyclable. In another area of the plant, paper and cardboard were sorted by hand.

Conventional bags for landfill are also processed at the same site and, as the bags split open, we saw bottles, cans, clothes, and many other items that could all have been recycled. But there's no way to sort

---

PROJECT **Reuse materials in the garden**

Household cardboard tubes make great biodegradable pots to start carrot and other root vegetable seeds—plant them in the soil, tube and all, without disturbing the roots. Plastic bottles make ideal mini cloches for individual plants.

YOU WILL NEED
- Cardboard tubes
- Potting mix
- Tray
- Seeds
- 2-liter soda bottle
- Scissors

BIODEGRADABLE POTS

MAKE A BOTTLE CLOCHE

1. Fill tubes with sifted potting mix after standing them in a tray. Sow one seed per tube. Water gently and leave to grow.   **2. Plant out** seedlings when they are growing strongly; bury the tube directly into the soil.

1. Cut the base off a 2-liter bottle.   **2. Place the bottle** over a plant such as a tomato, to make an instant mini cloche. Use the cap as a ventilator and take it off on warm days when condensation collects in the bottle.

through it all once it's reached this stage. Recycling has to be done as far as possible in the home.

Get organized at home

Try our top tips (see box, right) to help you sort out your recycling at home—either ready for collection by your local service, or to take to your nearest recycling center when you are next passing by.

Some enlightened municipalities collect food waste separately for processing (see anaerobic digesters, pages 88–89), but the easiest thing to do at home is to compost your raw vegetable and fruit scraps to make a wonderful soil conditioner (see pages 104–107 for a guide to what you can and cannot compost). We collect composting material in a little bin in the kitchen, and have found we don't need a lid as it doesn't smell—the sheer volume of vegetables we eat means that it is emptied regularly, and we rinse it in the stream on the way back to the house. We also use a bokashi tub (see page 104) to compost all of our waste cooked food.

Generally, it's best to send textiles and clothes to charity stores or sell them at garage sales for reuse, but they can also be recycled if there's no useful wear left in them. Some recycling centers ask you to separate textiles into synthetic and natural fibers before recycling.

Shoes that still have plenty of life in them can be repaired and used by people in developing countries, as can pairs of eyeglasses.

RECYCLING TIPS

Recycling can be messy if you don't have a well-ordered system. We have a unit in the kitchen that is labeled, lined with the required recycling bags, and easy to empty. It saves lots of hassle and is a reminder to recycle every time we walk past it.

Ready for recycling

■ **Wash cans and tins**, and flatten them before recycling.

■ **Plastics** may need to be sorted into different types—not all services take every type of plastic. Wash and flatten bottles and containers before recycling.

■ **Plastic shopping bags** can be put in recycling bins in supermarkets or other stores. Bags made from recycled plastic use one-third of the energy needed for virgin plastic.

■ **Glass** can be recycled hundreds of times, so there is no need for any waste. Recycle metal lids as cans.

■ **Paper and cardboard** are easy to recycle, and reclaimed waste paper now makes up more than half of the fiber used to produce paper and cardboard in the US.

■ **Foil-lined beverage cartons** and Tetrapaks are hard to recycle, but in some areas you can take them to your local recycling center.

Recycling *begins at home with the sorting process.*

1. Reuse old gutters *to start pea seeds under cover (see page 142).* **2. CDs and bottle tops** *threaded on string and hung between stakes so that they move in the breeze make good bird scarers.* **3. Turn an old window frame** *and some lumber into a cold frame.* **4. Cardboard boxes** *laid flat make a great biodegradable mulch (see no-dig gardening on page 100).*

93

PRODUCTIVITY Growing your own food is probably one of the most satisfying things you can do. We love the idea of not only being productive but also growing in harmony with nature. When you get the balance right, you'll discover just how awesome nature can be and how much it is on your side. This chapter provides you with all the information you need to make the most of your property, large or small. We put a particular focus on how to save time in the garden and extend your growing season—so you can sit out in the summer sun and still enjoy homegrown food in the depths of winter.

Approaches to growing

Growing your own food is a big step for first-time gardeners, and the range of techniques can be daunting. However, the fact that there are so many methods points to one simple truth: there is no right way to do it. Experiment with whatever appeals to you—some methods take so little effort, you won't even need to lift a spade—and you'll find an approach to suit you and your garden.

Keep an open mind

You don't have to live on a five-acre lot to follow organic principles or design a permaculture plot. These are simply the "tools" that can be used to cultivate your space, large or small.

Techniques have changed drastically over time, from traditional methods to intensive pesticide-based systems, and back again to natural approaches. As with many aspects of sustainability, the traditional methods are often more valuable.

We have found it worthwhile to keep an open mind about growing. We try anything once: in our opinion, once can be an accident, twice a mistake, and three times is an enemy action. If a method doesn't work for you, then try an alternative. Remember, sustainability is about getting the most out of your space without damaging its future productivity.

Growing organically

Organic cultivation is based on the belief that the environment and the way we grow our food are interdependent. Its principles take into account soil and climate, while avoiding the use of toxic chemicals.

How it works

■ **Enhancing soil health** by composting is one of the foundations of organic practice, mainly because there is lots of life in the soil compared to artificial fertilizers. These lack the humus content— the decayed plant material and soil organisms—of compost, which brings vitality and holds moisture.

■ **Crop rotation** (see page 108) reduces buildup of soil-based diseases and pests.

■ **Weeds** are controlled mechanically— by hoeing or hand-weeding—or by mulching (see page 100).

■ **Using green manure**—fast-growing crops that are dug back into the soil to improve fertility—is another key organic method (see page 106).

■ **Pest control** is based on minimizing the opportunities for pests to flourish, using techniques such as companion planting (see page 101) and encouraging natural predators (see pages 120–123).

Permaculture

Permaculture means different things to different people. We understand it as working with nature rather than against it. Permaculture uses natural ecosystems as a model for growing food, linking plants, animals and microbes. By designing your garden around what is already growing, permaculture can fit any situation.

How it works

■ **A no-dig policy** and low-energy approach are often followed. However, it's not just lazy gardening! In permaculture, disturbing the soil is

1. **Organic tomatoes** *taste great—and no chemicals involved.* 2. **Using every bit** *of space productively, by tucking a row of lettuce in front of peas.* 3. **Crop rotation** *is the natural way to avoid pests and diseases.* 4. **Straw mulch** *conserves moisture and suppresses weeds, and keeps produce off the ground.*

Permaculture forest garden

A forest garden is made up of mainly perennial plants, growing as they would in the wild. A well-managed garden will yield fruits, nuts, and herbs, and annual crops such as salads can be sown in between the perennials. Growing a mix of diverse plants side by side reduces disease and pest attack: it's companion planting on a large scale.

Making a forest garden

A forest garden is ideal for well-established yards as it can incorporate mature trees. But don't let that limit your imagination. You can create a forest garden in pots on a patio by planting a dwarf fruit tree, a grapevine, herbs, and salads. Forest garden plants benefit each other: vines use trees for support; wild garlic grows in the shade of fruit bushes, leaving no space for weeds.

A forest garden *is planted in layers of edible perennials. Here gooseberry bushes are planted alongside fruit and nut trees with lavender as low-growing groundcover.*

A low-maintenance garden
Perennial plants need far less attention than annual crops. Once they are planted, there is very little digging to do in a forest garden, apart from preparing small salad beds.

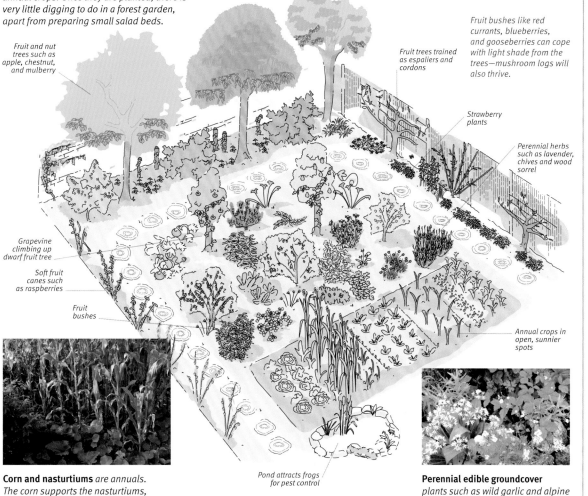

Fruit and nut trees such as apple, chestnut, and mulberry

Fruit trees trained as espaliers and cordons

Fruit bushes like red currants, blueberries, and gooseberries can cope with light shade from the trees—mushroom logs will also thrive.

Strawberry plants

Perennial herbs such as lavender, chives and wood sorrel

Grapevine climbing up dwarf fruit tree

Soft fruit canes such as raspberries

Fruit bushes

Annual crops in open, sunnier spots

Pond attracts frogs for pest control

Corn and nasturtiums *are annuals. The corn supports the nasturtiums, which shade the soil and keep it moist.*

Perennial edible groundcover
plants such as wild garlic and alpine strawberries help suppress weeds.

thought to destroy its natural fertility and lead eventually to erosion.

■ **Growing perennial crops** is an important feature of permaculture. When they are well established, they use up less energy than sowing a new crop each year, and weeds are less of a problem as there is less bare soil for them to colonize.

■ **Zoning** is another fundamental. Whatever needs most attention—vegetable beds, salads, and herbs—is grown close to the house. Orchards and livestock zones are farther away; farther still you come to field crops.

■ **Mulching** is one of our favorite permaculture principles—see below.

No-dig gardening

The normal reasons for digging are to incorporate manure and compost, remove or bury weeds, and create a good tilth for sowing. However, in no-dig gardening, all manure, compost, and other organic material is applied to the surface two or three months before sowing, and is gradually incorporated by worms and other organisms. No-dig gardening feeds the soil, not the plant.

How it works

■ **Worms and their allies** do the digging for you. Earthworms work on a permanent and ongoing basis that is arguably far more efficient than using a spade or a fork!

■ **Weeds** are dealt with by taking preventive action. Shallow hoeing or mulching removes weeds before they have time to seed. A decent layer of light-excluding mulch left in place for at least a growing season can be used to clear the ground of tougher weeds. You can plant through the mulch—see below.

■ **Conserving your energy** is one of the key reasons for adopting a no-dig approach. Some people love digging but others are put off gardening by this strenuous aspect. For those who are elderly, less able, or less inclined

PROJECT **Easy no-dig mulching and planting**

This is the easy way to plant a vegetable bed, with no digging or weeding. It relies on mulching: blocking the light so weeds can't grow. Cardboard is an ideal mulch as it's readily available and biodegrades over time.

YOU WILL NEED
- Cardboard
- Large stones
- Watering can
- Topsoil
- Spade
- Sharp knife

1. Lay the cardboard mulch directly on uncultivated ground, overlapping the pieces so that there are no gaps for weeds to grow through.   **2. Weigh down the edges** with stones to stop the cardboard from blowing around.   **3. Water** thoroughly.

4. Cover with a layer of topsoil around 6 in (15 cm) deep.   **5. Leave for two weeks** and then make a planting hole by digging into the soil and cutting away a circle of cardboard. **6. Plant** (a squash is shown) and firm the soil.   **7. Water well** and let grow!

to get muddy, no-dig is an accessible entry into the world of growing your own produce.

No watering

We first encountered this technique when we visited the Lost Gardens of Heligan, the award-winning garden restoration project in southwestern England. It saves water in the garden and saves a lot of effort too. We've had great success with this method on our zucchini.

How it works

■ **Once a young plant** has been transplanted and thoroughly watered in, it is left to grow without being watered again. At first the plant will look a little unhealthy and may struggle, but this is only while the roots go down deeper in search of the natural water table.

■ **A strong taproot** develops as a result, and the plant thrives in dry periods due to its resilient root formation, without extra watering.

Square-foot gardening

Square-foot gardening is a new approach that evolved from the need to optimize space and reduce maintenance. It is ideal in an urban environment with limited space but works just as well for an intensively planted plot or in an experimental farmstead or community garden.

How it works

■ **The basic concept** is to grow crops in a series of squares instead of rows. Each is about 12 in (30 cm) square and has a different vegetable, herb, or flowering plant in it.

■ **Obvious benefits** include companion planting (see box): pest-deterrent plants like marigolds, onions, garlic, and chives are so close to the surrounding crops that their effectiveness is magnified.

■ **Succession planting** (see page 134) is much easier with this method: once a square has produced its harvest, it is easily replanted with a brand-new mini crop.

Biodynamics

First propounded by the philosopher and scientist Rudolf Steiner at the beginning of the 20th century, biodynamics treats a plot of land as an interdependent and self-nourishing system. It has a lot in common with organic principles, but biodynamics is still regarded as being at the wacky end of gardening.

How it works

■ **Biodynamics goes a step further** than the usual ecological gardening practices such as companion planting, green manures, and composting, by using a series of herbal remedies to treat the soil, plants, and even the compost pile.

■ **An astronomical calendar** is used to plan sowing and harvesting times.

■ **The dynamic aspect** takes note of biological processes. A typical biodynamic technique is to take sap rising in the morning as a sign that leafy vegetables should be harvested first thing when they are fresh.

COMPANION PLANTING

Companion planting is based on crops that grow together in a beneficial partnership, reducing the time needed for pest control and maintenance. Here are a few tried and tested combinations—experiment with your own and plant your beds with a bit more companionship.

■ **Corn, beans and squash** This American Indian tradition is one of the oldest and most famous forms of companion planting. The corn serves as a trellis for the beans to climb up; the beans fix nitrogen for the corn;and the squash grows around the base, keeping in the moisture and suppressing weeds. Try substituting sunflowers for corn.

■ **Onions and lettuce** Rows of onions or garlic next to lettuce and other salads create a "smell" barrier that helps stop slugs and snails from approaching the salad plants.

■ **Poached-egg plant and peas** Poached-egg plants are a perennial you can move each spring to your legume bed. The flowers attract lots of

hoverflies, which keep down the aphids that would otherwise ruin your peas.

■ **Basil and tomatoes** Aphids hate basil, so plant it next to your tomatoes. It's a great combination on the plate too.

■ **Nasturtiums and cabbages** Nasturtiums are a favorite food plant of cabbage-white caterpillars. Grow them as a trap crop to lure the butterflies and caterpillars away from brassicas. Add aphid-free flowers and leaves to salads.

■ **Radishes and cucumber** Reduce the risk of cucumber beetle by planting a ring of radishes around cucumber plants.

■ **Carrots and onions** One of nature's matches made in heaven: the onions drive away carrot flies and the carrots keep away the unwanted onion flies.

Keep aphids under control
Sow poached-egg plant (Limnanthes douglasii) at the same time as your peas.

101

Growing with hydroponics

Imagine a method of growing plants that doesn't need soil, uses a fraction of the water, and has yields up to four times greater than traditional soil-based growing. It sounds almost too good to be true—and in the past hydroponics has suffered from being associated with white-coated scientists. Today it's a technique that anyone can try, and we have been researching how to use it at home.

What is hydroponics?

Hydroponics is a method of growing plants without the need for soil, by directly feeding the roots with a mineral nutrient solution. Setting up a system at home does involve an initial outlay of time and resources, but in the long run, it saves labor and conserves water.

We first became interested in hydroponics because of the challenge facing many people living in densely populated urban areas, with little space to grow their own food. Hydroponics makes efficient use of space and labor, and has a low impact on the environment.

At Newhouse Farm we recommend the Nutrient-Film Technique (NFT), where a very shallow stream or "film" of nutrients, less than ⅛ in (1–2 mm) deep, provides plants with all the nourishment they require for healthy growth, and because the nutrient flow is so shallow the roots are still able to access oxygen, without which they would rot.

The advantages

▓ Hydroponics can be employed on stony or otherwise **difficult sites**.

▓ No risk of **soil-borne diseases**.

▓ There are **no weeds** to compete for space, nutrients, and water.

▓ **Nutrients are delivered directly** to the plants' roots, so up to four times more plants can be grown than on the same area of land.

▓ **Tailoring the nutrient mix** to suit each particular crop increases yields.

▓ Because hydroponics **uses water efficiently**, consumption can be reduced by up to 90 percent.

▓ **Combining hydroponics** with a greenhouse or hoophouse stretches the growing season, enabling you to eat out-of-season produce without the air miles.

What to grow

Plants grown hydroponically require a constant stream of diluted nutrients washing around their roots. Crops we have had success with are herbs, zucchini, salad greens, tomatoes, chili peppers, and eggplant. It is important to support tall-growing vegetables with wire or string as they grow, as you would normally.

The only vegetables we would not grow hydroponically using NFT are root vegetables: there simply isn't space in the growing channels for large roots. The bottom line with hydroponics is to experiment and learn as you go along.

CARING FOR CROPS

With hydroponics, successful growing depends on monitoring the nutrients and pH level of the solution.

Starting plants off

The seed-germination medium we use is coconut fiber, a by-product of the husking industry, which comes shaped into cubes or plugs. Germination is up to five times faster than in using traditional methods because the fiber retains water more effectively than soil. Place seeds in the middle of the plugs and feed them on a starter nutrient (you can order this online) for a couple of weeks.

Transferring plants

Once a plant reaches a decent size and the tips of its roots are poking through the bottom of the cube, move the cube and plant into a growing channel.

Feeding with nutrients

Organic nutrients can be bought online from hydroponics suppliers: worm castings, krill, alfalfa, and kelp are all suitable. If you want to make your own, use the liquid fertilizer from the bottom of a worm bin (see page 127) or comfrey concentrate (see page 107).

A 12-gallon (45-liter) tank will be large enough for a small-scale domestic growing system. It will need to be topped off every few weeks to keep the water level high and to replenish the nutrients absorbed by the plants as they grow.

Monitoring pH levels

Check the pH of the nutrient solution in the tank regularly using a waterproof pH monitor. Adjust the pH by adding "pH down" powder (handle it with care), or by altering the amount of nutrients you add.

Tomato plants thrive *when grown hydroponically. With a constant supply of water and nutrients you need never worry about the fruits splitting and it saves lots of time. Set up your system under cover and you can extend the growing season and eat tomatoes for most of the year.*

Setting up a system

A hydroponics system involves growing plants in channels fed by a stream of nutrient-rich water pumped around in a continuous cycle. Kits are available, but to really understand the process, we recommend putting together a system yourself. You can grow plants hydroponically outside, but growing under cover gives maximum yields.

The irrigation system

To pump the nutrient solution to the growing plants, we use a simple plant irrigation system available from garden centers. This uses electricity, so there can be a small running cost. We run a 12V pump from a battery powered by a solar panel and/or wind turbine.

Growing channels

You can buy special growing channels, but we've found that flat-bottomed rain gutters work just as well. Make covers from white plastic to keep the inside dark; this reduces algal growth and simulates the normal environment for roots. A thin layer of capillary matting down the length of the channel gives an even flow rate and healthier roots.

Growing channels need to slope gently down toward a collection channel; we adjusted their height with slivers of wood until the solution was trickling slowly down. If the gradient is too shallow, the solution collects in puddles around the roots and increases the risk of disease.

The length of the channels is up to you. Ideally they will have closed ends with small drainage holes, but open-ended channels do exactly the same job, just with more splashing!

The shape of a geodesic dome *prevents warm air pockets from forming, making it ideal for growing plants under cover.*

Grow in winter *with a growing lamp to simulate summer light, an aquarium heater to warm the nutrient solution, and bubble wrap to insulate the channels.*

A typical setup
A simple trestle table is ideal for the growing channels, leaving plenty of space for the nutrient tank underneath.

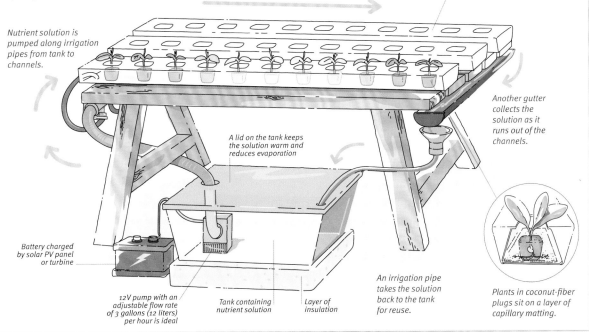

The nutrient solution trickles down the growing channels, which are raised slightly at one end.

Growing channels made from flat-bottomed gutters

Nutrient solution is pumped along irrigation pipes from tank to channels.

Another gutter collects the solution as it runs out of the channels.

A lid on the tank keeps the solution warm and reduces evaporation

Battery charged by solar PV panel or turbine

12V pump with an adjustable flow rate of 3 gallons (12 liters) per hour is ideal

Tank containing nutrient solution

Layer of insulation

An irrigation pipe takes the solution back to the tank for reuse.

Plants in coconut-fiber plugs sit on a layer of capillary matting.

Achieving a productive plot

Growing your own food is relatively easy; plants require little more than nutrients and water to survive. But to improve productivity and get impressive harvests, a little more effort is needed. Regular watering, feeding, and thorough maintenance make your plants stronger and more resistant to weeds and garden pests. Providing your crops with optimum soil conditions is the key.

Caring for the soil

It's good gardening practice to think of the soil structure as the foundation of a productive garden. Whether you have a raised bed in an urban area or a small farm, you'll get better results if you add plenty of rich organic materials to the soil. At Newhouse Farm we make huge amounts of our own compost every year to replenish our raised beds. We enrich our soil with green manure crops and animal manure, and make our own liquid fertilizers to boost certain crops in the growing season.

Nurturing the soil is a bit like mixing together the right ingredients in a cake: it directly determines how well your fruit and vegetables "rise." We find it is a very hands-on aspect of growing and really gets you back to the roots of a productive plot.

Make your own compost

Composting is the process whereby the natural decomposition of organic matter is accelerated to create a rich growing material. Bacteria, fungi, and microorganisms thrive in the right conditions and will break down waste quickly to provide a great source of quality compost to use around your yard. Successfully making your own compost depends on getting the mixture just right.

Any compost pile will naturally break down eventually and turn into something useful, but to avoid a smelly wet mix or a pile of dry matter, you must get the balance right between materials high in carbon and those that are high in nitrogen. At Newhouse Farm we always try to mix one part "greens" with at least one part "browns." We also add

activators to speed it all up (see box); most work by providing a nitrogen boost to kick start the process.

Browns (high in carbon)
- Straw
- Dead leaves
- Cardboard
- Shredded paper
- Toilet paper rolls
- Egg cartons and egg shells
- Twigs and plant stems
- Sawdust

Greens (high in nitrogen)
- Grass cuttings
- Uncooked fruit and vegetable scraps and peelings
- Tea bags and coffee grounds
- Manure
- Urine
- Weeds and fresh plants

COMPOST COOKED FOOD

Above all, you should never waste food and always try to be inventive with leftovers. If you do have cooked food, meat, fish, and dairy products to dispose of, however, it's possible to compost them using the bokashi system. This turns cooked food waste into compost in an odorless, compact unit, using a type of bran that contains microorganisms. The process is anaerobic, so the container must be airtight. The microorganisms ferment the waste, then you can add it to your conventional compost bin.

Add cooked food scraps and a handful of bran. Bokashi also makes strong liquid fertilizer: dilute with water to feed plants or use neat to unblock drains!

TRY THIS

- **Add an activator** Compost just happens, but if you want it in a hurry, add an activator to speed up the process. Try any of these.
- **Urine** Men's works better than women's (it's the hormones).
- **Grass cuttings** Add sparingly in thin layers.
- **Comfrey leaves** Even the old ones left over from making concentrate (see page 107).
- **Seaweed** Collect it fresh, from below the tide line.
- **Manure** Add a little at a time.
- **Nettles** Don't forget to wear gloves when picking.
- **Topsoil** Contains lots of microorganisms that will help get the pile going.
- **Compost from an old pile** Also full of microorganisms.

Cool composting

The cool composter is probably the most common style of compost bin. It does not retain much heat but instead encourages a large worm population to break down materials, along with a huge collection of microorganisms. Just lift the lid and add small amounts of waste regularly. Don't add weeds with seed heads: these must be hot-composted to destroy the seeds or you will end up sowing weeds on your vegetable beds when you dig in the compost.

Cool composters are easy to use. We recommend emptying them out every couple of months and turning the compost before putting it back in. Use a fork to mix it up. If it looks too wet add more "browns"; if it's too dry and fibrous, add more "greens." We have several cool composting bins that we use in rotation for a ready supply throughout the year.

Hot composting

Composting at higher temperatures kills weed seeds and reduces the spread of plant diseases, but you won't find many worms in the mix—it's too hot for them. Heat-loving anaerobic microorganisms do all the work in a hot compost pile.

When we first arrived at Newhouse Farm, we cleared a lot of uncultivated land for vegetable beds. This in turn presented the challenge of what to do with all the unwanted weeds. We didn't want to waste the plant

1. Green plant material *is rich in nitrogen, so add it to your compost pile.* **2. Mix it** *50:50 with dry "brown" material such as straw.* **3. Plastic cone-shaped bins** *are ideal for cool composting.* **4. Cool compost in progress.** *The bottom layer is ready to use but the top goes back in the cone for a bit longer.* **5. Retain the heat** *in a hot compost bin with a layer of old carpet.* **6. Spread** *homemade compost on a vegetable bed, then fork it in.*

material, so we built a few big hot-composting systems out of pallets.

Wooden pallets are available all around the world—free of charge if you scavenge them. Put them together using big nails or string to create two adjoining wooden boxes that can be used in rotation, each about one cubic yard (cubic meter) in volume. The wood helps retain the heat created by the composting process. For extra insulation, line the insides of the boxes you have built with big bits of cardboard and stuff bubble wrap inside the hollow part of each individual pallet.

It may also be worth using a shredder to cut up some of the materials if you are processing large quantities. To maintain the temperature in a hot compost pile, you need to turn the compost regularly to aerate it. Use a fork to shift the outside to the inside and vice versa; it's hard work but well worth it. Covering the pile with black plastic or some bits of old carpet helps retain the heat too.

Using a worm bin

One of the main advantages of composting with a worm bin is that when it's designed in vertically stacked tiers, it takes up so little space. In an urban environment we would recommend one as your first choice. Build your own or buy one (see page 127). The other attraction is the liquid fertilizer or "worm tea" that collects in the base. It's high in nitrogen and phosphates—rocket fuel for growing plants.

Making leaf mold

Leaf mold is an excellent form of compost, either to use as a soil conditioner, to improve both drainage and water retention, or for potting seedlings. Simply collect fallen leaves and place them in black plastic bags with some small holes. Leave them for about a year and then enjoy—a simple compost recipe, but worthwhile. If you are making leaf mold on a larger scale, we recommend building a big cube-shaped cage using four wooden

posts and some chicken wire. Shred the leaves before adding or collect them using a lawn mower: it chops the leaves up and mixes them with grass, which is high in nitrogen, creating a magic compost mix full of microorganisms and water.

Using green manures

Green manures are crops grown specifically to help build a good soil structure and maintain fertility. They are not harvested; instead, they are dug straight back into the soil. Once considered a large-scale agricultural technique, growing green manures is increasingly popular with small-scale organic gardeners.

At Newhouse Farm we have been using them for a few years as part of our crop rotation and have been pleased with the results. Not only do they look attractive, they also help protect bare soil from erosion, as well as providing a good covering blanket to keep the beds free of weeds. Green manuring is simple. Choose a suitable crop from those listed on

---

PROJECT **Dig a compost trench**

Compost trenches are a really good alternative to a conventional compost pile, particularly in winter when normal compost bins have cooled down and are slower to deal with waste. They are completely odorless, quick, and easy, and are a great source of food for young plants; the decomposed material provides a rich supply of nutrients right where it's needed, at the growing plants' roots.

1. Choose a space in a vegetable plot that will have runner beans or peas growing in it next season. In fall, dig a trench one spade deep and a spade's width across.
2. Fill it gradually by adding vegetable scraps and kitchen waste, covering them with the original soil from the trench as you go.   **3. Once the trench is full** leave it for a couple of months, then sow seeds or plant directly into it. Pumpkins and zucchini also do particularly well on top of compost trenches.

PROJECT **Make comfrey fertilizer**

Comfrey is an excellent plant to grow in the garden. Not only does it attract a whole host of bees and pollinating insects but, by following a few simple steps, you can turn the leaves into a liquid fertilizer rich in nitrogen, potash, and phosphorus—essential for healthy plants. Comfrey is a deep-rooted herbaceous perennial that absorbs nutrients from way down in the soil. It grows best in full sun and can be cut down four or five times in a season, but remember to stop by early fall to allow enough regrowth before winter. In our opinion, the only negative issue with composting comfrey is the smell—but that just adds more character.

TRY THIS

■ **Cut the bottom** off a large plastic bottle and pack it with comfrey leaves. Stand the bottle—without its top—upside down in another container. In two weeks you'll have comfrey concentrate on a smaller scale.

■ **Substitute nettles** for comfrey in either method if you don't have any comfrey in your yard.

1. Pick handfuls of comfrey leaves. It grows prolifically so don't worry about stripping the plant. **2. Build a stand** for your comfrey distillery—we used old cinder blocks. Place a container such as a watering can underneath to collect the concentrate. **3. Drill** a hole in the base of a rain barrel or large plastic container with a lid, capable of holding approximately 10 gallons (40 liters).

4. Pack the comfrey leaves tightly into the container. **5. Weigh the leaves** down with some bricks to speed up the process. As more leaves grow back on the comfrey plant, pick them and add to the container. **6. After about 10 days** the leaves will start to decay into a black liquid. You should collect about 4–6 pints (2–3 liters). **Store the comfrey concentrate** in a bottle in a cool dark place, but don't seal the bottle too tightly as it may ferment in warm weather. Once the concentrate has stopped dripping into your collector, add the leftover comfrey leaves to the compost pile as an activator. Dilute the concentrate 1:15 with water and feed your plants for amazing results.

the crop rotation plan opposite, and allow it to grow for a short time. Then dig it back into the soil with a sharp spade to replenish the nutrients.

You must dig green manure back in while it is young and sappy. If you leave it too long, then it defeats the purpose and looks more like you have planted a bed full of weeds! Several green manures—including alfalfa, clover, trefoil, and fenugreek—belong to the legume family and can actually take up nitrogen from the air, adding extra goodness to the soil. We allow a month or so after digging them in before we plant up the beds.

A few favorite green manures

Alfalfa Sow from spring to mid-summer and grow for a few months.

Crimson clover Sow from early spring to late summer. The flowers attract insects, especially bees.

Fenugreek Sow from early spring to late summer. One of the fastest-growing green manures; useful if you have a tight crop rotation.

Trefoil Sow from spring to late summer. Does well in shade; use it to undersow corn or Brussels sprouts.

Mustard Sow from spring to summer to grow for about eight weeks. Goes to seed quickly in hot weather, so dig it in nice and early.

Grazing rye Sow late summer to late fall. Ideal over winter, when it suppresses weed growth.

Crop rotation

Before we head out into the garden at the beginning of each year, we plan an organized system of crop rotation. This sounds complicated but it makes sense. Simply put, some families of plants are more prone to particular diseases and have specific pests that

prey on them. In addition, different plant families also need different nutrients from the soil. By moving the crops from plot to plot each year, you can give them a better chance to get strongly established before problems start. At the same time the soil gets a chance to replenish itself.

Working out a rotation plan

Trying to work out a definitive rotation plan proved nearly impossible when we first started, as different experts give different advice. So we tried to understand exactly which elements of each system we liked and what logic we agreed with. After many headaches we came up with a plan that suited us and appeared to be in line with most expert advice. We divided our crops into groups, shown in the chart opposite. Green manures are included in our crop rotation too.

1. Crop rotation *stops soil from getting depleted and avoids a buildup of pests too.*
2. Sow clover *as a weed-suppressing green manure.* **3. Labeling is crucial:** *you've got to be organized for crop rotation to succeed.*

CROP ROTATION PLAN

We divide our crops into six groups but follow a four-year, four-bed rotation by fitting salads in wherever we can and letting alliums and umbellifers share a bed. We don't include potatoes in our crop rotation because they are prone to blight where we live and need to grow entirely separately.

	YEAR 1	YEAR 2	YEAR 3	YEAR 4
BED 1	A&U	L	B	M
BED 2	L	B	M	A&U
BED 3	B	M	A&U	L
BED 4	M	A&U	L	B

GROUP	CROPS INCLUDE		SOIL REQUIREMENTS
Alliums (A)	▪ Garlic ▪ Leeks	▪ Onions ▪ Shallots	High organic matter; may need lime added to the soil to reduce acidity.
Umbellifers (U)	▪ Beet family (quinoa, spinach, Swiss chard, beet tops) ▪ Carrots ▪ Celeriac ▪ Celery	▪ Fennel ▪ Parsley ▪ Parsnips ▪ Potatoes—unless blight is a problem where you live	Root crops need stone-free soil, a fine tilth. Soil should not be freshly manured. Some root crops also help break up soil structure, especially potatoes.
Legumes (L)	▪ Alfalfa (green manure) ▪ Broad beans ▪ Clover (green manure) ▪ Fenugreek (green manure) ▪ French beans	▪ Lupines (green manure) ▪ Peas ▪ Runner beans ▪ Tares (green manure) ▪ Trefoil (green manure)	Well-drained and moisture-retentive, but not nitrogen-rich. Legumes fix nitrogen in their roots for future crops. When harvesting, leave the roots.
Brassicas (B)	▪ Broccoli ▪ Brussels sprouts ▪ Cabbage ▪ Calabrese ▪ Cauliflower ▪ Kale	▪ Kohlrabi ▪ Mustard (green manure) ▪ Oriental brassicas ▪ Radish ▪ Rutabaga ▪ Turnip	Leafy crops need nitrogen-rich soil; may need lime added to soil to reduce diseases like clubroot.
Miscellaneous (M)	▪ Buckwheat (green manure) ▪ Zucchini ▪ Cucumbers ▪ Grazing rye (green manure) ▪ Peppers ▪ Phacelia (green manure) ▪ Pumpkins	▪ Squash ▪ Sweet corn ▪ Tomatoes	Some plants have so few soil-dwelling pests or diseases that they can be fitted in anywhere in the rotation.
Salads (S)	▪ Chicory/endive ▪ Mache (lamb's lettuce) ▪ Lettuce ▪ Miners' lettuce ▪ New Zealand spinach	▪ Purslane ▪ Salsify ▪ Scorzonera	Not fussy. We put them in as needed, rotate within beds, and grow lots under cover—that's why they're not in the rotation plan. Succession plant.

Set up a greenhouse irrigation system

When you grow plants outside, you don't have to worry too much about watering, as you expect nature to do it for you. But once you start growing plants in hoop houses, greenhouses, cold frames, or cloches, they depend on you for water. Installing an automatic irrigation system will make life an awful lot easier at the height of the growing season.

Getting water where it's needed

To set up an irrigation system, you first need a water source. Rain barrels are an ideal, simple solution: we have one inside our greenhouse that is filled from gutters attached to the greenhouse roof. But bear in mind that rain barrels have a limited capacity; in a dry spell you may find yourself topping off the barrel with water from the hose or elsewhere.

Water is heavy, and it takes a lot of energy to move it. If you can collect and store water on land that is higher than your greenhouse, then you can use gravity to help with the watering. If you cannot use gravity to reduce your workload, then technology can come to your rescue.

A simple little demand pump is all it takes to move water to exactly where you want it. A demand pump can run off a wall outlet or be battery-operated, and will only pump—and therefore use energy—if a tap is turned on, in this case by an electronic timer. The pump is controlled by a pressure switch: when the tap is turned off again, the water pressure builds up and switches the pump off.

Delivering the right amount

The key to irrigation is to deliver the right amount of water. You'll know when you get it wrong. "Splitting" tomatoes are a telltale sign: if a tomato plant receives too little water, then is deluged with it, the fruits can't handle the sudden surfeit and the skins will split. Don't forget that plants only need water during the day when they are photosynthesizing. Water in the morning and harvest in the evening when flavors are at their most concentrated. Don't take our word for it—try it with your tomatoes!

Irrigation in action *A combination of sprayers and drippers in our greenhouse saves us valuable time each day, and the plants get watered very gently, without disturbing the soil.*

TRY THIS

If you have only a few plants, these small-scale systems will keep them watered for a couple of days.

■ Take a **plastic container** with a lid. Make a hole in the lid, drape the ends of longish strips of fabric through the hole, and insert a piece of pipe. Spread out the fabric strips and bury the container in soil with the pipe sticking out so you can use it to fill the container with water. The fabric "wicks" transfer moisture from container to soil.

■ Cut the bottom off a 2-liter **plastic bottle,** turn it upside down, and push the neck into the soil next to a plant. Fill it with water, which will seep into the soil.

■ **Lay a piece of fabric** on a tray and stand plant pots on top. Drape the fabric into a container of water so that the plants can draw up moisture by capillary action.

PROJECT **Install an automatic watering system**

A few hours arranging hoses, drip lines, and sprayers and connecting them to a water supply will save you many more hours of watering. Your system will pay for itself in terms of increased yields.

YOU WILL NEED
- Drip line system, soaker hose, spray system, or a combination of these
- Water source
- 12V demand pump
- Rechargeable 12V deep-cycle battery
- Garden hose
- Battery-powered pump timer
- Small block of wood

INSTALLING DRIP LINE

1. Install the system before planting. Lay the drip line on the soil in a way that will distribute moisture to the maximum growing area. Use small sticks to hold it in position and serve as markers. **2. Bring both ends together** and connect them to the water supply hose using a T connector. Connect the supply hose to your automated system (see below). **3. Add soil** to cover the pipe. **4. Plant the bed,** avoiding the sticks marking the drip line.

INSTALLING DRIPPERS AND SPRAYERS

1. Arrange sprayers so the nozzles deliver water to each pot. **2. Continue** building up the system; drippers are ideal for hanging baskets. **3. Add dual-purpose** attachments to act as misters or drippers. **4. Add an end cap** when you get to the end of a run of piping.

CONNECTING TO THE WATER SUPPLY

1. Make a float from a block of wood for the hose drawing water from the barrel, so it takes water from the top, rather than the bottom where sediment collects. **2. Mount the pump and timer** to a wooden box unit using the supplied hardware. Our unit has a sloping roof to keep the battery dry, and you could mount a solar panel on the roof to charge the battery. Connect the pump to the battery; the timer has its own internal battery. Connect the timer to the pump with a length of hose, and connect a supply hose to the timer. **3. Connect the pump** to the rain barrel with another length of hose, keeping the distance between them as short as possible. **4. Bring all the supply hoses** to a single junction close to the timer beside the pump. You can run several systems at once but the water pressure will drop. Connect the junction hose to the timer. Switch on and experiment.

Growing under cover

Growing under cover is not a gardening technique for secret agents. It's the process of extending the growing season by using a greenhouse, hoop house, or smaller-scale options such as cloches and cold frames to create warmer conditions for your plants. This allows you to produce fresh vegetables for longer, grow some foods out of season, and grow exotic crops from warmer climates.

Why do it?

To become self-sufficient, you need to maximize the growing potential of your land, starting crops early to ensure successive harvests, and avoiding lean periods later on. A greenhouse or hoop house may be expensive, but the benefits soon pay off—from growing salads in winter to giving tender plants a head start in spring. Some foods travel around the world to reach us, leaving a trail of environmental issues in their wake. A greenhouse is a way to grow them at home, rather than giving them up or feeling guilty every time we eat a strawberry out of season.

Small-scale options

From mini cloches for individual plants to homemade cold frames, you can still give plants in smaller yards extra protection without putting up a hoop house or greenhouse. Even city dwellers growing herbs and salads on windowsills can experience the benefits of growing under glass.

Cloches

Cloches are essentially protective covers for plants. We have tried tent-style cloches covered with plastic, low plastic tunnels with inverted U-shaped wires, glass frames, and hard corrugated plastic sheets bent

into a curve. One of our favorite methods is simply to place a clean jelly jar over a newly transplanted seedling—a modern take on a Victorian glass bell cloche. We also cut the bottom off big plastic bottles and place the top half over the plant, unscrewing the cap for ventilation in warmer weather.

Cold frames

Traditionally used for hardening off seedlings before planting out, we've found they're also ideal for raising seedlings from scratch and for extending the season of salads and herbs. A cold frame's key design

1. **A traditional glass cloche** *to protect a single plant.*
2. **The shape of a geodesic dome** *prevents frost pockets from forming.* 3. **DIY cloche** *made from a cut-down plastic bottle.* 4. **Harden off** *plants in a cold frame before planting out.* 5. **Open vents** *and door in a greenhouse to keep the air circulating.*

feature is that it can be accessed easily for watering and harvesting. Using an old window for the top saves lots of effort and is a great way to recycle (see pages 116–117).

Windowsills

Growing plants on a windowsill may not sound like the most ambitious approach to growing food under cover, but it is one of the most successful. Young plants thrive in a warm, slug-free environment and, because you see them regularly, they get more attention and grow well.

Large-scale structures

With the warmth and protection of a hoop house or greenhouse, we think it is more than viable to become self-sufficient in a range of vegetables. What you may lose in ground space on your property, you more than make up for with the extra weeks of growing time that you gain.

Greenhouses

A greenhouse has to be one of the nicest places to work in winter. The warmth and smells make it a bit like going on vacation.

As with all methods of growing under cover, choosing where to site it is crucial. Our greenhouse is oriented east–west on a south-facing wall, which gives lots of light and the wall acts as a heat sink.

Greenhouses are expensive to buy new but may be available second-hand if you are prepared to dismantle one. They can be surprisingly productive for their size if you get the layout right. Optimize vertical space by installing tiers of shelves for pots and trays, and by hanging baskets inside. Try growing tomatoes, herbs, eggplants, chili peppers, and salads, and starting off all sorts of seedlings.

In winter the temperature shouldn't fall below about 40°F (4°C) at night, and we find it can get

6 STEPS TO SUCCESS

Follow these guidelines to get the best from plants grown under cover

■ **Ventilate often**, even in winter, to prevent pests like red spider mite from proliferating. A heat sink (see pages 118–119) helps to keep air circulating, or open the door and roof vents to draw air through.

■ **Don't overplant**: too many plants, too close together, are more susceptible to pests and diseases.

■ **Nourish the soil** in permanent beds with a good supply of liquid fertilizer or new compost. Intensively used soil can become depleted of nutrients.

■ **Monitor the temperature**: frost is still an issue under cover. Even a rain barrel or small pond will help retain heat, but a fan-assisted heat sink is ideal (see pages 118–119).

■ **Clear away detritus** from dead plants and fallen fruits to reduce the chances of pests and diseases building up.

■ **Water automatically** by installing an irrigation system and plants need never go thirsty (see pages 110–111).

UNDERCOVER JOBS

Tender plants such as chili peppers have to be grown under cover in cool regions; you'll get an earlier harvest from many crops if you start off seedlings in a greenhouse or hoop house; and a protected environment can fool other vegetables into cropping out of season.

Take cuttings *from chili peppers. Remove a few leaves to increase the chances of success, and pot in a rehydrated coir plug or cutting medium (see page 135).*

Start off corn *seedlings under cover for an earlier harvest. Harden them off (see page 134) before planting outside when there is no longer any risk of frost.*

Harvest rainbow chard *all year round by growing it in beds under cover in a hoop house or by putting cloches over plants outside.*

113

surprisingly warm in sunny weather. Installing a heat sink (see pages 118–119) keeps the air warm in winter, and also circulates air in summer to keep the temperature down and reduce the risk of disease. To stop a greenhouse from overheating, hang a damp towel in the open doorway and keep the roof and side vents wide open.

Hoop houses

Commercial hoop houses are a familiar part of our landscape, but they're not just for farmers and market gardeners. We built our first one in a small suburban garden.

Hoop houses are often made from clear plastic stretched over metal frames and are simple to put

together. Dig down around the frame and lay some sod over the edges of the plastic; this keeps it stretched tight and avoids any embarrassing kite fiascos in high winds.

At Newhouse Farm we have built raised beds down either side and installed benches for potting up seedlings. We added a pond to help retain heat and encourage frogs to keep down pests. In summer the pathway down the middle is full of pots holding the taller plants like tomatoes and cucumbers, which grow incredibly well tied up to the center of the frame and are easy to harvest by walking along the rows.

Geodesic domes

Geodesic domes are not new; they have been around since the beginning of the 20th century. Championed by inventor Buckminster Fuller, they are designed to have a minimum external surface area but with far fewer internal building supports, giving maximum growing space.

Geodesic domes also make the most of solar energy. Sunlight shining into a conventional structure like a greenhouse creates warm air pockets that can damage plants. A dome shape aids air circulation and prevents pockets from developing.

We ordered our geodesic dome in kit form. Putting together a building that gains its strength only when the last piece is put in place is a bit of a nightmare, but a lot of fun. We think it looks like a spaceship. For more on geodesic growing, see pages 102–103.

Sunrooms or conservatories

Most sunroom owners know that they are excellent places to grow plants. You can start off an array of seedlings in a sunroom and make it a permanent home for exotics. Citrus and olive trees, grape vines, and physalis plants do particularly well in sunrooms.

TYPE	PROS	CONS
Cloche	▦ Cheap to construct—free if you make it out of scrap. ▦ Ideal for gradually hardening off seedlings (see page 134). ▦ Protects vulnerable young plants from pests.	▦ Can get easily knocked over or blown away. ▦ Only useful when plants are small. ▦ Time-consuming technique.
Cold frame	▦ Easy access for weeding, watering, harvesting. ▦ Simple and cheap to make.	▦ Not enough room for tall plants such as tomatoes.
Windowsill	▦ Almost everyone has one. ▦ Big plants like tomatoes will be extremely productive.	▦ Tall plants may reduce the amount of daylight getting into the room. ▦ Stand pots in a tray to protect woodwork when watering. ▦ You must rotate the pots.
Greenhouse	▦ Productive growing space with the right layout. ▦ Relatively easy to assemble.	▦ Can be expensive.
Hoop house	▦ Cheaper than a greenhouse. ▦ Large space available for growing.	▦ Not as durable. ▦ Not a good option on a windy site.
Geodesic dome	▦ No warm air pockets. ▦ More space for tall plants. ▦ Admits maximum amount of light. ▦ Aerodynamic shape—great on windy sites. ▦ Fits into the landscape because of its completely curved outline.	▦ Challenging to assemble from a kit or build from scratch. ▦ Expensive.
Sunroom	▦ Great for exotics. ▦ Part of the house so plants get maximum care.	▦ Very expensive. ▦ Temperature control is essential.

Using a hoop house

Hoop houses are great places to grow everything from spinach to salad, but their usefulness doesn't end there. Use the space to dry garlic, onions, and herbs before storing, and to bring tender plants such as citrus trees under cover in winter—and make a workstation where you can repot plants or take cuttings. Our hoop house is a carefully planned mix of permanent plantings such as vines and olives, crops such as tomatoes and cucumbers that will spend their entire life under cover, and others that benefit from a warm start but are destined for the vegetable plot. We even have a propagator in the hoop house, which acts as a double skin to retain the sun's heat and is ideal for starting tomato and melon seedlings.

Hang up garlic *to dry in the airy warmth of a hoop house before storing it.*

Maximize productivity
Use your undercover space to start plants early, keep salads and herbs producing over winter, and grow more crops such as melons and eggplants that won't survive outside in a cool climate.

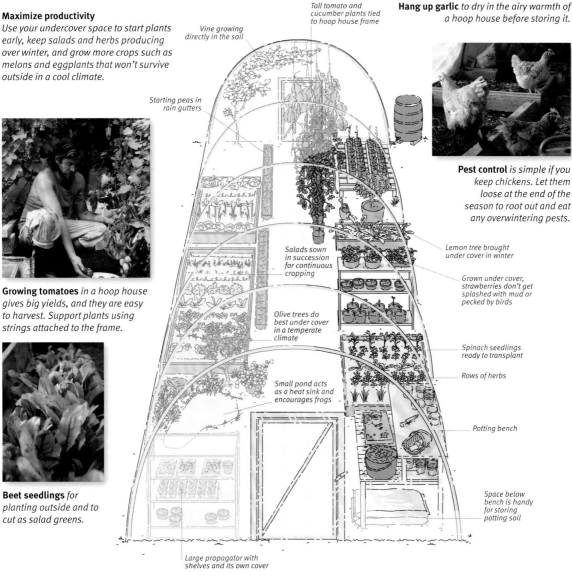

Vine growing directly in the soil

Tall tomato and cucumber plants tied to hoop house frame

Starting peas in rain gutters

Salads sown in succession for continuous cropping

Olive trees do best under cover in a temperate climate

Small pond acts as a heat sink and encourages frogs

Large propagator with shelves and its own cover

Lemon tree brought under cover in winter

Grown under cover, strawberries don't get splashed with mud or pecked by birds

Spinach seedlings ready to transplant

Rows of herbs

Potting bench

Space below bench is handy for storing potting soil

Growing tomatoes *in a hoop house gives big yields, and they are easy to harvest. Support plants using strings attached to the frame.*

Beet seedlings *for planting outside and to cut as salad greens.*

Pest control *is simple if you keep chickens. Let them loose at the end of the season to root out and eat any overwintering pests.*

115

PROJECT **Build a cold frame**

In its simplest form, a cold frame is a box with a glass lid that helps seedlings to grow by enhancing the environment they are in and protecting them from extremes of weather. Instead of buying new materials to build one, we always recommend looking around to see what odds and ends you have available. Reusing old windows or panes of glass is a much greener option—and it's cheaper.

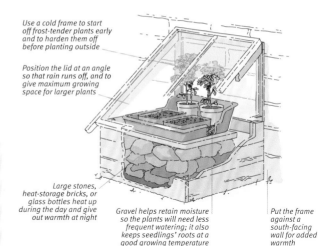

Use a cold frame to start off frost-tender plants early and to harden them off before planting outside

Position the lid at an angle so that rain runs off, and to give maximum growing space for larger plants

Large stones, heat-storage bricks, or glass bottles heat up during the day and give out warmth at night

Gravel helps retain moisture so the plants will need less frequent watering; it also keeps seedlings' roots at a good growing temperature

Put the frame against a south-facing wall for added warmth

YOU WILL NEED
- Drill
- Level
- Hammer
- Nail set
- Tape measure
- Hand saw
- Screwdriver
- Wood: planks, uprights, and battens
- Old window plus extra glass or plastic
- Sliding hinges
- Nails
- Screw anchors
- Screws
- Stones or glass bottles

MAKING THE BASE

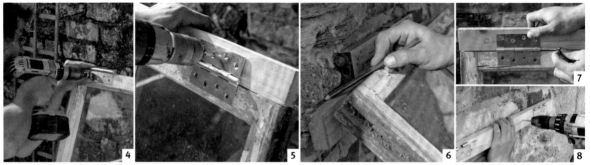

1. Make a simple box by screwing horizontal planks to a framework. The size of your box will depend on what you use for a lid. We based ours on an old window. Make the uprights from standard 1 x 2 in (50 x 25 mm) lengths of wood. We used some leftover planks for the sides—1 x 6 in (150 x 25 mm) are ideal—and we saved on wood by positioning the cold frame against a raised bed and wall.   **2. Make sure the sides** are level.   **3. Add a brace** across the back of the box to keep it square.

MAKING THE LID

4. Use an old window for the lid. Screw two sliding hinges to opposite ends of the top edge of the window frame. Slide on the other half of each hinge.   **5. Screw the other hinge halves** to a length of wooden batten the same width as the lid. **6. Flip the hinges shut** and hold the lid in its final position, resting it against the wall and the front edge of the cold frame base. Mark the position of the batten on the wall, then put the lid down.   **7. Slide the bolts** out of each hinge to separate lid and batten.   **8. Drill** the batten to the wall using screw anchors and screws, following the guide marks you made earlier.

CONSTRUCTING THE SIDES

9. Measure and cut lumber for the triangular side-wall frames, with the lid in place. Remove lid. **10. Mark the angle** of the joint for the side-wall frame. Do this at both ends. Cut the angles. **11. Drill** the side frame in place using long screws at an angle. Measure the triangular space and cut a pane of glass to this size. **12. Nail narrow battens** to the inside edges to stop the glass from falling inward. **13. Fit glass** against inner battens and nail additional narrow battens onto the outside to hold it in place. Take care not to smash the glass. Use a nail set to keep your hammer a safe distance away! If you don't feel confident about cutting glass to fit, use tough, clear plastic sheeting or bubble wrap and staple it to the frame.

USING THE COLD FRAME

14. Fill the cold frame to within 4 in (10 cm) of the top with large stones, heat-storage bricks, or glass bottles filled with water, allowing space for warm air to circulate and be absorbed. **15. Place an old paving slab** on top of the stones, again leaving room around the sides for air circulation. Adjust it until it's level. **16. Fill a plant tray** with gravel and level the surface. Place it in the cold frame. **17. Slide the lid** back onto the hinges. Set trays and pots of seedlings on the gravel—taller plants at the back, small ones at the front. Keep a length of wood handy to prop the lid open, to acclimate plants gradually and harden them off (see page 134).

ALTERNATIVE USES
Make maximum use of your cold frame with these ideas.

Make a hotbed
Line the base with plastic, then half-fill it with fresh horse manure. Mix in some straw and leave to ferment. Wait until the strong smell of ammonia disappears, then add about 1 ft (30 cm) of topsoil. Plant or sow when the soil temperature is about 80°F (27°C). Great for initial germination of plants.

Drying seeds
Use your cold frame to speed up the drying process when preparing seed to store. Keep the lid slightly open to allow moisture to escape.

Cold frame turned solar dryer
Spread seeds thinly to dry. Use trays to keep different varieties separate.

Making a greenhouse heat sink

Even growing under cover, plants still need extra protection from frost. Greenhouses and hoop houses heat up quickly but, sadly, cool down just as fast. The challenge is to find a way of keeping the temperature above the danger zone where plants can be damaged—we're not saying warm, just warm enough. That's where the heat sink comes in.

What is a heat sink?

A heat sink is something that can capture the sun's heat and store it during the day, then release the heat when temperatures drop at night.

Instead of trying to generate heat to keep our greenhouse frost-free, we like the idea of capturing it. Even in the depths of winter, the sun warms greenhouses and hoop houses, but the lack of insulation means the heat disappears quickly as the sun sets.

So we decided to stop some of that free heat from escaping and store it. Our system uses a small fan that runs continuously. During the day it blows warm air through a box buried in the ground and filled with lumps of glass—the heat sink. At night it blows cooler air through the warm glass, which warms the air. This warm air stops the temperature in the greenhouse from falling below freezing. For added frost protection we also built our lean-to greenhouse against a south-facing stone wall, which itself acts as a heat sink.

Construction

Our heat sink is a hole roughly 1.3 cu yd (1 cu m), dug in the floor of the greenhouse. We figured this would be big enough for our 8-x-13-ft (2.4-x-4-m) greenhouse. We insulated the hole with discarded polystyrene to stop heat from being lost to the ground, before filling it with imploded glass to absorb the heat. Imploded glass has amazing thermal properties, but we realize it's not easy to get ahold of this special type of glass: rocks, stones, glass bottles or jars—filled with water—will work just as

well. Making the pipework is a great opportunity to recycle odd bits of leftover plumbing. You'll need a variety of connectors and lengths of standard plastic piping. Drill holes to perforate the pipes before assembling. Start with a T-connector where the inlet pipe enters the ground and connect a series of pipes to form a big loop that returns to the T-connector. There's no need to apply sealant between joints.

The benefits of a heat sink

▨ **Very little power** is needed to run the system, which relies on an inexpensive computer fan designed to run for years on very low power. You can generate the power yourself if you use a solar PV panel to charge up the battery.

▨ **No nasty fumes** from conventional kerosene or propane heaters.

▨ **Unexpected frosts** won't catch you off guard. The heat sink runs regardless, so no need to constantly check the weather forecast.

▨ **Prevent diseases** such as botrytis by keeping the system running year round to circulate air.

The results

It's very hard to say exactly how efficient our system is, but combined with the south-facing rear wall, it has managed to keep our greenhouse frost-free. Salads continue to grow deep into the winter—no mean feat considering we regularly have frosts with temperature sometimes dipping as low as 21°F (−6°C). A winter of extra productivity and the system paid for itself: not a bad investment.

How the heat sink system works

We all know hot air rises, and that's what this system relies on. During the day a fan sucks hot air from the apex of the greenhouse roof, down through some piping, and into a network of perforated pipes to warm up the heat sink. At night the fan draws down cool air, which is then warmed by the heat sink and in turn warms the greenhouse—simple!

A frost-free greenhouse
Store the sun's energy in a heat sink and use it to warm up your greenhouse at night.

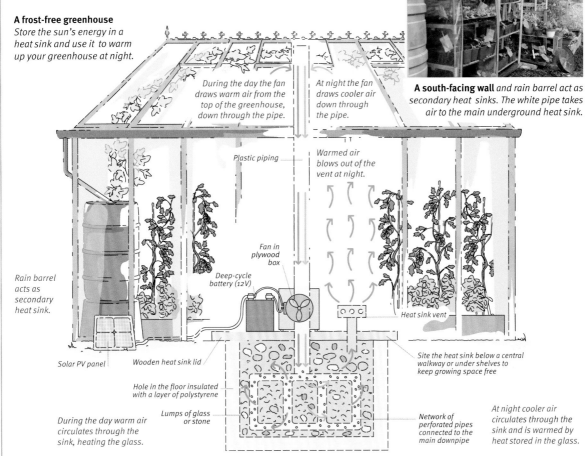

During the day the fan draws warm air from the top of the greenhouse, down through the pipe.

At night the fan draws cooler air down through the pipe.

A south-facing wall *and rain barrel act as secondary heat sinks. The white pipe takes air to the main underground heat sink.*

Plastic piping

Warmed air blows out of the vent at night.

Fan in plywood box

Deep-cycle battery (12V)

Rain barrel acts as secondary heat sink.

Heat sink vent

Solar PV panel

Wooden heat sink lid

Site the heat sink below a central walkway or under shelves to keep growing space free

Hole in the floor insulated with a layer of polystyrene

During the day warm air circulates through the sink, heating the glass.

Lumps of glass or stone

Network of perforated pipes connected to the main downpipe

At night cooler air circulates through the sink and is warmed by heat stored in the glass.

INSTALLING THE FAN

1. Wire up the fan.   **2. Make a small plywood box** to house the fan. Make a lid to seal the box. Cut out holes in the sides to fit the air pipes, and drill holes for the wiring.   **3. Connect the fan** to a deep-cycle battery using alligator clips. Screw the lid onto the fan box. Keep the battery and fan box in a plastic crate to protect from moisture. Cut holes in the crate to match the holes in the fan box for the air pipes.   **4. Push the pipes** through the holes in the crate and into the fan box.
5. Connect the battery to a small solar panel outside the greenhouse and the system is up and running.

Gardening in harmony with nature

We encourage wildlife on our land because improving biodiversity is an effective method of controlling pests and boosting productivity. This dedicated wildlife garden illustrates different ideas and the benefits they bring, so that you can choose suitable elements to add to your own yard. And don't forget, urban gardens can be wildlife havens, too.

KEY TO GARDEN PLAN

1. Nettle patch
2. Bird nesting box
3. Bat box
4. Small pond
5. Rock-pile habitat for garter snakes
6. Bee B&B
7. Flowers for beneficial insects
8. Ladybug hotel
9. Nectar station for bees and butterflies
10. Mason bee house
11. Bird feeder
12. Toad house
13. Log-pile habitat
14. Mini wildflower meadow

Flowers for butterflies (7)
Attract butterflies with flowers such as New England asters and they'll move on to pollinate your crops.

A wildflower meadow (14)
Plant a traditional meadow to benefit all wildlife—tall grasses provide safe cover for little creatures, and birds like to eat the seeds, while wildflowers attract butterflies and bees.

Make a log pile (13)
Stack up logs, vines, and other twiggy trimmings, securing the pile in place with strong branches hammered in vertically, to create a habitat for frogs and toads, which shelter in the gaps.

Birds as pest control
Some birds snatch insects on the wing; other species eat at ground level—sparrows love to munch aphids and caterpillars.

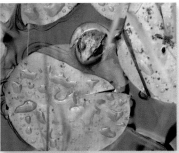

Feed the birds (11)
Hang up suet blocks packed with nuts and seeds.

Dig a pond (4)
Frogs and toads need water to breed—and the good news is that they all eat slugs and other garden pests.

Bee hotel (6)
Bamboo canes in a flower pot will encourage solitary bees to take up residence.

A dew-covered spider web
Spiders are an important part of a garden's ecosystem, playing their part in keeping down insect pests and being in turn a valuable food source for small backyard birds like wrens.

Encouraging wildlife

Simply by gardening organically, without chemicals, you've already made your property wildlife-friendly, even if you do nothing else. By adding a few extras such as nectar-rich flowers and a small pond or bird feeder to attract the right wildlife, we've noticed a positive effect on the productivity of our cultivated areas for little effort and outlay.

Making habitats

Different creatures like different environments. A shady log pile will shelter frogs and toads, while a rock pile in a sunnier spot will encourage garter snakes. You need them in your yard because they all eat slugs.

A nettle patch attracts ladybugs. Adults and larvae eat huge amounts of aphids (up to a 100 a day!) and polish off pests such as potato beetles, mealybugs, and whiteflies.

Set up a toad house—a bottomless wooden or ceramic container with a small entrance hole—to attract toads. They eat slugs and other pests such as cutworms and mosquitoes.

Create wildlife corridors

Use these to link habitats and help insects and small animals to move around the garden. All you need to do is leave to grow unchecked areas along boundaries, under hedges, and against fences. You could even ask your neighbors to do the same and the result would be a natural wildlife highway across your neighborhood.

Planting for wildlife

Native plants are the best choice for encouraging biodiversity as they support a wider range of wildlife. Bees like flowers that are rich in nectar, such as borage, lavender, lemon balm, mint, chives, and other herbs. Useful insects such as hoverflies and parasitic wasps, which prey on aphids, prefer flat flowerheads packed with lots of tiny flowers, so plant dill, fennel, yarrow, daisies, asters, and zinnias.

Don't deadhead flowers—seedheads make good snacks for small seed-eaters. Coneflowers and sunflowers are ideal.

Feeding

Put seeds and nuts out when natural food is in short supply, then birds will be used to visiting your garden by the time insect pest populations build up. Feed early bees and butterflies when flowers are scarce by investing in a nectar station. It looks a bit like a bird feeder but it holds a sponge soaked with sugar water and is bright yellow to attract insects.

Nest boxes

We see birds as both friends and foes. It's great to have their company in the garden, but our fruit bushes need netting to prevent them from harvesting before us. On the other hand, birds like to eat insect pests, and so we encourage them to visit. Nest boxes help: set them up out of reach of cats, and facing between southeast and north so they don't overheat in strong sunlight.

Insect houses

As well as the bee B&B (opposite), leave clay pots stuffed with dry grass at ground level for bumblebee queens, which hibernate underground.

Cater to overwintering ladybugs by opening a ladybug hotel. You can make your own by drilling a log full of holes (see the bee B&B for tips) and setting it vertically on a pole. Or cut short lengths of hollow bamboo and twigs, tie them into bundles, and hang them around your yard.

These small changes can make a big difference to a useful insect's survival rate.

1. Oxeye daisies *have flat, open flowers that attract useful insects.* **2. Teasels** *are great dual-purpose wildlife plants: bees like the flowers and birds eat the seeds.* **3. Poppies** *are another favorite of bees and other beneficial insects.*

PROJECT **Construct homes for wildlife**

There are occasions when you can improve on nature. A homemade bee B&B makes an ideal shelter and nesting site for solitary pollinating bee species such as mason bees. And we'd say that digging a pond is one of the most wildlife-friendly steps you can take on your property: it's a water source for small birds and mammals, and a vital breeding habitat for frogs.

YOU WILL NEED
- Saw
- Hammer
- Drill with various-sized bits
- Scrap plywood and a fairly thick log
- Bracket, nails, screws

BUILD A BEE B&B

1. Use a flat piece of wood for the base. Cut a log section to fit the base. **2. Drill** a variety of holes in one end of the log using drill bits of various sizes. Drill at a slight upward angle so that rain can't drip in. **3. Add a bracket** to the base and screw the base to the log. **4. Make a roof** with some spare wood. **5. Attach the B&B** to a south-facing wall or fence, near bee-attracting plants, and wait for the bees to move in.

MAKE A WILDLIFE POND

Dig your pond at least 2 ft (60 cm) at its deepest. It must have a shallow area, too. Rake the soil to remove sharp stones, then spread out the underlay and liner. Use one or two rocks to hold them in place while you fill with water. Edge with stones or rocks.

YOU WILL NEED
- Spade, rake
- Underlay such as carpet
- Pond liner
- Edging stones or rocks

Fill your pond with rainwater if possible; if you have to use city water, let the pond stand for a week to drive off any chlorine before adding plants.

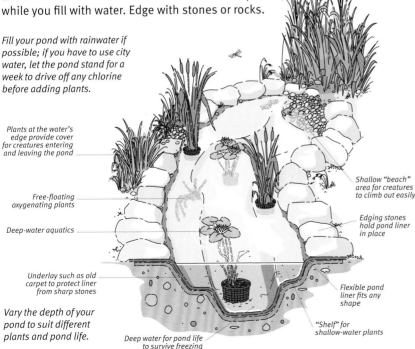

Plants at the water's edge provide cover for creatures entering and leaving the pond

Free-floating oxygenating plants

Deep-water aquatics

Underlay such as old carpet to protect liner from sharp stones

Vary the depth of your pond to suit different plants and pond life.

Deep water for pond life to survive freezing

"Shelf" for shallow-water plants

Flexible pond liner fits any shape

Edging stones hold pond liner in place

Shallow "beach" area for creatures to climb out easily

Add oxygenating plants *A bucketful from another pond will also contain creatures from pond snails to water beetles, and will boost biodiversity.*

Dragonflies *spend part of their life cycle under water. They eat midges and other insect pests.*

Growing in urban spaces

Space may be restricted in towns and cities, but it's still possible to grow some of your own food in a small garden or even on a balcony or large windowsill. By using simple and intensive gardening methods, you'll soon be picking salads and herbs, or even fruit and vegetables. And they can all be grown conveniently just outside your back door.

CROPS FOR URBANITES

If you have limited space, use these guidelines to decide what to grow.
■ Is it something you love to eat?
■ Is it expensive to buy?
■ Is it easy to grow?
■ Is it little work for a high yield?
If a crop checks all of these boxes, go ahead and grow it!

Our suggestions

■ **Salads** are expensive to buy but easy to grow at home. Try arugula and lamb's lettuce, or cut-and-come-again varieties, the leaves of which can be picked all summer.
■ **Easy growers** include garlic, onions, and carrots.
■ **Quick croppers** like radishes work well in between rows of slower-growing crops.
■ **Perennials** can be low-maintenance and highly productive. Try perpetual spinach and soft fruit, as well as a selection of hardy herbs.
■ **High-yielding crops** should be your staples. These include runner beans, carrots, zucchini, leeks, rutabagas, chard, and tomatoes.

Salad plants *Keep picking arugula (top) all summer long; nasturtium flowers add a peppery tang to salads.*

Think outside the box

Balconies, flat roofs, and even sloping roofs can all help to optimize your area for growing food, while using vertical walls makes sense in an urban environment where space is severely limited.

But you don't have to sacrifice everything for food production. Balancing productivity with a place to relax after work is easy to achieve if you rethink what is considered ornamental. Chard with colorful stems, architectural artichokes, and peas and beans grown for flowers as well as crops will all make your space more beautiful. And include flowers that work harder; some act as natural pest controls (see page 101) while others can be eaten (see page 157).

Growing in containers

Almost any fruit or vegetable will grow in a container, and this form of gardening offers a manageable introduction to growing your own. Container growing is cheap, easy, suitable for any size of yard, and movable. We spent years moving from house to house with our collection of kitchen-garden plants in pots, ranging from herbs to fig trees.
■ **Use any type of container** for growing plants, from terra-cotta pots and plastic bottles cut in half to old paint cans and buckets.
■ **Drill drainage holes** in the bottom of your containers, and cover the holes with a layer of broken pots or small stones to stop them from clogging up.
■ **Plants in pots are not self-reliant:** water them regularly, feed them, and replace the potting mix each spring.

Growing in raised beds

Raised beds are ideal for areas where there's no soil or it's of poor quality. Building a raised bed (see page 126) makes planting and harvesting so convenient; you can even make beds at waist height to avoid back strain.
■ **A wide range of materials** can be used to build a raised bed.
■ **Raised beds on hard surfaces** are like containers, and you'll have to water and fertilize plants regularly.

Growing in hanging baskets

Hanging baskets aren't just for flowers—you can grow fruit and vegetables in them, too. Strawberries, tumbling tomatoes, salads, and herbs will thrive in them. Use a bracket to fix baskets to a wall, or hang edible baskets from a trellis or fencing.
■ **Pests like slugs and snails** find scaling hanging baskets a mission impossible, especially if suspended from copper wire, which they will be reluctant to cross.
■ **Baskets dry out quickly,** which means they need regular watering, so consider an automatic irrigation system (see pages 110–111).

Growing vertically

Vertical growing imitates the natural world, which has three productive layers: trees, shrubs, and herbaceous plants (see forest gardens, page 99).
■ **Try interplanting.** Grow tall, thin vegetables between short, bushy ones to maximize your space.
■ **Add climbing plants**—anything from runner beans to grapevines—to transform walls, fences, arbors, and trellises into productive areas.

PROJECT **Plant a hanging basket**

We used a basket we made from willow stems, but you've probably got one lying around that will do just as well. You also need a tough plastic liner, such as a piece of an old potting soil bag. We planted our basket with alpine strawberries—they're easy to grow from seed and produce fruit the same year. Or try salad mixes, herbs such as thyme and basil, and tumbling cherry tomato plants.

YOU WILL NEED
- Basket
- Plastic for liner
- Potting mix, straw
- Copper wire
- Strawberry plants

1. Line the basket with plastic, and poke a few holes in it for drainage. Fill with potting mix. Use the copper wire to make a handle to hang the basket. **2. Make holes** in the soil and insert plants. Firm soil around plants. Water well. **3. Mulch with straw** to reduce evaporation and keep soil moist. **4. Hang** the basket in a sunny spot. Water daily.

1. Urban backyards *can hold an awful lot of produce, using a variety of raised beds and containers. Trellises and an arbor make frames for climbing beans; wall pots are ideal for herbs and salads. There's even room for a fig tree in the center.* **2. A raised bed** *edged with chamomile for infusions (see pages 266–267) and to attract pollinating insects, beans at the back, and salad in between, plus a squash cascading over the edge.* **3. Hanging baskets** *in tiers triple your growing space. These are planted with a cut-and-come-again spicy salad mix, which you can pick for many weeks over the summer.*

125

PROJECT **Build a raised bed**

Building a raised bed is a great way to turn a small space, even one where there is no soil, into a productive plot. Of all the different gardening methods we've experimented with, our raised beds take the least effort to maintain. They are easy to weed and water, there's less bending involved (ideal for older gardeners), and the soil doesn't get compacted because it is never walked on.

YOU WILL NEED
- Hammer
- Ruler
- Pencil
- Saw
- Electric drill
- Nails, screws
- Wood—salvaged floorboards are ideal and cheap
- Pond liner or tarp
- Crushed stone
- Potting soil and compost

Decide where to build your bed. *We made ours against a south-facing wall to absorb more heat during the day and retain it overnight. It's shown planted with squash, chamomile, lettuce, and runner beans.*

BUILDING THE FRAME

1. Cut wood to length. Vary the lengths of the pieces, so that in the first layer the front overlaps the sides, in the second layer the sides overlap the front, and so on. Staggering the end joints in this way strengthens the frame. The average size for a raised bed that is easy to reach from all sides is 2 ft x 3 ft (60 cm x 90 cm).   **2. Screw** each layer together. We used long POZIDRIV screws.   **3. Build up the frame** in layers.   **4. Strengthen** the finished frame by adding corner posts.

LINING AND FILLING THE BED

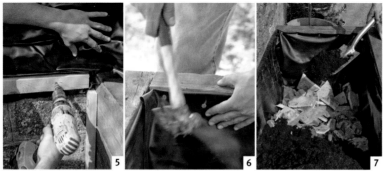

5. Line the bed. We used a piece of old pond liner and attached it to the wall using a wooden batten.   **6. Fold the liner** to fit, then nail the edges to the frame. The liner stops moisture from soaking into the wood and keeps it in the soil.   **7. Fill** the bottom 4 in (10 cm) with broken pottery and stones for drainage. Add good-quality potting mix, water it well, and start planting.

TRY THIS
- **Lift some slabs** on your patio and use them to build a raised planter. Stand them on end and bury them up to half their depth for stability.
- **Dismantle an old rock wall** and reuse the stone—it stores heat and keeps your plants' roots warm.
- **Experiment:** build walls from old car tires (see page 48) or glass bottles cemented together. Or stack a few tires on top of each other for an instant raised bed or potato tower.
- **Add "keyholes"** to a deep raised bed. This creates an E-shaped bed, with recesses that allow you to reach plants at the back easily.

PROJECT **Make a worm bin**

Conventional compost bins take up a lot of space and the process can be slow. A worm bin turns kitchen waste into superb compost quickly, thanks to the action of redworms. These aren't earthworms, but worms that live in leaf litter on top of the soil. A worm bin recreates their ideal habitat, which is warm, dark, and damp. The easiest thing to do is to buy a kit, which consists of a series of stackable units, and comes with a tub of worms. As you fill each unit with waste, you simply add another on top. The worms also produce a liquid nutrient that filters down through the worm bin—we call it worm tea. Dilute it about 1:10 with water before feeding it to your plants.

A worm bin in action *takes up minimal space and even has room for a plant. Copper tape keeps slugs away.*

DO FEED YOUR WORMS
- Fruit and vegetable peelings
- Tea bags and coffee grounds
- Paper and cardboard (shredded)
- Old socks (not synthetic fabrics)
- Flowers
- Pet and human hair
- Fallen leaves
- Small amounts of grass cuttings
- Dust from the vacuum cleaner
- Raw eggshells

DON'T GIVE THEM
- Meat, fish, and dairy products
- Dog and cat feces
- Too much citrus or too many onions
- Cooked food

ASSEMBLING THE WORM BIN

1. Stand the base unit with the spigot on a level piece of ground close to your kitchen. Push one of the corrugated rings firmly into place. These stop worms from escaping. **2. Stack the unit** with the fine-mesh bottom on top of the base unit and add the tub of worms to it. **3. Feed the worms** with some fresh kitchen scraps. Chop up any big pieces first. Feed them small amounts until they settle in. **4. Cover them** with shredded paper. Lift the paper up to add food. You can tell when the worms are coping with waste you give them: they will be active and you'll see that they are composting what you put in.

5. Add another corrugated ring and composter unit. Add a final ring to the top unit and put the planter on top to act as a lid. **6. Fill** the planter with potting mix. **7. Plant** the planter with vegetables or herbs. We added a zucchini. The top planter doesn't benefit from the worms below; it's just a way of making every bit of space in your plot productive and a neat finishing touch to your worm bin.

CARE TIPS

- **Start using** the unit above when the bottom composter is full of scraps. Take a couple of handfuls of worms and waste from the bottom layer to start up the next one. When the worms are in full production they will compost scraps within a couple of weeks.
- **Drain off** the worm tea weekly.
- **Inspect** your worms regularly. If the bin's contents dry out over the summer, add a little water. If it gets too damp, then add more paper, cardboard, or a bit of straw.
- **Don't add more scraps** if there are no worms on the surface of your food waste. Too much food will starve your worms of air, leading to a soggy, slimy mess and eventually even worm fatalities.

Joining a community garden

If you have a tiny yard, or none at all, a community garden provides valuable space in which to grow your own food. Most are also social places, where you can swap seeds, exchange produce, and pick up tips from other gardeners. The extra room allows you to practice planting on a larger scale, too, and you can grow enough to preserve and store your produce for year-round use.

WHAT TO GROW

Try our recommended annual crops for first-time community gardeners.

▪ **Garlic** is very easy to grow and can be stored for months.

▪ **Leeks** are high-yielding crops for a late fall harvest.

▪ **Beets** are another high-yielding crop. You can use the young greens in salads, as well as the roots.

▪ **Squashes** store well for winter, but they require a lot of space to grow.

▪ **Rainbow chard** is one of our favorites. It has incredibly colorful stems, and it grows quickly.

▪ **Radishes** grow rapidly—sow them between slower-growing crops.

▪ **Broad beans** can be sown in early spring and fall for a steady seasonal supply, but watch out for pest damage and disease.

▪ **Climbing and runner beans** make the most of vertical space. Grow them at the northern end of your plot so they don't shade other crops.

▪ **Zucchini and summer squashes** need little work for a high yield. Try a no-watering policy (see page 101).

▪ **Potatoes** are a no-brainer in a community garden. To optimize your space, try growing them in stacks of tires, barrels, or old potting soil bags, as well as in the ground.

Squash tastes best *small; try to find hidden ones before they get too big.*

Assess your time

The problem with community gardens is their popularity. Waiting lists can be long, and by taking a plot, you will inevitably be delaying someone else's chance to grow their own food, so if your garden at home is not used for crops, cultivate that first. Also think about how much time you will be able to give; if you don't keep your plot looking ship-shape, you might be asked to give it up. The obligation to keep your area tidy and productive is a great incentive to get the most out of it, but the pressure can be daunting. We recommend joining your first community garden with a friend or neighbor if you are in any doubt about how you will cope.

Read the rules

Community gardens are governed by by-laws that vary widely. In general, you can expect restrictions on planting trees, putting up fencing or a shed, or using the plot for business purposes. You may be barred from using pesticides or materials such as black plastic mulch. And many community gardens require you to participate in group work days or spend a certain amount of time maintaining common areas.

First steps

You rarely get to choose your plot, and will probably be forced to work with what you're given. This presents a great opportunity to do a mini site survey (see pages 170–171). Look at the slope of the land and type of soil. Note which areas get the most sunshine and which are shady.

Before you start planting, condition the soil with plenty of well-rotted manure and fertilizer (see pages 104–109), and perhaps some sharp sand, mushroom compost, or wood ash if it is heavy clay.

When deciding what to grow, think about what will be most suitable for each of your productive sites. For example, grow herbs and salads that you use most days at home—perhaps on a balcony or windowsill—and plant crops that require less attention on your community plot. You can also start seeds off at home and then transplant them to the plot.

Grow perennials

One of the great things about perennials is that they need little maintenance—ideal if you don't have much time. They are also relatively hardy. You could go for soft fruit such as strawberries, raspberries, and gooseberries, and a variety of vegetables, including perennial arugula, perpetual spinach, globe and Jerusalem artichokes, and, of course, rhubarb. Although it's not edible, comfrey is also worth growing as a useful fertilizer (see page 107).

If your site has restrictions on planting trees, try dwarf varieties, or train trees as cordons or step-overs—you may be able to fit them in without breaking the rules.

Access to water

Keeping your plants well watered can be a challenge. Sites usually have hoses, but you should plan your water use wisely. To preserve water, plant your crops farther apart than the recommended spacing, giving the roots more room to search for moisture. Also mulch between rows to reduce evaporation and help retain soil moisture.

Sheds and structures

If you are allowed to put up a shed, it will save you from carrying tools back and forth from home. Add a decent lock to store equipment safely. If you have a garden at home, you'll need to double up on basics, such as a spade and fork. For the ultimate well-organized shed, see pages 130–131.

Other permanent structures to consider are a cold frame to protect small plants (see pages 112–113 and 116–117), and a double compost bin made out of old pallets to recycle all of your plot's organic waste.

1. All the features *of an ideal plot, including shed, compost pile, and bean supports.* **2. Rain barrels** *collect a significant amount of rainwater from a shed roof.* **3. Plant runner beans** *at the north end of your plot so they won't cast shade.* **4. Fruit cages** *and floating row covers protect plants from pests.*

Setting up a well-equipped shed

The shed is the hub of Newhouse Farm, the store for the tools and equipment we need to keep it all going. We love our tools and tend to favor manual over mechanized. Of course, some modern machines are best suited to getting a job done, yet in general, especially on a small farm, we believe the more traditional tools really do help you become more connected to the land and thus more productive overall. Hand tools are also almost always cheaper and easier to maintain.

KEY TO SHED

1. Spades
2. Garden fork
3. Rake
4. Post driver
5. Scythe
6. Long-handled shovel
7. Ax
8. Broom
9. Pitchfork
10. Sledgehammer
11. Hoe
12. Mattock
13. Pickax
14. Tool rack
15. Fishing rod *(pp.215–216)*
16. Shelving
17. Squashes storing over winter *(pp.164–165)*
18. Egg incubator, infrared lamp *(p.194)*
19. Beekeeping equipment *(pp.212–213)*
20. Demijohns for brewing *(pp.254–261)*
21. Hand trowel
22. Hand fork
23. Watering can
24. Gas can
25. Plant pots
26. Dibber
27. Bin for animal feed
28. Wheelbarrow
29. Bucket
30. Spare boots
31. Sieve
32. Lawnmower
33. Bee suits *(pp.212–213)*
34. Screw press *(pp.256–261)*
35. Apple chopping box *(pp.260–261)*
36. Straw for animal bedding
37. Hand truck
38. Sprouting potatoes *(p.146)*
39. Industrial wood chipper *(pp.82–83)*
40. Rotary tiller

Hanging tools up *saves space in a small shed.*

Spades (1) *get a lot of use, and it's worth investing in really solid ones that won't bend.*

A dibber (26) *is useful for repotting small plants and for planting onion sets. Look for different sizes.*

A sieve (31) *is ideal for sifting soil or homemade compost to get rid of stones and bits of twig.*

Store squashes (17) *on the shelves if your shed is frost-free. Turn them regularly so they don't rot.*

Shelves and hooks *keep a big shed tidy and well organized. Use a floor-standing rack to stop tall tools from falling over. Put trays and boxes on the shelves to store small items neatly.*

A screw press (34) *for squeezing fruit for wine, hard cider, and juice.*

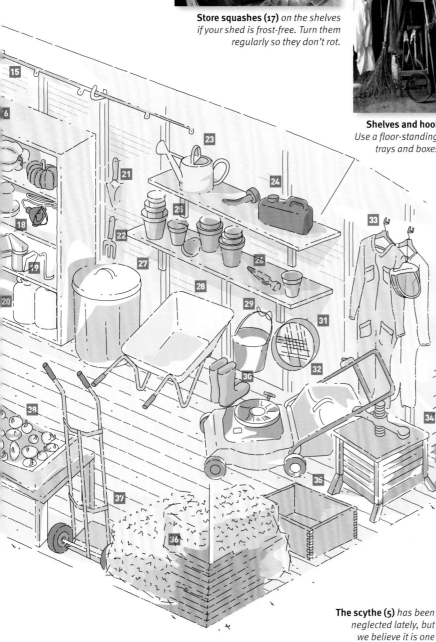

The scythe (5) *has been neglected lately, but we believe it is one of the small farm's greatest tools.*

131

WHAT TO GROW The variety of plants that you can grow for food is absolutely amazing, from quick-growing salads to slow-maturing walnut trees. By growing under cover, you can also try out some more exotic crops, for the sheer fun and challenge of it but also to reduce your food miles and still be able to enjoy a few tropical treats. Our philosophy is: try growing anything once, and if it grows well and you enjoy eating it, grow it again! There's something very special about planting fruit and nut trees that you know will provide produce for generations to come. And don't ignore nature's pantry of wild foods to forage...

Sowing and planting

Successful sowing and planting is all about getting the timing right—from starting seeds off under cover so that the seedlings are ready to plant outside when there's no risk of frost, to waiting for the soil to warm up before sowing outside. You also need to keep sowing every month to guarantee harvesting throughout the growing season. See pages 136–139 for a calendar to help plan your year.

Preparing the soil

Choose a warm area for a seed bed and add plenty of well-rotted organic matter, such as homemade compost, to improve it. Spread compost over the soil in fall and fork it in or allow the worms to do it for you. As well as adding nutrients, compost improves the soil structure, making clay soils easier to work and sandy soils more moisture retentive.

Dig heavy clay soils in fall and leave it to the frost to break up large clods. Any left in spring can be easily broken up with the back of a rake. Another option, if your soil is clay or full of stones, is to build raised beds on top of it (see page 126).

Before sowing seeds, rake the soil to achieve a crumbly, stone-free structure, known as a "fine tilth."

From seed to bed

Buy seeds from a catalog or garden center; we also save our own seeds from vegetables we have grown (see page 164). Having space to start seeds off under cover is invaluable. Hoop houses, cloches, and cold frames protect seedlings from frost and pests (see pages 112–115), and in northern regions, they let you start your growing season earlier and make the most of short summers.

We sow seeds in a range of trays, pots, and cell packs, using our own homemade compost, sieved to remove lumps and twigs. Pots are ideal for big seeds such as zucchini and beans; cell packs or egg cartons allow you to sow small seeds in individual units, which minimizes root disturbance when transplanting.

Thinning out

Seedlings grown in trays need thinning out so that they have more room to grow. Water them first, then hold a seedling between your thumb and forefinger and pull gently. Leave seedlings at 1–1½-in (2.5–4-cm) spacings. Transplant thinnings into seed trays to grow on—or eat them.

Hardening off

Plants grown under cover need to be acclimatized before transplanting outside. Set trays outside and bring them in at night, or open the lid of a cold frame during the day and close it at night, until there is no risk of frost.

Succession sowing

Sowing at intervals throughout the year maximizes the growing season and avoids gluts. For example, start peas under cover in February to harvest in May; then sow a few rows each month from March to July.

1. Thinning and transplanting *basil seedlings, to give them space to grow.*
2. Raking *to create a fine tilth ensures good contact between seed and soil.*
3. Use a drill marker—*string tied to two stakes—to sow seed in a straight line.*
4. Add compost *before planting seedlings to give them a nutrient boost.*

Basic techniques

When you can see that a pot or seed tray is full of roots, it's time to transplant seedlings. Sow seed outside when the soil has warmed up and is not too wet: follow package instructions, but as a general rule, sow thinly and not too deep. Plant fruit trees and bushes in winter when they are dormant.

TRANSPLANTING SEEDLINGS

1. Gently ease the seedling (here, an alpine strawberry) out of the cell. Hold the base of the stem and push up from below. **2. Use a dibber** to make a hole—in a pot of growing mix or outside in the soil—and set the plant at the same depth it was growing at in the tray. **3. Firm the soil** around the roots and water well.

SOWING OUTDOORS

Use a spade to make a ridge in the seed bed. **1. Sow seeds** thinly into a shallow drill made by drawing your hand or the side of a rake through the top of the ridge. These are radish seeds. **2. Cover** with finely sieved soil tilth. **3. Tamp down** the sides of the ridge with a spade. Water and leave to grow. Thin out the seedlings after a week or two, if overcrowded.

PLANTING CUTTINGS

1. Measure out equal volumes of homemade compost and sharp sand. Sieve the compost to remove lumps. **2. Mix the compost and sand** well. Sand improves drainage and reduces the risk of rotting. **3. Use the mixture** to fill pots, and push one cutting—these are gooseberries—into each pot. Water well and leave them to grow in a sheltered spot. Do not allow the pots to dry out.

PLANTING TREES

Dig a hole twice as wide and as deep as the rootball. Drive a stake into the hole before planting. **1. Plant the tree** at the same depth it was growing at—you'll see a soil line on the stem. Mix the excavated soil with compost and use it to fill in around the roots. Firm in gently with your foot. **2. Tie** an old bicycle inner tube around the trunk and nail it to the stake. **3. Water well**. Add mulch, avoiding the stem.

PLAN THE GROWING YEAR: VEGETABLES

Our aim is to be able to harvest something to eat from our vegetable beds virtually all year round. And for the most part we succeed, especially as we have a greenhouse and hoop house as backup. One of the keys to achieving our aim is succession sowing (see page 134). By sowing a couple of rows of salad greens every few weeks throughout the summer, the plants mature at different times, giving us a staggered harvest instead of a single glut. In fall we carry on sowing and harvesting in the greenhouse for winter salads.

Use these charts to help you plan when to sow and when to harvest crops. We've indicated the best spacings

CROPS	SPACINGS ROWS	PLANTS	WINTER E	M	L	SPRING E	M	L	SUMMER E	M	L	FALL E	M	L
Asparagus	18 in (45 cm)	18 in (45 cm)					P	H						
Beets	9–12 in (23–30 cm)	4 in (10 cm)				S	S	S	S H	S H	H	H	H	
Broad (fava) beans	10 in (25 cm)	10 in (25 cm)			S	S	S	S	H	H	H	H		S
Broccoli, sprouting	24–30 in (60–75 cm)	24–30 in (60–75 cm)	H		S	S	S	S	T	T		H	H	H
Brussels sprouts	14–18 in (25–45 cm)	14–18 in (25–45 cm)	H	H		S		T					H	H
Cabbage	12–20 in (30–50 cm)	12–20 in (30–50 cm)	H	H			S	S					H	H
Carrots	6 in (15 cm)	2–3 in (5–8 cm)	H		S	S	S	S H	S H	S H	H	H	H	
Cauliflower	20–30 in (50–75 cm)	20–30 in (50–75 cm)					S	S		T	H	H	H	H
Celeriac	18 in (45 cm)	12 in (30 cm)				S	S	T				H	H	
Chard	18 in (45 cm)	12 in (30 cm)	H	S H	S H	S H	S SH	S SH	H	H	H	H	H	H
Chile peppers	pot grown					S	S					H	H	
Cucumber	18–30 in (45–75 cm)	18–30 in (45–75 cm)				S	S	S	T		H	H		
Eggplant	24 in (60 cm)	24 in (60 cm)		S	S	S	T	T			H	H	H	
French beans	18 in (45 cm)	4 in (10 cm)						S	S H	S H	H	H	H	
Garlic	6 in (15 cm)	6 in (15 cm)	S	S					H	H	H			S
Ginger	pot grown					P	P					H	H	
Globe artichokes	36 in (90 cm)	36 in (90 cm)					P		H	H	H			
Horseradish	12 in (30 cm)	12 in (30 cm)					P		H	H	H			
Jerusalem artichokes	36 in (90 cm)	18 in (45 cm)	H	H	P	P								H
Kale	12–24 in (30–60 cm)	12–24 in (30–60 cm)	H	H	H	S H	S H	S H	S	T				
Kohlrabi	12 in (30 cm)	6 in (15 cm)				S	S	S H	S H	S H	H	H	H	

between rows and between plants in a row. We've also indicated where you can gain extra time by starting seeds off undercover before transplanting outside—or where a tender crop has to spend its entire life in a greenhouse. See pages 140–147 for more specific growing instructions on each vegetable.

KEY TO CHART			
S	sow	**S**	sow under glass
P	plant	**P**	plant under glass
T	transplant	**T**	transplant under glass
H	harvest	**H**	harvest under glass

CROPS	SPACINGS		WINTER			SPRING			SUMMER			FALL		
	ROWS	PLANTS	E	M	L	E	M	L	E	M	L	E	M	L
Leeks	12 in (30 cm)	6 in (15 cm)	H	H	H	SH	SH	H	T	T		H	H	H
Onions	12 in (30 cm)	2–3 in (5–8 cm)				S	S	S	S	H	H	H		
Parsnips	8–12 in (20–30 cm)	4–6 in (10–15 cm)	H	H	SH	S				H	H	H	H	H
Peas	18–24 in (45–60 cm)	3–4 in (8–10 cm)			S	S	ST	ST	SH	SH	H	H		
Peppers, bell	12–20 in (30–50 cm)	12–20 in (30–50 cm)			S	S	S			H	H	H	H	
Potatoes	18–30 in (45–75 cm)	12–15 in (30–38 cm)				P	P	P	H	H	H	H		
Pumpkin/squash	24–48 in (60–120 cm)	24–48 in (60–120 cm)					S	ST	S	H	H	H		
Radishes	6 in (15 cm)	1 in (2.5 cm)		S	S	S	S	SH	SH	SH	SH	SH	H	H
Rhubarb	36 in (90 cm)	36 in (90 cm)	P		H	PH	H	H	H	H	H		P	P
Runner beans	18 in (45 cm)	9 in (23 cm)				S	ST	S	H	H	H	H		
Rutabaga	15 in (38 cm)	9 in (23 cm)	H	H	H			S	S				H	H
Salad greens	10–18 in (25–45 cm)	10–18 in (25–45 cm)	H	H	SH	SH	SH	SH	SH	SH	SH	SH	SH	H
Scorzonera/salsify	12 in (30 cm)	6 in (15 cm)	H	H	H	S	S					H	H	H
Shallots	9 in (23 cm)	4 in (10 cm)				S	S			H	H	H		
Sorrel	15 in (38 cm)	15 in (38 cm)			P	P				H	H	H	P	P
Spinach	12 in (30 cm)	3–6 in (8–15 cm)	H	H	H	H	SH	SH	H	H	SH	SH	H	H
(Sweet) Corn	12–24 in (30–60 cm)	12–24 in (30–60 cm)					S	ST	H	H				
Tomatoes	10–18 in (25–45 cm)	10–18 in (25–45 cm)			S	S	S	T	H	HH	HH	HH	H	
Turnips	6–9 in (15–23 cm)	6–9 in (15–23 cm)	H	H	H	SH	S	S	S	S				H
Wild garlic	4 in (10 cm)	4 in (10 cm)				H	H	H					P	P
Zucchini	24–48 in (60–120 cm)	24–48 in (60–120 cm)						S	S	T	H	H	H	

PLAN THE GROWING YEAR: FRUIT AND NUTS

We've given spacings for between rows and between plants in a row for mature fruit and nut trees in case you're planning an orchard. But we realize that even one sweet chestnut is too many for average gardens. Patio varieties of fruit trees and pots of strawberries and blueberries make fresh fruit available to all.

KEY TO CHART

P	plant	P	plant under glass
H	harvest	H	harvest under glass
X	prune	X	prune under glass

CROPS	SPACINGS ROWS	PLANTS	WINTER E	WINTER M	WINTER L	SPRING E	SPRING M	SPRING L	SUMMER E	SUMMER M	SUMMER L	FALL E	FALL M	FALL L
Apples, pears	8–18 ft (2.5–5 m)	8–18 ft (2.5–5 m)	XP	XP	XP	P					XH	XH	H	P
Apricots, peaches	12–20 ft (3.6–6 m)	12–20 ft (3.6–6 m)	P	P	P	P	X		H	H	H	H	H	P
Blackberries	6–7 ft (1.8–2.2 m)	6–7 ft (1.8–2.2 m)	P	P	P	P				H	H	H	X	
Black/red currants	6 ft (1.8 m)	6 ft (1.8 m)	P	P	P	P			H	H	H	H		XP
Blueberries	5 ft (1.5 m)	5 ft (1.5 m)	P	P	P	XP				H	H	H		P
Cape gooseberries	14–18 in (25–45 cm)	14–18 in (25–45 cm)				S	S					H	H	
Cherries	20–25 ft (6–7 m)	20–25 ft (6–7 m)	P	P	P	XP			H	H	H	H		P
Figs	12 ft (3.6 m)	12 ft (3.6 m)	P	P	P	P	X				H			
Gooseberries	4–5 ft (1.2–1.5 m)	4–5 ft (1.2–1.5 m)	P	P	P	P			XH	XH	H			XP
Grapes	6 ft (1.8 m)	4 ft (1.2 m)	P	P	P	P							H	XP
Hazel nuts	15 ft (4.5 m)	15 ft (4.5 m)	P	P	P					X		H	H	XP
Kiwifruit	10 ft (3 m)	10 ft (3 m)	P	P	P	P								H
Lemons		pot grown	P	XP	P	P				H	H			P
Medlars, quince	12–25 ft (5–8 m)	12–25 ft (5–8 m)	P	P	P	P					H	H		XP
Mulberries	13 ft (4 m)	13 ft (4 m)	P	P	P	P					H	H		P
Olives	6 ft (1.8 m)	3ft 3 in (1 m)	XP	P	P	P								HP
Pecans, honey locust	6–33 ft (1.8–10 m)	6–33 ft (1.8–10 m)	P	P	P	P						H	H	XP
Plums, damsons	8–15 ft (2.4–4.5 m)	8–15 ft (2.4–4.5 m)	P	P	P	P		X	X		H	H		P
Raspberries	6ft 6 in (2 m)	12–15 in (30–37 cm)	P	P	XP	P				H	XH	H	H	H
Strawberries	3 ft (90 cm)	18 in (45 cm)	P	P	P	P				H	H	H		P
Sweet chestnuts		16 ft (5 m)	P	P	P	P						H	H	P

PLAN THE GROWING YEAR: HERBS

Herbs do well in pots, window boxes, and indoors on a windowsill, so everyone can grow them. Some can be picked all year round; others are annuals. We've indicated the best spacings between rows and between plants in a row. If you've got space to grow rows of annual herbs, you'll be able to dry some for winter.

KEY TO CHART

S	sow	S	sow under glass
P	plant		
T	transplant	T	transplant under glass
H	harvest	H	harvest under glass
X	prune		

CROPS	SPACINGS ROWS	SPACINGS PLANTS	WINTER E	WINTER M	WINTER L	SPRING E	SPRING M	SPRING L	SUMMER E	SUMMER M	SUMMER L	FALL E	FALL M	FALL L
Bay		4 ft (1.2 m)	H	H	PH	PH	H	H	H	XH	XH	H	PH	PH
Basil	12 in (30 cm)	8 in (20 cm)				S	S	S	TH	SH	SH	H	H	
Chives	12 in (30 cm)	12 in (30 cm)					S	S	H	H	H	H	H	
Cilantro	12 in (30 cm)	6 in (15 cm)	SH	H	H	S	S	S	SH	H	H	SH	SH	SH
Dill	12 in (30 cm)	9 in (23 cm)					S	S	SH	SH	H	H		
Marjoram	8 in (20 cm)	24 in (60 cm)	T				S	S	H	H				
Mint	12 in (30 cm)	12 in (30 cm)	T	H	H	PH	PH	H	H	H	H	H	H	H
Parsley	9–12 in (23–30 cm)	9–12 in (23–30 cm)						S	SH	SH	SH	H	H	
Rosemary	6 in (15 cm)	36 in (90 cm)	H	H	H	H	S	H	H	XH	XPH	H		H
Sage	6 in (15 cm)	24 in (60 cm)				S	S	P	P	XH	XH	H	H	
Tarragon	24 in (60 cm)	24 in (60 cm)	T					P	H	H	H			
Thyme	24 in (60 cm)	6 in (15 cm)	H	H	H	H	H	P	PH	XH	XH	H	H	H

Plant basil thinnings *and grow them for even more plants. Growing Mediterranean herbs such as basil under cover guarantees success.*

Pruning and training *apples and other fruit trees boosts the crop, helping fruit ripen by opening up the tree and letting in more light (see pages 154–155).*

Squash and zucchini *are staples in our kitchen. We enjoy zucchini in summer and store squash for winter soups (see pages 164–165).*

VEGETABLES TO GROW

Nothing beats the satisfaction of picking and cooking your own homegrown produce, from the first runner beans to late winter leeks. The biggest problem is deciding what to grow in the first place. We see it as a matter of balancing the "must-haves" with the "should-haves" and adding a few of the vegetables we think are a bit decadent, such as globe artichokes. You also need to take into account the suitability of your soil: there's more information on this on pages 104–109.

The must-haves

These are the basics that give you crops to eat all year (for tables of the growing year, see pages 136–139). With a little planning and succession planting you'll be able to run out to the garden to harvest something useful at any time of year. Sow seed outdoors, unless otherwise stated.

Beets (1)
Beta vulgaris
■ **How to grow** Beets have a long season: succession-sow monthly throughout spring and summer, starting in April. Sow thinly, a couple of seeds every 4 in (10 cm), about 1 in (2.5 cm) deep, and set them in rows about 1 ft (30 cm) apart. Thin out when the seedlings are about 1 in (2.5 cm) tall.
■ **Problem solving** Beets need regular watering or they will be tough and woody to eat.
■ **Harvest, cook, store** When harvesting, twist off the leaves 2 in (5 cm) above the roots to prevent bleeding. Store in clamps or in a box of sand in a cool place (see pages 164–165). Young greens can be used in salads, and when thinning rows the small beets are tasty, too.

SUPPORTING BROAD BEANS

Taller varieties of broad beans need support to stop them from flopping over and becoming an easy target for slugs. A trellis laid horizontally does the trick. Drive in stakes about 1 ft (30 cm) tall at each corner of the bed to hold it in place.

Broad beans (2)
Vicia faba
■ **How to grow** It is mild in Cornwall in the far southwest of England, so we sow our broad beans in November for an early harvest. Elsewhere, sowing is usually February to May. Sow about 8 in (10 cm) apart and 2 in (5 cm) deep. We plant in blocks so we can use trellises to support the growing beans (see box), though staggered pairs of rows with a 2-ft (60-cm) gap between them also work well.
■ **Problem solving** The biggest pest is aphids: pinch out all the growing tips where they gather. If you do this before they really take hold, you should have lots of succulent, untouched bean tops to eat.
■ **Harvest, cook, store** You should be able to pick beans from late spring through early fall. They can also be dried for winter use; they'll need to be soaked for 8 hours and boiled for 40 minutes. In spring, steam bean tops or cook them in butter.

Broccoli (3)
Brassica oleracea
Cymosa Group
■ **How to grow** Purple-sprouting is the hardiest and most prolific variety—that's why we grow it. It's a great vegetable for late fall and winter. We sow the seeds in individual plugs or very thin drills in April under cover. When robust enough, transplant seedlings to their final growing position outdoors: leave about 18 in (45 cm) between them, as the mature plants are huge.
■ **Problem solving** Birds love broccoli too, so hang up a bird scarer or protect plants by stringing thread between twigs to stop birds from landing. Stake plants as they grow, or try the trellis support system (see box): they can get top-heavy.
■ **Harvest, cook, store** Cut stems before flower buds open. Cut the central spear first. Keep cutting and plants will continue producing until harsh winter weather sets in, provided you don't strip all the stems at once. Purple sprouting is great stir-fried. Broccoli can be frozen, but the result is such a poor imitation of the fresh vegetable that we don't bother.

Brussels sprouts (4)
Brassica oleracea
Gemmifera Group
■ **How to grow** For us, it wouldn't be Christmas without Brussels sprouts. Sow your Brussels sprouts around Easter in individual plugs or thinly in drills under cover; transplant seedlings at the end of May, leaving at least 2 ft (60 cm) between them, and then wait for winter.

5 **6** **7** **8**

■ **Problem solving** Brussels sprouts are low-maintenance, but watch for birds, which will eat seedlings as well as helping themselves to the final crop. Protect seedlings by stringing thread between twigs; hang bird scarers near mature plants.

■ **Harvest, cook, store** Start picking sprouts from the base of the stem—use a sharp knife. Don't forget, sprout tops are also good eating. Sprouts can be frozen (blanch them first) but we prefer to eat them in season.

GROW CARROTS IN PAPER ROLLS

Grow carrots in cardboard tubes from the middle of toilet paper rolls. They make great biodegradable pots: fill them with seed-starting medium and plant seeds in the top. The narrow tube encourages long, straight root growth and makes transplanting really easy.

Carrots (5)
Daucus carota

■ **How to grow** Sow carrots thinly in rows 6 in (15 cm) apart and set the seeds about ½ in (1 cm) deep. Sow in succession from late winter through early summer. There are lots of varieties, from carrots shaped like golf balls to roots that come in shades of yellow, white, and purple. They all have one thing in common—they taste great.

■ **Problem solving** Companion-plant with onions to deter carrot flies; this will also help protect the onions against onion fly.

■ **Harvest, cook, store** You should be able to harvest from June to December if you have succession-planted. Lift maincrop carrots before the first frost and store in a clamp (see page 165) or root cellar (page 181). Pulled straight from the ground, wiped on a sleeve, and then crunched, carrots are a good way to get kids to eat vegetables. We like roasting carrots and grating them into carrot cake.

Celeriac (6)
Apium graveolens var. *rapaceum*

■ **How to grow** There is no doubt that every kitchen garden needs celery or celeriac—the flavor is invaluable in so many dishes. We chose celeriac because it's easier to grow.

Raise seedlings under cover in early spring. Plant them outside at the end of May, about 12 in (30 cm) apart and 18 in (45 cm) between rows.

■ **Problem solving** Generally maintenance-free, though slugs can be a problem.

■ **Harvest, cook, store** Harvest the roots from fall through winter in mild regions—leave them in the ground rather than lifting and storing. Eat them raw or cooked: they are a pain to prepare because it is difficult to scrub all the dirt off, but practice makes perfect. The leafy tops can be used in warming winter broths.

Zucchini, squashes, and pumpkins (7)
Cucurbita family

■ **How to grow** Sow squash and zucchini seeds under cover in April, in individual pots. Plant them outside at the end of May. We follow a no-watering policy (see page 101), which saves lots of hard work. Squashes and pumpkins take up a lot of space, but are good trailing down over raised beds, or grow them up netting and trellis.

■ **Problem solving** Slip a square of old carpet or slate under larger fruits to keep them clean and prevent rotting.

■ **Harvest, cook, store** It's essential to keep picking zucchini and summer squashes

while they are young: miss a couple of days and all of a sudden you have unappetizing monsters. Frying garlic, zucchini, summer squashes, and a handful of tomatoes in olive oil makes a very quick and easy, colorful meal. Store squashes and pumpkins on open shelves in a frost-free place. They will keep for months and are a useful standby for winter soups.

Kale (8)
Brassica oleracea
Acephala Group

■ **How to grow** Kale is an old-fashioned vegetable that has recently come back in favor—and we think it deserves it. It is hardy and tasty, plus it's easy to grow nearly anywhere. Sow seed in May and transplant seedlings in July to their final position.

■ **Problem solving** More or less trouble-free.

■ **Harvest, cook, store** Pick kale from November all the way through to the following May in mild regions. It's a great standby—we run out and whip off some nice-looking leaves when we need greens in a hurry. There are a number of different varieties—we like the curly kale. Like most brassicas, it can be frozen, but we think it is only truly tasty and appetizing when freshly picked.

141

1

2

3

4

Leeks (1)

Allium porrum

■ **How to grow** Growing prize leeks is a mystical art, but we're just interested in growing them to cook with. We sow them in drills about 6 in (15 cm) apart and ½ in (1 cm) deep. When they are big enough to transplant—when they are about 8 in (20 cm) tall—we get a handful of the plants, twist off all but 2 in (5 cm) of the green, and separate them. We make holes in the ground, about 2 in (5 cm) deep, using a dibber, and then place one leek in each hole. A good watering will fill the hole sufficiently— there's no need to firm the soil in place. They grow well, even in cold, wet areas.

■ **Problem solving** More or less trouble-free.

■ **Harvest, cook, store** Leeks may look like they're growing in the plot most of the year, but that's because they can be left in the ground and lifted as needed, from September to May in warm regions. It's comforting to know they are out there to be harvested all winter. Always ease the plant out of the ground with a fork or you will end up tearing off the outside layers or even pulling the leek apart. Please don't forget exactly how good the green part of the leek is. For some reason supermarkets have a tendency

to chop off all the greenery to make it more convenient—what they are really doing is throwing away the goodness. By all means chop off the tips, but cook the rest!

Onions and shallots (2)

Allium family

■ **How to grow** Onions are usually pretty cheap to buy, but there is something special about having a braid of your own homegrown hanging up ready to use. We grow onions from sets—miniature onion bulbs—rather than from seed, because the plants have better disease resistance. We plant them in late winter, spacing them 4 in (10 cm) apart, in rows about 10 in (25 cm) apart.

■ **Problem solving** Onions grown from sets have a tendency to "bolt," or flower too early. If this happens, cut off the flower stalk and use the onion right away.

■ **Harvest, cook, store** The delicate flavor of shallots makes them popular with chefs, but we mainly use them very early in the season as a substitute for green onions— mature shallots are small and fussy to prepare. Green-onion-size shallots are usually ready long before the first true spring onions. Main-crop onions are ready to harvest around July.

Parsnips (3)

Pastinacea sativa

■ **How to grow** We know parsnips are not as popular as they were, but we felt they had to be on our must-have list. Our efforts at growing them have been quite hit or miss. The little seeds can blow away easily, so take care when planting: we spread them very thinly, a couple of seeds every 6 in (15 cm), in rows 12 in (30 cm)

apart, at a depth of ½ in (1 cm). We sow them around Easter. They are slow to germinate. Thin out when the parsnips are the size of a golf ball.

■ **Problem solving** Dig over the soil and pick out stones to avoid growing misshapen roots. Improving the soil with well-rotted compost helps produce long, straight parsnips.

■ **Harvest, cook, store** We dig our parsnips from October

GROWING PEAS IN RAIN GUTTERS AND SUPPORTING WITH WILLOW STICKS

When starting peas under cover, we grow them in waste lengths of plastic rain gutter, with holes drilled in it for drainage. Sow the seed in zigzag formation. When the seedlings are big enough and the risk of frost is past, it is really easy to slide them off the gutter into a prepared trench outside.

Support peas with sticks to stop them from trailing on the ground and becoming slug food. There is absolutely no point in buying bundles of garden sticks: any twigs and small branches will do the job of keeping the pea plants off the ground and growing upward. We use willow offcuts left over from pollarding our trees: we like to find a use for every scrap.

5

6

7

8

to the following Easter. The parsnips are happy sitting in the ground waiting for you to come and get them, but the tops wither away, so you have to remember where you planted them. We really enjoy eating them roasted or curried in soup. They are a family favorite—and let's not forget they were a staple food in the Old World before the potato arrived. The thinnings are lovely cooked in butter.

Peas (4)
Pisum sativum

▧ **How to grow** Sow peas under cover in late winter and plant out when the risk of frost has passed. Continue sowing every couple of weeks until early summer, sowing outside once the weather warms up.

▧ **Problem solving** Using sticks to support plants helps reduce slug damage (see left). Taller varieties may need further support, such as netting stretched between posts.

▧ **Harvest, cook, store** Start picking in June and continue until September. The first peas of the year are great to eat straight from the plants; even when the peas are tiny we munch the whole pods like snow peas. The growing tips are tasty sautéed in butter and the empty pods cans be made into country wine (see page 258).

Radishes (5)
Raphanus sativus

▧ **How to grow** It is so quick and easy to grow radishes that many gardeners think it beneath them. By summer you may have had a surfeit, but we always keep a row or two on the go. Sow seed in drills about 6 in (15 cm) apart and ½ in (1 cm) deep, from February to August. Radishes are also great sown as a quick crop in between rows of slower-growing veggies.

▧ **Problem solving** Flea beetles may attack the leaves but the

FORCING RHUBARB

We "force" rhubarb by covering a plant with a heap of well-rotted manure in spring and putting an old half-barrel on top. We take the barrel off when the pale shoots emerge from the top of the rich manure. Tradition says that once a plant has been forced, it needs to rest for two years before you do it again, but we force our rhubarb plants every year and they are fine!

radishes themselves aren't usually affected.

▧ **Harvest, eat, store** Pull radishes while they are still small: the larger they are, the tougher and hotter they get. Enjoy them fresh in salads – you can't store them for any length of time.

Rhubarb (6)
Rheum x hybridum

▧ **How to grow** Yes, we know you eat it like a fruit, but rhubarb is a stalwart perennial of the veggie garden. It's easiest grown from crowns—rooted pieces of plant. Set them 3 ft (90 cm) apart. Create more plants by dividing every five years.

▧ **Problem solving** Generally trouble-free.

▧ **Harvest, cook, store** Leave new plants to establish for a year. Then harvest any time up until July. Pull the stalks; don't cut them. As well as pies and crisps, rhubarb can be used in chutney and jam. It freezes well. Don't forget the leaves are toxic.

Runner beans (7)
Phaseolus coccineus

▧ **How to grow** Sowing runner beans in pots in the greenhouse and transplanting them out as early as the frost allows is one of our yearly rituals. You can also sow straight into the ground later on. We grow

ours on teepees; leave 9 in (23 cm) between plants, stick in bamboo canes, and tie them together at the top.

▧ **Problem solving** Lots of people avoid runner beans because they think they are tough and stringy. There is absolutely no reason to suffer tough beans. You can buy "stringless" varieties, but by far the easiest answer is to pick them young and often.

▧ **Harvest, cook, store** Keep picking so the plants keep producing: surpluses can be blanched—briefly plunged in boiling water—and frozen.

Salad greens (8)
Lactuca and others

▧ **How to grow** Growing salad, especially lettuce and arugula (*Eruca*), is one of the easiest things to do well. Sow thinly in drills 12 in (30 cm) apart and ½ in (1 cm) deep. This ensures that the seeds are well spread out and not as much thinning is needed. Choose "cut and come again" varieties and sow in succession and you'll be cutting salad all summer long.

▧ **Problem solving** Use beer traps and plastic collars made from cut-down bottles against slugs, and encourage natural predators (see pages 166–7).

▧ **Harvest, eat, store** Cut the leaves in the morning when they are freshest.

Spinach (1)
Spinacia oleracea

■ **How to grow** We figure Popeye had the right idea; spinach is good for you—and it's very easy to grow. To pick spinach over a long period, keep succession-planting in rows about 12 in (30 cm) apart and at a depth of 1 in (2.5 cm). Don't be tempted to plant too much at once, as the leaves are best eaten young. There are varieties of perpetual spinach, but in our opinion they don't taste anywhere near as good as annual spinach.

■ **Problem solving** Can "bolt" or go to seed if it doesn't get enough water.

■ **Harvest, cook, store** We cut off handfuls with a pair of scissors: it will grow again quite quickly, allowing for a second harvest. Sadly, after all the effort of picking and washing, spinach cooks down to very little. The young leaves are great raw in salad. Blanch the leaves before freezing them.

Tomatoes (2)
Lycopersicon esculentum

■ **How to grow** Tomatoes are an easy crop to grow on balconies, window sills, under cover, or outside. At Newhouse Farm, we grow the majority of our tomatoes in the greenhouse, starting them in small pots and trays in March, and transplanting them to bigger pots as they mature. Keeping them in pots does require quite a lot of potting mix and watering, but they do extremely well. Tomatoes need regular feeding. We use our worm tea (see page 127) and comfrey fertilizer (see page 107); they help the tomato plants to remain healthy for significantly longer each season. Support plants with canes or tie them to strings running down from the greenhouse roof.

■ **Problem solving** We have problems with blight, a disease that damages tomatoes and potatoes: we've tried to counter it by growing the plants upside down—which is supposed to prevent blight from establishing. Use a hanging container and plant young tomato plants through a hole in the base. The plants' roots grow upward. In our experience it's reasonably effective—and a good talking point.

■ **Harvest, cook, store** Pick tomatoes when they are completely ripe: cut them just above the flower stalk. Try growing different varieties for cooking, salads, etc. If you have a glut, freeze tomatoes—skin them first, then cook them for 10 minutes or so and strain to make your own homemade sauce; they also can well (see page 240). At the end of the season, green tomatoes make great chutney, or ripen in a bowl with a banana.

The should-haves
If time and space are tight, you may have to sacrifice some of the should-haves. But if you can squeeze them in, they are all worth growing.

Asparagus (3)
Asparagus officinalis

■ **How to grow** It is worth having an asparagus bed for the sheer seasonal indulgence, even though it takes time for the plants to establish. Plant one-year-old "crowns" in April (see box opposite).

■ **Problem solving** Go out after dark with a flashlight and pick off any slugs—feed them to your hens or ducks.

■ **Harvest, cook, store** Cut your first spears two years after planting and then annually in late spring. Start cutting when spears are 4 in (10 cm) long. Use a knife to cut the spears off just below the surface of the soil. Stop cutting in June and allow the plant to grow. We love the spears simply steamed and served with butter. You could freeze some if you have spare.

Cabbage (4)
Brassica oleracea
Capitata Group

■ **How to grow** Some people may class cabbage as a must-have, but there are other brassicas that we would rather grow. Of course, there is nothing nicer than a neat row of cabbages if you have the space. Sow spring cabbages in summer and Savoys in spring for winter eating.

■ **Problem solving** Birds will peck at the seedlings, so set up a bird scarer (see page 167). Caterpillars can be a problem later on; pick them off by hand and feed them to your hens.

PINCHING OUT TOMATOES

Pinching out the diagonal side shoots that grow at an angle between the side shoots and the main stem of a tomato plant encourages the plant to form fewer, bigger fruits. If you don't do it, you get lots of smaller fruits. You can pot the pinched-out side shoots and grow them into new plants, if you have time.

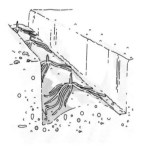

Harvest Cut spring cabbages from April onward and Savoys in winter. As before, we don't think brassicas freeze that well from a taste point of view.

Cucumbers (5)
Cucumis sativus

How to grow Cucumbers are relatively easy to grow and every year we marvel at how many we get from each plant. In our first year at Newhouse Farm, we picked well over a hundred from one plant!

Okay, it's confession time: our cucumbers look nothing like the ones you buy at the store. They tend to be a lot shorter and fatter and, dare we say, tastier. Sow seed under cover in April or outside in June.

Problem solving Spray greenhouse cucumbers with water to increase humidity and discourage spider mites.

Harvest, cook, store Keep cutting cucumbers until the first frost. Try pickling them if you have a glut, or make tzatziki.

PLANTING ASPARAGUS CROWNS

Dig a trench, then make a shallow mound at the bottom of it. Set the crowns on the shallow mound, placing them at least 18 in (45 cm) apart. Spread out the roots and cover them with soil. Keep mounding up the soil as the plants grow, so that you end up with them growing on a ridge. This will get higher over the years as you add

mulch and well-rotted manure. Asparagus plants are perennial, so site the bed carefully—you can't start moving it around. For the same reason, you must first remove every bit of quackgrass, thistle, burdock and any other pernicious weeds before you plant: they will be impossible to dig out later.

French beans (6)
Phaseolus vulgaris

How to grow French beans are less prolific than broad or runner beans. From a 10-ft (3-m) row you can expect 20 lb (9 kg) of broad beans, 60 lb (27 kg) of runner beans, and a mere 10 lb (4.5 kg) of French beans—however, they are very fine eating. Sow seeds outside in May and keep succession-sowing until late June.

Problem solving Young seedlings are vulnerable to slugs, so set plenty of beer traps. Support your beans with trellises or willow teepees to keep them off the ground and away from the slugs.

Harvest, cook, store Pick beans from July to October. Like runner beans, you can leave the pods on the plant to fatten up and then dry the beans for winter use. Or blanch and freeze the tender young beans.

Globe artichokes (7)
Cynara scolymus
Scolymus Group

How to grow Globe artichokes are magnificent, thistlelike perennial plants that take up a lot of space for very little produce. That said, we love them and they taste great. For best results, plant rooted offsets (like suckers taken from the base of a mature plant): it's easier than growing from seed.

Problem solving Set beer traps for slugs while plants are small. Once they reach full size, they can cope with a few tattered leaves.

Harvest, cook, store Wait a year before harvesting the heads, then cut them every summer. Pick them before they flower, when they become a popular hideout for insects. You can pickle the bases or hearts, but preparing them is a bit tricky and time-consuming.

Jerusalem artichokes (8)
Helianthus tuberosus

How to grow Jerusalem artichokes are prolific, but we know very few people who consume the whole harvest. Our pigs usually benefit from part of ours. Although they are tasty, we have nicknamed them "fartichokes" because of their propensity to cause gas. Think carefully about where you site them: these 7-ft- (2.2-m-) high daisies are invasive, and once you've planted them, they are nearly impossible to get rid of. But on an exposed site they make a great, productive wind-break with pretty flowers.

Problem solving More or less trouble-free.

Harvest, cook, store Dig up tubers from November onward. Roast them with other veggies or make them into soup.

145

1

2

3

4

Kohlrabi (1)

Brassica oleracea
Gongylodes Group

■ **How to grow** Kohlrabi is not very popular in North America but has a following in Europe and Asia. Sow seed April to July.

■ **Problem solving** Use a bird scarer to keep birds away from the young plants.

■ **Harvest, cook, store** Leave in the ground and dig up as needed from midsummer on. Simply trim off the leaves, scrub, and slice. They make a good gratin, or mash with butter.

Potatoes (2)

Solanum tuberosum

■ **How to grow** Space is the only reason we have not listed spuds as a must-have, as you can buy local potatoes in season. But they never taste as good as those dug from the garden and put on the plate within the hour! Plant seed potatoes from late March to April, depending on whether they are earlies or maincrop.

■ **Problem solving** Protect against frost by drawing soil over leaves with a hoe.

■ **Harvest, cook, store** Dig earlies from June, maincrop from September. Harvest promptly before slugs move in. Homegrown potatoes are sweet and tasty with a little butter. Store maincrop varieties in a clamp (see page 165).

Rutabagas and turnips (3)

Brassica napobrassica
and *B. rapa*

■ **How to grow** We plant more than we will ever need of these great winter staples and use the less perfect ones to feed our pigs. Sow seed in May.

■ **Problem solving** Keep birds away from the young plants.

■ **Harvest, cook, store** Dig up roots from October onward. Store in a clamp (see page 165). Some of us love mashed rutabagas; others claim it is punishment, not nutrition.

SPROUTING POTATOES

Seed potatoes *should be encouraged to begin sprouting (or "chitting") before you plant them outside. Several months before planting, lay the potatoes out in a dry, cool, frost-free place. It should be light, but out of direct sunlight—a garage with a window is ideal.*

Corn (4)

Zea mays

■ **How to grow** Corn needs plenty of sun to ripen the cobs successfully. Sow under cover in April and plant after danger of frost has passed.

■ **Problem solving** Stake plants on windy sites.

■ **Harvest, cook, store** Pick the cobs in late August/September. Eat as soon as possible after picking before the sugar content turns to starch.

Why not try

We wouldn't give these top priority, but you may have more success in warmer climates with the following vegetables.

Eggplant (5)

Solanum melongena

■ **How to grow** Here in the far southwest of the UK we can get away with growing eggplants outside, but we usually have some in the greenhouse too. Start seed in pots in March under cover. Stake and feed plants as for tomatoes.

■ **Problem solving** Spider mites can be a problem. Reduce the risk by spraying with water to keep the humidity up.

■ **Harvest, cook, store** Pick eggplants once they are at least 4 in (10 cm) long and the skin is shiny. Watch out for the prickles on the little green caps and on the stalks.

Cauliflower(6)

Brassica oleracea
Botrytis Group

■ **How to grow** Cauliflowers are challenging to grow, needing well-manured soil that hasn't been recently dug and, above all, regular watering. Grow different varieties and you can cut cauliflowers from spring to fall. Sow seed in spring and thin seedlings as they grow. Transplant so mature plants will be 2 ft (60 cm) apart.

■ **Problem solving** Keep birds away from the young plants with homemade scarers.

■ **Harvest, cook, store** To eat them at their best, cut them while the heads are still tightly packed—loose florets mean they are past their prime. Fold in the leaves and cover with a piece of slate for a week first. We particularly like to eat the florets raw with dips. If you want to freeze cauliflowers, separate the florets and blanch them first.

Chile peppers (7)

Capsicum annuum

■ **How to grow** Chile peppers are really easy to grow. At Newhouse Farm we have tried everything from small Scotch bonnets that blow your socks off to more refined banana peppers. All are fast-growing annuals that do best in warm summers and like a bit of

5 6 8

humidity. In temperate climates they are definitely best grown under cover and sown in spring.

■ **Problem solving** Look out for spider mites—misting with water can help prevent attacks and the peppers like humidity.

■ **Harvest, cook, store** We use chile peppers in salsas and curries, and mixed with roasted seeds and nuts. To dry, string them up and hang in a dry, airy spot. You can freeze chopped peppers—remove seeds first.

SPROUTING SEEDS

Sprouted seeds *are nutritious and tasty in salads. Our favorites include radish, broccoli, sunflower (shell them first), and chickpea. First, soak them in water for 24 hours. Lay them in a sieve in a well-lit location. Every day rinse the seeds with clean water and tip them back in the sieve. They will sprout in 4–5 days. Rinse, shake, and store in the refrigerator— eat within two days.*

Ginger
Zingiber officinale
■ **How to grow** If you like fresh ginger, try growing your own from a root from the grocery store. Look for a portion of root that has a bud on it. Start it off in a small pot in spring and repot as it grows. Grow ginger under cover in temperate climates. It's a tall plant with grasslike leaves.

■ **Problem solving** As ever, in the greenhouse, spider mites are a problem. Spray with water.

■ **Harvest, cook, store** Dump out the pot in fall and harvest your roots. Replant a bit and use the rest. We use it to make ginger beer (see pages 254–5). You can freeze ginger.

Horseradish
Amoracia rusticana
■ **How to grow** Horseradish grows in moist, rich soil and can tolerate a shady location.

■ **Problem solving** It is highly invasive: plant it in a secluded part of the garden where you can easily restrain it.

■ **Harvest, cook, store** Instead of buying jars of horseradish sauce, we now make our own. You can dig up and harvest horseradish about nine months after planting: save the smaller roots for replanting. It tastes extremely good with smoked mackerel. Freeze the roots or store in a clamp (see page 165).

Chard (8)
Beta vulgaris var. *flavescens*
■ **How to grow** Chard is easy to grow—we often find it self-seeds and pops up in the veggie bed unannounced. Sow seed in April and thin the seedlings to 1 ft (30 cm) apart. Rainbow chard has ruby red, orange, yellow, and pink stems.

■ **Problem solving** Trouble-free, apart from the occasional bit of slug damage to leaves.

■ **Harvest, cook, store** Pick leaves all summer long. We like chard because you get two veggies for the price of one: steam the stalks and cook the leaves separately like spinach. Freeze them the same way too.

Sweet peppers
Capsicum annuum
■ **How to grow** Grow peppers just as you would tomatoes but keep them in the greenhouse.

■ **Problem solving** If stems flop over, stake them up.

■ **Harvest, cook, store** Pick peppers in late summer.

Salsify
Tragopogon porrifolium
■ **How to grow** These root vegetables look like small, thin, darker-colored parsnips but taste vaguely mushroomlike. Sow in April.

■ **Problem solving** Plant seeds in a deep compost-filled hole for straight roots.

■ **Harvest, cook, store** Dig up in October and cook immediately. Peel them once they're cooked.

Scorzonera
Scorzonera hispanica
■ **How to grow** A root vegetable similar to salsify, but with black skin. Sow in April.

■ **Problem solving** See salsify.

■ **Harvest, cook, store** Dig up in October. Blanch and eat in salads. Store salsify and scorzonera in a clamp or root cellar (see pages 165 and 181).

Sorrel
Rumex acetosa
■ **How to grow** Sorrel likes a shaded, damp spot.

■ **Problem solving** If a plant starts to look a bit tired, divide it and replant the pieces.

■ **Harvest, cook, store** Pick regularly and add to soups and salads. It has a lovely lemony flavor and is good for making your own pesto.

Bear's garlic
Allium ursinum
■ **How to grow** Order plants from a nursery. Plant in a shady, damp spot to mimic its habitat.

■ **Problem solving** Generally trouble-free.

■ **Harvest, cook, store** Pick leaves in spring for best flavor and add to soups, salads, and risottos. The flowers are edible too: add them to salads.

147

1 2 3 4

FRUIT AND NUTS TO GROW

Growing a wider range of fruit and nuts is one of the advantages of a small farm. In an average-sized garden, it's easy to add climbers such as grapevines and kiwis, while blueberries and dwarf fruit trees thrive in pots on a deck or patio.

Soft fruit

The great thing about soft fruit is that you don't have to wait long for results. Unless otherwise stated, plant as bare-root plants in fall or spring. They need little maintenance other than weeding and mulching, and yields can be phenomenal.

Blackberries (1)

Rubus fruticosus

■ **How to grow** Here at Newhouse Farm we would never plant blackberries—but that's because we are lucky enough to have lots in the fencerows. Once a year they cease to be thorny invaders and become prickly baskets of tasty fruit. If you need to buy plants. look for thornless varieties—ideal for smaller spaces—and juicy hybrids like loganberries and tayberries. Grow on wires and posts or train against a wall.

■ **Problem solving** On a small farm and in many larger yards,

brambles can be a nightmare. If you inherit some wild brambles on your plot, try to tame them by shaping them into easily accessible blocks.

■ **Prune** If growing blackberries on wires, cut out all dead wood in fall and tie in new canes.

■ **Harvest, cook, store** Pick fruit in mid- to late summer. As well as crumbles, we always make jams and jellies, and open-freeze surplus berries on trays before bagging them.

Black currants and red currants (2)

Ribes nigrum, R. rubrum

■ **How to grow** Black currants are easy to grow and thrive in cool, heavy soil, even in clay. Mulch them generously each spring using well-rotted manure. Bushes are heavy-fruiting and the fruit has a high vitamin C content. Red currants are yummy and they are particularly useful to grow against awkward north-facing walls and in shady areas—ideal for a city garden.

■ **Problem solving** Put up netting to stop birds from stripping your crop. Watch out for currant borer damage on the leaves in summer. Cut off and destroy infested stems if symptoms appear.

■ **Prune** For black currants, prune in late fall or early spring. Remove one-third of the stems:

stems can become overcrowded in the middle of the bush. For red currants, see gooseberries for instructions.

■ **Harvest, cook, store** Pick in mid- to late summer. Separating the small berries from their trusses is tedious. Some people prefer to cut off entire fruiting branches and strip the berries in the kitchen. We pick ours by hand so that the stored energy in the branches can return to the plant. We make our black currants into pies, jams, and jellies. Red currants are great in summer desserts and in jellies to serve with roast lamb. Both berries freeze well.

Blueberries (3)

Vaccinium corymbosum

■ **How to grow** Blueberries are a mountain fruit that does really well in a temperate climate. They grow best in groups so that they can cross-fertilize each other; you'll need two varieties that flower at the same time for pollination. Unless your soil is acidic, you'll need to grow them in raised beds or big tubs filled with acidic potting mix. Plant bushes in mid- to late spring.

■ **Problem solving** Always water bushes with rainwater to keep the soil pH low.

■ **Prune** Not necessary.

TAKING GOOSEBERRY CUTTINGS

Increase your stock of fruit bushes by taking cuttings. Gooseberry cuttings are simple to take in early fall. Choose a stem that grew this year and make an angled cut across it (see left). Your cutting should be about 6 in (15 cm) long. Push it into a pot of growing medium and keep it in a sheltered spot or cold frame. It will start producing fruit in two years. Or grow new bushes from suckers—new shoots that grow from the parent bush. Cut off a sucker (see left), making sure you take some roots with it, and pot it up.

■ **Harvest, cook, store** Pick berries from late summer to early fall when they have turned from light blue to a pewtery deep blue-black and are soft to the touch. We like fresh blueberries in fruit salads or muffins. We freeze any surplus for making smoothies.

Cape gooseberries and tomatillos (4)
Physalis peruviana,
P. ixocarpa
■ **How to grow** These are annuals with a difference—each cape gooseberry is enclosed inside a papery lantern. The tomatillo (pictured) is a close cousin. Plants must be grown in a greenhouse or inside. Sow seed in late winter or early spring. Care for plants like tomatoes: use canes or string to support the growing plants.
■ **Problem solving** Spray regularly with water to reduce spider mites.
■ **Prune** Not necessary.
■ **Harvest, cook, store** Pick from late summer to mid-fall when the berries have turned bright orange. Tomatillos are excellent in salsa. Cape gooseberries taste sweet but smell rather odd.

Cranberries (5)
Vaccinium oxycoccos
■ **How to grow** We grow cranberries to go with our

home-reared holiday turkey. Plant bushes in spring. They grow well in a sunny, sheltered position and need regular watering. If growing them in a pot, set it in a wide saucer topped off with water, and use low-pH potting mix, as cranberries need acidic soil.
■ **Problem solving** Use rainwater rather than tap water, to keep soil pH low.
■ **Prune** Not necessary.
■ **Harvest, cook, store** Pick berries in early to mid-fall. Cranberries are easy to freeze for Thanksgiving or Christmas.

Gooseberries (6)
Ribes uva-crispa
■ **How to grow** Gooseberries need rich, moist soil and regular watering. Plant bushes in fall: mulch with leaf mold.
■ **Problem solving** Pick off currantworm larvae by hand and buy plants resistant to American gooseberry mildew.
■ **Prune** Cut back old wood in winter; prune strong lead shoots by half to an upward-pointing bud. Cut out cross shoots and shorten laterals. Summer-prune so that fruits have maximum exposure to sunshine to ripen. Aim for an open cup shape so you can reach in to pick the berries.
■ **Harvest, cook, store** Pick from late spring to midsummer. The smaller the berries, the

more sour they are. We also grow dessert varieties, which are red and much sweeter and don't need cooking. Gooseberries freeze well.

Grapes (7)
Vitis vinifera
■ **How to grow** We have planted a small vineyard on a south-facing slope and have had a few vines growing under cover for years. We water indoor vines regularly and give them liquid tomato fertilizer once a week in spring. Outside we feed our vines by mulching in spring

TRAINING GRAPES

Train the main stem upward with a cane. Train some lateral stems horizontally on wires. In late winter, prune the laterals to two or three buds from the main stem. In summer, stop them from getting too long by "nipping" out the growing tip three or four leaves beyond each developing bunch of grapes.

and fall. They grow on thin topsoil on a clay-based subsoil.
■ **Problem solving** We grow mulberry trees at the end of the rows of vines. They have an antifungal property that helps protect the vines from disease.
■ **Prune** Shape the frame in the first few years. Then prune annually in late fall (see box).
■ **Harvest, cook, store** Pick grapes from late summer to mid-fall. Grapes are one of the fruits we grow for their fermenting potential—they taste great too.

Kiwi fruit (8)
Actinidia deliciosa
■ **How to grow** Kiwi fruits are exotic but do well in a temperate climate. Choose a self-fertile variety so you only need one plant. For best results grow against a south-facing wall or in a hoop house.
■ **Problem solving** Generally trouble-free.
■ **Prune** You don't have to prune them, but if you don't, kiwis take up lots of space; pruning also encourages more fruit. Do it in late fall or late winter. Train sideshoots on wires and, after a few years, nip out growing shoots 6 in (15 cm) beyond the last fruiting buds.
■ **Harvest, eat, store** Pick fruits from mid-to late fall. They can be eaten straight from the vine—they don't keep too long. 149

1 **2** **3** **4**

Melons (1)

Cucumis melo

■ **How to grow** We pride ourselves on our melons. Melons grow best in warm climates. We sow seed in pots in April and add a cane for each plant to grow up and some netting to support the fruit, but you can grow them on the ground.

■ **Problem solving** Plant melons on mounds to avoid neck rot—damage between the base of the stem and the top of the root brought on by wet conditions at soil level.

■ **Prune** Pinch out growing tips two leaves after a developing melon. This stops the plant from wasting energy on growing and puts it back into the fruit.

■ **Harvest, cook, store** Melons ripen from late summer to mid-fall. They don't store well.

Raspberries (2)

Rubus idaeus

■ **How to grow** Raspberries are always expensive at the store. But luckily they grow well even in wet and cold areas, and have a long picking season. Raspberries like well-drained soil in a sunny position. Support them with a couple of stakes at each end of the row with some wire running between them.

■ **Problem solving** Cover with netting to prevent bird theft.

■ **Prune** In winter, prune the majority of canes all the way back to just 1 ¼ in (3 cm) above the ground. Leave a few unpruned. As time goes on, leave more and more canes unpruned. Try pruning the canes at different levels so that you have a nice spread of fruit.

■ **Harvest, cook, store** Raspberries ripen in mid-summer or early fall, depending on variety. They are fun to pick, but they don't all make it safely to the kitchen—gardener's perks! They are delicious just as they are or made into jam or preserved in liqueurs for a winter treat (see page 241).

Strawberries (3)

Fragaria x *ananassa*

■ **How to grow** Strawberries are one of our must-haves. Plant them in spring on ridges for drainage. Plants have a relatively short life of cropping (three to four years) so try to propagate some of your own from runners—mini plants on the end of a long stem.

■ **Problem solving** Avoid slug attack by growing plants in hanging baskets—but they will need heavy watering. When growing conventionally we mulch plants with straw in summer to keep the fruit off the ground and prevent rotting. Net plants to stop birds from getting the fruits before you do.

■ **Prune** Not necessary.

■ **Harvest, cook, store** Pick fruits in midsummer. If you have a glut, make some jam or freeze whole berries on trays before bagging them up.

Fruit trees

Fruit trees are an excellent long-term way to cut down on your food miles—especially if you store some apples for winter eating. Plant varieties that suit your local environment: consult a specialty nursery for help. Many dwarf varieties of fruit trees will even grow well in a container on a deck or patio. All are best planted when the trees are dormant, in mid-fall or early spring (see page 138). Fruit trees are an investment for the rest of your life, so take your time and do it properly. Training fruit trees not only saves space but increases yields too. We explain some common training methods on page 154.

PICKING APPLES FROM TALL TREES

Pick apples before they fall to reduce problems in the orchard—rotting windfalls attract wasps and can spread disease. This homemade contraption is ideal for picking apples individually from traditional tall trees. Cut the bottom off a 2-liter soda bottle. Push a broom handle through the neck of the bottle and hold it in place with duct tape. Maneuver the bottle so that an apple sits inside, then shake gently to detach it from the branch. This method takes longer than shaking the apples down, but you'll have fewer bruised fruits, which don't store well.

5 6 7 8

Apples and pears (4)
Malus domestica
and *Pyrus communis*

■ **How to grow** Both trees like annual heavy mulching with rich compost. Pears like to grow in a more sheltered spot than apples and are more fragile. Pears normally need another tree within 100 yards (110 m) to serve as a pollinator, or buy a multi-variety pear tree that has several different varieties grafted onto one trunk that will self-pollinate. Apples and pears are available in dwarf varieties.

■ **Problem solving** Codling moth larvae burrow into apples. Use pheromone traps to catch adult moths before they mate.

■ **Prune** Pears don't need specialized pruning. Trim long shoots in summer and again lightly in winter. For apples see information on page 155.

■ **Harvest, cook, store** Pick from midsummer to mid-fall. Depending on variety, some apples are best eaten early, others will keep into next year. Store apples and pears in trays in a cool, dry place. As well as tarts and pies, apples make a good base for herb jellies.

Apricots, peaches, and nectarines (5)
Prunus armeniaca, P. persica
and *P. persica* var. *nectarina*

■ **How to grow** Apricots, peaches, and nectarines like a sunny, sheltered position. We are fan-training our nectarines on a south-facing wall.

■ **Problem solving** Flowers open early when pollinating insects are rare, so hand-pollination helps. If short on space, grow patio apricots in pots—they produce full-sized fruit even though they are barely 3 ft (1 m) tall.

■ **Prune** Remove dead wood as necessary.

■ **Harvest, cook, store** Pick from midsummer to early fall. Apricot jam is delicious. Eat the best peaches and nectarines; preserve the rest in brandy or dry them (see pages 242–245).

Cherries and plums (6)
Prunus avium
and *P. domestica*

■ **How to grow** Cherries and plums are easy to grow. They work best fan-trained against a south-facing wall or in a sunny, sheltered position.

■ **Problem solving** Protect fruit from birds with netting. Plums are a wasp's favorite food, so pick ripe fruit daily.

■ **Prune** Pruning only during the growing season to reduce the risk of bacterial canker.

■ **Harvest, cook, store** Pick cherries in midsummer, plums in late summer or early fall. We make plum jam and chutney, and try to save some cherries for preserving in brandy.

Figs
Ficus carica

■ **How to grow** Figs are a solid Newhouse Farm favorite and do remarkably well in our mild climate. They grow well in containers and do even better if you move them under cover in winter and water and fertilize regularly. They grow best when their roots are restricted: it improves fruiting.

■ **Problem solving** Generally trouble-free.

■ **Prune** Between December and January. Make sure you remove all unripened fruit and fruitlets or they will reduce next year's crop.

■ **Harvest, cook, store** Harvest figs in late summer or early fall, when they feel soft and the "eye" on the bottom of the fruit has opened up a bit. They should be moist, sweet, and fragrant. The right time to pick them is just before they would fall off the tree naturally. Eat immediately.

Lemons (7)
Citrus limon

■ **How to grow** Lemons are the easiest citrus trees to grow in a temperate climate. In cold-winter areas, grow them in large pots and bring them inside over winter. When growing lemons in pots, you need to topdress them every year or so by removing the top 1 in (2.5 cm) of soil and replacing it with fresh. This is best done in spring.

■ **Problem solving** Mist with water to reduce spider mites.

■ **Prune** Shear back in winter to a compact shape. Try rooting the prunings.

■ **Harvest, cook, store** Pick lemons from July to October. Watch out for their spiky bits when harvesting.

Why not try?
We wouldn't give olives top priority, but that doesn't mean you shouldn't give them a try. Our experiment is still in its early stages, but here's what we've found out so far.

Olives (8)
Olea europaea

■ **How to grow** We have yet to get a decent crop from our olive trees, but patience is a virtue and so we will wait. In all but the warmest areas, they need to be grown under cover. Olives grow particularly well in sandy soil interspersed with clay layers. You may need to water small trees in hot summers.

■ **Problem solving** Grow olives on a slope to avoid their roots sitting in too much water.

■ **Prune** Heavy pruning needed; consult a specialty book.

■ **Harvest, cook, store** Pick olives in late summer. You can't eat them straight from the tree: try pickling them in brine first (see page 236).

151

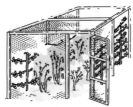

Old fruity favorites

These less well-known fruit trees are returning to popularity in the UK—and about time, too.

Medlars (1)

Mespilus germanica

■ **How to grow** Medlars are medium-sized trees with highly unusual fruits that look like little wooden rose hips. They are hardy trees and like a sunny open spot. You can even grow them in a large container.

■ **Problem solving** Generally trouble-free.

■ **Prune** Avoid pruning as the fruit is produced at the tips of the branches.

■ **Harvest, cook, store** Pick in October when the fruits have almost rotted—or "bletted"— to a rich golden yellow. Eat the flesh with a teaspoon—enjoy it with cheese and a nice glass of port, but don't eat the seeds. Medlars don't keep: make jelly with any surplus.

Mulberries (2)

Morus nigra

■ **How to grow** Mulberries don't travel well, so really the only way to taste them is to grow your own. We grow the black variety rather than white mulberry whose leaves silkworms eat. We've planted them alongside our grapevines. They come into flower quite late, avoiding any frost damage.

■ **Problem solving** Generally trouble-free, though birds help themselves: you'll know about it when you find mulberry-stained bird poop on the paths—or, worse, the laundry.

■ **Prune** Thin branches in winter if necessary to maintain the tree's shape.

■ **Harvest, cook, store** Pick in late summer and early fall. Watch out for juice stains: wear old clothes when harvesting. The fragrant fruit tastes of raspberries dipped in red wine. The berries soon deteriorate once picked, so freeze any surplus immediately or make them into jam, jelly, or wine.

Quinces (3)

Cydonia oblonga

■ **How to grow** Quince trees grow to about 16 ft (5 m) high and produce fruit like enormous golden pears. They like damp soil and prefer a sheltered spot. They don't flower until late spring, so are usually safe from frost damage.

■ **Problem solving** Thin the fruits as they develop to get bigger, better quinces.

■ **Prune** Not required.

■ **Harvest, cook, store** Quinces ripen in fall. They are too hard to eat raw, so they have to be cooked. They won't last much longer than a few weeks, so use them quickly: try adding a few slices to an apple pie. We enjoy quince poached in rosewater syrup with elderflower cream.

Nut trees

Nuts are a great source of protein and relatively easy to grow. Plant trees in fall or spring. Harvesting normally takes place in fall. Most nuts can be stored for about six months in a dark, dry environment. Here are some of our favorites that we grow at Newhouse Farm.

Almonds (4)

Prunus dulcis

■ **How to grow** Best grown as fans on south-facing walls. Almonds are just like peach trees—you can hardly tell them apart—and need similar conditions. They have beautiful blossoms that appear before the leaves in spring.

■ **Problem solving** Almonds do poorly in wet winters and will not survive a hard freeze. In all but the warmest, driest climates, grow in containers.

■ **Prune** Try to avoid pruning: it increases the risk of diseases such as bacterial canker. As a last resort, prune in spring after new growth starts.

■ **Harvest, cook, store** Pick almonds in fall and rub off the leathery skin (wear gloves to do this); then dry and store.

PROTECTING YOUR FRUIT CROP

A fruit cage is extremely effective as a defense against birds. We leave the door to our fruit cage open in early summer so that birds can eat any pests, but close it when the currants and raspberries are ripening. We keep it closed in winter too, when birds like to snack on the buds of the currant bushes.

Netting fruit bushes or rows of strawberries is another option. Make a tunnel by pushing bent hoops of plastic piping into the ground and stretching netting over the top. Peg netting into the soil to stop birds from sneaking underneath. Don't lay it directly on top of fruit—birds will peck straight through it!

Hazelnuts (5)
Corylus avellana

■ **How to grow** Hazelnuts or filberts are very tasty and the trees can be used for hedging and coppiced for firewood, plant supports, and making your own hurdles.

■ **Problem solving** Birds and squirrels love the nuts and often strip the crop before you get a chance to pick. You can't get ahead of the game and pick unripe nuts—they need to ripen on the tree. Visit trees daily and start picking as soon as the husks start to turn brown.

■ **Prune** Keep trees to a manageable height by pruning in winter—or follow a coppicing routine (see page 182).

■ **Harvest, cook, store** Pick nuts when ripe in fall. Eat them right away or, if you are going to store them, take off the husks first.

European chestnuts (6)
Castanea sativa

■ **How to grow** A low-maintenance tree that erupts with loads of yummy nuts in spiny shells. They are huge trees and not suitable for a small space.

■ **Problem solving** Generally trouble-free.

■ **Prune** No pruning necessary.

■ **Harvest, cook, store** Knock down the nuts in fall and take them out of their shells—wear gloves! You will find up to three nuts per shell. Leave them to dry, then store. If you roast chestnuts on an open fire or in the oven, pierce the shells first with a skewer or they'll explode—messily.

Walnuts (7)
Juglans regia

■ **How to grow** Walnut trees are definitely a long-term investment. They are very slow-growing and can reach 100 ft (30 m) high, so consider the location carefully before planting. Grafted varieties can crop within three to four years, but with traditional types it's more like 10 to 15 years.

■ **Problem solving** Grow in a sheltered spot to avoid frost damage to flowers.

■ **Prune** Shouldn't be necessary, but if you need to take out a branch or two, do it in fall to avoid the sap bleeding.

■ **Harvest, cook, store** If you want to pickle walnuts, harvest them before the shell forms. Otherwise, pick them later, rub off the sticky skin, and dry them—they store well.

Why not try?
Here are a couple of other trees that we plan to try. They are a long-term investment but look to be worth experimenting with, especially using permaculture principles in a forest garden (see page 99).

Pecans (8)
Carya illinoinensis

■ **How to grow** We tend to associate pecans with the South, but some varieties are hardy to USDA Zone 5. The main drawback is how long they take to mature and produce nuts—anything from 10 to 20 years. A mature tree can be 110 ft (30 m) tall and 65 ft (20 m) wide.

■ **Problem solving** Keep well watered while establishing to avoid powdery mildew.

■ **Prune** Rarely needed, but if you do have to take out a branch or two, do it in fall to avoid bleeding.

■ **Harvest, cook, store** Pick in mid-fall when husks open.

The nuts keep best if frozen. Dry them at room temperature for a couple of weeks first.

Honey locust
Gleditsia triacanthos

■ **How to grow** These multi-purpose trees are native to North America. The seedpods are edible, the flowers attract bees, and trees can be coppiced and leaves used as fodder.

■ **Problem solving** Protect young trees from severe frost until established.

■ **Prune** Shouldn't be necessary. Watch out for thorns on mature trees.

■ **Harvest, cook, store** Collect pods as they fall. The pulp inside is edible—use it to make beer!—but the pods are more commonly used to feed sheep, cattle, or pigs.

ORCHARD BIRDS

Letting geese, ducks, and hens have the run of an orchard or allowing them to forage under fruit and nut trees benefits both birds and trees. The birds supplement their diet with insects and stop pest populations from building up. Geese are traditional orchard birds and will also keep grass under control by grazing. Keep them away from young trees, or use tree protectors.

Pruning, training, and grafting

Pruning will make your fruit trees more productive, increasing yields and fruit quality, as well as making harvesting a whole lot simpler. Training is a more specialized form of pruning and is used to restrict a tree's growth to create formal, space-saving shapes; grafting is a method of making more fruit trees, which mature quickly and bear fruit sooner, for very little outlay.

Pruning fruit trees

The point of pruning is to increase yields and create an open tree shape that is more convenient for harvesting. It is also needed when a tree is suffering from any of the three Ds: Dead, Dying or Diseased branches. Pruning has many more complex quirks depending on different trees and it's worth consulting a book that's entirely dedicated to the subject.

Pruning generally falls into one of two categories: either summer or winter pruning. Winter pruning is a great time to tidy up the tree and remove any dead or diseased parts.

Summer pruning

This stimulates growth of fruit buds for next year and opens the tree up to sunlight so the fruit will ripen better. Summer is also a good time to prune trees that you are training into espaliers, fans, and cordons, because the shoots are more flexible then. Do it once the leaves are dark green and the bark has started to turn brown and woody at the base of the shoots—toward the end of summer. In cold areas it may be fall before shoots are mature enough to prune. See the directory on pages 148–153 for specific advice on different trees.

Tools to use

For pruning thin shoots up to around ¾ in (2 cm) in diameter you need pruning shears. To deal with bigger branches, invest in a pruning saw and a pair of long-handled loppers. You'll need them for coppicing woodland too (see pages 182–183).

Training

Training fruit trees is an ideal way to grow fruit in a small space. It can take advantage of warm south-facing walls and fences that help fruit ripen quicker, and makes harvesting easier. All trained shapes need support of some sort. Run horizontal wires across a wall or fence; use posts and wires for freestanding trees (see below). Once established they are easy to maintain.

Grafting fruit trees

We tend to leave grafting to the experts, but it's worth learning. Grafting combines the properties of two different varieties: strong roots and trunk (the rootstock) with top-quality fruit (the scion). All fruit trees you buy have been grafted.

Budding is useful for grafting a favorite apple, for example, onto a less-productive tree. Whip-and-tongue grafting creates a new tree.

Popular styles of training
By training fruit trees into neat space-saving shapes, you can fit them into small spaces and improve productivity.

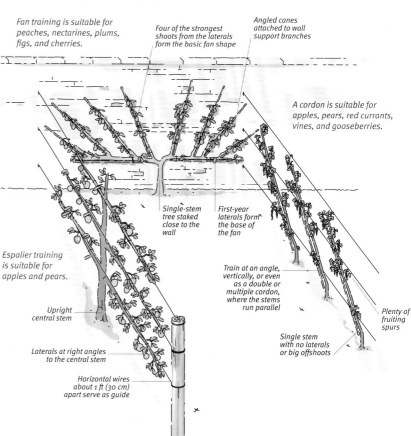

Fan training is suitable for peaches, nectarines, plums, figs, and cherries.

Four of the strongest shoots from the laterals form the basic fan shape

Angled canes attached to wall support branches

A cordon is suitable for apples, pears, red currants, vines, and gooseberries.

Single-stem tree staked close to the wall

First-year laterals form the base of the fan

Espalier training is suitable for apples and pears.

Train at an angle, vertically, or even as a double or multiple cordon, where the stems run parallel

Plenty of fruiting spurs

Upright central stem

Single stem with no laterals or big offshoots

Laterals at right angles to the central stem

Horizontal wires about 1 ft (30 cm) apart serve as guide

PROJECT **Prune an espalier apple tree**

Summer pruning is crucial to maintain the shape of a formally trained espalier tree. The basic techniques shown here apply to other styles of training, as well as to pruning straightforward bush-type fruit trees. Use sharp shears and always cut above an outward-growing bud.

1. Cut cleanly with the shears at a shallow angle facing away from the leaf. Leave a small gap between the cut and the last leaf bud.   **2. Cut back leafy shoots** that have grown up directly from the main horizontal branches to three leaves above the base clump of leaves.   **3. Tie in sideshoots** growing out of the vertical stem by training them along a wire and incorporating them into the shape. **Or remove them completely if the tree is becoming overcrowded**.

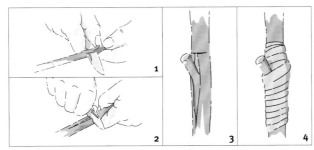

4. Trim back any shoots that are growing out at an angle from the espalier instead of along its length.
5. Take off the top of the tree.   **6. The finished tree** has a precise tiered shape that makes harvesting easy and saves space in the garden.

PROJECT **Grafting techniques**

BUDDING

To be successful, budding needs to be done in midsummer. Choose a healthy cutting about 12 in (30 cm) long for the scion and graft it to a strong healthy branch of your rootstock tree.

1. Cut a piece of bark with a leaf bud from the scion   **2. Cut a T-shaped slit** in the bark of a branch of the rootstock tree.
3. Peel back the flaps of bark and insert the bud. Fold the flaps of bark back down around the bud.   **4. Bind the stem** with grafting tape. Your chosen variety will grow from the newly grafted bud. As the bud grows, cut back the old stem of the rootstock above the grafting point so that all the energy goes into the new variety.

WHIP-AND-TONGUE GRAFTING

For this technique, best carried out in late winter, you will need a year-old rootstock. Start by taking a healthy cutting about 9 in (23 cm) from the scion tree in late fall. Heel it into the ground to keep it dormant. Rootstock and scion should be roughly the same diameter—ideally about 1 in (2.5 cm).

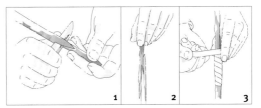

Cut off the rootstock at 6–12 in (15–30 cm) above ground level.   **1. Make a sloping cut** across the rootstock 2 in (5 cm) long and slice into it thinly to form an upward-pointing tongue. Make a similar cut in the scion, just behind a bud, to form a downward-pointing tongue.   **2. Interlock the tongues** on scion and rootstock.   **3. Bind together** with grafting tape.

1 2 3 4

HERBS TO GROW

Herbs usually do extremely well in pots and containers and are a great starting point for growing your own produce. Grow herbs that you like eating, and remember, you are more likely to use them if they are close to the kitchen. Here are some of our favorites.

Bay (1)
Laurus nobilis

■ **How to grow** Bay is an evergreen that requires very little maintenance. It grows extremely well in pots or containers and is a great herb for an urban space.

■ **Harvest, cook, store** You can dry bay leaves, but in our mild climate, we pick fresh leaves from our tree year-round. In cold regions, you'll need to move your bay indoors for the winter.

Basil (2)
Ocimum basilicum

■ **How to grow** Basil can be grown as a perennial in warmer regions, but in cooler climates it is usually grown as an annual. The fact that we have been growing basil from seed every summer for years says something about how tasty we think it is. Basil grows extremely well in a sunny position, provided it is watered regularly. It is good practice to pinch out

the growing tips to help preserve the plant's bushy shape and to remove the flowering shoots to ensure a decent supply of young leaves.

■ **Harvest, cook, store** There's nothing better in summer than a snack of our own tomatoes and basil on fresh bruschetta. The big mature leaves are the tastiest. Basil doesn't really dry and store well, so the leaves are best used fresh.

Chives (3)
Allium schoenoprasum

■ **How to grow** Chives are hardy perennials and a member of the onion family. They grow in small clumps. Sow seed outside in spring when the soil warms up, in a warm, sunny position. Or propagate by dividing up existing clumps and replanting in good soil. Chives will grow in almost any soil but they like humidity, so we tend to plant them next to our ponds. If seed is sown under cover, leaves can be harvested in just a couple of weeks.

■ **Harvest, cook, store** The hollow, grasslike leaves are great snipped over potato salads and omelets. We also use the pinky-purple flowers as a tasty garnish in summer salads. Yes, chives can be frozen or dried, but nothing beats the taste of the freshly picked herb.

Cilantro
Coriandrum sativum

■ **How to grow** We love cilantro. Sow seed from late spring into fairly rich soil in a sunny position. We succession-sow to guarantee a steady supply. We are also lucky enough to be able to grow cilantro and other annual herbs under cover in winter thanks to our greenhouse heat sink (see pages 118–119).

■ **Harvest, cook, store** The leaves and seeds can be used in a huge range of dishes including lots of spicy Mexican and Asian cuisine. Follow the instructions for dill, below, for harvesting the seeds (known as coriander).

Dill
Anethum graveolens

■ **How to grow** Dill is a hardy annual with highly aromatic dark brown seeds and lively tasting leaves. Sow dill seeds *in situ* and be sure to keep the area very well weeded—the seedlings don't grow well with competition. To ensure a good seasonal supply, succession-sow dill from late spring to early summer.

■ **Harvest, cook, store** The leaves are delicious with fish, and our favorite recipe has to be the Scandinavian salmon dish gravlax. Dill is also excellent with cucumber or fresh in salads. To harvest the

seeds, simply cut the base of the plant when the flower-heads turn brown and tie the stems into loose bunches. Cover the heads with brown paper bags and hang upside down somewhere airy for a few days. Open the bag and you'll find plenty of dry ripe seeds ready to store in a glass jar. If you want to dry the leaves for use in winter, make sure you cut them when the plants are about 12 in (30 cm) tall and before they start flowering.

Marjoram
Origanum majorana

■ **How to grow** There are lots of different varieties of marjoram, and to make things even more confusing, some of them are called oregano. As a general rule, marjoram varieties are hardy perennials while oregano varieties (*Origanum vulgare*) are usually tender plants. Gourmets claim the latter have the finest flavor. Both do well in pots or in a sunny spot in the garden.

■ **Harvest, cook, store** Both marjoram and oregano are vital herbs for pasta sauces and for sprinkling over pizzas. The leaves dry successfully (see pages 242–243), but you should be able to keep a pot or two going on the kitchen windowsill or on a shelf in the greenhouse over the winter.

5 **6** **7** **8**

Mint (4)
Mentha species

■ **How to grow** There are lots of different varieties of mint, and most of them are tasty. Mint spreads very quickly and is best planted away from other herbs, either against a wall or in a sunken pail or box in the herb bed to control its roots—cut out the bottom of the pail to allow drainage. Mint can tolerate a degree of shade and needs lots of water.

■ **Harvest, cook, store** We use our mint to make everything from mint sauce for lamb to tzatziki, to help us get through our summer cucumber glut. We also enjoy it freshly picked in a cup of mint tea. Mint can often be harvested all year in mild-winter areas, but it's worth potting up a few roots for winter and bringing them indoors to a kitchen windowsill, just in case.

Parsley (5)
Petroselinum crispum

■ **How to grow** Parsley is one of the best-known herbs and has made its mark in culinary circles with its unique taste and versatility. It is also a very good source of vitamin C and iron. We sow parsley each year into rich soil that has a fine tilth; it also likes to be kept well watered.

■ **Harvest, cook, store** Dry the leaves at high temperature by blasting them in a microwave for a few minutes. Add fresh parsley as a garnish: it loses its flavor in slow cooking.

Rosemary (6)
Rosmarinus officinalis

■ **How to grow** Rosemary is a delightful evergreen shrub in mild climates: some species can grow to about 5 ft (1.5 m), so choose carefully—you might consider using it for a hedge. It likes light and dry soil. Sow seeds in spring or take some cuttings from a friend's plant (ask first!). Take them in late summer from nonflowering shoots and push into a pot of potting mix. Keep in a frost-free environment until the following spring when they can be planted outside. Prune established plants in spring after the first flowering.

■ **Harvest, cook, store** Late summer is probably the best time to pick leaves for drying, but as we can harvest rosemary year-round, we don't tend to bother. We often use rosemary when cooking meat or roasted vegetables and almost always as a fragrant addition to the outdoor grill.

Sage (7)
Salvia officinalis

■ **How to grow** Sage is an aromatic perennial. It grows to about 2 ft (60 cm) in the right sunny position with well-drained soil. For best results, grow from cuttings taken in late spring. Cut bushes back at the end of the summer to prevent them from becoming too woody.

■ **Harvest, cook, store** Sage is great for flavoring stuffing and makes a very tasty pesto mixed with garlic and pine nuts. Cut leaves and hang up to dry at the end of summer. Be warned: they take a long time to dry.

Tarragon
Artemisia dracunculus

■ **How to grow** Tarragon is a very untidy but vibrant perennial herb that usually comes in two varieties: French and Russian. We recommend growing the French variety rather than the coarser Russian. Take cuttings and keep them indoors, as French tarragon is susceptible to cold weather and may die over winter. Drainage is important: plant it on sloping ground in a sunny position, or near the top of an herb spiral (see pages 158–159).

■ **Harvest, cook, store** Leaves can be dried, but they are best frozen. Add to chicken dishes or infuse a sprig in vinegar to use in salad dressings.

Thyme (8)
Thymus species

■ **How to grow** Thyme is another great perennial that thrives in a well-drained, dry position. It is best grown from cuttings taken in early summer, rather than from seed. For best results, cut shoots about 6 in (15 cm) long from the tips of the plant, avoiding the woody base stems. Prune it after flowering to stop it from getting straggly.

■ **Harvest, cook, store** Thyme can be dried successfully but as it is evergreen in our area, we pick it even in winter. It's great in all tomato recipes.

EDIBLE FLOWERS

We like to liven up our salads with a scattering of edible flowers. While most British people are familiar with borage flowers floating in their summer Pimm's Cup, they are often surprised to find nasturtiums, calendula or pot marigolds, wild garlic flowers, and heartsease in among the lettuce. Chives add a nice touch of pink. Shake flowers free of insects before adding.

157

Create an herb spiral

Growing herbs in a 3-D spiral uses the plants themselves to create the ideal conditions for each other, in a kind of compatibility arrangement. The other advantage if you have only a small plot is that the spiral structure makes maximum use of vertical space as well as horizontal—almost like a gardening skyscraper. But don't let that put you off: it's fantastically simple to build.

How it works

An herb spiral works on the premise that some plants require more sunlight and drainage, while others like shade and damp soil. The clever thing about the spiral is that it allows for a variety of different conditions in such a small space, giving each herb its own little microclimate.

Permaculture in action

A spiral also means you can plant more densely, which is a major principle of permaculture (see pages 98–101): high-yield growing in as little land as possible. The height of the spiral creates drainage for herbs like rosemary, thyme, and sage, and also provides cover and allows moisture to collect on the lower north side for herbs like chives and wild garlic that prefer damper, shadier conditions. As the herbs grow and become established, the spiral casts shade—even in full sun.

Getting started

Consider the location of your herb spiral carefully. For the spiral to work and the sun-loving plants to thrive, it needs to be placed in a sunny location, ideally south-facing to receive sun throughout the day. The spiral will cast its own shade, but it can't create its own sun!

You can figure out the sunniest areas in your yard by observing where the sun falls throughout the day, but a compass is useful when you're planning the planting scheme.

"Zoning" is another key design principle of permaculture: plants that need most attention or are in frequent use should be grown closest to the home. So try to position the spiral close to the house.

Gathering the materials

An assortment of medium-sized stones is ideal for building up the spiral walls, thanks to their stability and heat-absorbing qualities— another clever aspect of the design that maximizes the growing year by encouraging early growth. But before going out and buying any materials, remember the mantra "Reduce, Reuse, Recycle." We used stones because that was what we had lying around (see box opposite), but there is no end to the different materials you could try— from wood to bricks to old wine bottles.

TRY THIS

■ **Experiment** with different herbs, planting them in the appropriate position in the spiral.

■ **Wine bottles** work well as a building material. Make sure you fill them with soil before you start to improve their strength and enable the walls to absorb and retain some of the sun's heat.

■ You could include a **small pond** at the bottom of the spiral on the northern side to grow watercress and encourage frogs into the garden to help with natural pest control. Dig a shallow hole, line it with impermeable material, and edge with additional stones (see page 123).

■ Add **alpine strawberries** to your herb spiral: they thrive in the shady gaps between plants and provide a great snack for whoever is picking the herbs.

SUGGESTED PLANTING PLAN

Use the plan to position herbs according to their preferred growing conditions.

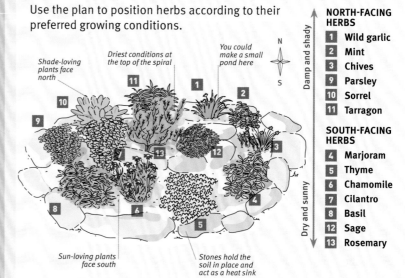

Shade-loving plants face north

Driest conditions at the top of the spiral

You could make a small pond here

Sun-loving plants face south

Stones hold the soil in place and act as a heat sink

Damp and shady

Dry and sunny

NORTH-FACING HERBS
1. Wild garlic
2. Mint
3. Chives
9. Parsley
10. Sorrel
11. Tarragon

SOUTH-FACING HERBS
4. Marjoram
5. Thyme
6. Chamomile
7. Cilantro
8. Basil
12. Sage
13. Rosemary

Build and plant the spiral

Laying a barrier below the spiral saves digging the ground beforehand and helps prevent weeds from growing up through your herbs. If your spiral is in the middle of the lawn, make a mowing edge with some slate like we have—you'll appreciate it in summer.

YOU WILL NEED
- String and pencil
- Tape measure
- Scissors/utility knife
- Trowel
- Watering can
- Pile of medium-sized stones
- Eco-mulch or cardboard
- Slate or tiles (optional)
- Potting mix or topsoil
- Herbs for planting

1. Measure out the circle on the ground to a diameter of about 5 ft (1.5 m); the age-old technique of using a pencil and string will give you a fairly accurate circle. Roughly mark out the edge with stones.   **2. Cut strips** of mulching material or cardboard slightly larger than the circle, so that they extend beyond the stones. Position the mulch under the stones.
3. Place slate or tiles, if using, under the stones to make a mowing edge.

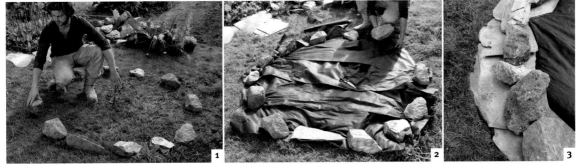

4. Lay an extra piece of slate in the center to weigh down the mulch, and then start building the spiral inward from the north-facing edge   **5. Add potting mix** or topsoil as you go, to give the spiral stability. Make sure that the lowest stones in the spiral are sitting directly on the mulch, not on a layer of soil.   **6. Spiral the stones** upward, adding height with soil and packing it between the stones as well. The herb spiral needs to be at least 20 in (50 cm) tall.

7. Make the spiral wall taller on the south-facing side by adding more stones. Position the herbs according to the planting plan.
8. Plant the herbs and water well.   **9. Harvest herbs** once they are established. Here, sage, chives, wild garlic, marjoram, and tarragon are thriving, with alpine strawberries filling the gaps.

PROJECT **Grow your own mushrooms**

One of the biggest worries about foraging for mushrooms in the wild is identifying the edible ones. Growing your own eliminates the risk. You can confidently sample lots of different types without needing to be an expert mycologist. They'll be cheaper than store-bought, and whichever of these two methods you try, you'll be reusing a waste product.

A fun and easy way to grow mushrooms uses an old paperback book. We tried pearl oyster mushrooms. In the wild, they grow on dead or dying hardwood trees, but we grew them on our windowsill at home.

Another method uses logs and dates back to China a thousand years ago. Back then, they simply placed freshly felled logs next to ones that had mushrooms growing on them and waited for them to spread. These days we can buy spawn plugs: small lengths of grooved wooden dowel that contain the mushroom's root system, or mycelium, to insert in a log. Look for shiitake, pearl oyster, or chicken of the woods spawn plugs.

YOU WILL NEED—BOOK METHOD
- Mushroom spawn (order online)
- Paperback book with 200–400 pages
- Plastic bag and rubber bands
- Mister spray bottle

YOU WILL NEED—LOG METHOD
- Ax
- Narrow spade
- Post-hole digger
- Pry bar
- Hand drill and ¼-inch (6.35-mm) drill bit
- Logs that have been felled within the last six months, about 4 ft (1.2 m) long and 6–7 in (15–18 cm) in diameter
- About 50 mushroom spawn plugs per log (order online)

BOOK METHOD

1. **Soak the book** in warm water for 20 minutes. Squeeze the bubbles out of the book while it is underwater to get rid of most of the air. **Take the book** out of the water and squeeze it again, so that it is wet but not saturated. **2. Carefully open the book** and break up the mushroom spawn. **3. Gently spread** some on the pages. **4. Press** the pages together. **Repeat this process** every 50 pages or so throughout the book, until you have used all the spawn.

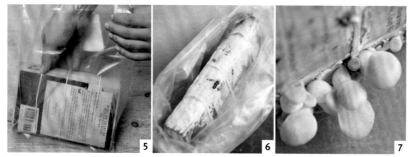

 5. Put a few rubber bands around the book and place it spine down in a clear plastic bag. Seal the bag and label it with the date. Keep in a warm place away from direct strong sunlight and drafts—about 68°F (20°C) is ideal. In winter, keep it near a heat register. After 24 hours the spawn will begin to activate. In about two weeks the paper will be covered in a white fuzz—the mycelium, or mushrooms' roots. When the edges of the book look white, place the bag in the refrigerator for two days.
6. Remove from the refrigerator and open, folding the bag down to just above the top of the book. Put it in a light position (indirect sunlight). Water regularly with a plant mister. **7. Harvest** oyster mushrooms when they are about 4 in (10 cm) across.

GROWING TIPS

- **Maintaining high moisture** levels is very important since mushrooms are mostly water. Growing them in a book means they need a bit of attention, but no more so than any indoor houseplant, and you can expect a harvest much faster than with the log method.
- You may get as many as **three crops** from your book. There's no need to put it back in the refrigerator—the mushrooms should just continue to grow as you harvest them.
- **Dry mushrooms** in a solar dryer (see pages 242–243), then store them in airtight jars.

LOG METHOD

1. Choose a disease-free hardwood log and trim off any side branches and twigs. Remove any lichen or moss. Try not to damage the bark: it will help to retain moisture when the mushrooms start growing. Moisture is a top priority for mushroom cultivation.   **2. Dig a hole.** Your site should be damp, shady, and sheltered from strong winds. Use a pry bar to get started.   **3. Finish off** with a post-hole digger: the hole should be about half as deep as the log's total length.   **4. Stand the log** in the hole and secure it firmly by backfilling with rubble and soil. The log will draw up water from the ground.

5. Drill holes at right angles into the log. Make them half again as deep as the length of the spawn plugs. Stagger the holes at 4–6-in (10–15-cm) intervals in a diamond pattern, going all around the log.   **6. Push the spawn plugs** into the holes immediately after drilling—make sure your hands are clean. Then tap them into place with a hammer.   **7. Water** the log thoroughly. Place a pot or a piece of plastic wrap with a rubber band over the top of the log. This will help to limit moisture loss by evaporation. Continue to water in hot weather. If the log gets too dry, the bark will flake off. If it sprouts green mold, you've overdone the watering.   **8. Repeat with more logs** if you have space. In 12 to 18 months your crop will be ready. Pick mushrooms when they form clumps of about 6 in (15 cm) across. Use a sharp, short knife and cut close to the bark.

Any hardwood log can be used for growing mushrooms, but we've had great success with beech, oak, and birch.

TRY THIS

■ **Tree stumps** are ideal for growing mushrooms, as their roots still draw up plenty of moisture from the soil, but you must inoculate the stumps within a few months of the tree being cut down. Drill only the outer ring of sapwood on the face of the stump, then insert spawn plugs.

■ **The north side** of a building can be ideal for the log method. The wall will keep the logs a bit warmer, but don't position them too close to the building or they won't get any rain.

■ **Tray culture** gets great results with button mushrooms. The trays should be about 8 in (20 cm) deep and filled with well-rotted horse manure. Sow dry mushroom spawn on the surface and cover with damp newspaper. Store the trays in a garage or shed. Remove the newspaper after about two weeks when the mycelium has grown. Cover the surface with 2 in (5 cm) of normal topsoil and water well. You should be picking mushrooms in two weeks.

FORAGING FOR WILD PLANTS

Foraging was once vital for the survival of hunter-gatherers. Now it's a popular pastime—even in cities, people gather free food from parks or bike paths. Before picking and eating any wild plants, however, be certain that you've correctly identified them. We recognize veggies in a supermarket but have lost the skills needed to scan a fencerow for edible treats. Get a plant identification book—and if in doubt about a plant, don't eat it!

FORAGER'S CODE

■ **Eat only** what you have identified as being edible.
■ **Leave plenty** for others, including wildlife—pillaging is bad foraging etiquette.
■ **Gather fruits widely** from scattered plants, not just from one individual. Leave some for plants to set seed.
■ **Be selective**—pick only the young, tender leaves or the best-looking fruits.
■ **Avoid roadsides** because of car fumes, and don't pick low-growing plants next to paths or sidewalks, where dogs may have sprayed urine.
■ **Take a bag** whenever you go for a walk—just in case.
■ **Give as well as take.** Volunteer to help plant trees or put up bird houses.

Spring salads and roots

This is the best time to pick the first green tops of nettles and unusual early salads, and to dig up various roots. Look for them in fencerows and field edges.

Nettles (1)

Urtica dioica
Excellent cooked or made into tea. Use the freshest tender top leaves, cook in a little water, and serve as a side dish with butter. Cooking destroys the sting so your tongue won't tingle!

Chickweed

Stellaria media
A low-growing, mat-forming plant and common lawn weed with small leaves and dainty star-shaped white flowers. Chickweed can be eaten in salads (when raw, the flavor resembles fresh corn) or cooked (when it tastes something like spinach). True to its name, chickens find it irresistible.

Fireweed (2)

Epilobium angustifolium
Steam the young shoots, or boil in a very small amount of water, as you would asparagus.

Purple clover

Trifolium pratense
Purple clover is widespread, abundant, and nutritious. Steam and eat the familiar three-part leaves; add young flowers to salad, or make tea from dried flowers.

Burdock

Arctium lappa
A tall plant with round purple flowers and rhubarb-like leaves—but it's the delicious root you want. Peel and cut into chunks to add to stews, or cut into thin sticks, fry in oil, and serve like French fries.

Dandelion

Taraxacum officinale
You've probably got dandelions growing in your yard, and you'll find them in open areas. The roots are very tasty in stews or stir-fries, and you can also roast and grind them to make a coffee substitute. Mix young leaves in with salads. They're tricky to uproot—a digging stick is a great help (see box).

Ramps (3)

Allium tricoccum
Ramps or wild leeks grow in woodland margins, and you can often smell them before you see them. Eat the leaves wilted in butter as a side dish, or mixed with potatoes and fried.

THE DIGGING STICK

One of the forager's oldest tools is a digging stick made from strong wood—hazel is ideal. Give it a sharp, beveled chisel end and harden it by heating in the embers of a fire. Excavate a deep hole alongside a plant. Dig all the way to the bottom of the root and on all sides and pry out the root. Fill in the hole afterward!

Wood sorrel

Oxalis stricta
This pretty plant grows on the woodland floor in spring and looks like oversized clover with delicate yellow flowers. The heart-shaped leaves have a strong lemony flavor, great sprinkled in soups or salads. Just don't eat too much, as the plant contains oxalic acid, which can upset digestion.

Summer fruits

On summer walks we fill our baskets with fruits, roots, and something succulent.

Glasswort

Salicornia depressa
A green succulent plant, it will often carpet areas around salt

5

6

7

8

marshes or mud flats. Delicious pickled, then served with ham on toast. Like many wild greens, the taste is hard to describe.

Horseradish
Armoracia rusticana
The leaves look like dock leaves: large, long, and coarse. Find them in fields and open areas. Grate the very strong-tasting root and blend with olive oil and lemon juice to make a basic horseradish sauce.

Blackberry
Rubus fruticosus
A fruit with a rich foragers' tradition; many of us have fond childhood memories of picking baskets full. Avoid gathering next to busy roads as the pollution will spoil the fruit.

Elderberry (4)
Sambucus nigra
Elderberries make very good wine. Earlier in the season we also pick some of the fragrant flowers to make our very own elderflower champagne (see page 259).

Wild strawberry (5)
Fragaria vesca
These little strawberries are very tasty—more delicate in flavor than the cultivated kind but well worth collecting. Find them on the edges of woodland and shady lanes.

Crab apple (6)
Malus sylvestris
This underrated fruit makes tasty jelly. It's easy to forage: just hold out a basket and shake the branches. Look for trees in mixed hedges.

Autumn harvest
Traditionally, fall was a time for gathering and storing nuts for winter, with people behaving very much like squirrels. It's also a good time for fungi, but they are notoriously difficult to identify. We haven't covered them here; instead, we recommend going on a fungus foray led by an expert.

Sweet chestnut
Castanea sativa
The nuts are contained in sheaths covered in hundreds of thin, green spikes. We think that these make the best stuffing for Thanksgiving turkeys. If you pierce them with a knife first, they are excellent roasted in front of an open fire.

Walnut
Juglans regia
Mature trees have huge crops. If you know where one is growing wild, keep it a secret and enjoy the benefits once a year. The compound leaves comprise several pairs of leaflets. See page 153 for tips on storing and preserving.

Hazel (7)
Corylus avellana
It takes a fast-draw forager to beat the squirrels to these yummy nuts. Hazelnuts are tasty cooked in all sorts of ways. We like to store them as winter treats, but make sure they are completely dry, otherwise they will rot and your crop will be wasted.

Winter fruit and seashore food
Wrap up warmly and, if fencerow pickings are thin, head to the seashore instead.

Sloes
Prunus spinosa
Sloes are the fruit of the blackthorn tree and look like clusters of tiny purple plums. Picking sloes is an annual ritual for us. Although they are too bitter to eat, we use them to flavor gin (see box).

Rose hips
Rosa canina
Rose hips are a great source of vitamin C and can be eaten raw if you scrape out the hairy seeds. They're also good for making syrup (see page 238).

Edible kelp
Alaria esculenta
Kelp has long brown fronds and is found in rock pools or deeper water. Cut into short lengths

and soak them in warm water for 5–10 minutes before adding to stir-fries.

Dulse
Rhodymenia palmata
A tasty seaweed from the intertidal part of the shore. Identify it by its rich red color.

Sea lettuce (8)
Ulva lactuca
Its stunning emerald green color makes sea lettuce easy to identify. We use it in stir fries.

SLOE PRICKER

We cut a cork from a wine bottle in half lengthways and stuck lots of pins through it to make a sloe-pricking tool. Use it to pierce the skin of sloes when making sloe gin; it helps the flavor and juice to infuse. To make sloe gin you need 8oz (250g) sloes and the same weight in sugar. Fill a wide-necked bottle halfway with pricked sloes and sugar and top off with gin. Shake for the first couple of days to dissolve the sugar. It'll be ready to drink after two months.

Storing the harvest

Growing your own produce is one of the most exciting aspects of living a more self-sufficient lifestyle, especially with an effective storage regimen to back it up. A well-thought-out system means your excess harvest won't end up as fodder for livestock or cause the compost bin to overflow. More importantly, it helps you to maintain a supply of fresh food year round.

Harvesting for storage

As a general rule, harvest produce for storage when it is at its peak. It should look healthy, ripe, and ready to eat. But there are a few exceptions. With vegetables such as squashes, wait until the stem has dried out and shriveled a bit, and the skin doesn't dent when you press it with your fingernail. Equally, wait a bit longer before picking apples and pears, which are best harvested for storing near the end of the growing season. For best results, store only late-ripening varieties and leave them on the tree for as long as possible. You'll know they are ready when they can be gently lifted off the branches.

Try not to damage crops as you pick them or dig them up. Don't waste time trying to store damaged or diseased produce—either send it to the compost bin, or give it to pigs or chickens as fodder.

Cleaning and trimming

Brush off most of the excess soil from root crops but don't scrub or wash them—you can do that just before you cook them. Similarly, don't trim off any unshapely knobby bits: the exposed cut could start to rot in storage. But do remove the leafy tops from roots before you store those, as they will take some of the moisture from the root and can turn slimy later, ruining anything they are touching.

In the storeroom

For thousands of years, people lived without refrigerators and plastic wrap. They used natural larders, pantries, root cellars, and storerooms to keep food edible. At Newhouse Farm we keep our produce fresh for months in our storeroom. A storeroom needs to be at a cool and constant temperature, and should be frost-free. It doesn't have to be dark like a root cellar (see pages 180–1), but it shouldn't have direct sunlight, which will make the room too warm and can discolor produce. The humidity should be ambient: too wet and produce will develop mold and fungal problems; too dry and your vegetables will shrivel.

Ventilation is important: window screen on windows and vents lets air in while keeping pests out.

SEED-SAVING TIPS

■ **Leave seeds to ripen on the plant,** but remove them before they scatter naturally. Cut the stalks and place the seed heads upside down in a paper bag, to collect seeds as they dry.
■ **Briefly soak seeds** from fruits like tomatoes in water to wash off the "jelly" before drying on a hard surface—on paper towels you'll never get the paper off the seeds!
■ **Shell peas and beans** from the pod before drying and storing.
■ **Dry seeds in a cold frame** to speed up the process (see page 117).
■ **Store seeds** in labeled paper envelopes in an airtight container. Keep in a cool, dry room.
■ **Save bags of desiccant** that come with electronic equipment and use to keep the moisture out of your store.

Runner bean pods *dry out and split to reveal ripe beans ready to store.*

1. Cut squashes *for storage when the stem attaching them to the plant has dried out.* **2. Beets** *will store for longer without their leaves.* **3. Dry onions** *thoroughly before storing them—this can take several weeks.*

Hanging produce

This is a great way of making stored food inaccessible to vermin while allowing good air flow. We hang vegetables like garlic, onions, and corn from strings, while suspending squashes in netting saves us from having to turn them regularly when they are sitting on shelves.

Using trays

Onions and apples store particularly well on trays with slats or chicken wire bases to allow air to circulate. Apples are best wrapped individually in paper to stop one rotten apple from spoiling the rest. Deeper trays can be used to store beets, Jerusalem artichokes, carrots, and parsnips in sand or sawdust. Put a layer of sand in the bottom of the tray and arrange the roots so that they don't touch. Layer sand and roots, finishing with a final covering of sand. Fill trays in situ to save the effort of moving them. You can also store roots in a barrel (see page 180). For other methods of preserving food, see pages 224–5.

1. Use deep trays to store layers of root vegetables in sand. **2. Hang** onions, garlic, herbs, and chile peppers from the roof. **3. Keep homemade** drinks, preserves, cured hams, and eggs, as well as fruit and veggies, in an organized storeroom. **4. Dimpled cardboard trays** are another way to keep apples separate in storage.

PROJECT **Make a potato clamp**

Clamping is a traditional way of storing potatoes if you haven't got a storeroom or root cellar. Put a clamp in a sheltered spot, as it isn't guaranteed frost protection. Store only top-quality potatoes, and watch out for slugs. You can use the technique to store any root vegetables and fodder beets for livestock.

YOU WILL NEED
- Fork
- Colander
- Straw
- Spade

1. Dig up your potatoes and leave to dry—a colander is ideal—for a couple of hours, before laying them on a base of straw. **2. Arrange the potatoes in a pyramid** and cover with more straw. Leave them to breathe for an hour or two. **3. Cover the pyramid** with a layer of soil 6 in (15 cm) thick. Allow some straw to poke through the soil, to let air get to the crop. Pat the sides flat with a spade: make them steep so that rain can run off.

Problem solving

Our way of dealing with pests, diseases, and weeds is to use an integrated approach that takes into account the soil and the crops themselves. This means getting to know your pests and their natural predators. It's a method that sets great store by the old expression "an ounce of prevention is worth a pound of cure." It's not perfect, but it's cheap—and there's no risk to people or the environment.

DEALING WITH WEEDS

Keeping on top of weeds before they become a problem is the best approach. Mulching is extremely efficient at suppressing weeds (see page 100). Where it isn't possible to mulch, hoe off weeds regularly when they are small, especially on dry, sunny days when they will shrivel and die. Bigger weeds may need removal with a small fork or trowel. Always deal with weeds before they set seed. Remember: "one year's seeds means seven years' weeds." Digging is a satisfying way of clearing overgrown areas but the benefits can be short-lived. It exposes dormant seeds that will germinate and create as many weed problems as you've solved. Try covering the ground with a cardboard mulch instead, let the weeds die down, then plant through.

Two ways to tackle weeds. *Mulching (top) suppresses weeds by blocking out light. Hand-weeding is the best way to get rid of long-rooted dandelions.*

Start with the plants

To get the best results from our crops, we start by buying seed of pest-resistant varieties—usually traditional, local, proven types. Then we grow strong, healthy plants that will be more resistant to attack. We boost our plants by feeding the soil. Worm tea (see page 127) is useful as it contains all sorts of beneficial fungi and bacteria, not just nutrients.

We also focus on the environment: crop rotation (see pages 108–109) reduces the buildup of pathogens in the soil, while good spacing between plants allows air to circulate, which helps reduce disease. Winter digging exposes pests to bird predators, and companion planting in spring and summer (see page 101) attracts beneficial insects to deal with pests. Interplanting—growing two crops together—is a neat way to confuse crop-specific pests like carrot flies. These preventive methods are highly effective, but keep a watchful eye too.

Animal pests

■ **Moles** are difficult to deal with. They eat huge amounts of worms, damage plant roots, and build mole hills in undesirable spots. Get a special trap and check it daily.

■ **Birds** can be deterred with a traditional scarecrow. Douglas, our scarecrow, works best if we move him around over the season. Plastic bottles make good bird scarers, or string up old CDs to create moving reflections. We use netting to keep birds off our soft fruit or young brassicas. Fine netting will also stop cabbage white butterflies and turnip moths from laying eggs on leaves.

■ **Rabbits** can devastate a garden. The best option is to fence them out with 1-in (2.5-cm) wire netting. Bury it at least 6 in (15 cm) below the surface and make it at least 2 ft (60 cm) high.

Small pests

■ **Aphids** can devastate a salad or bean crop. We interplant with calendula (*Calendula officinalis*). It works by attracting syrphid flies that will eat the aphids. Other predators include ladybugs, which you can encourage by building a simple ladybug hotel and placing it near crops (see page 122). When aphids appear on broad beans or peas, we pinch out the tips where they cluster, and throw to the pigs.

■ **Caterpillars** are easy to spot and pick off by hand. Or use barriers such as fine mesh or floating row cover, which allow light to reach plants but keep out butterflies and other insect pests, and even birds and rabbits.

■ **Colorado potato beetles** can destroy entire potato, tomato, and eggplant crops. Handpick beetles, protect crops with floating row cover, or ask your local extension office about using biological controls.

■ **Slugs and snails** If you don't like the idea of squashing them, try copper tape around individual plants or pots. It works wonders but is expensive. We have tried other deterrents, such as egg shells, coffee granules, and soot, but good old-fashioned beer traps work best for us. The smell attracts slugs and snails, which fall in and drown. Empty regularly to avoid a nasty concoction.

Wireworms are beetle larvae that live in the soil and eat plant roots. Cultivate the ground and feed the wireworms to your ducks or chickens.

Diseases

Cleanliness helps avoid problems in the first place. Scrub pots and trays before using, pick up fallen fruit and leaves, and burn diseased plants.

Bacterial canker sometimes develops on stone fruit trees, killing buds and branches. Cut out and burn all affected parts immediately.

Blight affects tomatoes and potatoes, causing brown and black marks on leaves and fruit. Remove and burn infected leaves quickly. It's a wet-weather disease, so provide plants with good drainage. We've dealt with the problem by growing our outside tomatoes upside-down.

Clubroot is a soilborne disease that affects brassicas. Avoid it by growing your plants in a cardboard box filled with fresh potting mix and sink it into the soil.

Gray mold, or botrytis, occurs in greenhouses and hoop houses. It affects all plants and starts with brown spotting on the foliage, followed by furry mold. Improve air circulation, avoid overwatering, and burn infected shoots.

Rust appears as yellow, red, and brown pustules on leaves. It can kill an entire onion crop. Burn affected leaves, don't wet the foliage when watering, and avoid high humidity.

1. **String up CDs** and bottle caps to deter birds.   2. **Make a bird scarer** from a plastic bottle. Cut side "wings" so it spins in the breeze.   3. **Pour beer** into jars set level with the soil to trap slugs and snails.   4. **Eject aphids** with a high-pressure blast of water.   5. **Pick off caterpillars** as you spot them and feed to your chickens.   6. **Netting** keeps birds and butterflies off brassicas.   7. **Jagged edges** on cut-down plastic bottles, plus copper tape, discourage slugs and snails from reaching lettuces.

WORKING LARGE AREAS If you are lucky enough to have a large property, you'll also have lots more decisions to make. This chapter is intended to guide you through the decision-making process and to give you some food for thought. Without wanting to sound too negative, you'll have to be careful not to bite off more than you can chew—and, to fully milk the eating analogy, it is important to remember that you can only eat an elephant a bite at a time! It's a real privilege to be the custodian of land, so enjoy your time and don't forget the generations who worked it before you.

Observing, planning, and designing

It's hard to resist jumping in with both feet and getting started, but creating a plan for your property can save you from expensive mistakes down the line. Gathering as much local information as you can and making a detailed site map will help you to make your dreams come true without too many false starts, and you may uncover some fascinating history at the same time.

Start by observing

Ideally, you should take notes throughout the seasons before making permanent decisions. In our first year, for example, we waited to see where frost traps developed before planting our fruit trees, and monitored wind speeds in different sites before erecting a turbine.

For a comprehensive picture of your land, speak to previous owners and neighbors, or research old photographs and maps. Part of our motivation to plant an orchard was discovering a 400-year-old map that showed the whole of our valley covered in fruit trees. Both local knowledge and the nature of the land itself should influence any decisions you make. The result will be a well-designed landscape that grounds your dreams and ambitions in reality.

Planning your plot

Now you're at the exciting stage. First decide which existing elements of your property you're going to keep, and which have to go. Then think about what you are going to produce on your land, and why. What kinds of fruit and vegetables do you like eating? Do you want to keep poultry?

Our advice is: don't overstretch yourself. Your energy and enthusiasm will fade if you take on too many projects and don't have time to step back, gain some perspective, and think to yourself: "This is the life."

Designing your plot

The design that you eventually come up with will never be a finished thing. Nature constantly moves the goal posts—anything from the weather to the local slug population has the power to alter your plans. But this unpredictability is what makes life fun. We often stray from the initial idea, but this is another advantage of the organic lifestyle—allowing yourself the luxury of diverging.

1. Assembling a geodesic dome *is a flat-pack nightmare.* **2. Digging a channel** *for the pipe that brings water from the spring to the buildings at Newhouse Farm.* **3. The water wheel** *starts to take shape next to the barn.*

DESIGN TIPS

▪ Site your **vegetable garden** in a sunny, sheltered place near the house.
▪ Keep **tool shed and compost bins** close to the vegetable garden.
▪ Align rows of fruit and vegetables from **north to south,** to catch the sun.
▪ On a slope, **plant across the contours** to prevent erosion.
▪ Plant **fruit bushes** densely to make harvesting and netting easy.
▪ Use **fruit trees** as a way of hiding ugly features.
▪ Earmark **south-facing walls** for delicate fruits like peaches and vines.
▪ Site **wind turbines** away from sources of turbulence, or plan to build them high enough.
▪ Keep **poultry** near the house so it's easy to let them out and put them away at night.
▪ **Geese** are noisy: site their pen near the entrance of your property and they'll act as watchdogs!
▪ A south-facing roof is ideal for **solar PV panels** or **thermal collectors**.

Conducting a site survey

Making a map is without a doubt the best way to get to know your land. A well-observed map fits everything together spatially and helps you visualize your plans. But resist the temptation to add your ideas onto the map at this stage—it makes the process much more confusing. Simply record what is already there, and always mark north and south.

Filling in the details

Record the dimensions of your lot as accurately as you can—to scale if you have the patience. Try using a printout of your plot from Google Earth and lay tracing paper on top. They you can add extra information such as the sunny and shady areas, and different soil types.

Consider drawing a separate map of your buildings at a larger scale to show details such as underground utilities and power.

Look beyond your boundaries. Are there tall neighboring trees or large buildings that cast shadows? Areas such as these may be harder to utilize, so highlight them on the map.

Newhouse Farm in the early days was in need of attention, from clearing the land of brambles and gorse to fixing the roof and updating the plumbing.

Mapping out the options
Annotate your map with lots of information, from soil types to prevailing winds and sun traps.

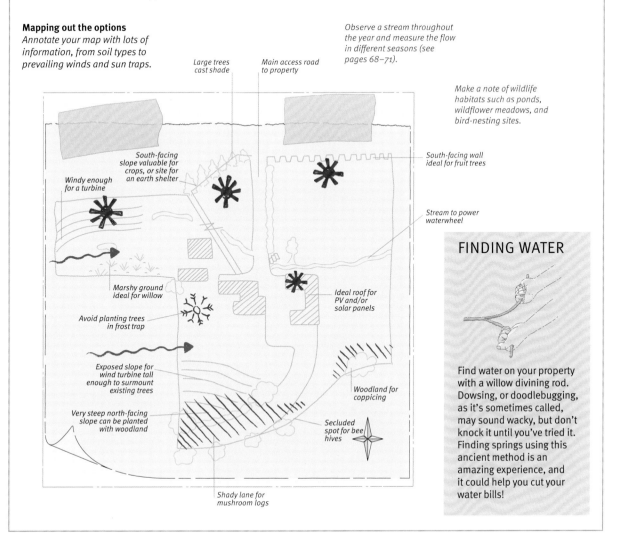

Observe a stream throughout the year and measure the flow in different seasons (see pages 68–71).

Large trees cast shade

Main access road to property

Make a note of wildlife habitats such as ponds, wildflower meadows, and bird-nesting sites.

South-facing slope valuable for crops, or site for an earth shelter

Windy enough for a turbine

South-facing wall ideal for fruit trees

Stream to power waterwheel

Marshy ground ideal for willow

Avoid planting trees in frost trap

Ideal roof for PV and/or solar panels

Exposed slope for wind turbine tall enough to surmount existing trees

Very steep north-facing slope can be planted with woodland

Woodland for coppicing

Secluded spot for bee hives

Shady lane for mushroom logs

FINDING WATER

Find water on your property with a willow divining rod. Dowsing, or doodlebugging, as it's sometimes called, may sound wacky, but don't knock it until you've tried it. Finding springs using this ancient method is an amazing experience, and it could help you cut your water bills!

171

Creating boundaries

Losing a crop of carefully tended vegetables to farm animals on the rampage is one of the most frustrating things that can happen on a small farm, so we always make sure our livestock is securely contained. A mixture of permanent hedging and fencing, together with easily assembled temporary enclosures, helps us keep animals where we want them.

Permanent enclosures

Hedges, walls, and fences are traditional permanent boundaries, used the world over to contain animals—or to keep them out. All need regular maintenance to keep them strong and secure.

How to plant a hedge

Hedges are bushes that have been trained to form an impenetrable mass that livestock cannot push through. Once planted, they are cheap to maintain. A traditional hawthorn hedge is planted with thorn bushes (normally midland hawthorn, *Crataegus laevigata*). Use seedlings about 6 in (15 cm) tall and set them in two staggered rows with about 18 in (45 cm) between each plant and 9 in (23 cm) between rows. Protect from livestock using conventional fencing for at least the first four years. This extra fencing is the most expensive aspect. Once the bushes are mature, you can lay the hedge.

Hedge-laying (see opposite) encourages the plants to produce dense growth that contains livestock efficiently and creates an important habitat for wildlife. It is ideal for many species of nesting birds.

Traditionally, a professional hedgelayer can lay a "chain" or 22 yd (20 m) a day. Seven years after laying a hedge, the regrowth can be as high as 15 ft (4.5 m).

Dry-stone walling

Dry-stone walls are built by laying together large, closely fitting stones without using mortar. The old walls on our boundary are animal-proof but need regular repairs. We also built a wall from scratch. The trick is to dig a level foundation trench and use flat, angular stones that fit together snugly. You can buy stone from landscape or building suppliers, but it is not cheap. It makes sense to build dry-stone walls only if you've got plenty of stone on your land.

Wire fencing

Wire is expensive but relatively durable and makes an effective boundary. A good wire fence needs to be tensioned, so buy a wire strainer to achieve this. This simple tool can also strain slack or broken wire, including barbed wire, and can exert up to 2 tons of pull, so the pressure

THE STONE HEDGE

Where we live in Cornwall in far southwestern England, this form of hedging is extremely popular. It is basically a cross between a stone wall and a living hedge.

Building a stone hedge

Use large, rounded stones to construct a pronounced batter—that is, two walls that lean toward each other. Make the walls around 4 ft (1.2 m) tall. Fill the gap between them with rammed earth and plant a thorny hedge on the top. Plants will also grow in gaps between the rocks. Stone hedges are valuable habitats for small mammals and reptiles, as well as plant life.

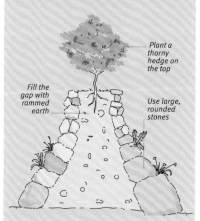

1

2

Plant a thorny hedge on the top

Fill the gap with rammed earth

Use large, rounded stones

A typical stone hedge *should be as wide as it is tall, and the width at the top of the wall should be half the width of the base.*

1. Fencing for sheep and goats *needs to be at least 3 ft 3 in (1 m) high.*
2. Dry-stone walls *should be twice as wide at the base as the top for stability. Different regions have distinctive styles.*

PROJECT **Lay a hedge**

A hedge needs to be at least 8 ft (2.5 m) tall for laying, and the technique is usually carried out when most of the leaves have fallen. The stems to be laid are called "pleachers" and should be the straightest, best-looking stems in the hedge. Remove dead or bent, twisted stems as you work your way along. This is the Blackdown style of hedge-laying, specific to a region of the West Country of England.

HEDGE-LAYING TOOLS
- Stafford bill hook (1) or bolo knife
- Tenterden bill hook (2) or bolo knife
- Short-handled slasher (3)
- Kent pattern hand ax (4)
- Hedging maul (5)
- Hedge rake (6)
- Leather gloves (7)

1. This hazel hedge was laid about eight years ago and is starting to look gappy. **2. Clear brambles and nettles** from the base using a bolo knife and slasher. **3. Select a pleacher** and, using a sharp bolo knife, make a vertical cut through the stem so that it is pliable enough to be laid down. Although the technique looks drastic, the pleacher continues to grow.

4. Trim the stob—the cut-away stump—and any whiskers of wood, to reduce rotting. **5. Lay the pleacher down** horizontally. **6. Roughly weave the pleacher** into those that have already been cut and laid, to hold it in place. **7. Cut a crook** from the hedgerow—look for a post with a natural hook at the end, to hold the pleachers in place. Sharpen the base with the bolo knife.

8. Hook the crook over the pleachers, facing inward. **9. Use the maul** to hammer the sharpened base into the ground. **10. The finished hedge.** The pleachers throw up vertical growth along their length and the cut stump will also send up six to eight stems.

on fence posts can be considerable and they will need careful anchoring (see box below).

Match fencing height to your livestock. Goats need fencing that is at least 3 ft 3 in (1 m) high so that they can't jump over. You can increase the height of standard stock fencing (square netting) by adding two extra lines of wire. Put up fencing about 45 in (1.15 m) high for cattle, and 30 in (80 cm) for pigs and sheep. To keep deer out, you need a fence that is at least 6 ft 3 in (1.9 m) high.

Post-and-rail fencing

if you have oak or chestnut trees to coppice, you could make your own post-and-rail fencing from stakes. Split them in half to make the uprights and into quarters to make the cross-rails. Post-and-rail fences are fine for most livestock and for marking out footpaths, but obviously won't keep rabbits out of a vegetable garden.

Temporary enclosures

When grazing sheep, cattle, or pigs on fodder crops, you need a way of confining them to one area at a time—something quick and easy to set up and dismantle. Temporary enclosures are also important when you need to corral sheep for shearing or lambing, or to inspect their feet.

Electric fencing

With electric fencing, it's easy to create a secure temporary boundary in no time at all. We always use electric fencing for our pigs and poultry. It helps protect poultry from potential predators if the voltage

WIRE FENCING

Wire fencing is only as strong as your posts. Use a post rammer to set them firmly in the ground. If necessary, add box anchors (see below). These stop posts from being pulled out again under tension when you use a wire strainer to take up slack in the wire.

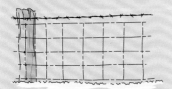

Bury a boulder or large stone *as a box anchor. Corner posts need two, to take the strain in each direction.*

Square-meshed stock fencing *with a single line of barbed wire on the top will stop pigs and cows from straying.*

Temporary wire fencing *such as diamond netting will contain sheep. Roll it up when not in use.*

TWO TYPES OF HURDLES

Lightweight gate-style hurdles can be used for instant pens; woven wattle hurdles make short-term fences. Make gate-style hurdles out of any wood that splits easily, such as ash or chestnut; thin stakes make lighter hurdles. Sharpen the end stakes, then use mortises to join horizontals. Nail crossbraces to the horizontals for strength.

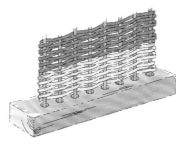 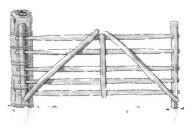

Use a frame *to make a wattle hurdle. Make holes 9 in (23 cm) apart and weave between stakes with willow or split hazel.*

To assemble an enclosure, *place solid posts in the ground at intervals and attach hurdles between them with twine.*

Wattle hurdles *make good temporary fences but don't last more than a few years. They also look good in the garden but take quite a long time to make. See pages 280–281 for basic weaving techniques.*

is high enough and the fencing is in good condition.

Electric fencing is also effective with cattle, but it doesn't always work with sheep as their thick fleeces don't conduct electricity easily. You can up the voltage to high levels of 4,000–5,000 volts with three strands of wire or consider using electric netting when your sheep are lambing to protect them from predators. But under normal circumstances the best way to secure sheep temporarily is with diamond wire netting or hurdles.

The simplest electric fence uses one strand of hot wire. Position it at nose level for pigs and cattle. For pigs, that's about 12 in (30 cm) off the ground.

If you set up a small solar panel to trickle-charge your battery, you won't have to take it back to the workshop every time it needs recharging. The whole setup can be rolled up and put away in minutes.

Hurdles

Lightweight and easy to move around, hurdles are ideal if you have a supply of coppiced wood (see pages 182–183), and are ready to build your own (see box opposite). Alternatively, you could make more permanent woven wattle hurdles, which make good, cheap, short-term fences (see box opposite).

Temporary wire fencing

Wire netting that can be rolled up is particularly useful as a temporary fence. Diamond netting is easiest to work with as square-meshed netting may get bent out of shape.

PROJECT **Set up electric fencing**

Electric fencing is cheap and effective, and can be set up or taken down in moments. It can be adapted for a range of livestock by varying the height of the live wire—the ideal position for any animal is nose height. Pigs are remarkably intelligent animals, for example, and it only takes one zap on the nose for them to learn it's best not to cross the line.

YOU WILL NEED
- Plastic stakes
- Electric wire
- Control unit and battery
- Watering can, plastic crate

1. Clear the grass around the perimeter to reduce "bridging"—losing electricity into the ground where grass touches the wire. Set out plastic stakes. Space them close enough so the wire doesn't sag. **2. Feed the wire** around the stakes. **3. Set the wire** at an appropriate height. In this setup, all the strands are live. **4. Check again** for grass touching the wire.

5. Firmly push the spike of the control unit into the ground. This acts as a ground, so wet the ground for good conductivity. **6. Connect the control unit** to the fence and the positive and negative terminals to a fully charged battery. We then cover our battery with a plastic crate. **7. Test the fence** by touching a piece of grass to the wire. If it's working, you'll know (get someone else to do this if you have a weak heart or a pacemaker). Remember to tell visitors that the fence is live.

FODDER CROPS TO GROW

Rearing livestock on a small scale is a great way of becoming more self-sufficient. However, animals often need more food than they can obtain from grazing alone, and this extra feed can be expensive. In the past this was why most livestock was slaughtered before winter when fresh food could not be spared. Agriculture then developed so that planting crops to feed livestock through the harder months became the norm. It is now perfectly viable for a small farm to supplement winter feeding with crops specifically grown as fodder. For some you will need to use a seed drill for best results; others can be broadcast-sown, by scattering handfuls of seed.

Fodder cereals

Cereals are not just a crop for farms with hundreds of acres; growing them on a small farm can easily be achieved with a bit of hard work. Most cereals grow quickly and should smother any weeds.

Barley (1)
Hordeum distichum
■ **How to grow** Barley will grow in surprisingly poor conditions. It does like a finer seed bed than other cereals and should be sown in spring, when the soil is warm and dry. Sow at 220 lb per acre (250 kg per hectare) using the same method as oats (see below).
■ **Harvest** Cut barley late when the ears are bent over, the grains have turned pale, hard, and yellow, and the straw is dry. Store loose in a stook (see box)

MAKING HAY

Leave a field of grass or an orchard to grow. Cut with a scythe in early summer when the grass is tall, either just before or just after flowering, but before it goes to seed. Make a 6-ft (1.8-m) tripod of wooden poles tied together at the top and around the structure. Place a bent piece of tin on the ground facing a windward side; this will keep the air flow circulating through the haycock. Cover the structure with hay and leave to dry. When dry, store in a hayshed and feed to livestock such as cattle, goats, and sheep, in fall and winter.

until it is completely dry. Then thresh it, which can easily be done by hand—by bashing handfuls against the back of a chair or by beating it with a homemade flail. Feed the grain to pigs or cattle. You should always soak grain for at least 24 hours before feeding. Don't waste the straw: your livestock will appreciate it for food and bedding.

Corn (2)
Zea mays
■ **How to grow** Corn is another excellent fodder crop. Sow in spring into light soil, about two weeks after the average last frost date for your area. Sow at about 33 lb per acre (38 kg per hectare) at a depth of 3 in (7.5 cm) in rows 15–30 in (38–75 cm) apart. Put up a scarecrow to stop birds from swooping down and eating all the freshly sown seed.
■ **Harvest** Ripe corn cobs are great for cattle, or you can feed them the whole plant in summer like grass. Corn can even make good silage: cut it when green, crush, and store it in plastic sacks so it ferments. Of all the fodder crops, corn is definitely one of our personal favorites—especially since we love eating it too! To harvest the cobs, simply walk along the rows, rip out the ears, and drop them into a sack.

They'll keep you and your livestock very happy indeed.

Oats (3)
Avena sativa
■ **How to grow** Oats grow well in damp, cold places. In wet areas they are best sown in spring, and in drier and warmer regions they are better suited to winter sowing—but make sure you have a scarecrow ready at this time of year, as birds like to snack on the newly sown oats. The seeds should be sown into a coarse seed bed with small

HOW TO MAKE A STOOK

To construct a stook, secure two sheaves together, standing them upright so that the grainy heads stick to each other. Add more pairs so that they will not blow over in the wind. Leave the stooks for about three weeks to dry thoroughly, then bring under cover.

clods about the size of a child's fist. Ground that has been turned over by pigs using their snouts is ideal. Sowing is most easily done in a biblical fashion by holding a bag full of seeds and broadcasting them over the ground. Sow oats at 88–110 lb per acre (100–125 kg per hectare). Then harrow the ground. Harrowing involves pulling—either by manpower, horse, or tractor—a spiky "bush" or attachment called a harrow to cover the seeds and mix them into the ground. When some of the oats reach 6 in (15 cm) tall, harrow again to kill weeds and open up the surface.

■ **Harvest** Cut the oats when there are still some green bits in the straw. Tie into sheaves: grab-sized bundles tied around the middle. Make a stook with the sheaves (see box). Sheaves can be fed directly to cattle alongside their grass diet, at a rate of one sheaf per animal per day. Oat straw is generally accepted as the best cereal straw for feeding.

Rye (4)
Secale cereale
■ **How to grow** Rye grows well in cold, dry conditions and light sandy soil. It is planted in a very similar way to oats. Sow in fall for best results as it grows fast.

Rye is known as a catch crop due to its quick-growing habit. The other excellent thing about rye as a fodder crop is that birds don't like it much, so the success rate is high.
■ **Harvest** If you plant rye right after a crop of potatoes, it will be ready to be grazed off by sheep or cows in spring when other greens are in short supply. This space can then be planted with another spring crop. It also makes good straw bedding or animal feed.

Fodder root crops
Roots are useful as winter fodder for animals, as well as being delicious in the kitchen. Root vegetables store up energy in the summer and retain all the nourishment as they lie dormant over the winter. They are packed with goodness and can significantly supplement your animals' diet.

Fodder beets and mangolds (5)
Beta vulgaris
■ **How to grow** Sow seeds at 9–11 lb per acre (10–12 kg per hectare) into a fine seed bed in mid-spring. Make rows 22 in (55 cm) apart and thin them to around 9 in (23 cm) between plants.
■ **Harvest** Mangolds (also known as mangels) can yield huge crops but are not as rich in

protein as fodder beet. Pull both in the fall before the first frost and place in piles covered with their leaves until you have time to clamp them (see page 164). Wait until after New Year's Day before feeding them to pigs and cattle: this reduces the risk of any toxins being present. Neither crop is good enough to eat—they're like bland-tasting, tough beets—but in England, some people do grow mangolds specifically to make wine.

Turnips and rutabagas (6)
Brassica rapa and *B. napus*
■ **How to grow** Turnips and rutabagas do extremely well in wet and cold conditions. Sow into a fine seed bed in late spring in drills at a rate of about 1 lb per acre (1 kg per hectare) and then thin out to one every 9 in (23 cm). Try to hoe between plants a couple of times as they are growing to reduce competition from weeds.
■ **Harvest** Lift both turnips and rutabagas some time after Christmas and store in clamps (see page 164). Or try grazing sheep directly on the growing crops in fenced strips, which you extend each day. After the sheep have finished, let your pigs out into the field to root up all the leftovers. Don't forget to lift and store some roots for use in the kitchen too.

Fodder brassicas
These tend to be nutritious hardy crops for fall and winter feed for lambs or cows; they also suppress weeds and so help clear the ground in preparation for future plantings.

Cabbage (7)
Brassica oleracea
Capitata Group
■ **How to grow** Sow in early April in drills 20 in (50 cm) apart, in well-manured soil.
■ **Harvest** You get double-value feeding when you grow fodder cabbage. You can cut and cart the cabbages to cows when they are ready to harvest—usually around October—then let your pigs out onto the ground and they will turn up all the edible roots with their snouts. Cabbages can also be stored in clamps throughout the winter (see page 164).

Kale (8)
Brassica oleracea
Acephala Group
■ **How to grow** Sow seed as for cabbage above. Kale tends to have a higher yield and is rich in protein.
■ **Harvest** As with cabbage, you get double value from kale, as you can feed livestock on both leaves and roots. Start grazing animals on kale from early fall onward, then let pigs into the field.

1 **2** **3** **4**

Mustard and rape (1)

Brassica juncea and *B. napus*
■ **How to grow** Sow mustard from early spring onward by drilling at 9–11 lb per acre (10–12 kg per hectare). Sow rapeseed (also called canola) in summer—drill 5 lb per acre (6 kg per hectare)—and it can be ready for your animals to graze in 12 weeks and will carry on producing until winter. If you grow rape and keep bees, be aware that your bees will harvest rape nectar voraciously, but the honey they produce is not at all palatable.
■ **Harvest** Like turnips and rutabagas, both mustard and rape are ideal for strip grazing.

Other fodder crops

Sunflowers and Jerusalem artichokes look stunning—the artichokes are also a member of the sunflower family. More importantly, they will fatten up your pigs in winter.

Jerusalem artichokes (2)

Helianthus tuberosus
■ **How to grow** Plant Jerusalem artichokes any time after Christmas. Set the tubers every 12 in (30 cm), in rows 3 ft (90 cm) apart. They are prolific and you will find that the following year, despite all your best harvesting efforts, tubers will sprout up again in the same place.

■ **Harvest** Instead of wasting time digging up your Jerusalem artichokes, simply put your pigs in an enclosure with them, giving them access to a few plants at a time, like strip grazing. They will root them up and happily eat them for weeks, while you save plenty of money on your normal feed costs.

Sunflowers (3)

Helianthus annuus
■ **How to grow** We grow sunflowers as a dual-purpose crop, harvesting the heads for the chickens—and ourselves—and letting the pigs in to forage on the stems and leaves. Sow 1–1½ in (2.5–4 cm) deep at roughly 3–4 lb per acre (4 kg per hectare).
■ **Harvest** The seeds are ready to harvest when the back of the flower head turns brown. We scrape out the seeds and dry them. Leave some heads for wild birds.

UNUSUAL CROPS TO GROW

Climate change is a reality. We have seen a noticeable change in conditions here in Cornwall, and evidence shows the same is happening all over the world. Wherever possible, we embrace changes to our advantage and try to focus on the glass-half-full

perspective. If it is warmer in the summer, we see it as an opportunity to grow unusual crops and reduce the amount of food we import. Growing more produce locally is clearly signposted on the road to self-sufficiency, but it relies on experimenting. It also happens to be quite a lot of fun!

Bamboo (4)

Phyllostachys species
■ **How to grow** Bamboo is an incredible crop. It grows quickly, is very strong, and is excellent in damp areas. Some species are even edible. We decided to plant it at the bottom of our plot where the land is fairly wet but well drained. Here it acts as a windbreak for the vines farther up the hill and thrives in the moist conditions. Bamboo can be grown all over temperate regions. It needs little care and attention, thriving naturally and spreading profusely through its root system. We planted *Phyllostachys nigra*, which has black canes, and *P. glauca*, which forms good clumps and spreads well. Choose species carefully; some bamboos are rampant and will spread rather too efficiently.
■ **Harvest** Cut canes regularly to remove older or decaying culms or stems and let in

enough light for the rest of the plant to flourish. Harvest canes annually near the end of summer. We love the idea of being self-sufficient in as many materials as possible, so never again needing to buy a single bamboo cane for the garden was reason enough to plant bamboo! Any larger growth that we get in years to come we plan to weave together and build with, for some form of garden shelter or seating area.

Flax or linseed (5)

Linum usitatissimum
■ **How to grow** Flax is used to make linen and also linseed oil, a rich source of omega-3s. Flax seed grows best in well-drained soil, rich in organic matter. Sow in drills in late spring and cover lightly with soil.
■ **Harvest** The seed capsules are ready to harvest in late summer when most have turned brown. Mow the crop, rake it up into sections, and let it dry. The dried seeds can be pressed to make oil or milled for flour. The husks make a rich oil cake for cattle and the rough straw a base layer for animal bedding.

Hemp

Cannabis sativa var. *sativa*
Hemp was a significant crop during the formative years of the United States; in fact,

5 **6** **7** **8**

because it was so useful, the Virginia Assembly passed a law in 1619 requiring all farmers to grow hemp. But by the 1930s, growing fear of drug abuse meant that hemp was lumped together with marijuana and regulated as a narcotic—even though agricultural hemp has negligible levels of cannabinoids, the psychoactive substances in marijuana. Despite attempts to legalize hemp production in the US, this versatile crop is still considered a drug and is illegal to cultivate. The environmental benefits of hemp compared to crops such as cotton are unquestionable. It is fast-growing, thrives with little water and no pesticides, and can be made into fabric, paper, rope, insulation, and animal bedding.

Hops (6)
Humulus lupulus

■ **How to grow** After a hard day's work, there are few things more enjoyable than going to the local pub and enjoying a pint of beer. By chance, we prefer our local brewery's ale over imported lager, so the ensuing "beer miles" are not too bad. However, if you are serious about becoming more self-sufficient, then growing your own hops is worth trying. Hops are relatively easy to grow in well-drained soil with plenty

of manure. First, remove any perennial weeds and grass growing in the area, and then lay bits of hop roots 1–2 ft (30–60 cm) in length, under a good layer of manure or compost. Space these bits of root 3 ft (1 m) apart. Male and female flowers are produced on separate plants. It's the female "cones" you need for brewing, and for best flavor they should be unpollinated, so dig up any male plants that grow.

TRAINING HOPS

To make picking easier and keep your plot neat, train hops on a traditional-style frame with 10-ft- (3-m-) tall strings; the hops race up them when they burst into life in spring. If you have space, try a "maypole" with strings running from the top of a central pole. Or train hops on an arbor instead of a grapevine and create a shady place to sit.

■ **Harvest** Cut the flowers when they are blooming and the inside is full of a yellow powder that will be the key ingredient in your very own beer (see page 254). Dry them thoroughly by hanging from wires over a stove or wood burner. Store the hops in a burlap sack until you are ready to use them.

Rice (7)
Oryza sativa

■ **How to grow** Although better known as an Asian crop, in fact rice is grown in large quantities in North America and southern Europe. The thing that makes rice difficult to grow farther north is that it requires summer temperatures of over 68°F (20°C) for most of its growing season of up to four to five months. Rice also needs plenty of water. We recommend growing it under cover (with a minimum temperature of 50°F/10°C) and using a ram pump to supply the irrigation system (see pages 74–75). Prepare a seed bed that has warmed up in spring and rake the seed in well after sowing. Flood the bed once. As the plants grow, keep the bed well watered, making sure that the water is below the top of the shoots. When they are about 8 in (20 cm) tall, thin to about 4 in (10 cm) between plants and continue to keep your

small-scale paddy field wet. Transplant the thinned seedlings to a second bed. Seeds can be difficult to source: we recommend growing mountain rice.

■ **Harvest** At the end of summer, when the rice spikelets are hard and yellow-colored or turn from green to brown. Drain the patch and allow the rice to dry for 2–4 weeks in the greenhouse.

Tea (8)
Camellia sinensis

■ **How to grow** Tea is indigenous to China and India but has more recently been grown in other parts of the world. It is an evergreen plant from the camellia family. Plants are best propagated from cuttings and grown under cover for the first couple of years. Outside on a south-facing slope, a standard tea bush will grow to about 3 ft (1 m) tall, and needs selective pruning to make it easy to pick the young leaves. Position tea plants about 5 ft (1.5 m) apart in rows, with 3 ft (1 m) between each row. We are growing our own tea thanks to the microclimate in the southwest of England.

■ **Harvest** Bushes take six years to mature before they can be picked. Pick the tender young tips every 7–10 days in the growing season.

179

Storing crops on a larger scale

When you're growing crops for animals and humans you need more storage space. A root cellar is designed to keep vegetables fresh for months on end. We think there is something very satisfying about eating a stored carrot in spring or having turnips to feed to our pigs on cold winter days. And if you've made hay in summer, you'll need somewhere weatherproof to keep it.

The hayshed

Once hay is harvested and dried (see page 176), you'll need a covered hayshed to keep it dry. Wet, moldy hay breaks down quickly and is not only unhealthy for animals to eat, it's a fire hazard—hay heats up as it rots. If it gets too wet, mix it into your compost bins or use as a mulch.

Site the shed close to livestock housing so you don't have far to lug the hay. Make the sides from vertical wooden slats about 3 in (7.5 cm) apart, to let the hay breathe but keep it from getting wet. Design the door so there is enough headroom to walk in while holding a pitchfork of hay—this will prevent backaches later! The shed should be solid and wind-resistant, but don't waste large sums of money on what is essentially a rain cover for dried grass.

Grain store

Grain that has been threshed to separate it from straw needs to be kept safe from vermin. Metal bins with lids are a good option, or try a traditional grain store bucket raised off the ground. Keep straw under cover in the same way as hay.

Some cereals, such as oats, can be fed to livestock without threshing. Store these in sheaves (see page 176) under cover.

Storing root vegetables

Root cellars are designed to store large quantities of produce all through the year without refrigeration. Their design is based on the fact that most root crops keep best in cold, humid, dark conditions, with plenty of room for air to circulate. Traditional root cellars were built wholly or partly below ground. The ideal site is carved into a north-facing slope. They don't need windows—roots must be kept in the dark, just as they were when they were growing. Site your root cellar close to the house. The last thing you want in winter is to get cold and wet fetching produce. Keep a wind-up flashlight hanging inside the exterior door to the cellar so you can see what you're doing.

Temperature

Put a thermometer in the cellar and check it regularly. The ideal temperature range is 32–40°F (0–4.5°C). Install an intake vent near the bottom of the cellar wall to draw in cool night air and, at the high point of the cellar, another vent to let out warm air. Use the vents to control the temperature: open at night if the cellar gets too warm.

Humidity levels

High humidity is best: about 90–95 percent will stop root vegetables from shriveling. Use a hygrometer to measure it accurately. The easiest way to increase humidity is by pouring water on the floor. Dirt floors maintain higher humidity levels than concrete.

Ventilation

Keeping air circulating in the cellar also helps remove ethylene gas produced by vegetables as they ripen. Left to build up, it can cause other veggies to ripen quickly, and make them smell bad or start to sprout. Use the air vents to control circulation and temperature.

MINI ROOT CELLAR

If you have an old wooden barrel, don't even think about cutting it in half and turning it into two planters! Sink it into the ground against a wall close to the kitchen and turn it into a mini household root cellar.

Converting the barrel to a store

Dig a slight dip in the ground next to the wall and start layering up rocks so that the barrel can be positioned at a 45° angle with the lid facing outward. Fill the barrel with harvested root crops, packing straw around them for insulation. Backfill with soil behind the barrel; add a layer of straw and another layer of soil, except above the barrel opening. Add a wooden board for a door.

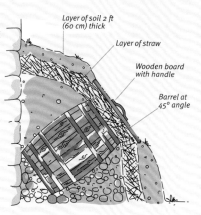

Layer of soil 2 ft (60 cm) thick

Layer of straw

Wooden board with handle

Barrel at 45° angle

Building a root cellar

If you haven't got a natural slope to house a root cellar, you can achieve a similar effect by building it partly below ground and heaping soil over the top to create an earth berm (see pages 48–49). You will need advice from a structural engineer to create a framework strong enough to hold the weight of the soil. Make your cellar at least 5 x 8 ft (1.5 x 2.5 m).

Finishing the cellar

Add plenty of shelves for storage. Make them from a durable hardwood such as oak that won't need treatment with wood preservatives, which can taint stored produce. Spread a thick layer of gravel on the floor to stop your feet from getting wet when you pour water on the ground. Or use large, shallow pans of water to adjust the humidity instead.

Traditional root cellars *in Canada built into the slope of a north-facing hill, with sod roofs and solid doors for insulation.*

Making use of natural factors
The design of a root cellar relies on soil's insulating properties combined with the tendency of warm air to rise.

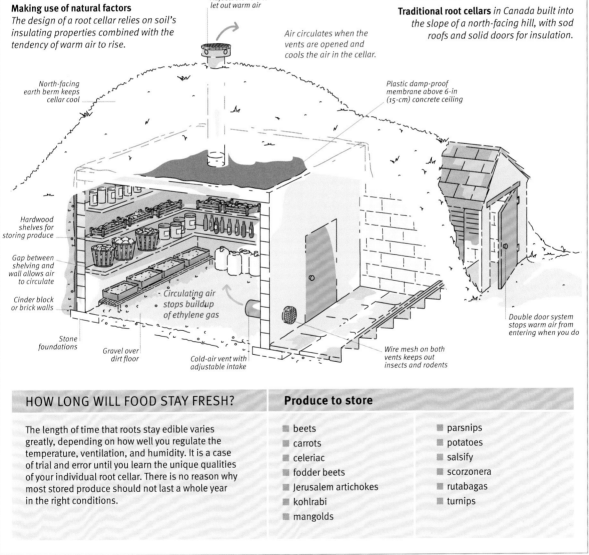

Adjustable vent to let out warm air

Air circulates when the vents are opened and cools the air in the cellar.

Plastic damp-proof membrane above 6-in (15-cm) concrete ceiling

North-facing earth berm keeps cellar cool

Hardwood shelves for storing produce

Gap between shelving and wall allows air to circulate

Cinder block or brick walls

Stone foundations

Gravel over dirt floor

Circulating air stops buildup of ethylene gas

Cold-air vent with adjustable intake

Wire mesh on both vents keeps out insects and rodents

Double door system stops warm air from entering when you do

HOW LONG WILL FOOD STAY FRESH?

The length of time that roots stay edible varies greatly, depending on how well you regulate the temperature, ventilation, and humidity. It is a case of trial and error until you learn the unique qualities of your individual root cellar. There is no reason why most stored produce should not last a whole year in the right conditions.

Produce to store

- beets
- carrots
- celeriac
- fodder beets
- Jerusalem artichokes
- kohlrabi
- mangolds
- parsnips
- potatoes
- salsify
- scorzonera
- rutabagas
- turnips

Managing a woodlot

Productive woodlands have been carefully managed in the UK for centuries, and we believe that some form of control is really beneficial, as it helps to keep trees strong and healthy, and can extend their life. It also makes good economic sense, allowing you to become self-sufficient in fuel, as well as providing a shelter belt for crops and playing an important part in nature conservation.

Woodlands for fuel

Small woodlands are most often managed to provide a source of firewood for the home. Season firewood by storing it under cover with good air circulation for at least a year—the longer you store it, the better it burns. If you have firewood to spare, you can sell it or make charcoal (see pages 184–185).

Construction and crafts

Roundwood is wood that's in the same state as it was when felled. It isn't worth much money, but is useful for building simple structures, like sheds and barns. Coppiced wood is ideal for fencing, basketry (see pages 280–281), and green woodworking techniques (see pages 282–283).

You may need permission from your state's department of natural resources or your county's zoning department to fell trees in certain areas, such as near shorelines. Trees with trunks less than 3 in (8 cm) in diameter when measured 4 ft 3 in (1.3 m) above the ground are safe to fell yourself. For all others, call in a professional.

Livestock and woodland

▨ **Pigs** kept in woodland enjoy eating acorns and beechnuts.

▨ **Cattle and sheep** allowed an occasional foray into the woods can help to regenerate the vegetation.
▨ **Chickens** are woodland birds.
▨ Holding an occasional **pheasant hunt** brings in extra income.

Managing a coppice

Coppice comes from the French word *couper*, meaning "to cut," and it's a sustainable way to harvest large quantities of lumber from your trees. Plant the trees close together and, when the trunks are about 9 in (23 cm) in diameter, cut them in winter to just above the ground. Tall, straight poles will grow from the stumps, and you can then repeat the procedure every few years and harvest the wood. Ash, hazel, and willow are ideal.

If you have an existing coppice that has been left for several years, divide it into "coupes" or areas to be coppiced. The diameter of a coupe should be about 1.5 times the height of the trees. For fencing and firewood, cut the trees every 10–15 years. Harvest one coupe at a time within this cycle; don't cut all the coupes at once, as this will disrupt the natural ecology. A short cycle of 3–4 years is known as a short-rotation coppice. Use willow for this, and turn the slimmer poles into wood chip biomass for heating (see pages 82–83).

1. **Coppiced hazel trees** *planted close together grow tall and straight toward the light.* 2. **Chickens** *enjoy foraging in the willow and dogwood coppice at Newhouse Farm.* 3. **Using a log splitter** *reduces logs from mature trees to a manageable size for a stove.*

Creating a new woodlot

Planting a mixture of conifers and broad-leaved trees helps to ensure biodiversity, and provides the best environment for wildlife. Your plot will benefit too, as woodland creates an effective windbreak for crops.

Getting started

Siting a new wood is easy. Choose land that is not good for much else, such as north-facing slopes, poorly drained land, and infertile soil.

Spacing is important. If trees are too far apart, they will grow with short trunks and too many branches, and if planted too close together, they will be tall and spindly. The best technique is to plant closely and then thin out the trees as they grow (see page 135). Buy bare-root trees from a nursery and plant in late fall or early spring, or grow your own saplings from seed (see below).

In a mixed woodland *of conifers and deciduous trees, the conifers create shelter for wildlife in winter, and early nesting sites for birds in spring. They also retain warmth in fall so that deciduous trees hold onto their leaves for longer, which improves their growth rates.*

Growing your own saplings *from locally collected nuts and seeds ensures your new trees are truly local species.*

Putting up boxes for birds *and bats is just one way of making your woodland more wildlife-friendly.*

Plastic tree guards *protect saplings from rabbits and woodchucks. Remove them as the trees mature.*

TOP TREES

Our suggested trees for planting a small-scale woodland for lumber and firewood:

- **Sweet chestnut** Awesome for lumber, fast-growing, strong.
- **Oak** Slow-growing and slow-burning too.
- **Ash** Tough and resilient with deep roots. Fast-growing. Excellent firewood as it splits easily and even burns when it's green.
- **Larch** An unusual deciduous conifer. Very fast-growing. Makes good fencing.
- **Cherry** A good hardwood for sweet-smelling firewood.
- **Elm** Great for making cutting boards or butcher's blocks; choose varieties that are resistant to Dutch elm disease.
- **Silver birch** One of our favorites for burning, but it must be well seasoned.

PESTS AND PROBLEMS

Newly planted saplings are most at risk from animal pests, such as deer and squirrels, which can damage mature trees too.

- **Deer** damage is easy to spot, as they eat all the leaves and nibble the twigs up to a definite, visible line. Put up deer fencing 6 ft (1.8 m) high.
- **Gray squirrels** munch on the bark of many broad-leaved trees and will often eat leading shoots of young saplings. Consult a wildlife control specialist if they become a major problem.
- **Rabbits** strip the bark of young saplings, which kills the young trees. Protect trees with guards or fencing.
- **Invasive trees and shrubs** such as buckthorn and bush honeysuckle can take over and wipe out biodiversity. Check the USDA invasive species website for more information (www.invasivespeciesinfo.gov).

Making charcoal

Nothing says summer like the scent of food cooking on a charcoal grill. But you don't have to lug home bags of manufactured briquettes from the grocery store to enjoy the experience. It's easy to build a kiln and make some natural charcoal on a small scale, so if you have a source of waste lumber, why not give it a try and enjoy even more satisfying summer barbecues?

What is charcoal?

Charcoal is made by heating wood with insufficient oxygen to burn, but to a temperature high enough to drive out water and volatile gases. Charcoal burns slowly at a very high temperature. In Europe it was used for thousands of years for smelting metals until coal took its place, and traditional blacksmiths still prefer to use charcoal in their forges. It is also popular with artists for sketching, but today its main use is for barbecues.

Its slow-burning properties make charcoal perfect for outdoor cooking, but never use it on an open fire indoors, as it produces toxic carbon monoxide when it burns.

Making your own charcoal

There are advantages to making your own lump charcoal instead of using commercial briquettes. First, you can be sure your charcoal contains no chemical additives; and second, it's easier to light without potentially hazardous charcoal lighter fluid.

In the US, most charcoal is derived from sawmill waste. If you live in an area where this industry thrives, you may have a rich (and inexpensive) resource for the raw material needed. Hardwoods like hickory, mesquite, and oak are good choices. These, and other fruitwoods, produce wonderful aromas and premium charcoal for grilling/cooking.

BARBECUE TIPS

■ **To speed up the cooking process** try this method of lighting. Take a piece of metal pipe and stand it in the grill to make a "chimney." Stuff the bottom with paper, add some kindling, and light it. Once the kindling catches, add charcoal via the top of the pipe. When the charcoal starts to burn, put on some barbecue gloves and carefully lift the pipe upward so that the glowing charcoals spread across the tray.
■ **Don't start cooking** until the bed of hot embers has been glowing for 10–15 minutes.
■ **When the charcoal is ash gray** it has reached the right temperature.

A TRADITIONAL CHARCOAL CLAMP

The clamp was built with logs arranged in a crisscross pattern around a central hole. More wood was stacked around the logs to form a mound about 12 ft (4 m) across, and topped with layers of leaves and sod, with a few vents at the bottom. A collier lit the clamp by throwing fire embers into the hole. He tended the fire day and night for two weeks until the smoke color signaled that the charcoal was ready.

Make a modern trench version

A charcoal pit is a good idea if you have the space and want to make a large batch. Dig a decent-sized trench and fill it with wood. Set fire to the wood, and when it is fully ablaze, cover the trench with a couple of sheets of corrugated iron. Then quickly shovel soil on top, burying the sheets of metal and cutting off the oxygen supply. Leave the heat to work its magic. After several days, open up the trench and remove your newly made charcoal.

A traditional charcoal clamp should smolder but never burst into flames.

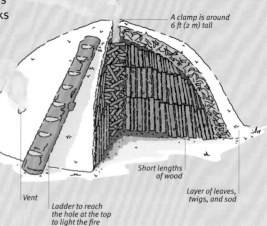

Logs are arranged in a crisscross pattern around a central hole to make the chimney

A clamp is around 6 ft (2 m) tall

Short lengths of wood

Layer of leaves, twigs, and sod

Vent

Ladder to reach the hole at the top to light the fire

DIY charcoal kiln

We made a small kiln out of an old oil drum, which produces more than enough charcoal for our summer barbecues. To keep homemade charcoal in good condition, store it in sealed bags so that it doesn't get wet. Use it for cooking, blacksmithing, or drawing.

Homemade charcoal *is cheap to make from wood that would otherwise go to waste, and it's also easy to light.*

Using the kiln

First, light a wood fire in the drum to burn off any remaining residue (see page 251). Then, using an angle grinder, cut off the base of the drum around the metal rim, leaving three protruding cams. This disk will later form the lid. Turn the drum over and drill five holes in what will now be the base. Place the base on some bricks and seal it with soil and sod, leaving an air vent 6 in (15 cm) in diameter. Fill the kiln by standing a wooden post in the middle and stuffing scrap pieces of construction lumber and hardwood around it. To light the kiln, carefully pull out the central post to leave a chimney, and drop lighted paper and kindling into the hole. Once the wood is burning, place the lid on the cams, and seal around it with sand. When the smoke from the kiln turns from white to blue, close off the air supply by rotating the lid to cover the cams. Leave overnight—your charcoal will be ready the next day. Take care not to inhale any dust when removing it.

Making charcoal
For best results, use hardwood scraps and monitor the air flow carefully.

The disk cut from the original base of the oil drum forms the lid

Smoke will change from a thick white plume to a blue-colored haze, normally after about three hours

Metal cams support the lid and close off the chimney holes when needed

Rotate the lid to close the chimney holes and leave the drum to stand overnight

Upside-down oil drum

Seasoned wood cut into wedges ¾–2 in (2–5 cm) thick

To make your own artist's charcoal, simply stuff a tin can tightly with 4-in (10-cm) lengths of willow and place the can in your kiln along with the other wood

Five well-spaced inlet holes in base of kiln

Soil and sod to seal base

Bricks to raise kiln off ground

Inlet hole for air 6–9 in (15–23 cm) in diameter

ANIMAL HUSBANDRY By keeping animals, you take a huge step toward leading a self-sufficient life. Even just a couple of hens can give you a real sense of independence. If you choose to produce your own meat, however, there are stark facts to be faced. Meat does not come sliced and wrapped in plastic, and we know lots of people who have problems killing their livestock. To give your animals the best possible life, and then to dispatch them with the least amount of stress, seems to us the sensible way to produce meat. You can be certain commercially farmed animals are not shown the same respect.

Keeping chickens

People have been keeping hens for thousands of years. The ancient Egyptians, Greeks, Chinese, and Romans all enjoyed the benefits of rearing chickens for eggs and meat. Nowadays they are still ideal domestic animals, whether you live in an urban or rural area. However you like your eggs in the morning, if they come from your own free-range chickens, nothing compares to their great taste.

Choosing the breed

The first decision to make is what breed you want and how many birds. We generally try to mix our small flocks to include pure breeds and some hybrids. Hybrids are great layers—they are used commercially and you can expect large amounts of eggs. Traditional breeds look more interesting and are useful to have as broody hens if you want to rear your own chicks. We tend to opt for bantams, which are small breeds: they are relatively cheap to feed and you don't need much space to keep them. Light Sussex and Rhode Island Red are also ideal for both eggs and eating but are ignored by commercial farmers because of their small eggs. For a small yard, especially an urban one, we would recommend getting only a few hens and not bothering with a rooster (see box opposite).

What age to buy?

What age to buy your chickens at is another important decision. Day-old chicks are cheap but may be sold as "straight run" (unsexed), so you won't find out which are roosters until later. This is fine if you want some birds for meat but bad news if you only want eggs. There is also the expense of heating their enclosure when they're young and giving them extra feed until they are ready to lay.

Pullets

Pullets are birds that can be anything from about eight to 20 weeks old. You can buy them in batches of all females—no worries about roosters.

OUR FREE-RANGE PHILOSOPHY

The key for us has always been to provide our chickens with as much free roaming space as possible. In our suburban yard, we let them out into the garden in the morning and locked them away at night. Now, on our farmstead, they have a substantial area to roam. Chickens are traditionally woodland birds and appreciate being in our willow coppice. They are also at home in open fields, where they supplement their diet with insect pests and weed seeds. However, there are disadvantages to the free-range lifestyle. Hens will start laying eggs in hidden places instead of their nest boxes. If it becomes a problem, keep them in their run till midday, until they start laying inside again.

Good to eat?
To check how old an egg is, put it in a bowl of water. A fresh egg lies on its side at the bottom (left); rotten eggs float (right).

They take a little more feeding before they start producing eggs but are a good age to buy.

Laying pullets

At 20 weeks old, hens start laying eggs. Their first season tends to be their most productive. You have to spend a bit more to get laying pullets, but we have occasionally found it worthwhile, especially when our existing hens are getting a bit old and we want a few more daily eggs.

Year-old ex-factory hens

Factory egg farms kill their hens after their first year of laying. After they have reached their productive peak, they are no longer valued. There are huge animal-welfare issues associated with factory hens. Often they spend their whole life in an area no bigger than a letter-size piece of paper; they lose their feathers, never learn how to scratch, and are often debeaked. We buy factory hens and give them a second chance. They are normally hybrids and egg-cellent layers. It is a humbling experience to see a maltreated animal rediscovering its instincts and enjoying its first dust bath or struggling to eat its first worm. The color of the hens' combs changes from a sickly pale pink to a healthy red in just a few weeks. Not only is it a feel-good thing to do, but factory hens are productive and cheap.

1. Marans *are one of our favorites. They tend to be very hardy and lay large, deep-brown eggs.* **2. Light Sussex** *are a lovely old English breed and are great layers as well as good table birds.*
3. Buff Orpingtons *are one of the most popular backyard breeds in the US. These placid birds lay brown eggs and do well in colder regions. They can be excellent hens for fostering chicks.*
4. Rescued hybrid battery hens *adapt quickly and soon thrive in their new free-range environment and are reliably good layers.*

ROOSTER PROS AND CONS

A rooster is great for keeping a free-range flock together; he will shepherd them and protect them from predators. Our latest, William, lost his tail feathers defending his ladies from a fox and walked around with an unsightly stump for a few months afterward. Another reason to keep a rooster is that it gives you the opportunity to rear more chicks, at little expense, if you let a hen go broody. The disadvantage in urban areas is the rooster's tendency to act as an alarm clock—for this reason, roosters are usually banned even in cities that allow backyard chickens.

Housing and basic care

Whether you keep chickens in an urban backyard or on a small farm, they have the same needs: a cozy nest box to lay in, a patch of ground on which to scratch and forage, and—most important—somewhere to sleep at night, safe from predators. We built our big chicken coop inside a shed with an outside run attached. This makes cleaning them out easy, even on a rainy day. We've also got a movable "ark" (see pages 192–193) down in the field. A movable system is ideal for lawns: it gives hens access to grass, and you can change its position when the land is looking a bit henpecked. All chickens need somewhere to perch during the day and to roost at night, constant fresh water and, of course, tasty food.

Chickens like to perch, *as they are woodland birds—ideally on a round branch to avoid injuring their feet.*

KEY TO CHICKEN RUN

1. Outside run
2. Dust bath under shelter
3. Mesh roof on outside run
4. Indoor run within shed
5. Pulley system to operate door
6. Door to outside run
7. Staggered perches
8. Nest box with access hatch
9. Hen access to nest box
10. Vermin-proof feed store
11. Access for humans
12. Sawdust on floor
13. Rat-proof feeder
14. Bowls of grit and oyster shell
15. Automated water supply

Dust baths are a vital way to get rid of parasites like lice; make one by filling a shallow wooden box with fine sand and keep it somewhere covered from the rain

Give grit and oystershell in small pans to aid digestion and avoid calcium deficiency

Chickens must have clean water, and an automatic watering system saves a huge amount of time—if you fill up their water manually, do it regularly

MAKING A PERCH FOR A MOVABLE RUN

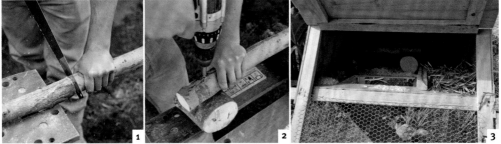

Even though the sleeping quarters are raised off the ground in a movable run (see pages 192–3), hens still need freestanding perches to roost on at night. **1. Saw** a piece of freshly cut wood to length. It should be around 3 in (7.5 cm) in diameter. Leave the bark on. Cut two supports from thicker trunks. **2. Attach** the perch to the supports with long screws, ensuring that no sharp edges protrude. **3. Install** the perch.

A simple movable run *with secure, sheltered accommodation for nighttime. If you have hens and ducks, they will happily share a run. Move to fresh grass every few days.*

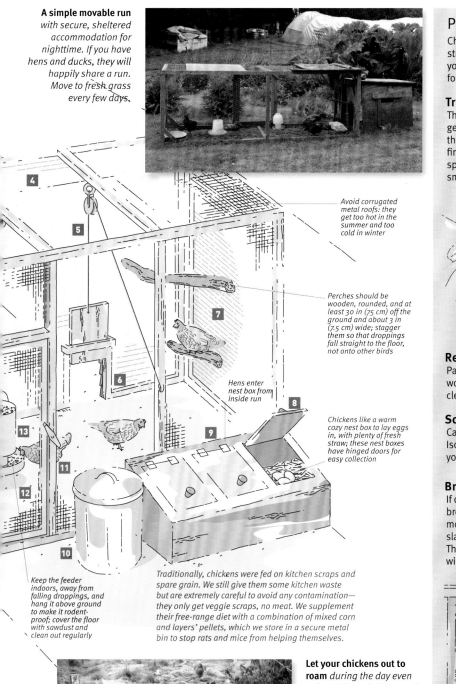

Avoid corrugated metal roofs: they get too hot in the summer and too cold in winter

Perches should be wooden, rounded, and at least 30 in (75 cm) off the ground and about 3 in (7.5 cm) wide; stagger them so that droppings fall straight to the floor, not onto other birds

Hens enter nest box from inside run

Chickens like a warm cozy nest box to lay eggs in, with plenty of fresh straw; these nest boxes have hinged doors for easy collection

Keep the feeder indoors, away from falling droppings, and hang it above ground to make it rodent-proof; cover the floor with sawdust and clean out regularly

Traditionally, chickens were fed on kitchen scraps and spare grain. We still give them some kitchen waste but are extremely careful to avoid any contamination—they only get veggie scraps, no meat. We supplement their free-range diet with a combination of mixed corn and layers' pellets, which we store in a secure metal bin to stop rats and mice from helping themselves.

Let your chickens out to roam *during the day even in frost. The only time you'll need to keep them shut in is when there is deep snow on the ground. Remember, egg production will drop in winter—it's controlled by the hours of daylight.*

PESTS & PROBLEMS

Chickens are generally pretty straightforward birds to keep, but you may need to use some of the following techniques.

Trimming a rooster's spurs

This will stop your hens from getting hurt during mating. Wrap the rooster in a towel and hold him firmly. Use wire cutters to trim the spurs a little at a time. File them smooth when you're done.

Making the cut
Avoid the vein: stop at the first sight of blood below the surface.

Red mites

Parasites that emerge from the woodwork at night. Keep the coop clean and dust with insecticide.

Scaly legs

Caused by a burrowing mite. Isolate affected birds and consult your veterinarian or feed store.

Broody hens

If one of your hens has gone broody and you don't want any more chicks, place her in a small slatted coop for a couple of days. The cold air circulating underneath will deter her from sitting.

The cooler
This coop has a slatted floor to stop the hen from sitting comfortably.

PROJECT **Build a chicken ark**

A movable chicken ark is ideal for small yards, as it keeps your chickens where you want them while giving them access to grass. When a patch wears out, you can simply lift the ark and move it on to pastures new. Raising the nest box above the run makes maximum use of the space available for the chickens to move about. This ark houses two or three hens comfortably.

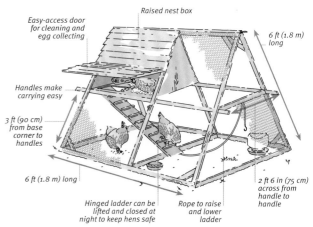

Raised nest box

Easy-access door for cleaning and egg collecting

6 ft (1.8 m) long

Handles make carrying easy

3 ft (90 cm) from base corner to handles

6 ft (1.8 m) long

Hinged ladder can be lifted and closed at night to keep hens safe

Rope to raise and lower ladder

2 ft 6 in (75 cm) across from handle to handle

YOU WILL NEED

- Handsaw
- Circular saw, jigsaw
- Power drill/driver
- Wire cutters
- Tape measure, pencil
- Hammer
- Pressure-treated planks, battens
- Plywood, feather boards
- Chicken wire
- Staples, pins, screws, nails
- Hinges, latch, clasp, rope

MAKING THE FRAME

1. Cut planks to size and screw them together. We used 6-ft- (1.8-m-) square frames that were a convenient fit for chicken wire of 3-ft (90-cm) width. Screw angled brace supports into the corners of each frame, except for the corner where the door will be located.   **2. Fit the final corner brace** on the inside edge of the frame, so that the door to the ark will fit flush in the corner. Rest one frame on the other while working for stability. **3. Fix a vertical strut** into the center of each frame. Attach longer horizontal struts to the inside of the frame, protruding at least a handspan on each side of the ark. These will be used to carry it, so put them at waist height and sand the ends to make them comfortable to handle.

4. Figure out the ideal width to maximize space for the chickens while making the ark easy to carry, and prop the frames against each other.   **5. Take measurements.** Ours was 5 ft (1.5 m) wide at the base and 2 ft 6 in (75 cm) wide at handle height. Cut horizontal central and base struts.   **6. Mark angles** and cut ends to fit.   **7. Fix base struts** to the inside edge of the long verticals, and central struts to the inside edge of the horizontals. Fix an additional horizontal strut higher up, to attach the nest-box door frame (see step 12).

MAKING THE NEST BOX

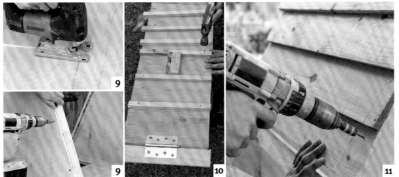

FEATHER BOARDING

To fit boards, secure screws without over-tightening, lift the edge, and slide the next layer under. Once in position, tighten top screws and repeat process.

8. Measure the floor for the nest box, and cut out from plywood using a circular saw or handsaw. Cut out a hen-sized access hatch using a jigsaw. Screw the floor to the supporting struts.   **9. Measure, cut, and attach** plywood end pieces for the nest box.   **10. Make a ladder** from a 1-x-4-ft (0.3-x-1.2-m) plyboard plank. Pin on rungs made from battens. Hinge the ladder to a section of plank and screw the plank to the underside of the floor, level with the access hatch.   **11. Shingle one side** of the nest box with feather boards (see box); fit them to about halfway down on the other side.

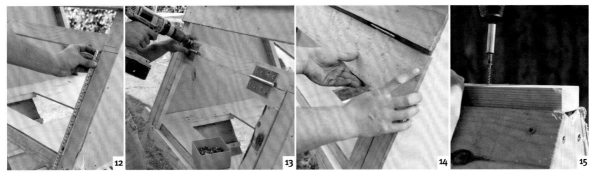

12. Construct a door big enough for you to collect the eggs; aim to make the height such that the bottom of a featherboard will fit over the top part of the hinges.   **13. Fit it flush** with the main frame and let it overhang the nest box floor to avoid drafts. Add hinges.   **14. Complete the feather boarding,** attaching those covering the door to its frame. You can also add a simple clasp for a padlock.   **15. Attach a capping timber** to the roof peak of the ark to stop rain from dripping through.

ATTACHING CHICKEN WIRE

17. Make another door to fit one of the bottom rectangles. Strengthen the door with two corner braces at opposite ends. Attach hinges to one of the vertical sides. Cut chicken wire to size and staple it in place.
18. Screw the door hinges in place and attach a latch to keep out predators.   **19. Continue** attaching chicken wire over the whole frame, taking care not to leave any loose edges. Snip off any sharp ends.
20. Install a drinker and feeder, and introduce your chickens!

How to increase your flock

Which comes first: the chicken or the egg? Well, we have always started with chickens and increased our flocks from their eggs—that's why we keep a rooster (see page 189). But for a beginner, we recommend buying fertilized eggs (do this online) and incubating them yourself. It's harder work than leaving it to nature, but it's the least risky way to build a flock.

Hatching your own

An electronically controlled incubator takes care of the temperature and humidity, but you'll still need to turn the eggs three times a day so that the embryo does not get stuck on the shell (see box). Incubation is about 21 days. After seven days, "candle" the eggs to check for fertility (see box). Stop turning them on day 19.

After hatching, leave the chicks in the incubator for the first 24 hours and don't worry about feeding. Then move them to a heated brooder, where they will live for the next six weeks. The brooder must be rat-proof, with wood shavings on the floor and an infrared lamp above. Initially the temperature should be 95°F (35°C); then reduce it by 5°F (3°C) per week.

The natural way

It is easy to tell when one of your hens is broody. She won't leave the nest box and fluffs up to twice her size when you peer in. She will make loud noises, and if you move her she'll go straight back to her eggs.

If you want her to hatch chicks, you must move her to her own house—first, so that the chicks are safe, and second, so that she doesn't discourage all the other hens from coming into the nest box to lay.

Her house should be warm and cozy, with food and water nearby. We find it easiest to move broody hens at night. After that, there is very little to do, other than provide chick mash and water for your new chicks.

DIY HATCHING

■ **An electronic incubator** allows minimal handling, which can cool the eggs or introduce bacteria.
■ **Warm it up** before the eggs arrive. In a still-air machine, the ideal temperature is 102.9°F (39.4°C), measured 2 in (5 cm) above the eggs. Set the humidity to 75–80 percent.
■ **Label eggs** with the date they were added to the incubator.
■ **Turning the eggs** Using your penciled date label as a helpful marker, rotate each egg through 180 degrees every time you turn it.
■ **Candling the eggs** Cut two holes in opposite sides of a cardboard box. Hold an egg in front of one hole and shine a flashlight through the other to examine the yolk. Discard infertile eggs and those with the blood ring of a failed embryo.

What to look for
From left: failed embryo, infertile egg with clear yolk, fertile embryo.

■ **In the brooder** Show your chicks where the water is by dipping their beaks in it, and drop food in front of them like the mother hen would.

■ **Using an infrared lamp** If it's too hot, chicks move away from the lamp; too cold and they huddle below.

Broody Buff Orpingtons *are great foster hens. Give them a clutch of fertilized eggs to sit on and they will hatch the chicks and raise them as their own.*

PROJECT **Prepare chickens to eat**

Killing one of your chickens and preparing it for a meal is relatively simple. The first time you do it, it's a good idea to get an experienced person to help so that the chicken is rendered unconscious immediately and doesn't suffer.

KILLING AND PLUCKING

DO

- Make sure that the bird has not been fed for 24 hours so that its digestive system is empty
- Get someone to help
- Stay relaxed
- Pluck the chicken right away, while it's still warm
- Wash your hands between plucking and drawing

DON'T

- Panic
- Use too much force
- Kill a bird in front of other chickens
- Tear at the feathers or you'll rip the skin

1. Take both legs firmly in your left hand and hold the head cupped in the palm of your right hand, with your index finger and middle finger on either side of its neck. **2. Stretch** the neck down so that the head bends backward. Stretch until the neck is broken: don't go too far or the head will come off. **3. Tie the feet** and hang the chicken. Start plucking immediately. It is far easier to do while the bird is warm. Pluck the wing feathers, followed by the leg feathers, then the body.

DRAWING

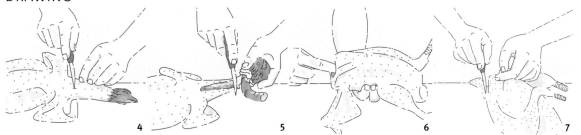

4. Cut from the bottom of the neck up to the head. **5. Sever** the neckbone and remove it, along with the head. **6. Put your finger** inside the gap and loosen the innards by moving your fingers inside the cavity. **7. Turn** the chicken and slit between the vent and tail, being careful not to pierce the rectum or you'll contaminate the flesh. Cut all around the vent.

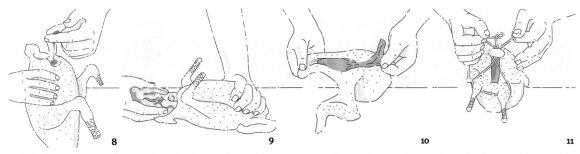

8. Pull the vent carefully away from the body; it should come away quite easily now that you've cut it free. **9. Draw out** the intestines, gizzard, lungs, liver, and heart with the vent as you keep pulling it steadily. **10. Remove the crop** from the neck end of the chicken, being careful not to pierce it. Tuck the flaps of skin back inside at either end of the bird. Gently singe the skin with a flame to burn off any remaining fluffy feathers. **11. Truss the bird** up ready for roasting. Cut off the feet and tie the wing tips to the legs, then wrap the string around the hocks and the end of the tail.

Keeping turkeys

The first Christmas at Newhouse Farm we ordered an organic turkey from our local butcher. It was a lovely bird but with a huge price tag. The next year we did the math and figured we could rear them for about a third of the price. So we fattened a dozen, giving them lots of room and organic feed, and it was a resounding success. Watching them grow is fascinating and they make great presents.

Choosing what to buy

We opt to buy 5–6-week-old birds rather than day-olds because it cuts down on the hassle of providing heat lamps and caring them when they are at their most fragile. We normally buy 12 Norfolk Black turkeys, which are too young to sex at a glance. We would expect to know which are toms and which are hens by 12–13 weeks.

Some good turkey breeds to choose from include:

▪ **Bourbon Reds** are an American breed that originated in Kentucky and Pennsylvania and can grow to an impressive 33 lb (15 kg). Their feathers are a reddish chestnut color with white tail feathers.

▪ **Bronze** are named after the unusual color of their feathers, which are a green copper-brown in the sunlight. Bronze turkeys often require artificial insemination to reproduce due to the large size of their breast meat. We have found them a calm bird that can grow very large indeed.

▪ **Giant Whites** are easy to dress thanks to their white pin feathers. Some toms may reach an astonishing weight of 45 lb (20 kg).

▪ **Narragansett** are an extremely tasty bird that is more hardy than most other breeds due to its mixed genetic selection (it originated as a cross between wild and domestic breeds). Narragansetts are known for having a calm disposition and making good mothers.

▪ **Wild turkeys** don't grow as large as domestic turkeys, but are tasty, colorful, hardy, and popular with hunters. You can buy wild-type birds from hatcheries, but check the rules for your state—you may need a permit to keep these birds.

CLIPPING WINGS

If you want to restrict your turkeys' movement, clip one of their wings. Clip both wings and they will put lots of effort into flying and eventually take off, whereas one wing makes them lopsided and spin back to earth. When clipping, cut off their primary feathers with a sharp pair of scissors at the point where they line up with the next layer.

Get someone else to hold the turkey as you clip the wing feathers.

1. Turkeys don't have great eyesight, *so don't get angry if they won't follow you into their shed at night; they may need a little coaxing.* **2. Give them organic feed** *and clean them out regularly.* **3. Turkeys** *require very little work and will thrive with plenty of room to enjoy.*

Midget Whites were bred in the mid-20th century as an alternative to the large domestic breeds. They're calm birds, and the hens make good mothers but can have difficulty laying the first of their relatively large eggs.

Housing and basic care

Turkeys must be kept separate from chickens to guard against the fatal blackhead disease. We keep our turkeys outside in a small paddock surrounded by electric fencing to keep out any hungry foxes (see page 175 for how to set one up). They have a decent-sized shed to shelter in and a big perch in the middle of their enclosure, which they sit upon and practice their vulture impressions.

We feed our birds with turkey grower's pellets, which have less protein in them than commercial turkey feed. The reason we are able to use this type of feed is that we usually get birds as early as possible in the season, so they have plenty of time to get big naturally and obtain a great deal of their protein by snacking on the insects and bugs in their enclosure.

When caring for turkeys, it is also vital to provide a good source of grit for them to eat. This aids the digestion of your birds, and enables them to mash up their food in their crop and digest the goodness, ensuring they grow nice and big during the year.

Top turkey tips

Keep your turkeys clean! Meaning the bedding and food containers—and give them plenty of fresh water. By keeping their house clean, you greatly reduce the chances that one of your birds will get sick.

Close them up at night. Sounds like common sense, but free-range doesn't mean providing the local fox with an early Christmas present.

Leave the ground to rest for 12 months before a new batch of turkeys return to the same spot. This helps avoid the dreaded blackhead, which is a parasite that lives in earthworms and gut worms. Signs of a problem are sulfur-yellow droppings and, more often than not, a dead turkey.

Consider homeopathic worming alternatives.

If you plan to keep breeding stock so you can enjoy turkey all through the year, buy some special leather saddles as protection for the hens. These sit on their backs and stop the stags from damaging them too much while mating. The saddles need to stay on in spring and come off in early fall.

KILLING LARGE BIRDS

Slaughtering turkeys needs to be fast and efficient. We calmly take the birds one at a time to a barn. Then we place them upside down in a suspended traffic cone. One of us holds the legs while the other two place a broom handle on either side of the turkey's neck. They firmly squeeze the handles together and twist and push them down while the person holding the legs pulls up. This separates the vertebrae in the neck, and then we immediately slice the jugular with a sharp knife. Once dead, the birds are hung up by their feet and plucked right away (see page 195).

Doing the deed alone

To kill a turkey solo, place a broom handle over its neck, twist and press down with your feet, while pulling it up by the legs.

The "suspended traffic cone" method *requires three people to make it as efficient and kind as possible.*

Working alone *requires greater coordination and strength to ensure the job is done quickly and humanely.*

Keeping ducks and geese

Geese are absolutely amazing to rear yourself. We find that they are hardy, tough, and surprisingly self-reliant—almost the perfect self-sufficient animal—but they can be noisy and a handful if you're not used to big birds. Ducks are also extremely useful animals to keep on your property, but you'll find they can be fairly messy.

Why keep ducks and geese?

Provided you have a source of fresh water, ducks are great to keep, not just for their delicious eggs—which make the best cakes in the world—or because they are tasty table birds, but because they are selective eaters that are less likely to scratch garden beds than chickens and can be useful at controlling pests like slugs. Geese are first-class grazers and great guard birds, their noisy honking serving as an intruder alert (actually, they're better than our two big dogs). They usually start laying enormous eggs in February and March. Soft-boiled for breakfast, you'll need a whole regiment of toast "soldiers" to dip

in them. Put in cold water, bring to a boil for six minutes—perfect! Bear in mind, though, that geese are large birds and need to be treated as such. Respect them when you pick them up or they'll wallop you with their wings.

Choosing which ducks to buy

Whether you are buying ducks or geese, you can buy them either as young birds or as eggs and raise your own. Among the best breeds of duck to choose from are:

▨ **Aylesbury** table ducks—famous as large birds for eating, weighing up to 10 lb (4.5 kg).

▨ **Indian Runners** don't have much meat on them but they are good egg layers—on average, you can hope for about 180 eggs a year. They have a distinctive upright stance and stroll around like penguins.

▨ **Khaki Campbells** can lay over 300 eggs a year!

▨ **Muscovy** ducks are heavy and placid, and make excellent mothers. They are very good fliers, so you will probably want to clip their wings (see page 196). Be careful when you pick them up as they have sharp clawed feet. Muscovies are thought to descend from a goose, but we class them as our favorite ducks.

▨ **Welsh Harlequins** are good all-around birds. They are decent layers and are big enough to be an impressive table bird.

Choosing which geese to buy

There are many breeds to consider:

▨ **Buff** geese are calm birds, a good choice if you have small children.

▨ **Chinese** geese are excellent egg

DUCKS TO WATER

We believe that it is only really fair to keep ducks if you have running water on your property or a pond that you can top off with fresh water regularly. Flowing water and a pond are ideal for keeping ducks, but if you don't have this, then you must ensure that you can provide them with a deep container of regularly changed water as ducks need to be able to periodically submerge their heads to clean their eyes and nostrils.

One of our Muscovy ducks *enjoys a paddle in the stream with her young.*

GREEN GEESE

Traditionally, rearing geese was inextricably linked with the growth and decline of green grass. Goslings begin grazing when the grass is fresh in spring and then, when the grass slows down in fall, we slaughter them. It is a harsh natural cycle, but efficient. In the past, they were called Michaelmas geese in Britain as their butchery tied in with November 29, and in North America geese were often bred to coincide with Thanksgiving feasts.

Keeping "green geese" *makes good financial sense and mows the lawn.*

layers and can be ready to slaughter as early as 8 weeks.

▨ **Toulouse** are good producers of down and dark meat and are the most popular breed in the US.

▨ **Embdens** are an excellent, very large table breed.

▨ **Romans** are particularly good if you want a goose that can be killed when it is young but still have plenty of breast meat to enjoy.

Housing

Housing ducks and geese is not very complicated.

▨ **Ducks will live happily** in a conventional hen house, easily adapted and placed near a pond or stream—water is essential to a duck's well-being. You may want to provide a ramp into the house, as ducks are clumsy and can easily injure themselves, but they don't need a perch. Additionally, the housing should be rat- and raccoon-proof, draft-free but well ventilated, and always have fresh dry bedding. Ducks like to wander, but we keep ours in a fenced area with a pond most of the time, to avoid stepping in duck poop when we leave the house.

◼ **Provide geese** with larger houses than ducks. The traditional design is an open, three-sided construction often made with straw bales, but we always protect them at night by locking them in a small shed. Geese are vulnerable to rats, raccoons, and foxes when they're young or when they're sitting on eggs. We use an electric fence with poultry wire to stop them from roaming (see page 175).

◼ **Geese require** a bit more space for grazing than ducks or chickens, and we have found that our small orchard is perfect for them. Although they are officially classed as water fowl, they don't absolutely need a pond; all they require is access to water to keep their nostrils and eyes clean by immersing their heads. A large container will do until you make something a bit more permanent, like a small pond, but it must be deep and the water changed regularly.

Feeding

◼ **Ducks aren't grazing birds** like geese, but they will supplement their diet with grass if you give them access. We feed our ducks corn daily to increase the number of eggs they lay and to fatten them up nicely. They are also partly carnivorous and will happily eat slugs, snails, worms, frogs, and insects. Therefore, in spring before we start the next round of crop planting, we allow our ducks

access to the vegetable beds to find and eat any hiding pests. Don't get carried away and give them free range of your beds all year round, though, as they will damage young brassicas and eat peas and lettuce like there's no tomorrow.

◼ **Geese eat grass** like living lawnmowers and can even be used for weeding between strawberry plants or vines, as they don't normally eat broad-leaved plants.

◼ **When you get your goslings**, feed them chick crumble for the first few months, reducing quantities after four weeks as they start to graze more

on grass shoots. Then, when the geese are full-grown, occasionally supplement their grass diet with corn feed if you want to fatten them up.

Slaughtering ducks and geese

For both ducks and geese we would recommend that you follow the methods described for large birds on page 197. Geese are larger and should be killed by a team effort, but some smaller ducks can be killed single-handed. You can kill your ducks at about 10 weeks old but we leave ours for much longer (see page 195). Kill geese at 5–6 months old.

1. Make sure you imprint yourself *upon goslings when they are young by being around when they hatch and over the first few days. You'll find they flock to you much more readily when they're bigger.* **2. Mesh and shutters on the window,** *plus a lockable door, will help secure your geese from predators. Always keep the floor clean and dry.* **3. These Indian Runner ducklings** *are particular favorites of ours as we enjoy their perky characters.*

Keeping pigs

Pigs are at the heart of our farmstead. They plow and manure the land as well as provide us with tremendous meat. Pigs are highly intelligent animals and are capable of coming when they're called and showing individual character. But here at Newhouse Farm we are omnivores and enjoy eating a bacon sandwich, so our pigs don't have names and we don't get too attached to them.

Choosing what to buy

Rare-breed pigs such as the Berkshire, Gloucester Old Spot, and Tamworth tend to be much hardier than specialized commercial hybrids and are better suited to natural outdoor living conditions. Ideally, you want your pig to put on weight fast and not have any health problems. You can often look at the history of certain pedigree animals in a pig breeder's records, to get an indication of the size they'll grow to and whether they will be better suited for making bacon or for processing into sausages.

Berkshire is one of the oldest pig breeds. They are early maturing and have a high proportion of lean meat.
Gloucester Old Spots were bred originally to live in apple orchards. They are hardy and make great bacon.
Landrace is a popular breed in Denmark and Sweden due to its long back for bacon production.
Large Blacks nearly became extinct in the 1960s but are making a comeback as a pasture-raised pig.
Large Whites provide top-quality back bacon and are extremely popular commercially.
Red Wattles are hardy, good-natured, and excellent foragers, well suited for pasture-based production.

Tamworth is a lovely, medium-sized, red-colored pig that is extremely hardy, even in northerly areas such as Canada and Scotland.

How to buy pigs

Before you think about getting pigs, make certain that your land is zoned for keeping livestock and that you'll be able to meet all requirements for proper housing and setbacks from adjoining properties.

We would not recommend buying your first batch of pigs from a local livestock market unless you are very experienced or have a knowledgeable friend to help you. Often farmers will auction off some of their inferior stock, and you won't know what you're looking for. Instead, develop a relationship with a reputable farmer who should then sell you good stock because, if the pigs don't do well, you won't go back to them again and they end up losing good business.

Gilt weaners

The easiest and most economical way to buy pigs is to get some 8-week-old weaners that have already been weaned for a couple of weeks and run around actively. Check whether the rear ends are clean and keep an eye out for any signs of lameness.

1. **We pick up our new weaners** *in a large cage on the back of our truck, and borrow a trailer from a friend when we take them to the slaughterhouse—an exchange involving plenty of sausages.* 2. **Choose weaners** *with long, lean backs.* 3. **Pigs from a reputable dealer** *are far more likely to remain healthy and grow quickly. You may be able to check out their history in the breeder's records.*

It is best not to buy breeding stock right away because, as a beginner, it will be nearly impossible for you to select genuinely good stock. Breeding pigs also involves much more in the way of equipment, attention, and expertise. We like to leave the complexities of breeding to local experts and concentrate our own efforts on the fattening-up side of things, always buying gilts. These are young female pigs that have not mated nor had any piglets. We opt for gilts rather than boars as the pork does not end up tasting "pissy"— a term for meat tainted by male hormones as the young boar matures.

Transporting your pigs

Getting your newly bought pigs home involves a bit of planning. In many states there are strict rules governing the movement of livestock and penalties if you don't adhere to them, so always check with your state's department of agriculture before transporting animals.

A key piece of equipment when moving pigs is a length of plywood with two holes cut in the top to hold it at each end. This simple tool will enable you to successfully shepherd your pigs in and out of trailers or to new pastures.

Housing and basic care

Most of the equipment that you will need to keep pigs is easily available from agricultural suppliers, but some equipment, such as feeders and electric fencing, can be expensive to buy new, so look for it at farm auctions. If you are buying second-hand equipment, make sure you disinfect it first and scour it with a wire brush. When choosing the pig sty, ensure it is well insulated against the cold. The more energy your pigs put into growing bigger instead of keeping warm, the better.

HAPPY PIGS

One of the main motivations for rearing our own pigs is that the animal welfare of factory-farmed pork can be horrendous. Commercial farming often denies pigs much space to move around, and their feed can be pumped with a cocktail of chemicals, resulting in cheap, tasteless pork. Such intensive farming has often escaped scrutiny, which is surprising considering we are so eager to get on our high horses about other meat production. If you can't rear your own pigs, you can still choose to eat free-range organic pork.

We are strong believers *that happy pigs are tasty pigs!*

PROJECT **Set up a pig pen**

The focal point of a pig pen will be the house or sty. We always place the door facing away from the prevailing winds and build it on a raised pallet to keep it dry. The shell is then covered by some corrugated iron. Don't go spending much money on pig housing, but do use large nails or screws and make it strong enough to withstand a full-grown pig enjoying a good back scratch!

YOU WILL NEED
- Electric fence
- Pigsty
- Straw
- Water bowl
- Stone weight
- Trough
- Organic feed

1. **Before moving your pigs** into their pen, surround the area with an electric fence (see page 175).   2. **Keep the pigsty** full of plenty of fresh straw, putting a whole bale in at a time.   3. **Ensure that there is plenty of water** in the pen to satisfy a pig's thirst. If possible, sink the container into the ground, as well as putting a weight in it, to prevent the pigs from knocking it over.   4. **To keep feed pellets** from being trampled into the ground in the animals' piglike enthusiasm to get to the food, put them into a trough twice a day.

POTENTIAL PROBLEMS

We find that keeping pigs on a small scale doesn't present many problems. However, here are some common ailments to watch out for:

■ **Erysipelas** can be fatal if not treated quickly. Symptoms include raised diamond patterns on the back and sides, which turn purple. Within 48 hours the pig can die, but a shot of penicillin in time can cure it.

■ **Lice** are not particularly dangerous to the pig, but they do cause great irritation. Buy lice wash from an agricultural supplier to treat them.

■ **Meningitis** will cause a pig to stop eating, lie on the ground and, if it walks around, hold its head to one side. An injection of antibiotics can produce a rapid cure, so act fast.

■ **Scour**, or diarrhea, mainly occurs in piglets. Reduce their feed and give them a course of antibiotics.

■ **The bottom line** with health problems of any kind is this: if you are in any doubt, call the vet.

1. Move your pigs *to fresh pasture from time to time so they can dig up and eat the crops.*
2. Throw fresh greens *into the pen for your pigs to forage for.*   **3. In hot summer weather**, *pour a few buckets of water on a muddy patch of ground to provide your pigs with a wallow.*

Pigs and water

Pigs drink large volumes of water and their container will need topping off regularly. We place it near the edge of the fence so that we can fill it easily. In hot weather you should also create an area of wet mud that the pigs can use as a "wallow." Wallowing helps the pigs to cool down, and the layer of dried mud on their skin offers some protection against sunburn.

Feeding pigs

The feed that we use is an organic pellet that contains plenty of protein and carbohydrates and is in addition to a foraging diet of grass, wild weeds, and roots.

When the weaners are young we allow them to eat as much as they want from an automatic feeder placed next to their house. When

they get to 10 weeks we start to feed them twice a day. Regardless of age we feed them 2¼ lb (1 kg) of food each morning and evening. For us, that means giving our two pigs a large full scoop of food twice daily and they do fine. We continue with this method of feeding until slaughter (see opposite).

You can throw the food over the ground for them to forage for, but as it is the most expensive part of the pig-rearing process, and they often end up urinating on it or trampling it into the ground, we pour it into their trough to avoid waste. Conversely, we do make a point of throwing fresh greens and fodder crops all over their enclosure for them to search for.

We like to give our pigs access to fresh pasture with plenty of roots for them to dig up and eat. It is also

a good idea to plant fodder crops on the land before they move in to save money on their feed bills.

Serving your pigs kitchen waste is complicated as there are now regulations restricting the feeding of pigs with any waste that has been in your kitchen. This is to avoid the spread of disease.

However, if you trim your vegetables in the garden and position your beds close to where the pigs live, then you will find they can still eat plenty of fresh peelings and spoiled vegetables.

When you feed them, call loudly each time with a distinctive noise. This will train them to come to you and makes it much easier to shepherd them if they escape. Our pig-calling noise sounds like "ShoooEee!", but it's completely up to you...

Slaughtering and butchering pigs

Once your pigs weigh 140–180 lb (65–80 kg) you can slaughter them at any time. We normally keep our girls for 9–10 months before slaughtering them, which is much longer than commercial farms, but gives us more of their digging and manuring power to help cultivate the land.

There are so many regulations covering the killing and eating of pigs on your own land, we recommend sending them to a slaughterhouse instead. Visit first to see if you are happy with the price and services they offer. This also takes the stress out of the visit on the day of the slaughter as you'll know what's in store. To move your pigs, tempt them into the trailer using pig boards, your signature pig call, and some food. At the slaughterhouse, escort them to their appointment and say your goodbyes. The next day you can collect a scraped carcass split into two halves to butcher at home, or ask a butcher to prepare the cuts for you.

Make your own sausages *with the aid of an electric meat grinder and prepared sausage skins.*

Some of our favorite cuts
One pig, so many different types of meat for you to enjoy. A chest freezer is especially useful post-butchering.

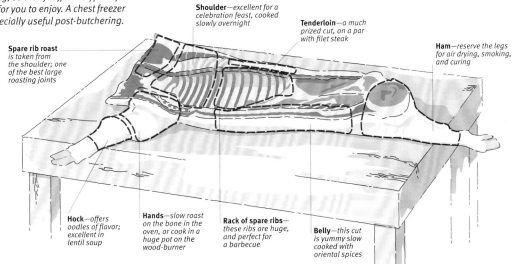

Spare rib roast *is taken from the shoulder; one of the best large roasting joints*

Shoulder—*excellent for a celebration feast, cooked slowly overnight*

Tenderloin—*a much prized cut, on a par with filet steak*

Ham—*reserve the legs for air drying, smoking, and curing*

Hock—*offers oodles of flavor; excellent in lentil soup*

Hands—*slow roast on the bone in the oven, or cook in a huge pot on the wood-burner*

Rack of spare ribs—*these ribs are huge, and perfect for a barbecue*

Belly—*this cut is yummy slow cooked with oriental spices*

BUTCHERING BASICS

Butchering meat requires a large wooden butcher's block, a meat saw, and some sharp knives. In addition, an electric meat grinder saves a huge amount of effort when making sausages—if you have a hand-powered one, good luck, and we bet you'll get an electric mincer next time.

Shoulder *To separate the shoulder, cut between the fifth and sixth ribs.*

Tenderloin *Remove this in one long strip from inside the backbone.*

Ham *Cut the flesh cleanly with a saw, then remove the aitch bone with a knife.*

Keeping sheep and goats

Rearing sheep reduces our reliance on imported meat and wool that travel thousands of miles to reach us. It takes commitment and skill to look after a small flock and is not something to undertake lightly. Goats tend to be hardier than sheep and are great at reclaiming a neglected property, as they eat anything, from brambles to weeds. Both sheep and goats produce excellent milk.

Choosing sheep

Geography is important. On an exposed site with poor grazing, a primitive hardy sheep such as Soay or Ouessant is the right choice. Some modern breeds of sheep are highly specialized, others are more general-purpose. For example, if you want sheep primarily for meat, go for a quality carcass breed like the Texel.

■ **Ouessant** are a primitive breed, which means they haven't been overbred and are very hardy.

■ **Dorset Horn** can lamb more than once a year. They produce good-quality wool and a high milk yield.

■ **Border Leicester** is an elegant English sheep. A prolific breeder, they produce good mutton and wool.

■ **Southdown** is a manageable size and matures early.

■ **Soay** are similar to wild sheep, with good milk yields and lean meat.

■ **Texel** is an excellent meat sheep. Both sexes have horns.

How to buy sheep

Buying good-quality sheep can be daunting for the first-timer. Visit local livestock auctions, and ask a farmer for advice before you start. Always look at the seller's performance records, and check that sheep have good teeth—they should be broad, short, and fit squarely in the mouth.

We recommend starting small—with three ewes, for example, or two orphaned lambs—until you feel confident that keeping sheep is going to fit in with your lifestyle.

■ **Your property must be zoned** for livestock if you intend to keep sheep and goats. There will also be paperwork to fill out when you buy your animals, and you'll need to keep records, tag each sheep and goat, and abide by regulations when transporting and slaughtering livestock. Check with your local extension office or state department of agriculture for details.

Choosing goats

Goats are gregarious animals, so you should keep at least two.

■ **Saanen** can get quite big, but have high milk yields on good grazing.

■ **Anglo-Nubian** have lower milk yields but of top-notch quality.

■ **Toggenburg** are fairly small but do well on larger, free-range areas.

■ **Golden Guernsey** are small, with lower milk yields than large breeds.

■ **Angora** are renowned for their soft mohair fleeces and high milk yields.

How to buy goats

As a rule, goats with strong legs, a wedge-shaped rear end, and strong backs are likely to be good animals. You can get more information by joining a goat-keeper's organization.

Buy weaned kids or goatlings that are 1–2 years old. Despite being a bit more expensive to buy, they are cheaper to feed than young kids that need milk.

1. Ouessant *sheep from France are small and easy to carry—ideal for a small farm. Primitive breeds like these don't flock together in the way other sheep do.* **2. Feed hay** *to sheep in winter if grazing is limited. Use a covered rack to keep the hay dry and clean.*

1. Well-brought-up goats *shouldn't butt their handlers.* **2. British Alpine goats** *produce milk with high butterfat.*

FEEDING GOATS

Goats need huge amounts of fiber, which they get from browsing on brambles, thistles, and twigs, and they require hay all year round—on average, a milking goat will need about a bale a week. Also give your goats a salt lick and a constant supply of fresh water.

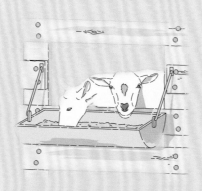

Supplement grazing *with special goat mix from your local feed mill or agricultural supplier for extra energy. Suspended feed troughs stop goats from fouling in their food and then refusing to eat it.*

Hay, straw, and, occasionally, kale *are best fed in a rack. The bars should be 2 in (5 cm) apart and at least 2 ft 6 in (75 cm) above the ground. Make it easy to reach from outside the goats' enclosure.*

Housing and basic care

■ **The land needed for sheep** varies greatly depending on the size of the breed and the quality of pasture—the grassland and mixed vegetation that grazing animals feed on. As a rough guide, you could keep about 10 ewes on 1 acre (0.4 hectare), but you must have more land available to move them onto. Moving sheep onto new pasture on a six- to eight-week rotation reduces the buildup of parasites on the land and also conserves the grass.

Sheep in southern regions shouldn't need housing beyond the natural shelter offered by outcrops of rocks and trees. In areas with severe winters, provide a run-in shelter from rain and wind, and a shed to move the ewes into when they are lambing.

■ **Goats don't like rain or cold.** Most need a draft-proof shelter to sleep in at night. If you are building one from scratch, put in a concrete floor to make cleaning easy—the manure is great to add to compost. Provide your goats with an outdoor daytime shelter as a bolthole in bad weather.

Securing your animals

■ **Good fencing for goats** is essential (see pages 172–175). Bear in mind a wise old saying: "Goats spend 23 hours of the day planning their escape and the last hour executing it." Anyone who keeps goats will soon become aware of the constant battle to stop them from escaping and eating the contents of the fruit and vegetable garden.

■ **Tethering goats** is another option, but it is time-consuming; as with sheep, you need to move them regularly to prevent the land from becoming contaminated with a buildup of parasites.

■ **For temporary sheep fencing** try hurdles (see pages 172–175). Use them to put together small enclosures when you need to examine their feet, give them medication, or round them up for shearing or at lambing time.

■ **For permanent boundaries** you can build stone walls, plant fencerows, or use wire-net fences topped off with a strand of barbed wire (see pages 172–175).

Feeding and drinking

■ **Sheep** should not require much supplementary feed if they have good grazing. If you have restricted access to grass, then feed them pellets—in troughs to avoid waste—or give them a rack filled with good-quality hay. They will also need a clean fresh supply of water, in a bowl raised at least 20 in (0.5m) above the ground to prevent them from fouling it.

■ **Goats** are best fed by grazing them on scrubland or pasture. They will thrive on brush-covered hillsides and deciduous woodland, but will not do so well in coniferous woods. They also require hay and supplementary mixes in addition to grazing.

205

Breeding sheep and goats

▓ **Mate or tup sheep** in the fall. For less than a dozen sheep, it's too expensive to keep a ram; we suggest borrowing one. Rub some reddle (any dark-colored soil) on his chest so that you can see when he has served all of your ewes. Keep your ewes on poor pasture for a few weeks before tupping—this is called flushing the flock—then move them onto good pasture with the ram.

▓ **Sheep's gestation period** is 147 days and lambing normally starts in late February or March. It can mean late nights and stressful days, much like being a doctor perpetually on call. A good shepherd allows sheep to get on with it alone, while remaining vigilant. The first signs of a ewe giving birth will be that they choose a place away from the rest of the flock and repeatedly lie down. A water bag appears first followed by

the feet and nose. When the lamb is born, the ewe licks away the mucus and membrane from its head to stimulate it. If a ewe has been in labor for more than an hour and is obviously in discomfort, call a neighboring farmer or vet.

When all the ewes have lambed, move them to the best pastures you have. New mothers and offspring will thrive on good nourishment.

▓ **Take goats to be mated**—it is usually cheaper than keeping a billy goat yourself. The advice for kids is the same as for lambing, although the gestation is a few days longer.

Castrating goats

If you plan to eat billy kids, castrate them before they're three months old, as this stops their meat from tasting too strong. The most humane method is to use an Elastrator, available from agricultural suppliers.

POTENTIAL PROBLEMS

▓ **Blowflies** lay eggs in the damp wool around the sheep's bottom. Cut away the affected fleece, and prevent a recurrence by spraying the back of the sheep with a suitable treatment from your vet.
▓ **Foot rot** can be a problem for both sheep and goats on damp ground. Keep hooves trimmed. If animals get foot rot, walk them through a foot bath of formalin.
▓ **Sheep's lungs** can fill with fluid and they may drown if they get stuck on their backs. Always tip them over if they're lodged upside down.
▓ **Intestinal worms in sheep** need treating. Invest in a gun for dosing a whole flock; if you only have one or two animals, use a syringe.
▓ **Abscesses in goats** are best lanced and kept clean with antiseptic solutions. Ask a vet to help with this procedure.
▓ **Dose goats against fluke** if they have access to wet or marshy land.

Butchering a sheep

Fat lambs are ready for slaughter at four months old; sheep for mutton between one and two years. We recommend finding a good local slaughterhouse to do the job. They may be able to hang the carcass for you for a few days, to improve flavor, but more often than not you'll need to find a cold spot to hang the meat at home. We think good lamb or mutton is underappreciated. These are our favorite cuts:

A good fatty leg of mutton *that's full of marbling is best for roasting.*

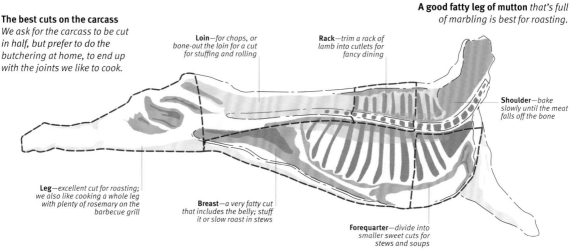

The best cuts on the carcass
We ask for the carcass to be cut in half, but prefer to do the butchering at home, to end up with the joints we like to cook.

Loin—for chops, or bone-out the loin for a cut for stuffing and rolling

Rack—trim a rack of lamb into cutlets for fancy dining

Shoulder—bake slowly until the meat falls off the bone

Leg—excellent cut for roasting; we also like cooking a whole leg with plenty of rosemary on the barbecue grill

Breast—a very fatty cut that includes the belly; stuff it or slow roast in stews

Forequarter—divide into smaller sweet cuts for stews and soups

PROJECT **Shear a sheep and dye wool**

Shearing takes lots of practice. Try learning the ropes on another farm first. We don't spin fleeces as it's easier to get it done by a professional—you'll find information on local spinning services online or at your nearest agricultural supplier. However, we do like dyeing our own wool with natural plant dyes. You can get an amazing range of colors from the unlikeliest sources, from onion skins to privet leaves. Treat the wool first with a mordant—a chemical that "bites" into the wool to fix the color.

YOU WILL NEED
- Hand shears
- Large saucepan
- Alum
- Cream of tartar
- Onion skins

HOW TO SHEAR A SHEEP

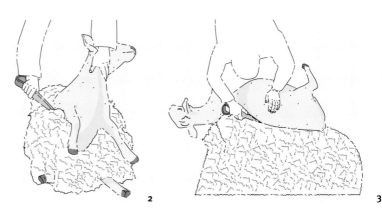

1. First clip all the wool off her stomach, down to the udders, taking care not to slice off the teats. **2. Next shear her down one side,** starting at the throat and around the side of her neck and head. Keep going as far down as you can reach; then roll the sheep over and shear down the other side. The fleece should now come right off her body except at the hindquarters. **3. Lay the sheep flat on the ground** and shear the fleece away from the back and hindquarters. Tidy her up with a trim of her hind legs and tail so that the other sheep don't laugh at her.

DYEING WOOL WITH NATURAL EXTRACTS

1. Weigh out the same amount of onion skins as the weight of wool. Let them sit in a big pan of water overnight, then boil for an hour. Strain the dye.
2. Wet the wool thoroughly, then boil it in a mordant solution of 4 oz (110 g) of alum in 4 gallons (18 liters) of hot water and 1 oz (25 g) cream of tartar. (Always keep a separate set of pans for dyeing; never use cooking pans.) **3. Add the mordanted wool** to the hot dye and soak for an hour, stirring occasionally. Drain and dry the wool. Onion skins give a rich orange color. Reuse the dye water for a paler, beige wool.

NATURAL DYES

Clockwise from left, wool dyed with natural plant colors:

- Apricot skein: **madder**
- Beige skein: **black currant**
- Beige ball: second use of **onion skin** dye.
- Primrose yellow: **weld,** or try **gorse shoots** or **privet leaves**
- Orange: **onion skin**
- Gray/blue: **black currant**
- Purple: **logwood** (a tropical tree), or try **willow roots** or **bilberries.**

Keeping cattle

Imagine how great it would feel to supply all of your own protein and dairy products! In our opinion, keeping cattle is the epitome of self-sufficiency, but before you take on any animals, remember that it is a serious commitment. Although one of the more complicated and time-consuming challenges, it can be extremely rewarding.

Choosing what to buy

Keeping cattle involves much more effort and a larger financial outlay than buying a few chickens. You will need extra sheds and an acre of pasture for each cow. Visit local farmers and experienced neighbors, to learn the ropes and think carefully about how many cattle you want to keep on your land. Do you want to produce beef to sell or just enough for your home, friends, and family? How much milk and dairy products do you use on average in a month? Do you want to add the job of milking cows twice daily to your routine? One cow will keep you in all the milk that you could possibly need. If you have a beef animal, you will also have more than enough meat.

You will have to decide between dairy cows, beef cows, or more traditional dual-purpose cows. We don't keep cattle because of lack of space, but we have good friends and neighbors who share an enthusiasm for older, dual-purpose breeds and natural rearing techniques. Our favorite heritage breeds for small farms include:

■ **Ayrshires** can be white and red and are perfect if you are looking for a tough breed that produces plenty of high-quality milk. They fatten early and can remain productive for up to 12 years.

■ **Dexter** is our favorite breed. Their beef is delicious and their small size makes them easier to butcher and preserve, and they satisfy the needs of a single family.

■ **Herefords** are excellent for beef.

■ **Jerseys** are docile, hardy, and produce excellent high-quality milk that's ideal for making butter and cheese. Jersey cows also live for a long time and can really become part of the family.

■ **Shorthorns** are excellent dual-purpose cows, suitable for a small herd. They are hardy, long-lived, rear calves very easily, and make good foster mothers.

How to buy cattle

Buying a cow is easier said than done, but before you even venture out to an auction, you must first make sure your property is appropriately zoned for cattle. There will be paperwork to fill out when you buy your cattle, and you'll need to keep records up-to-date, tag each animal, and abide by regulations when you transport your livestock and take them to the slaughterhouse. Call your local extension office or state department of agriculture for more information.

The first time you visit an auction, go with an experienced friend or farmer. You can find good deals at auctions, and the best cows to choose between are a "first-calver" and an older cow.

■ **A first-calver** is a heifer that has had just one calf and is therefore producing lots of milk. The farmer will probably have bred her specifically to sell, so you know that she will be a good cow and you can start milking her right away. The disadvantage of buying a first-calver is that you are both beginners, and she may be a bit flighty at first, and as nervous as you are when being milked. Also, her teats will be smaller and harder to squeeze than those of a mature cow.

■ **An older cow** is more likely to have a placid nature and elongated, well-milked teats, making her easier to milk. The drawback is that she won't be with you for so long.

Housing and basic care

Cattle usually only need to come in under cover to be milked or to eat dry hay. Look over the fence and see what your neighbors do at different times of the year; they will know the individual climate and conditions better than any weather forecaster,

---

EXAMINING A HEIFER

Ask to see the mother as well as examining the younger heifer; this will give you a good indication of what she's going to end up like.

■ **Make sure that she is calm** and reasonably tame.

■ **Feel the udder** carefully to see if you can detect any lumps; these can be caused by mastitis, which blocks the flow of milk.

■ **If the cow is in milk,** then ask if you can try milking her. Check the workings of each teat and see how calm she remains. She is likely to be a bit frisky as you will be a stranger to her, so cut her some slack before passing judgment.

■ **Go on to check** the cow's teeth to determine her age. A mature cow at five years old has eight incisors on the lower jaw. As the cow grows older, her age can be gauged by the wear, but this takes an experienced eye.

■ **Ask if she is tuberculosis tested** and also free from brucellosis.

■ **Don't buy her** if the farmer tells you upfront that she has a problem, such as a blind quarter, where one quarter of her udder has no milk in it.

and be able to advise you about extra shelter that your cattle may need.

More fussy breeds that produce high milk yields will want to go inside to eat extra food when the weather is bad or if the grass is not in prime condition. If you intensively rear cattle indoors over winter, you can have great results, but it is much more expensive to supply them with straw and extra food.

If you have spare outbuildings on your property, you may choose to use one as a designated milking shed, and another house for your cattle to sleep and eat in over winter.

The amount of food you will need for your cattle depends on the breed, their size, and their ability to adapt to the environment. Equally, they will need different-sized rations at different times. Normally, cattle receive a "maintenance" ration and then a little bit more, known as a "production" ration, when they are being milked. Add food according to how much milk they are giving. We prefer hardy breeds, such as Dexters, that thrive on grass and a simple supplement of hay.

If your cows are looking fatter or thinner, adjust their feed of hay and pellets accordingly. Watch how much milk they produce, how hungry they are, and if they appear healthy. If in doubt, ask other farmers, your feed store, or your vet for advice.

Mating

Smaller cows can be mated after 15 months but most bigger cows should wait until 20 months. They can only can be mated when they are in heat or "bulling." At this time a cow will have a slightly swollen vulva, moo more noisily than normal, and mount other cattle or allow another cow to mount her. Bulling occurs at 21-day intervals, and only lasts for about 18 hours, so keep your eyes open if you want to catch your cows at the right

1. Dexters *are small, hardy, dual-purpose, and love to browse, and they produce a high-quality gourmet meat.* **2. High-fiber cattle pellets** *supplement the basic dietary requirements of cattle producing high milk yields.* **3. Keep a salt lick** *in your cattle's field; it is an easy source of sodium and other minerals.* **4. Dexter cattle** *are ideal to rear traditionally as a suckler herd that lives as a family group. Regular handling ensures that the cattle are calm and easy to care for.*

time. Once you have chosen a cow that you want a bull to mate with, take her to a neighbor's farm or bring the bull to her. Alternatively, you can arrange to have your cow artificially inseminated.

Calving

Outdoor hardy cattle will normally calve on their own, with no real trouble. You're fairly likely to go out one day and see your cow licking a newborn calf. If, however, the calf has not sucked from its mother's teat within an hour of birth, hold it to its mother and make it suck. It may be necessary to tie up the mother while you do this. If you are bringing your cows in regularly, make sure it is a draft-free environment so that the calves don't get too cold. Never turn out calves without their mothers into cold, winter fields.

Milking

Milk your cows twice a day, preferably at 12-hour intervals. You will quickly find your own routine, bringing them in for an hour's milking in the morning and evening. Normally one cow will have to produce one calf a year if she is to produce milk. This means that you will not only have to milk them daily, but also have calves to keep an eye on.

Encouraging milk flow

To get milk from your cows, you will have to take calves away from their mothers early on. The mother will bellow loudly for a couple of days after this. Substitute yourself for the young one, so that your cow allows you to milk her as a calf would. Feed the calf separately with milk in a bucket. This may seem cruel, but cows are not human; they have shorter memories and it's just one of the realities of milking your herd.

Alternatively, you may prefer to remove one calf from its mother and try to pass it off as a twin on to another. If you can persuade the foster mother to accept a young calf alongside her own, you will free up the original cow for milking. You have to be a bit lucky to get away with this, but try tying up the foster mother to a post and coaxing her with some good food as a distraction.

Yet another option is to reach a balance where the calf takes its share of milk and then you take the rest.

PROJECT **How to milk a cow**

Before you start milking, wash the cow's udder, massaging it to stimulate the flow of milk as you clean. Then wash the rear end of the cow to prevent any nasties from dripping into your nice clean milk pail. Also wash the teats and your hands before you begin, and make sure that you give the cow something tasty to eat to distract her.

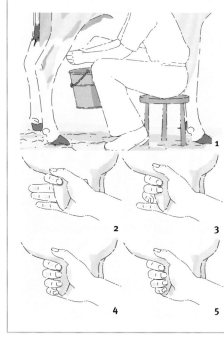

YOU WILL NEED
- Washing equipment
- Small stool and pail

1. Position a small stool on the right-hand side of the cow and grip the pail between your knees. **2. Grasp the two front teats,** one in each hand, and squeeze them at the top with each thumb and forefinger to trap the milk in the teats. **3. Move your hands down,** bringing in your middle fingers. **4 Bring in your little fingers** so your whole hand is around the teat. **5. Squeeze the milk** from the bottom of the teats. Then release the teats and repeat the process in a rhythmic rolling action. Use common sense to squeeze at the right pressure.

1. A calf *reaches puberty at about 9 months and is ready to breed from by 15 months.* **2. Teaching a calf to suck** *milk from a bucket may sound easy (see right), but you may need to persevere until it becomes second nature.*

Slaughtering and butchering beef

As with all livestock, before you kill an animal, ensure you have a place to store the carcass. Unless you're having a feast, you will need to keep cuts of beef in the freezer or salt them until you're ready to eat them.

The slaughtering method for cattle is the same as for pigs (p.203). The slaughterhouse may hang your beef for you, which can radically improve the texture and taste. We leave beef in a cold store at 35–41°F (2–5°C) for between two and four weeks. Everyone has their preferences, but we ask for the carcass back in quarters. This makes the meat marginally easier to handle and means we can carefully decide on the cuts we want for making hamburger, curing in salt, and packing away as treasured roasts in the freezer.

Invest in a large butcher block if you are doing your own butchering and preparing your meat. Watch for secondhand ones, as new ones can be expensive.

Beef cuts are numerous *and cooking times vary depending on which part of the animal they come from.*

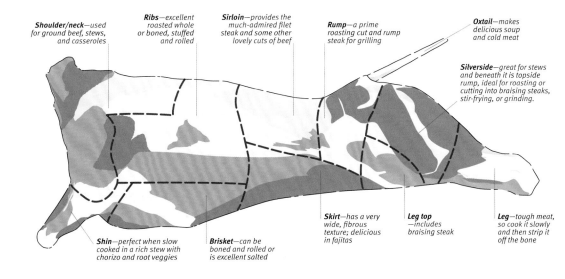

Shoulder/neck—used for ground beef, stews, and casseroles

Ribs—excellent roasted whole or boned, stuffed and rolled

Sirloin—provides the much-admired filet steak and some other lovely cuts of beef

Rump—a prime roasting cut and rump steak for grilling

Oxtail—makes delicious soup and cold meat

Silverside—great for stews and beneath it is topside rump, ideal for roasting or cutting into braising steaks, stir-frying, or grinding.

Shin—perfect when slow cooked in a rich stew with chorizo and root veggies

Brisket—can be boned and rolled or is excellent salted

Skirt—has a very wide, fibrous texture; delicious in fajitas

Leg top—includes braising steak

Leg—tough meat, so cook it slowly and then strip it off the bone

Teaching a calf to suck

If you want to feed the calf from a bucket, you will need to teach it to suck. To do this, try putting two fingers in its mouth and getting it to suck them. Then tease its head down into the bucket of milk, still sucking on your fingers, and once it starts sucking the milk, remove your hands. Feed a calf twice daily on one part warm water to three parts milk. After two weeks, introduce good-quality hay, and after four months wean it off milk and put it out on good pasture.

Keeping cattle for beef

Herds of cattle that are primarily kept for beef are likely to be successful if you allow the calves to remain with their mothers to suckle. These family groups are often referred to as "suckler herds." They take less effort to keep and, if you opt for a hardy heritage breed, they have a greater tendency to put on fat and produce marbling in the meat. Suckler herds also seem to do much better than other cattle in changeable weather conditions.

POTENTIAL PROBLEMS

■ **Mastitis** is a common complaint among cows where one or more teats become blocked and the resulting milk is useless.

■ **Other problems** include lameness, worms, foot rot, and milk fever. If your cattle suffer from any these, call your vet right away!

■ **Ask your vet** for information on the recommended vaccines in your area and keep your cattle well fed, with a clean water supply. Fortunately, cattle that are reared outdoors and kept naturally rarely get sick.

Keeping bees

Honey is the food bees produce for themselves from nectar. We started keeping bees 15 years ago in the garden of our suburban home because the honey we produce is far superior to anything from the supermarket, and the majority of imported honey. However, be wary of taking up beekeeping if you suffer from anaphylactic reactions to stings or have extreme allergic reactions.

Establishing your colony

To get started, you can order "package bees," essentially a swarm in a box—queen included—that arrives without brood or frames; establish a colony from a nucleus or small hive of about five frames that includes a laying queen; or you can buy yourself a colony that is already up and running, which is what we did.

Secondhand hives regularly come up for sale and your local beekeeping association will know what equipment is available. If you have never kept bees before, it is essential to spend time with a beekeepers' group, where you can get advice and share tips.

The elements of a hive

There are several styles of hives, but they all have the same main parts.

◾ **The brood box** is located at the base and is where the queen lives and new bees are hatched and tended. The queen lays eggs in the brood nest and, once hatched, the larvae are fed with pollen and honey stored around the nest.

◾ **The supers** stand above the brood and this is where the honey is stored. Some honey is stored in the brood, but a beekeeper takes the harvest of surplus honey from the supers. Make sure that there is a ¼ in (6 mm) gap, also known as "beespace," between

each frame in the super so the bees can move through the hive. Spacers are needed between some types of frame to maintain good "beespace." Smaller spacers are used in the brood box and larger spacers in the gaps of the supers.

◾ **The queen excluder** is a grill between the brood and supers and does just what it says: it prevents the queen from going up to the supers. It has holes wide enough for the worker bees to travel up and down but, due to her larger abdomen, the queen can't pass through the narrow gaps.

◾ **Frames** sit inside the brood and supers, and are the building blocks that enable your bees to start the honey-storing process. They normally have wooden sides enclosing a sheet of wax in hexagonal cell shapes to give the bees a head start.

Siting your hive

The position of your hive is of prime importance. Point it away from the prevailing wind and, if possible, facing east or southeast to catch the early morning sun.

If you live in an urban area, put a barrier made out of a willow hurdle in front of the entrance to your hives. This will help to force the bees' flight

1. Bees leave and enter the hive through small bee spaces in the sides of the super. 2. An open hive exposing the frames that stand upright within the super as it rests on the brood below. 3. Wear a bee suit with everything tucked in, as bees tend to crawl upward. Wear boots and gloves too. Hives are best positioned at least 3 ft (1 m) apart.

PROJECT **Gather honey**

Harvest your honey in late summer or early fall, but seek advice from a local beekeeper before you enter a hive. A smoker and centrifugal extractor are essential pieces of equipment. The smoker simulates a forest fire and encourages the bees to eat honey, making them nice and docile. The centrifugal extractor can be expensive to buy, but often you can borrow one from a beekeepers' association.

YOU WILL NEED
- Smoker
- Sharp knife
- Centrifugal honey extractor
- Glass jars

1. **Fill your smoker** with a fuel that smokes for a long time. We use dried rotted wood and rolled-up cardboard.   **2. Blow a few wisps** into the front of the hive and leave it for a few minutes while word spreads through the colony that it's time to get eating.   **3. Take out the heavy frames** and start scraping out the honey as quickly as possible—before the bees find out what you're up to!   **4. Use a sharp knife** heated in boiling water to cut just under the surface of the capping on each cell. This will allow the honey to ooze out.   **5. Secure four frames** that have had the caps cut off into a centrifugal honey extractor. Gently spin the handle until all the honey is flung onto the edges of the tub and drips down the sides to a sump with a spigot.   **6. Filter the honey** through a sieve to remove waxy bits, and store in sealed glass jars in a dark place.

path upward into the air when they exit the hive, rather than straight across your neighbors' yards. Provide a source of water near the hive so the bees don't become a nuisance around someone else's pond.

Maintaining the colony
Regularly check on the health and progress of your bees. The best time to inspect your hives is on warm afternoons when most of the colony is out gathering nectar and pollen. Make a routine inspection every week from April to October, checking that:
- **the queen** is still laying.
- **the brood** looks healthy and disease free.
- **the bees** have enough space for their honey—be prepared to add an extra super.

If you don't visit your hive regularly, you may find your bees have produced queen cells (by feeding selected larvae royal jelly) and they

may swarm, which means you will lose a large portion of your honey-producing worker bees. In addition, your bees will have glued everything together with layers of propolis. Moving them then jolts the other frames and you are likely to disturb your bees.

In years when the weather has been bad or the bees have suffered from disease, we don't harvest honey as it is the best food for your colony. When you do harvest, or when your bees are short of honey, you need to feed them so they survive the winter. Fill a plastic container with cold syrup made from 2¼ lb (1 kg) sugar heated in 2 pints (1 liter) of water. Cover the container with fine gauze and then add a lid with a small hole in it. Turn it upside down and place on the crown board on top of the uppermost super. The vacuum formed by the syrup in the container stops it from dribbling onto the hive.

POTENTIAL PROBLEMS
Stay up-to-date with information issued by beekeeping groups.
- **Varroa mite** This tiny parasite enters a brood cell and feeds on the larva. Check for infestation by inspecting brood cells and counting dead mites that have dropped out of the bottom of the hive. Control with pyrethroid strips, carefully following package instructions.
- **American foulbrood** This serious bacterial disease kills bee larvae, leaving them sticky and stringy. Antibiotic treatments are available, but spores can survive for decades, and badly infected hives may need to be destroyed. Call your state bee inspector for advice.
- **Swarming** Hives containing an older queen are more prone to swarming. A colony about to swarm can be distracted by moving the hive 6 ft (2 m) and turning it 180°. Put an empty hive in the original location and the bees should fill the new hive. Feed both until the colonies reestablish.

Game, fish, and vermin

Many city-dwellers struggle to come to terms with hunting for their food, while those of us brought up in the country take for granted that some animals are "fair game" when it comes to filling the pot. That said, gone are the days when anyone could have a gun or rod and help themselves to the bounty of the countryside. Licenses and permits are required.

SHOOTING TIPS

To become proficient, you need plenty of practice and attention to safety. Use these tips as a guide to key safety practices, controlling your pests, and becoming a better shot.

Safety
▪ **NEVER** point your gun at a person.
▪ **Do not** climb over fences or gates with a loaded weapon.
▪ **Never fire** at animals on the horizon.
▪ **Clean your gun** regularly and take it to a firearms dealer if there is a problem rather than risk using it.
▪ **If in doubt**—don't!

Practice
▪ **Always** zero your weapon before going shooting.
▪ **Buy plenty** of paper targets and practice on your groupings so that when you do go out you achieve a clean kill.
▪ **Keep practicing** until you are consistently accurate.
▪ **Try to lie down** or adopt a kneeling position.
▪ **Always aim** for head shots or shoot through the shoulder to hit the heart.
▪ **Control** your breathing and squeeze the trigger when you have half-exhausted your out-breath.

Stealth
▪ **Wear** warm, camouflaged clothing.
▪ **Stick to** fencerows when moving around.
▪ **Remain quiet** and try to avoid strong smells—which means no smoking, aftershave, or perfume.
▪ **Be patient** and don't rush a shot.
▪ **Take** your time.
▪ **Take a sharp knife** to swiftly dispatch an injured animal.
▪ **Invest in a night vision** sight if you go hunting regularly at dawn or dusk when light levels are low.

Hunting

Whatever your stance is on hunting, it is worth noting that a great deal of money and management goes into maintaining habitats for game species that might not otherwise have been invested if there was not a sporting tradition.

A certain amount of knowledge and skill is required before you start hunting. You can, of course, read about the subject, but there is no substitute for experience. If you wish to shoot with shotguns, most clay pigeon clubs welcome novices and will take the time to teach you from first principles. Until you are proficient and understand how to handle a weapon and traverse obstacles, you should not even contemplate going shooting. Even then, it is best to go out initially as an observer so you can learn from those with more experience.

Tools and equipment
▪ **If you are beginner**, buy an under-lever or break barrel .177 caliber or .20 air rifle, both of which have a straight trajectory and a knockdown power capable of killing rats, rabbits, and squirrels. For foxes you would need a shotgun or a more powerful .22 rifle.

1. We have years of experience *fishing rivers for trout and, since coming to Cornwall, salmon. If we were to be very honest, the time spent fishing compared to the catch we achieve is far from productive, but it is very relaxing.*
2. Rabbits *may be vermin, and cause untold damage to the vegetable patch, but they make fair game and are extremely tasty once skinned, butchered, and stewed (see page 217).*

Different weight air pellets suit different guns. We use dome head pellets as they offer greater accuracy.

Types of shoots

The two types of shoots that you may like to explore are:

Driven shoots, where a team of beaters walk through an area of land, driving the game in front of them toward the guns (who are static, standing at allotted pegs).

Rough shoots, where there is the opportunity to walk the land and to take whatever comes within range and is in season. This is always more of a lottery than driven shoots, but therein lies the excitement. And, of course, any vermin that present themselves can also be shot.

Before you hunt

There are a multitude of different recreational hunting and fishing licenses available across the US, including trapping, angling, shellfish, and so on. Some states require mandatory classes be completed prior to obtaining some licenses and permits. Check with your state's department of natural resources to be certain you get the necessary permits and follow all applicable laws and regulations relating to season dates and hours, bag limits, and disease reporting, where applicable.

Local knowledge and contacts are invaluable, so we recommend asking at your agricultural supplier or gun shop for some good leads. Never hunt on land that is posted, and remember that you should always get the landowner's permission before hunting or pursuing wounded game on private property, even if the land is not posted.

Fishing

As we live on an island and are also lucky enough to have masses of rivers, lakes, and lochs, a fishing

MAJOR NORTH AMERICAN FISH AND GAME	
Game	**Region**
American Bison	Wyoming, Montana, Alberta
Bass	all of US and Canada
Bear	all of US and Canada
Coyote	all of US and Canada
Deer	all of US and Canada
Duck	all of US and Canada
Goose	all of US and Canada
Groundhog	US Northeast, Southeast, Midwest; Canada
Moose	US Northeast, Northwest; Canada
Pheasant/Quail	all of US and Canada
Rabbit	all of US and Canada
Raccoon	all of US and Canada
Salmon	US Northeast, Northwest; Canada
Squirrel	all of US and Canada
Trout	all of US and Canada
Turkey	all of US and Canada
Wild Boar	US West, Southwest

opportunity is never far away. There are laws and regulations governing freshwater fishing, but shore fishing is free to all in the UK. In the US, you'll need to check with your state's department of natural resources to find out which types of fishing require you to buy a fishing license.

Freshwater fishing

Most freshwater fishing is for trout or salmon, which are classed as game fish, but that is only because we have forgotten that other types of fish are edible. British stock ponds used to be filled with species that are now only caught for sport and seem to have gained the reputation of being inedible. But eels, pike, carp, and perch—to name but a few—are eaten

in many parts of the world today, and are still classed as good food.

If you do decide to splash out on a rod license, you may also have to buy a permit to fish your chosen waters, and it will have to be in season. There are local variations to fishing seasons. All you will then need is the correct tackle and some skill and luck—easy, really.

Sea fishing

Our local fishmonger stocks fish that have been caught within a 40-mile radius of us, so we are spoiled for choice for fresh local fish. However, every once in a while we pop over the hill for a bit of fishing. We have a selection of rods, reels, and tackle that we have picked up from the classified ads or garage sales, so we have not spent much money on our equipment. That said, it's more than good enough. When fishing, we divide into groups, as follows:

■ **Those who wish to stay active** will either use spinners or mackerel feathers and cast and retrieve to their hearts' content. When there are mackerel around, this is a very successful method, and they make great fish for a barbecue or to stock the freezer. Truly fresh mackerel, simply filleted, seasoned, and popped onto the grill, are usually tasty enough to convert even the most skeptical of fish eaters.

■ **The less active group** bait fish, either on a float rig or ledgering on the bottom. This would appear to be the simpler option, but it does involve a little organizing of the bait. We keep some sand eels, squid, and mackerel in the freezer so we can go out fishing at any time.

Vermin

It is worth establishing the difference between game and vermin: game are animals that are hunted for food or sport (sometimes both), or for profit, whereas vermin are animals that spread disease or are unwelcome because they prey on (or have some other detrimental effect on) game animals. Of course, let's not forget that some vermin, like rabbits and pigeons, taste great too.

These small mammals, birds, and rodents can cause real problems around your property. From eating your crops to killing all of your chickens, vermin can really ruin your day. You can control them, however, as long as you keep within the boundaries of the law. Responsibility for controlling animal pests normally rests with you, the occupier of the land, and we have tried most of the methods below, normally with excellent results. We've even had a go at the theory that meat-eating men should pee around the perimeter of the plot to deter foxes.

■ **Rabbit populations** can be controlled in various ways (see box below). If your plot is under siege and your vegetables or grazing pastures are suffering, get a hound, buy an air rifle, and consider raising some ferrets. If you are shooting at a group of rabbits, start with the one farthest away, and then work your way back until they scatter. We would also suggest investing in an electronic "shot detector" to avoid breaking a tooth if you are planning on eating them. Common signs of rabbit activity in your area, as well as actual sightings, include closely grazed grass, fresh droppings, and rabbit-sized holes in fencing.

■ **Rats and mice** are all around us, and although they deserve to be seen as a threat to productivity and as a health hazard, we also accept that they are simply competing for space and don't need to be completely eradicated, just kept in check. For us, "rat warfare" on the farm involves setting a series of traps and sometimes putting poison down on their known routes.

■ **Foxes** have had a huge amount of press coverage in recent years with the abolition of fox hunting in the UK. Our stance is that prevention is better than cure. We prevent foxes from becoming a problem by protecting our animals with well-maintained electric fences, putting our poultry away every night, and owning two big dogs. If this doesn't work for you,

1 & 2. The normal balance of cat and dog *control seems to work for us; a hound is a particularly good rabbit chaser, while cats are, of course, superlative mousers.* **3. To protect our geese and ducks** *from predators, we make sure they are behind a wire fence by day and in their houses by night.*

TRY THIS

■ **Keeping ferrets** can be fun and functional. There is plenty of literature on the subject and we think it is a fairly natural way to reduce the rabbit populations over the winter months.

■ **Setting snares** can be effective, but it could also be considered cruel and is subject to legal restrictions. Properly practiced, it can quickly solve a pest problem. We recommend talking to local pest control experts and checking with your state's department of natural resources first.

■ **Shooting vermin** is our preferred method for dealing with rabbit and rat problems.

■ **Poisoning rats** and mice is only used as a last resort.

PROJECT Skin, draw, and butcher a rabbit

If you have been out controlling your rabbits and intend to eat them, the first thing to do with your dead animal is to hold it up by its front legs and stroke firmly down its abdomen a couple of times to empty the bladder. To allow them to cool, keep your rabbits separate rather than piled up or bundled into a bag.

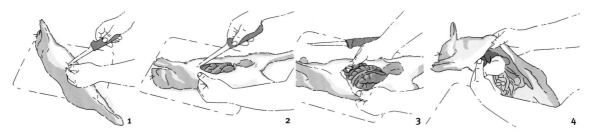

1. Place the rabbit on its back and pinch a bit of the belly skin to pull it away from the body cavity. Nick it with the knife, without sticking it into the belly.   **2. Carefully cut** the skin along the belly and, if you wish, cut down to the feet, without damaging the internal organs (or it can get messy).   **3. Pull back** the skin to expose the intestines.   **4. Turn the rabbit** belly-side down and shake out the innards.

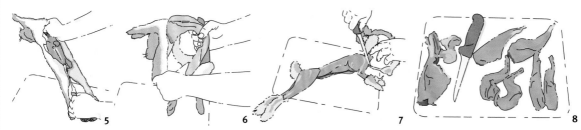

5. Cut around the "vent" and remove all droppings and lower intestines.   **6. Ease the skin** from the back and, holding the carcass in one hand and the skin in the other, pull them apart like a set of chest expanders.   **7. The skin** will roll down over the legs and come off, leaving fur on only the feet and tail. Chop off the head and trim off the feet and tail. **8. Carve the rabbit** with a sharp knife: back bones and hips for stock (left), rear legs (top), front legs (middle), and loin (right).

consider setting snares or shooting them (see below).

Squirrels can do some serious damage in areas where their numbers get out of control. If you need to cull the local population, we suggest setting up live traps, shooting them, and raking their drays with a long pole before they nest. You can eat them, but they are a nuisance to skin.

Prevention is better than cure

Dealing with vermin can be a complex process, but the best thing to do is to keep your property as neat and well maintained as possible. It is good practice to keep your feed stored in sealed bins or containers with lids, and suspend feeders for poultry slightly above the ground. Other forms of prevention include:

Fencing. If you have a vegetable garden that is being ravaged daily by rabbits, you could try putting up fencing to deter them. Buy fine metal mesh about 4 ft (1.2 m) wide. Bury at least 8 in (20 cm) below the ground in a trench, with 3 ft (1 m) above the ground. This option works for some people, but we would be wary of spending lots of money on fencing that is unlikely to completely prevent rabbits from getting to your carrots. Instead, we perceive a small-scale rabbit problem as a delicious source of free food waiting to make the journey from your garden to the kitchen. On the other hand, electric fencing offers good protection for poultry from foxes (see page 175).

Dogs and cats. We keep cats here at Newhouse Farm primarily as a form of vermin control. We always make sure that our cats are spayed to avoid fulfilling that farmyard stereotype with hundreds of cats and kittens hiding in every barn! The cats keep down the numbers of rats and mice, as well as being lovely pets. Our dogs are useful for deterring foxes, rabbits, and sometimes rats. The ideal breed of dog for catching rats is definitely a terrier, particularly a Jack Russell or other small terrier. Our two dogs are a pleasure to have as pets, but it's also great that they earn their keep by patrolling the property.

IN THE KITCHEN We practically live in our kitchen. Eating freshly cooked, high-quality food is a real pleasure, and we love to run out into the garden, see what's ready, and plan supper around the best produce. Even if you don't have enough space for a kitchen garden, you can still enjoy food at its best by buying fresh, local, seasonal produce. In this chapter, you'll learn about lots of traditional kitchen crafts, and may even discover that you're a natural cheese-maker or artisan baker. With a pantry full of homemade chutneys and colorful jams, you'll find yourself smiling every time you open the cupboard.

Eco-kitchens

The kitchen is the heart of many homes—it's where we have our morning cup of coffee, preserve garden produce, enjoy family meals, and entertain guests. But the kitchen is also where we use the most energy, and conserving it by preparing and cooking food with care is one of the easiest ways to reduce the bills. We also minimize food waste and ensure that none ends up in a landfill.

Avoiding food waste

The first step to creating an eco-friendly kitchen is to avoid any food waste and prevent any from reaching a landfill site. This means eating products before their expiration dates and buying in bulk, which reduces packaging and travel costs to and from stores.

Sort the contents of your pantry by food type and arrange products like the aisle of a supermarket so that you can easily see what you have and what needs replacing. In our pantry we have one clearly labeled shelf for open condiments and another marked "Closed for storage," which prevents us from opening too many jars at the same time. You may also find that pull-out baskets are useful for fresh produce.

We have invested in sealed plastic containers to store bulk buys, such as sugar, flour, and oats. If you don't have space to store large amounts of food, then you can try to set up a share arrangement with friends or family, which allows you to save money on bulk deliveries but have smaller quantities to store.

Remember, too, that "best before" dates on products simply refer to the time when food is at its best, so it will usually be okay to eat for a while after that date. The only foods you should avoid after their expiration date are eggs and mayo. If more perishable food is close to its expiration date and you are going away for a few days, or have other plans, freeze it.

Another great way to reduce food waste is to be creative and make meals with leftovers. Try established leftover recipes or experiment with your own. You could try throwing old apples into a pan with sausages or using some stale cookies as a crumble topping. The possibilities are endless.

Low-energy cooking

Most ovens are powered by gas or electricity. Electricity is the most inefficient option, as energy is converted from fossil fuels to electricity and then back to heat; taking energy directly from gas to heat is more efficient. However, the most sustainable choice is an electric oven powered by renewables on a "green" energy plan.

Another green fuel option is wood. Wood is a carbon-neutral fuel and modern wood burners are highly efficient (see pages 82–83). Although we find that using a wood burner for cooking only makes sense on colder days, it is at these times when a warm hot pot is just what we want. When cooking on a wood burner, make sure you use a pan or pot with a thick base, and start nice and early, as cooking times are much longer. When the wood burner is fired up, we also use it to boil a kettle, and to heat water for washing the dishes.

Earth ovens also burn wood as fuel. However, we only really use our outside oven in the warmer months.

USING A HAY BOX

One way to save energy while cooking is to turn off the oven or burner just before your food is completely cooked, and allow the heat in the pan to continue the process for you using a traditional method called a hay box.

■ **You will need** a box made from plastic or metal. Fill it with dry hay.
■ **Cook your food** in the usual way until it is hot but not completely cooked.
■ **Turn off the heat**, then quickly place the pot or pan into the hay box on a layer of straw. Make sure you cover the pot with more hay and seal the lid.
■ **Leave for a few hours** while your food continues to cook in your insulated homemade oven. Plan well ahead—the normal cooking time for this method is about 4–5 hours, though it varies greatly depending on what you're cooking. Experiment, but make very sure that any meat is fully cooked through.

Best for liquid-based food, hay boxes use the heat energy already in the pan to finish the cooking process. Line the box with hay and cover the pan with plenty more. The lid should fit tightly to keep the heat in.

1. **Slow cooking** *on a wood burner is perfect for a warming stew, and to boil a kettle for tea.* 2. **Shallow shelves** *allow us to see all our food so none festers at the back of the cupboard.* 3. **Buy flour in bulk;** *it has less packaging and you will always have some on hand to make fresh bread.*

Pressure cookers

Old-fashioned pressure cookers used to be a bit scary, but modern versions are absolutely safe and very easy to use. They are far more energy-efficient than conventional pots and pans because the higher internal temperature and pressure they exert cooks food in a third of the time. In addition, more of the vitamins and minerals in foods are retained when cooked in a pressure cooker. If you want to live a greener life and save a bit of money at the same time, then a pressure cooker is a must-have eco-gadget for the kitchen.

Engine cooking

When traveling, food available at service stations or rest areas can be a real disappointment. It often has lots of packaging and the only choice available is unhealthy fast food. The eco answer is "engine cooking," after which road trips will never be the same again. Simply find a spot under the hood of your car with no moving parts that heats up while driving. Then, before you set off, wrap the meal you wish to cook in two or three layers of foil and start your journey. By the end of your trip your meal on wheels should be ready.

Kelly kettles

Ideal for making hot drinks while you are working outside, a kelly, or volcano, kettle has a double-walled chimney that you fill with water. Then fill the fire base with twigs and dry grass, and light. Heat goes up the chimney, and the good surface contact area with the water leads to faster boiling.

QUICK TIPS

Try these simple tips to reduce food waste, transport costs, and your energy consumption.

Shopping

■ **Order food in bulk**; we order ours from an organic wholesaler, allowing us to enjoy the benefits of organic produce at a cheaper rate. The food also has far less packaging.

■ **Buy from local shops** rather than supermarkets. This reduces your transport costs and the food may also contain fewer preservatives. We are lucky to have local butchers, grocers, and a man who brings fresh local fish to the village.

■ **Buy a good variety of food** to make cooking more exciting and create different menus every day.

■ **Make a shopping list**; check your pantry before you go, and only replace items that you've used up. Stick firmly to your list.

■ **Opt for recyclable packaging** by choosing juice and condiments in glass rather than plastic bottles. Glass can be recycled infinitely and you can reuse jars at home to make more preserves or chutney.

■ **Choose long-life products** like canned beans, dried fruit, nuts, pasta, noodles, rice, and grains, which are unlikely to spoil before you have a chance to use them.

Cooking

■ **Just cover veggies with water** ; the less you use, the quicker it will boil. Don't throw excess water away after cooking; allow it to cool and use it to make stock, or feed it to your plants.

■ **Cover pans,** as the lids prevent heat loss. Also ensure that pots and pans cover the stove burners to maximize their efficiency.

■ **Try using a solar dryer** for cooking in the summer (see pages 244–245).

■ **Try one-pot cooking** like stews and soups that take one burner to cook and produce fewer dishes to wash.

■ **Allow food to cool** before freezing or refrigerating, as previously cooled food won't need as much energy.

■ **Don't fill teakettles**—only use as much water as you need.

■ **Keep the oven door closed**—opening it to check on food wastes energy. Leave the oven door open after cooking to heat the room, or use the heat to dry mushrooms or herbs.

Preserving the harvest

Certain times of the year bring with them a bountiful supply of produce, but the harvesting season is often short and sweet. However, you can make the most of these seasonal gluts by storing and preserving your produce, allowing you to enjoy it all year round. Some preserving methods also intensify flavors and make tasty treats to cheer you up on cold winter days.

Filling the pantry

If you are living and eating in tune with the seasons, you will notice a change in the types of food available locally at different times of the year. Yet by eating purely seasonal produce you could find yourself with a vitamin deficiency in the cold dark days of winter, which a supply of stored summer crops can help to remedy. Besides, there comes a time in the depths of winter when all you really want is a fruity dessert or some fresh tomato sauce with pasta. To achieve this, you need to look ahead in summer and early fall, and store your produce when it is ripe. Get the technique right, too, so that you don't end up with a jar of inedible mold.

Best preserving methods

▪ **Pickling and making chutney** (see pages 236–237) can actually improve the taste of your produce, as well as preserve it. The processes rely on preserving food in vinegar and flavoring it with spices and other ingredients. Both pickles and chutneys are delicious with cold meats, cheese, and curries.

▪ **Making jams and jellies** (see pages 238–239) is a great way to preserve all those fruits that grow in excess during the summer and early fall.

▪ **Canning** (see page 240–241) needs precision and attention to detail, but yields colorful jars of summery fruit and vegetables.

▪ **Drying** (see pages 242–245) is the oldest method of preserving produce, and it is also one of the cheapest and simplest. Here at Newhouse Farm we frequently dry herbs, tomatoes, seeds, chile peppers, salamis, and hams, and have built a solar dryer (see pages 244–245).

▪ **Curing** (see pages 246–247) is a preserving technique that is normally reserved for meat and fish. It usually involves using large amounts of salt to draw the moisture out of meat or fish and so make it inhospitable to harmful microorganisms.

▪ **Hot and cold smoking** (see pages 248–251) are methods used to preserve food, but are more reliable if you cure or dry it first. Today, smoking is primarily used for flavoring, rather than as a preserving technique. Having said that, if you smoke something for long enough, it will also dry out enough for storage.

▪ **Clamping** and using a sand box (see pages 164–165) are other traditional storage techniques that are very easy to do at home.

▪ **Freezing** allows you to store a wide selection of meats, fish, fruits, and vegetables. We also often freeze soups and leftovers once they have cooled down. The benefit of freezing fruit and vegetables is that most of the nutritional value is retained, but the drawback is that the texture of foods can be lost. Make sure you label and date your bags and containers, and that you organize your freezer well, with the newest produce at the back, or you will end up losing last year's frozen peas until the next ice age.

1. Vegetables *and other garden produce are best preserved as soon as possible after picking.* **2. Canning** *is a good way to preserve fruits, but vegetables require pressure canning.* **3. Freeze berries** *on trays before putting them into bags.*

THE PRESERVING YEAR

Winter/early spring

■ **Brussels sprouts** These can be blanched and frozen, but we try to time the growing season so they are harvested fresh on Christmas morning.

■ **Cabbage** Pickling is an effective preserving method, especially for red cabbage.

■ **Rutabagas** Set up a clamp or store in a sand box.

Mid-spring

■ **Asparagus** If you have an abundance of spears, blanch them for 2 minutes and then freeze them.

■ **Spinach** You could freeze it, but do so as soon as possible after harvesting.

■ **Sage and rosemary** Drying is the quickest and most effective method for most herbs.

Late spring

■ **Mushrooms** Dry in a solar dryer or oven and then store in jars in a dark cupboard. They will need rehydrating before you use them for cooking, but they last for ages.

■ **Radishes** Slice and pickle them in vinegar.

■ **Gooseberries** Frozen berries retain their original taste.

■ **Dill** We store dill alongside salmon when we make our own gravlax. This involves placing salt, dill, and salmon under pressure in a small press.

■ **Mint** Consider drying it to make a tin of tea leaves for a refreshing herbal tea.

Early summer

■ **Rhubarb** Stems of rhubarb can be canned, retaining much of their flavor.

■ **Broad beans (fava beans)** These are best blanched and then thrown into the freezer.

■ **Carrots** You could place them in a sand box or a clamp—or freeze them.

■ **Onions** Dry on a wire tray and then braid to hang up and dry. Don't leave them in the dark or they will start to sprout.

■ **Peas** No contest: freeze them if you have a glut.

■ **Red currants** Freeze red currants or turn them into a deliciously sweet jelly.

■ **Strawberries** Making strawberry leather is a nice way to preserve strawberries for a little longer. Pulp the fruit, mix with sugar, and then roll it into thin strips and lay them on muslin to dry in the sun. The result is a chewy fruit snack.

■ **Beets** Either pickle them or place in sand trays ready for roasting or turning into mash.

Midsummer

■ **Cucumber** Cucumber pickles are very tasty and popular.

■ **Chile peppers** We either preserve our fiery peppers in spicy chutneys or dry them on lengths of string and then store them in sealed jars.

■ **Potatoes** These are best stored in a clamp or in a big paper sack in a dark and dry place (1).

■ **Runner beans** Trim them, slice diagonally into thin strips, blanch for 2 minutes, and,

when they have been drained and cooled, freeze them.

■ **Tomatoes** We add them to chutneys, make canned sauces, and sun-dry them.

■ **Raspberries** Turn them into jam or store in the freezer if you have a glut (2).

■ **Thyme** Store stems using the traditional drying method, and make salt rubs for barbecues.

■ **Chives** Chopping them up and freezing in ice cube trays works really well.

■ **Lemon verbena** Dry some of this aromatic herb and use it to make a relaxing tea.

Late summer

■ **Garlic** Heads of garlic are stored at Newhouse Farm in braids that hang just outside the kitchen for easy use. We also pickle some cloves.

■ **Globe artichokes** We like to cook them with herbs and other delicious flavorings and then store them in oil.

■ **Blueberries** These freeze particularly well.

■ **Blackberries** An amazing crop to forage for around your fencerows if they grow wild in your area; they freeze well.

■ **Coriander (cilantro) seed** Simple to dry, and they add huge amounts of flavor to curries, dressings, and oils.

Early fall

■ **Horseradish** Around this time of year we make jars of horseradish sauce.

■ **Grapes** The only methods of preserving grapes that we

are prepared to consider are adding them to chutney, or using them to make our own wine (see pages 256–257).

Mid-fall

■ **Apples** Cider is one way to preserve apples (see pages 260–261) (3). Or wrap them in newspaper and keep in the storeroom, or slice and make sun-dried apple rings.

■ **Squash** Just before or right after the first frost, harvest the squashes by cutting them off the stems and store them in nets or on shelves in a dark place; they should last until the following year.

■ **Cranberries** We are traditionalists when it comes to cranberries. We try to make our own cranberry sauce and keep it untouched until Christmas day to enjoy with our home-reared turkey.

■ **Sweet chestnuts and walnuts** These nuts are very easy to freeze.

■ **Leeks** Freeze them, but they are happy left in the ground— the simplest storage of all.

■ **Cauliflower** Use to make your own piccalilli (4).

Late fall

■ **Parsnips** Best stored in clamps or in sand boxes.

Making cream, butter, and yogurt

If you have a cow or goat, then making cream, butter, and yogurt is a great way to make the most of their milk. It's also enormously satisfying to make your own dairy products, even if you live in the city with no animals and have to go out and buy the milk. We often whisk up a batch of butter to go with some home-baked bread, and always make enough to freeze some for later.

Skimming milk for cream

If you milk a cow or goat and then leave a bowl of the milk to stand at room temperature, the cream will separate naturally and rise to the surface. You can then skim it off with a skimmer—a flat, saucer-shaped utensil about 8 in (20 cm) across, traditionally made out of wood or tin, and perforated with small holes to allow the excess milk to drain away.

The alternative way to separate cream from milk is to use a specially designed shallow trough, often made of slate, with a drain in the base. Pour the milk in and wait for the cream to rise. Once the cream is almost solid, pull the plug and the milk runs away into a vessel below, leaving you with a trough of cream.

If you are buying milk to make cream, you need nonhomogenized (cream-top) whole milk. Some farm stores, supermarkets, and home-delivery dairies sell it. You can't use homogenized milk because the homogenization process stops the fat, or cream, from separating out.

Souring milk for yogurt

Yogurt is milk that has been soured with lactic-acid bacteria. It's easy to make your own: simply stir about 2 tbsp (30 ml) of store-bought live yogurt into about a quart (liter) of full-fat or reduced-fat milk. Cover the container and leave in a warm environment to work overnight. We recommend using a hay box (see pages 222–3). The yogurt is ready to eat when it has a thick consistency, at which point it's probably best to move it to the refrigerator. However, if you want to keep your yogurt culture alive and use it to make more than one batch, keep it in the hay box, and every time you take out some yogurt to eat, replace it with the same quantity of fresh milk.

Souring cream for butter

Cream can easily be turned into butter. First, you need to sour the cream by encouraging bacteria to turn some of the lactose into lactic acid. This will happen naturally in warm weather; for a quicker result and on cooler days, add a few teaspoons of already soured cream or yogurt to the cream and stir to mix.

Clotted cream

Clotted cream is made by heating milk so that the cream becomes very thick and forms a yellow crust. Leave fresh milk for 12 hours at room temperature, then heat it to 197°F (92°C). Cool it immediately by pouring it into a bowl. Once cool, leave it in the refrigerator for a further 24 hours, then skim off the delicious homemade clotted cream.

FLAVORED BUTTER

Freeze flavored butter for up to three months. Add slices to fish or steak for an instant sauce. Try:
- Dried thyme and salt
- Chopped chives
- Chopped parsley and lemon zest
- Sage and whole-grain mustard

Add salt and herbs *to fresh butter and roll up in wax paper.*

1. Fresh homemade butter *that was made in a traditional wooden mold.*
2. Thick clotted cream *is great with strawberries and shortbread.*

RECIPE **Homemade butter**

Shaking sour cream (see opposite) turns it into butter. You can simply use an electric mixer to do this—you don't need a butter churn. If the cream is at a temperature of about 68°F (20°C) then the butter will "come" (change from cream to butter) in a matter of minutes.

YOU WILL NEED
- 1 quart (1 liter) heavy cream
- 3 tsp live natural yogurt
- Salt
- Electric mixer
- Wooden cutting board
- Butter pats and stamp
- Mold or wax paper

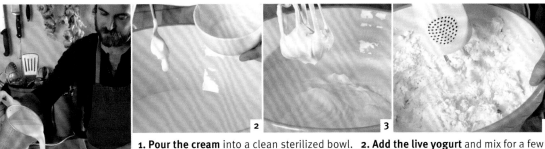

1. Pour the cream into a clean sterilized bowl. **2. Add the live yogurt** and mix for a few minutes. **3. The consistency** starts to change to make soft peaks. **4. Continue mixing** until the cream looks like scrambled eggs and turns pale yellow. After 2–3 minutes more, small globules of butter form. Add a little cold, clean water when the mixture looks like a firm mass of butter globules and keep mixing for 1 minute on low speed. Pour off the milky by-product (buttermilk) and keep it for making pancakes (see box).

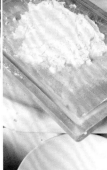

5. Use butter pats or wooden spatulas to transfer the butter to a wooden cutting board for washing. (Butter pats are grooved paddles.) **6. Mix and squeeze** the butter with the pats. Keep adding more water to wash the butter—this stops it from turning rancid later on. **7. Collect the buttermilk** as it washes off. Continue rinsing the butter with water and collecting buttermilk until the liquid runs clear.

IRISH BUTTERMILK PANCAKES

Soda flour mix
- 1 lb (500 g) all-purpose flour
- 1 tsp (5 ml) cream of tartar
- 1 tsp (5 ml) baking soda
- ½ tsp (2.5 ml) salt
- ½ tsp (2.5 ml) sugar

For the pancakes
- 4 cups (500 g) soda flour
- 1½ cups (300 ml) buttermilk
- 2 small eggs

Make a well in the flour and crack the eggs into it. Whisk together with a fork, gradually adding the buttermilk to make a batter. Oil and heat a griddle or frying pan and drop in spoonfuls of the batter. Cook for 2–3 minutes on each side.

8. Layer the butter in a mold, salting it with at least 2 percent of its weight in salt. **9. Push the layers** down to drive out air bubbles. **10. Stamp** the butter to decorate. If you don't have a mold, roll up the butter in wax paper instead.

Making your own cheese

Making cheese originally began as a way of using up surplus milk, and it's a useful technique to learn if you keep cows or goats. Even if you don't produce your own milk, making cheese is still extremely creative and gives you the chance to experiment by adding homegrown herbs to flavor your own delicious soft and hard cheeses.

What is cheese?

Cheese is milk that has been left in a warm place, or has had additives mixed with it, which increases its acidity and causes curds and whey to form. Cheese is made from the curds.

Delicious and a great source of protein, cheese is also very high in calories, even more so than some cuts of meat, although soft cheese made from reduced-fat milk is a less fattening option.

What milk to use

If you don't own milking animals, buy whole or reduced-fat milk to make cheese (avoid fat-free milk). Unlike making cream (see pages 226–227), you can use homogenized milk. Pasteurized milk is fine for cheese-making, as long as you use an effective starter (see right) and allow the lactic-acid bacteria to develop overnight before you begin.

Making soft cheese

You can make soft cheese by allowing some milk to curdle naturally on warm days in summer, or by adding a coagulant. It is fairly tasteless, which gives you the opportunity to be adventurous with flavorings (see recipe opposite). Cream cheese is a soft cheese made with curdled cream instead of milk. It has a smoother texture and more buttery taste.

Making hard cheese

A great way to preserve the summer glut of fresh milk for the winter, hard cheese was traditionally made from the milk from more than one cow, and from an evening and a morning's milking. The process was started off with evening milk and morning milk was added next day. But don't worry if you have no cows—we get great results using organic supermarket milk (see pages 230–231).

Using a starter

"Starters" are batches of milk that are very high in lactic-acid bacteria, which speeds up the cheese-making process. You can buy milk-based starters from a cheesemaking supplier or make your own. We make ours by leaving a quart (liter) of reduced-fat milk at 81–86°F (27–30°C) for 24 hours to go sour—this is known as the "mother culture."

Then skim off the top layer of the starter and add it to another pint of reduced-fat milk. Cover with a cloth and leave for another 24 hours at 70°F (21°C) to create the culture.

Using a coagulant

Rennet is a key ingredient in cheese-making. It comes from the stomach of a calf, goat, or lamb, and is the enzyme that causes milk to coagulate into curds and whey. Milk that is curdled with rennet without further processing is known as junket.

For vegetarian cheese, buy rennet made from fermented microorganisms, plant extracts, or synthetic animal rennet—or use lemon juice.

1. Soft cheese *doesn't need rennet to help the milk curdle—lemon juice will do the job—making it an ideal vegetarian option. Serve it with rustic slices of hot buttered toast.* **2. Homemade hard cheese** *will keep for months if stored correctly, but in practice it gets eaten all too quickly. This version has been rolled in finely chopped fresh chives for a mild oniony flavor. Serve with a stack of traditional oat cakes.*

RECIPE Soft cheese

Soft cheese is quick and easy to make, and is ready to eat in less than 24 hours. It doesn't keep for long and needs to be eaten quickly. Its mild taste gives you the chance to jazz it up with different flavorings, from classic crushed garlic and chopped fresh herbs to coarsely crushed peppercorns.

YOU WILL NEED
- Large pan
- Slotted spoon
- Muslin bag
- String
- 1 quart (liter) milk
- Juice from a lemon
- Chopped herbs
- Chopped garlic
- Salt and pepper

1. Bring a pan of milk to a gentle simmer. Remove from heat immediately and add the lemon juice. Stir the milk, which will start to curdle. **2. Use a slotted spoon** to put the curds into a muslin bag. Tie up the bag with string. **3. Hang the curds** above a bowl or sink overnight, to allow the whey to drip out.

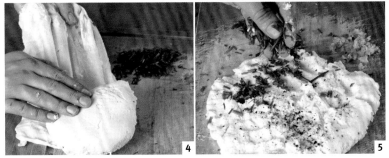

4. Unwrap the curds and you'll see that they have turned into a homemade soft cheese. **5. Spread the cheese** out on a work surface and mix in some flavorings. We used chopped fresh chives, crushed garlic, and salt and pepper. The soft cheese lasts a few days when stored in the refrigerator.

CREAM CHEESE

Warm some cream slowly until it is curdled. Leave the curds in the whey overnight. Then drain the whey off and cut up the curd with a long-bladed knife. Add some salt and some butter if you want it to taste a bit richer, and tie it up in a muslin bag. Hang the bag for a day to drip. The following day, tighten the bag up and leave it to hang for a month. You can leave it for up to four months to mature, but we are never that patient!

BUY LOCAL

We don't have time to make as much cheese as we would like, so we buy a selection of local cheeses. There has been a revival in small-scale dairies who take pride in producing truly delicious cheese. Look around and do some research into which regional specialties are available in your area, instead of opting for a bland block of Cheddar from some distant factory. Another option when choice is limited is to buy ordinary, uninspiring cheese and smoke it at home to add rich, exciting flavor (see pages 250–251).

RECIPE **Hard cheese**

We used to think that making cheese was only possible if you had all sorts of high-tech equipment and scientific knowledge, but in fact cheese can be made in the comfort of your kitchen. Clean all equipment thoroughly with scalding-hot water before starting. If you've got enough self-restraint, you'll find the taste of cheese greatly improves with age.

YOU WILL NEED

- Large settling pan to hold 2 gallons (8 liters)
- Cooking thermometer
- Muslin
- Long-bladed knife
- Sieve, ladle, slotted spoon
- Mold, heavy weight

- 2 gallons (8 liters) whole milk
- 1 heaping tablespoon of starter
- Small carton live yogurt
- 1 tsp (5 ml) rennet
- Salt
- Chopped chives or other fresh herbs

SEPARATING THE CURDS AND WHEY

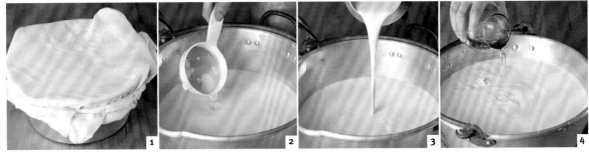

1. Pour 1 gallon (4 liters) of whole milk into a settling pan. Heat it to 68°F (20°C). Remove from heat, add the starter and half a cup of live yogurt, cover the pan with muslin, and leave it overnight. **2. Skim off the cream** with a sieve and heat it in a separate pan to about 86°F (30°C). Stir this back into the first pan of milk. **3. Add another** gallon (4 liters) of milk. Heat gently to 90°F (32°C). **4. Mix a teaspoon of rennet** with a cup of cold water. Remove pan from heat and pour in the rennet.

5 & 6. Stir the milk for 5 minutes using your hands. Stop stirring when the mixture starts to stick to your fingers as it separates into curds and whey. **7. Stroke the surface** of the mixture with the rounded bottom of a sieve to stop cream from rising to the surface. Do this for a good 5 minutes so that the cream gets trapped in the curds. Leave the curds and whey to stand for an hour. **8. Ladle off the whey** into another pan and reserve a little of it for step 10. **9. Dice the curds** into ¼-in (5-mm) cubes using a long-bladed knife, to release more whey. Ladle off the whey.

PITCHING THE CURDS

10. **Heat the curds with a little whey** to 97°F (39°C), stirring with your hands, to cook the mixture. It should look like scrambled eggs. **11. Test the acidity** of the curds with the pitching test. Stretch a small amount between your fingers: if it doesn't snap before it reaches ½ in (1 cm), it's ready. If it fails the test, leave it for a bit longer. Break the curd up into small pieces about the size of a walnut. You can do this using your fingers. This stage is known as "milling." **12. Let the curds settle.** Add herbs and spices and other flavorings at this point if you want to.

MOLDING, PRESSING, AND SALTING

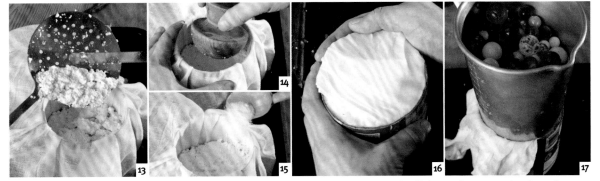

13. **Lift the curds** into a muslin-lined mold using a slotted spoon. Use a knife to slide off the curds. We used a clean tin can as a mold. You should be able to make 2 small cheeses. **14 & 15. Press the curds** into the mold in layers (we used a wooden garlic crusher) and add salt between layers—1½ tbsp (25 g) for every 1 lb (500 g) of curds. **16. Bring in the ends** of the muslin to cover the top of the cheese. **17. Place a weight on top,** such as a mug filled with marbles. Leave overnight.

18. **Unwrap the cheese** and wash in warm water. Turn it upside down, rewrap, and weigh it down again for another day. **19. Unwrap the cheese** and roll it in chopped chives or any fresh herbs. **20. Wrap it back up** in the muslin and weigh down for another two days. Remove the old muslin and wrap the cheese in a fresh piece. Store on a shelf at about 55–61°F (13–16°C). Turn the cheese daily for the first week and then weekly after that.

Baking bread

Even if you're a long way from the self-sufficient life, the smell of freshly made bread is reason enough for baking it regularly at home instead of buying it. There is an amazing variety of breads you can make in the comfort of your kitchen, and whatever kind you decide on, and whichever type of grain you use, the process is simple. So experiment, be inventive, and have fun.

Variety is the spice of life

Bread can be broadly divided into two types plus sourdough:

▨ **Leavened breads,** such as white or whole-grain bread, rye bread, and bagels, each of which use yeast as a rising agent.

▨ **Unleavened breads,** such as pita bread and flour tortillas.

▨ **Sourdough** (see pages 234–235) is a rising bread that doesn't use yeast.

Yeast

Yeast-leavened breads are the most commonly found breads; they rise when the yeast converts the sugars in the flour into alcohol and carbonic gases. After the alcohol has evaporated, the carbon dioxide makes bubbles in the dough, giving it that unmistakable fluffy texture. Yeast is a temperamental ingredient that needs warmth to flourish, but don't expose it to temperatures over 95°F (35°C) or you'll kill it.

Fresh yeast looks like soft putty with a strong yeasty smell. Refrigerate it or freeze it in 1-in (2.5-cm) cubes. We prefer it to dried yeast, but if you are using dried, use half the weight stated for fresh in the recipe.

Kneading

Pummeling your dough is not only a very important part of the bread-making process; it is also a superb stress-buster. While you're dissolving your pent-up tension, you're also distributing the yeast evenly through the dough and developing the gluten strands, without which the bread simply wouldn't have the elasticity and strength to be able to rise properly. It can be treated harshly and will love you for it. Push and pull the dough until it becomes silky and elastic. After a while, do the window pane test: stretch a portion of dough between your hands until it forms a thin sheet that you can see light through. (If it tears, it's not ready.)

Now put the dough aside until it has doubled in size. You'll know the bread is fully risen if it springs back to its original size when you stick your finger in it.

Experiment with flours

Try traditional breads from your local bakery and a variety of flours in your baking instead of buying tasteless, fluffy loaves from the supermarket. Here are some of our favorite flours:

▨ **Wheat flour,** which is a rich source of fiber as well as protein and vitamins B and E. It is also rich in gluten, rises very well, and produces a workable, stretchy dough.

▨ **Rye flour,** a traditionally dark, heavy flour with a slightly sour taste and an excellent chewy texture, is a favorite in much of eastern Europe. It is low in gluten and a popular choice for people with wheat intolerance.

▨ **Barley flour** is extra-delicious if you toast the barley flour first. It makes a lovely, sweet-tasting bread. We mix one-third barley flour with two-thirds wheat flour for a good loaf. Barley is also low in gluten.

▨ **Spelt flour** is made from the earliest known grain and is especially high in protein, vitamins, and minerals as well as being naturally low in gluten. The loaf can be fairly dry, so add some wheat flour if you want it to rise well.

WHOLE-GRAIN BREAD

▨ 1½ lb (600 g) spelt or whole-grain flour
▨ 2 tsp yeast
▨ 1½ cups (400 ml) water
▨ 3 oz (100 g) mixed seeds
▨ 2 tsp salt

▨ **Mix the flour and yeast** in a bowl and add the water (in cold weather, use tepid water to activate the yeast).

▨ **Work the mixture into a dough,** spread it on a work surface, and knead it thoroughly until it is elastic. Sprinkle the salt over it and then most of the seeds.

▨ **Use a scraper** to bring in the edges of dough. Consolidate it into a neat shape.

▨ **Put the dough in an oiled bowl,** spray with oil, cover with a damp dish towel, and leave it in a warm place to rise.

▨ **Knock back the dough,** divide it into halves, and put them in oiled loaf tins.

▨ **Spray with water** to make a sticky surface, and sprinkle with seeds. Cover with plastic wrap and leave for 2 hours.

▨ **Bake at 400°F (200°C)** for 20 minutes. Knock out of the tins and bake on a tray for another 10 minutes to form a crust.

RECIPE **Herby white rolls**

There will be bread-baking purists wondering why we have included white rolls here, but we have never found another sort of bread that makes quite such good toast. Use the herbs listed, or forage for others, such as wild garlic, or add seeds or honey.

YOU WILL NEED
- 2 lb (1 kg) bread flour
- 1 pint (600 ml) warm water
- 1 oz (30 g) fresh yeast
- 3 tbsp olive oil
- 1 tbsp (20 g) salt
- Handful of mixed herbs, such as sage, rosemary, and thyme
- Oil spray, loaf tin, plastic wrap

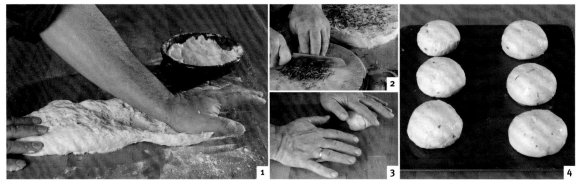

1. Mix together all the ingredients except for the salt and herbs. Turn onto a work surface, flatten the dough, then knead it well and flatten again. Sprinkle on the salt. **2. Chop the herbs** and sprinkle them on. Work the dough again twice, doing the windowpane test each time. Consolidate the dough by folding it into a smaller, neater mushroom shape. Put the dough in an oiled bowl and spray it with oil. Cover the bowl with a warm, damp dish towel and leave the dough to proof. **3. Turn the dough** onto a work surface and pull off pieces to make rolls. **4. Flour them** or wet them and sprinkle with seeds and leave them to rise. Cook in a preheated oven at 400°F (200°C) for about 20 minutes until golden.

RECIPE **Soda bread**

Soda bread is easy to make because it doesn't need to be left to rise. In Northern Ireland we eat flattened triangles of soda bread called soda farls. They are delicious toasted and extra-special when fried in bacon fat and served with an "Ulster fry-up."

YOU WILL NEED
- 1 lb (450 g) bread flour
- 1 tsp cream of tartar
- 1 tsp baking soda
- ½ tsp salt
- 1½ cups (350 ml) buttermilk
- Mixing bowl
- Griddle, palette knife
- Loaf tin

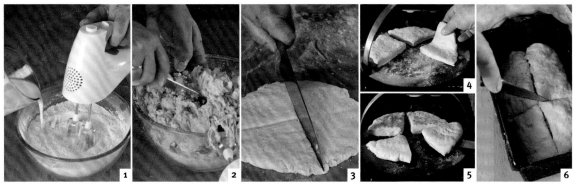

1. Put the dry ingredients into a mixing bowl, then whisk in the buttermilk. **2. It will be crumbly** at this stage, so work it together with a palette knife. **3. Turn the dough** onto a work surface and divide in two. Flour your hands and firm up each half, then roll one half into a rough circle. Cut in four to make triangular soda farls. **4. Flour a hot griddle,** lay on the farls, and let them cook for about 10 minutes until they are golden. **5. Turn them over** and cook for a further 10 minutes. **6. Shape the other half of the mixture,** put it in an oiled loaf tin, and cut a cross on top. Bake in a preheated oven at 400°F (200°C) for about 30 minutes, until golden.

RECIPE **Sourdough bread**

Sourdough is a halfway house between unleavened flatbreads and yeast-based bread. It's made using a natural fermenting process, so you don't need to add yeast. However, you do need to make a "starter" 2–3 weeks ahead of when you plan to start baking sourdough for the first time. A plastic scraper is a versatile little tool to use when making bread. It is great for getting dough out of the bowl, for cutting and dividing it, and for cleaning hands and work surfaces.

YOU WILL NEED
- 1 lb (500 g) bread flour
- ¾ lb (400 g) sourdough starter (see below left)
- 1 cup (250 ml) water
- 3 tsp salt
- 1 tsp brown sugar
- Mixing bowl
- Plastic scraper
- Oil spray
- Couche cloths
- Lame (razor)

MAKING THE STARTER

■ **Mix equal quantities** of bread flour and water—say, 1 lb of flour and 1 pint of water (500 g of flour/500 ml of water) in an open container. Cover with a cloth and leave somewhere out of harm's way at room temperature.

■ **After 2–3 weeks** the starter will start to ferment and increase in volume. You will also see air pockets in it. A wild yeast culture has been formed and is ready to use.

■ **After using** some of the starter, you have to replace it—called "feeding" it. If you use ½ lb (400 g) of starter in your recipe, replace with ¼ lb (200 g) of flour plus 1 cup (200 ml) of water, whisked into the original starter.

■ **If you are not** baking every day, keep your starter in the refrigerator and take it out 24 hours before you need to use it. This will bring it back to room temperature and kick-start it back into action.

■ **You can also freeze** the starter, which puts it into a suspended state. To bring it back to life again, let the liquid defrost and then leave it at room temperature for a day before topping it off to feed it.

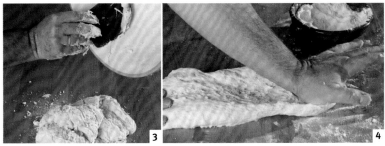

1. Put the flour and starter into a bowl. There's no need to sift the flour.
2. Work the flour into the starter with your hands, using the plastic scraper to remove the sticky stuff from your hands every now and then.

3. Turn the dough onto a lightly floured work surface. **4. Flour your hands** and work the dough thoroughly by stretching it with the heel of your palm. Be brutal with it and don't be afraid—you won't hurt it. The dough will feel wet but don't be tempted to add more flour. Flatten the dough once again and sprinkle with the sugar and then the salt, which will absorb any excess moisture.

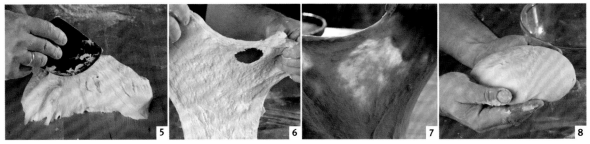

5. Fold the dough in with the scraper and start working it again. You will feel it starting to dry up.   **6. To test** whether the dough is ready to be left to rise, apply the windowpane test. Stretch a portion of the dough between your hands. If it tears, the dough is not yet elastic enough and you should continue kneading.   **7. If it stretches** to form a thin sheet that you can see the light through, then it is ready. This test is much more accurate than any instruction on exactly how long to knead for.
8. Consolidate the dough by folding it into a mushroom shape to make it smaller and neater.

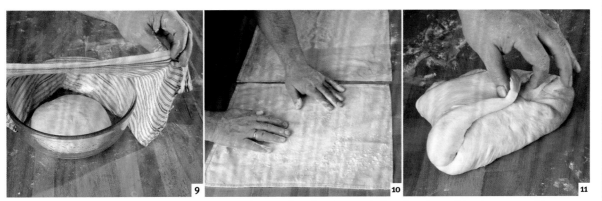

9. Oil a large bowl and put the dough into it. Spray the dough with oil to stop it from forming a skin, then cover with a warm, wet cloth or plastic wrap to stop the dough from drying out. Put it somewhere warm but not hot, to proof for at least 2 hours. Unlike most breads, sourdough won't double in size, but you should see some movement. **10. When the sourdough has risen**, prepare the couche cloths. These are made of tightly woven, unbleached cotton cloth. Work flour into them with your hands. **11. Turn out the dough** onto a floured surface and consolidate it by folding in the edges.

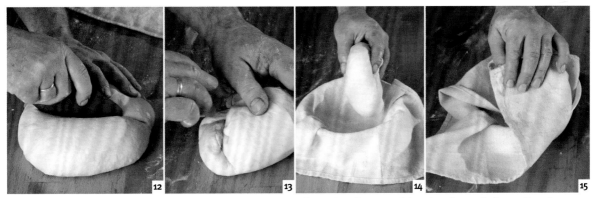

12. Halve the dough using your scraper. **13. Then pull in the edges** of each piece of dough to form a ball. **14. Put the prepared couche cloths** into bowls and drop each ball of dough into the cloth. Leave the "untidy" seam side of the dough uppermost. **15. Loosely fold** over the edges of the cloth and leave to rise again in a warm place for 2 more hours.

16. Peel off the couche cloth, putting the loaves onto floured baking trays, seam side down. (Never wash your couche cloths; just leave them to dry and then put away.) **17. Make several slashes** across with the lame—this will encourage the sourdough to burst open in the steam when being cooked. We use an old straight razor; a knife is not sharp enough. **18. Then flour the sourdough loaves** and put in a preheated oven at 350°F (180°C). Set a small bowl of water directly on the oven floor and shut the door quickly before any steam escapes. Bake for about 15 minutes, or until golden.

Making pickles and chutneys

The difference between pickles and chutneys is quite simple: pickles are pieces of vegetable or fruit preserved in vinegar, whereas chutneys are made from fruit or vegetables cooked in vinegar. Vinegar is used because its high acidity inhibits the actions of harmful microorganisms that cause food to spoil, and it adds a tangy flavor to your preserves.

Pickles

Generally, pickling is quicker and easier than making chutney, and makes use of young, undamaged, fresh fruit or vegetables. When pickling vegetables, it is important to first ensure that they are moist, and to then soak them in brine or pack them in salt for 24 hours to draw out some of the water in them. To make brine, mix 1/3 cup (100 g) of salt with 1 quart (liter) of water.

Place the veggies into sterilized jars (see opposite) and completely cover them with vinegar. Distilled vinegar is the strongest preservative, but also one of the most expensive; the more you pay for your vinegar, the tastier your pickles and chutneys will tend to be. However, you can always take the homemade option and make your own vinegar (see page 260) and flavor it with a selection of your chosen herbs and spices (see opposite).

Pickled eggs If you find yourself with more eggs than your family or friends can eat, pickling them is a great option. Hard-boil the eggs, then shell them and pack into large jars with about 1 quart (liter) of spiced vinegar to every dozen eggs. Close the lids tightly. The eggs should be ready to eat after about one month.

Pickled onions To achieve a sweet pickled onion, we add a little sugar to the vinegar (we use white sugar to keep the pickle clear and light). Before peeling the onions, soak them in a brine solution for 12 hours, then skin them and submerge in fresh brine for another two days before packing them into a jar. Cover them with spiced, sweet vinegar and seal the jar. Resist eating the onions for at least two months after pickling them.

Chutney

The chutneyfication process is one of the most satisfying and exciting aspects of growing your own food. We turn huge volumes of our produce into chutney, and it can be made from almost any fruit or vegetable. We have used apples, grapes, radishes, rhubarb, red and green tomatoes, chile peppers, eggplants, pears, squashes, and turnips—to name but a few. Then there are all the various spices that add those distinctive chutney flavors: cumin, coriander, allspice, cloves, ginger, peppercorns, paprika, mustard seed, and garlic are some of our favorite selections.

BRINING OLIVES

We grow our own olives in the hoop house, but raw olives need to be pickled to make them palatable. To remove any impurities, cut each olive to the pit, place in sterilized jars, and cover with water. To keep the olives submerged, place a small plastic bag filled with water on top. Change the water every day for a week and then pickle them in brine—1/4 cup (75 g) salt to 1 quart (liter) of water—for five weeks. Add a thin layer of olive oil for an airtight seal.

1. The perfect pickled onion *should be both sharp and sweet.* **2. Spooning chutney** *into sterilized jars is a good deal easier with an old-fashioned funnel.* **3. Crunchy vegetables** *like cucumbers and cabbage can be pickled directly in cold vinegar; they don't need to be soaked in brine first.*

RECIPE Spiced pickling vinegar

There is a wide variety of vinegars suitable for pickling, such as malt, wine, or cider vinegar. You can also add your own spices and herbs to clear distilled vinegar. For the contents to remain recognizable and look attractive, use whole spices, as ground spices make the vinegar turn cloudy.

YOU WILL NEED
- Dried chile peppers
- Juniper and sumac berries
- Cinnamon sticks
- Star anise
- Muslin squares
- Bottle of distilled vinegar

1. Lay two squares of muslin on top of each other on a work surface. Crush the chile peppers and berries, and then put the spices in the center of the fabric. Gather up the corners and tie with string to form a spice bag. Make sure the string is long enough to loop over and hang from the handle of the saucepan. **2. Put the bag** and vinegar in the saucepan and bring to a boil. Remove from the heat and leave the vinegar and spices to cool for a couple of hours. Take out the spice bag. The flavored vinegar is now ready to use. **3. Use the vinegar** to pickle garlic, onions, cabbage, or eggs, for example.

RECIPE Newhouse Farm chutney

The key to making chutney is to cook the fruit and vegetables for a long time so that most of the moisture evaporates and it has a thick, jamlike consistency. The colors will change and the flavors intensify in the process. A good chutney also benefits from bold and contrasting flavors, so be experimental and don't be afraid to mix together fruits and vegetables.

YOU WILL NEED
- 2 large pumpkins
- 6 large cooking apples
- 3½ lb (1.5 kg) tomatoes
- 5 onions
- 1 tsp red pepper flakes
- 1 tsp allspice
- 1 tsp mustard seeds
- 1 tsp red peppercorns
- 1 tsp paprika
- 1 small bowl of raisins
- 2¼ lb (1 kg) turbinado sugar
- 4 quarts (liters) red wine vinegar
- Muslin
- Mortar and pestle

1. Peel and roughly chop the pumpkins, apples, tomatoes, and onions. **2. Crush the spices** with a mortar and pestle. **3. Place all the ingredients** in a large pan, mix, and bring to a boil. Then turn down the heat and leave to simmer for 3 hours or until the contents take on a jamlike consistency and a wooden spoon drawn across the base of the pan leaves a trail. **4. Spoon into sterilized jars**, seal, and label. To sterilize jars, wash in hot, soapy water, put in a boiling-water canner, cover with water by 1 inch (2.5cm), and boil 10 minutes. (Add 1 minute for each 1,000 ft. of altitude over 1,000 ft.)

Making jam and jelly

Jam-making is really enjoyable and captures those delicious fruity summer flavors for use all year round. Our pantry is lined with rows of gleaming jars and top-quality condiments that are expensive to buy at the store, but are made from fruits like apples and berries that are easy to grow or forage for. Jams and syrups also make use of your surplus crops, ensuring that nothing goes to waste.

Jam-making ingredients

Good jam-making relies on three key ingredients: good-quality fruit, pectin, and sugar.

■ **Prime-quality fruit** is better for jam than overripe fruit. If you don't have your own fruit trees or soft fruit canes, visit a local "pick your own," or forage fencerows for a bumper crop of fresh blackberries.

■ **For jam and jelly** to set properly, you need the correct balance of pectin, acid, and sugar. Fruits that are rich in pectin (see the table, opposite) set well without any added ingredients, but those with medium to low pectin levels will need some pectin stock (see box below, right). Alternatively, you can add granulated or liquid pectin, or use gelling sugar, which has pectin included in it. Lemon peel contains pectin, offering another option, but be wary of adding too much as this can affect the final flavor of the jam or jelly.

■ **Sugar preserves** fruit by inhibiting the growth of yeasts. The sugar content must be more than 60 percent to stop the jam from fermenting. A rough guide is to add 1¼ lb (550 g) of superfine sugar to every 1 lb (450 g) of any fruit that you know is rich in pectin; 1 lb (450 g) sugar to 1 lb (450 g) fruit that is fairly rich in pectin; and only 12 oz (350 g) sugar to 1 lb (450 g) of fruit that is low in pectin.

■ **Any kind of sugar** can be used to make jam. Preserving sugar is more expensive, but very easy to use as it dissolves quicker and needs less stirring. Brown sugar produces darker jams with a slightly different flavor.

Making jelly

Jellies are made in much the same way as jam, but you don't need to throw away all skins, stones, and seeds before heating the fruit. This is because they are removed, along with any pulp, when you strain the mixture to obtain the juice.

RECIPE **Plum and cinnamon jam**

Plums contain particularly high pectin levels (see box opposite), especially when they are not quite ripe, so there is no need to add a setting agent to this recipe.

YOU WILL NEED
■ 5 lb (2.5 kg) dark plums or damsons, halved and pitted
■ 2 cinnamon sticks
■ 6 lb (3 kg) granulated sugar
■ Heavy-bottomed pan and canner

1. Put the plums, cinnamon sticks, and 1 quart (1 liter) of water into a pan and heat gently for about 20 minutes until the fruit is really soft and the syrup is reduced. **2. Remove the pan** from the heat, add the sugar, and stir until dissolved. Bring back to a rapid boil for about 10 minutes, stirring occasionally, until the gel point is reached. Test (see box, right). **3. Spoon the jam** into sterilized jars (see page 237). Process 5 minutes in a boiling-water canner.

ACHIEVING A SET

■ **Test for the gel point** When you think your jam is ready, test it to see if it will set. Spoon a little jam onto a cold plate and allow it to cool. Push your finger across the surface of the jam; if it wrinkles, remove the jam pan from the heat. Alternatively, remove some jam from the pan on a wooden spoon. If, after cooling, the jam sets in the spoon and any drops on the edge form into flakes, it is ready.

■ **Make pectin stock** This helps to set fruits that have a medium or low pectin content (see the table opposite). Put 2¼ lb (1 kg) chopped, unpeeled (the peel contains the pectin) cooking apples into a preserving pan and just cover with water. Cover the pan, bring to a boil, then simmer for 20 minutes or until soft. Remove the pulp by straining the apples over a clean pan. Simmer the juice gently once again until reduced by half. Pour into small freezer tubs. Generally, ⅔ cup (150 ml) of pectin stock is sufficient to set 4½ lb (2 kg) of fruit.

RECIPE **Apple and blackberry jelly**

Try this easy jelly recipe—you don't need to add pectin, as the apples contain enough to make it set. Remember when making jams and jellies to always remove the pan from the heat before adding the sugar, and warm the sugar before mixing it with the fruit so that it dissolves more quickly. Take care when boiling your jam, too. Boil it for too long and it will set rock hard; boil it too little, and it will be a runny mess.

YOU WILL NEED
- Equal quantities of cooking apples and blackberries
- 1 lb (450 g) superfine sugar for each 1 pint (600 ml) of jelly liquid
- Heavy pan, jelly bag, funnel, canner

REDUCING THE FRUIT

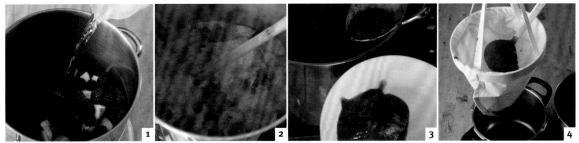

1. Core and chop the apples but leave unpeeled. Place in a large pan and add the blackberries and 3 pints (1.5 liters) of water.
2. Bring to a boil, turn down the heat, and leave to simmer for about an hour.   **3. Remove any scum** and then test the jelly consistency on a plate. It should be a pulpy mass. If not, simmer another 10 minutes and retest.   **4. Ladle the liquid** into a jelly bag suspended over a pan. Leave to drip several hours. Resist squeezing the bag because the jelly will turn cloudy.

MAKING THE JELLY

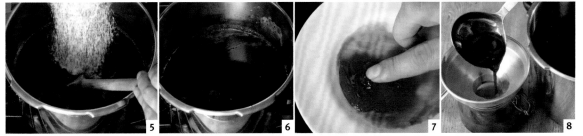

5. In the morning, remove and compost the pulp. Measure the juice and weigh the correct amount of sugar for the volume of liquid. Gently heat the syrup. Remove from the heat, and stir in the sugar until it has dissolved.   **6. Boil the jelly** for about 10 minutes, stirring occasionally. Turn down the heat and skim off any further scum that rises to the top.
7. Test the jelly for set (see box).   **8. Ladle into sterilized jars** (see page 237). Fill them to the top, as the jam will shrink when cool. Add lids and process 5 minutes in a boiling-water canner.

PECTIN LEVELS

Fruits high in pectin
- Black currants
- Citrus fruits (mainly in the peel)
- Cooking apples
- Crabapples
- Cranberries (unripe)
- Gooseberries
- Plums (unripe), damsons
- Quinces
- Red and white currants

Fruits with medium pectin levels
- Apricots
- Cherries (sour/cooking)
- Cranberries (ripe)
- Grapes (unripe)
- Loganberries
- Medlars
- Plums (ripe)
- Raspberries

Fruits low in pectin
- Blackberries
- Blueberries
- Cherries (sweet)
- Figs
- Grapes (ripe)
- Melons
- Nectarines
- Peaches
- Rhubarb
- Strawberries

Canning fruit and vegetables

Canning was invented in 1809 by Nicholas Appert, who won the prize offered by Napoleon Bonaparte to anyone who could invent a method for preserving food to provide his troops with rations while marching. Since then, canning has enabled people to store produce easily and safely, and to make winter meals tastier and more nutritious with summer and fall fruits and vegetables.

Canning fruit

You can use one of three bases—syrup, water, or fruit juice—to can all the lovely excess fruit from your garden. The jars must be sealed immediately after canning to prevent bacteria or pathogens from tainting the food. You will also need to heat the fruit in the jars since the high temperature destroys harmful microorganisms.

Fruits with a high acid content can easily be canned safely. Low-acid and borderline fruits (including tomatoes) require you to add acidity in the form of lemon juice or ascorbic acid (vitamin C) powder or tablets.

The **water-bath method** involves washing the jars and sterilizing them by submerging them in a boiling-water canner or large stockpot for 5 minutes. Then pack the jars with fruit—hot or raw, depending on the fruit type (see table). Wipe the jar rims clean, remove any air bubbles, place a flat lid on top of each, and secure them to fingertip tightness with the screwbands. Cover the jars by at least 1 inch (2.5cm) with hot water and process in the canner or pot for the recommended time (see table). Remove and let cool for 24 hours, checking to make sure each jar has sealed (the button in the center of the lid will be depressed).

When it comes to eating your produce, if the lid comes off too easily, or there are bubbles in the jar, or if the fruit smells wrong or has turned moldy, don't eat the contents. In fact, if there is any doubt, throw the fruit away.

Canning vegetables

Preserving vegetables at home is possible if you have a specialty pressure canner, which is like a large pressure cooker. Vegetables contain very little acid, and to avoid all risks you need to heat the jars beyond the boiling point of water under high pressure. A pressure canner enables you to accomplish this feat by increasing the temperature of the water inside it.

The most popular vegetables for pressure canning include asparagus, green beans, legumes, carrots, corn, okra, and potatoes.

Pressure canning is a big step up for home canners and requires an investment in equipment and learning, so many find it easier to just preserve vegetables by freezing them, although it causes a change in texture and flavor.

PROCESSING TIMES (AT 1,000 FT ALTITUDE; ADD 5 MIN FOR EACH 2,000 FT)

Fruit	Pack method	Processing time
Soft fruit e.g., soft berries, grapes, rhubarb	Place raw fruits in the jars.	Pints: 15 minutes Quarts: 20 minutes
Orchard fruit e.g., peaches, apricots, plums, apples, pears	Cook the fruit before packing it into the jars.	Pints: 20–25 minutes Quarts: 25–30 minutes

1. Buy canning jars *with two-part lids. Metal must not come in contact with the contents of your jars.* **2. Flat lids** *should only be used once for a perfect seal. Discard them after using the jar's contents.*

RECIPE **Strawberry jam**

You'll find that jam and preserves are the easiest and most forgiving of canning projects. All you need are perfectly ripe, sweet strawberries and sugar to create this delicious jam. Strawberry jam is fantastic in cookies or doughnuts, or simply spread on a slice of toast made from homemade bread.

YOU WILL NEED

■ 3lbs (1.5kg) strawberries, washed and hulled
■ 6 cups sugar
■ 6–8 sterilized half-pint jars (see p237) and boiling-water canner

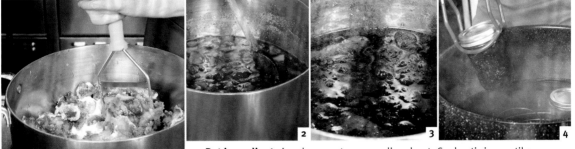

1. Put ingredients in a large pot over medium heat. Cook, stirring, until sugar dissolves. Crush berries with masher. **2. Increase heat to medium-high** and bring to boil, stirring frequently. **3. Cook up to 30 minutes** to 220F (104C). **4. Ladle into sterilized jars,** add lids, and process 5 minutes in a boiling-water canner.

RECIPE **Canned tomatoes**

Tomatoes are delicious when used in a winter meal, as they provide a rich, summery taste and plenty of vitamins. Canning tomatoes is also an excellent way to store any surplus produce you may have.

YOU WILL NEED

■ 22–24 lbs (10–10.75 kg) tomatoes
■ 1 tbsp bottled lemon juice per pint jar
■ $^1/_2$ tsp salt per pint (optional)
■ Sterilized jars (see p237) and boiling-water canner

1. Core and score tomatoes, then blanch in boiling water and remove skins. Add lemon juice to jars. **2. Put the tomatoes** in a large pot and cover with water. Bring to boil and cook 5 minutes. Pack tomatoes in jars and cover with liquid, leaving $^1/_2$ inch (2.5cm) space at top of jars (contents will expand).

CANNING PEACHES IN SIMPLE SYRUP

■ **Blanch and peel 11 pounds (5kg) fresh peaches.** Remove pits and cut into halves or slices. Dip in a treatment solution to prevent browning (such as Fruit-Fresh, or diluted ascorbic acid/vitamin C or bottled lemon juice).

■ **Cook $2^1/_4$ cups sugar and $5^1/_4$ cups water** in a large pot over medium heat, stirring until dissolved (approx. 10 minutes).

■ **Add peaches to syrup,** return to boil, reduce heat to medium-low, and cook 5 minutes.

■ **Pack peaches and syrup** into 9 sterilized pint jars, remove bubbles, wipe rims, and affix lids.

■ **Process in a boiling-water canner** for 25 minutes. Allow jars to cool before storing them.

3. Wipe jar rims, add jar lids, and secure in place with screwbands at fingertip tightness. **4. Put jars in canner** and cover with boiling water by 2 inches (5cm). Process 40 minutes. If jars don't seal, eat or freeze contents immediately.

Drying fruit, herbs, and vegetables

Sun-dried tomatoes and dried mushrooms and strawberries are sold at a premium as luxury foods, but drying food is a traditional way of preserving produce for winter use that's easy to do at home for little effort or cost. The drying process also often intensifies the flavor of the food, and apple slices and vegetable chips make delicious, healthy snacks.

How it works
Drying is a really effective way to preserve food. It prevents the development of unwanted enzymes, bacteria, yeasts, and fungi by removing the moisture they thrive on. There are various ways of doing this, from using the sun's heat or an oven on a low setting, to mixing food with desiccants (drying agents) such as salt and sugar.

Air drying
Air drying is one of the oldest and simplest ways to preserve produce. All you need is a dry, dark, well-ventilated place to hang herbs, fruit, and vegetables. Avoid hanging food where humidity levels are high, as it will turn moldy and rot.

Leave herbs to hang for a week or so, then crumble the leaves between your fingers to remove them from the stems. To collect herb seeds, hang stems upside down in a paper bag.

Sun drying and solar dryers
Laying out food on racks to dry in the sun is an effective preserving method, but it is more difficult in regions where a few days of back-to-back sunshine without rain are rarely guaranteed. You also need to bring racks under cover every evening to prevent the produce from rehydrating. A solar dryer can simplify the process (see box opposite).

Oven drying
You can dry sliced vegetables and fruit in a convection oven at about 120–130°F (45–55°C). (To make sure air is circulating in a conventional oven, prop the door open fractionally by slipping a skewer between the door and frame.) To dry mushrooms, brush off any dirt first, but do not wash them. They take 4–6 hours to

1

2

3

DRYING TIPS
■ **The freshest, best-quality** fruit and vegetables are best for drying.
■ **Use sharp tools** when harvesting and slicing produce.
■ **Always harvest produce** in the afternoon. Produce covered in dew takes longer to dry and could become moldy.
■ **Test food frequently.** Bend herbs or chile peppers in your hand: if they snap, they're ready; if they flex, leave them for a little longer. Squeeze fruit and veggies—no juice should come out.
■ **Store dried foods** in airtight containers in a cool, dark place. We take eco-pride in saving every glass jar that comes into the house and reusing it for storing our dried produce.

1. Hang herbs *in an airy place to dry. Suspend chile peppers by their stems, tying them to a length of string at 2-in (5-cm) intervals.* **2. Salt** *draws out moisture from fresh herbs and helps preserve them.* **3. Dry cranberry beans** *in pods until brittle, then shell and dry.*

dry and are ready when they shrink to half their size but are still pliable. Tomatoes take longer as they are fleshier—in the range of 8–12 hours. Apples and pears may take up to 24 hours. If you want to save fuel, use an earth oven (see pages 252–253). Leave all oven-dried foods to cool before storing in airtight jars.

Using a microwave

You can also use a microwave to dry produce. Slice fruit and vegetables, wrap them in a paper towel, and cook for a minute at a time on a high temperature setting. Test between each session. Use the microwave to dry herbs too; wrap them in paper, and make sure you place a small cup of water in the microwave at the same time—herbs (and some vegetables) don't contain much moisture and could damage your microwave.

Electric dehydrator

Electric food dehydrators are table-top units with a heating element, a fan, and a series of trays or racks that stack on top. They are efficient but expensive—the perfect present for an enthusiast who likes gadgets.

Desiccants

These draw the moisture out of produce while preserving color and flavor. Salt and sugar are the most commonly used. This is a more expensive method, as you need enough salt or sugar to fill a container and completely cover the food.

We use the technique to make aromatic herb "rubs" for cooking joints of meat. Layer rosemary, marjoram, oregano, and salt in a container, and leave the herbs to dry. Then crumble them up with the salt and store in an airtight jar for a very tasty herb mix.

DRY THIS

- **Apple and pear rings** Use a solar dryer, or thread them on a length of string and hang above the stove.
- **Peas and beans** Air-dry ripe pods until brittle to the touch, then shell the beans or peas. Finish drying in a solar dryer. Rehydrate before cooking, or save and sow in spring.
- **Beet, carrot, and parsnip chips** Slice thinly and dry in the oven or in a solar dryer.
- **Herbs** Air-dry bunches of herbs, such as rosemary and sage, before they flower, when aromatic oil levels are highest.
- **Strawberries** Try this Native American technique. Mash ripe berries and add 2 tbsp sugar. Roll the mixture out to a depth of about an eighth of an inch (2–3 mm) on a piece of muslin. Air-dry on a rack for a few hours to a couple of days, then slice into tasty snack-sized pieces.
- **Chile peppers** Hang up to air-dry.
- **Mushrooms** Slice large ones, leave small ones whole. Dry in the oven or a solar dryer.

PROJECT **Using a solar dryer**

A solar dryer needs no fuel and costs nothing to run. Place it in direct sunlight, facing south, and move it every couple of hours to track the sun. If you know you're not going to be able to do this, position the dryer to face the sun when it's at its highest point. See pages 244–245 for how to make a dryer.

YOU WILL NEED
- Sharp knife
- Cutting board
- Apple peeler, corer, and slicer

1. An apple peeler, corer, and slicer is a handy gadget that does all the functions at the turn of a handle. It works on pears, too.   **2. The apple** comes off in a continuous spiral. Cut into rings and dip in a solution of water, lemon juice, and a teaspoon of sugar. Pat slices dry before putting in the dryer.   **3. Cherry tomatoes** are simply cut in half.   **4. Arrange food** on wire shelves to allow air to circulate. Poppy seedheads don't need any preparation. Close the door, position the dryer, and leave for a few days. Test foods regularly (see box opposite).   **6. Store dried foods** in airtight jars.

PROJECT **Make a solar dryer**

Solar drying is an ancient cooking method. Sunlight is converted to heat in the solar collector—an insulating box with a glass front—and the hot air rises into the dryer or cooking chamber. A solar dryer is not nearly as powerful as a conventional oven. We use ours for drying fruit and vegetables (see pages 242–243), rather than cooking a full meal—you would need a very sunny day for that.

YOU WILL NEED
- Glass-fronted cabinet
- Plywood, spare lumber, battens
- Drill and various-sized bits
- Ruler
- Saw and hacksaw
- Corrugated iron
- Black paint, white paint
- Mesh—metal, plastic, or muslin
- Level
- Doorknob, hinges, catch

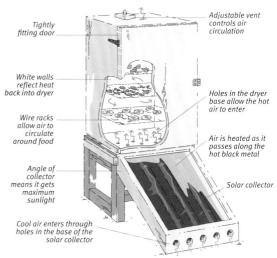

Tightly fitting door

Adjustable vent controls air circulation

White walls reflect heat back into dryer

Wire racks allow air to circulate around food

Holes in the dryer base allow the hot air to enter

Air is heated as it passes along the hot black metal

Angle of collector means it gets maximum sunlight

Solar collector

Cool air enters through holes in the base of the solar collector

MAKING THE SOLAR COLLECTOR AND STAND

1. Reuse an old cabinet. The glass door will form the top of the solar collector and the cabinet the dryer. Drill a hole at one end of the cabinet using a 1-in (25-mm) hole saw, to form the air vent (see step 16).   **2. To find the best angle** for the solar collector, prop it against a wall at noon. Adjust the angle of the glass door until a small notebook held upright on the frame casts virtually no shadow. At this point the collector is at the optimum angle to receive the maximum amount of sunlight all day.   **3. Measure the height** of the door against the wall; this will be the height of the dryer base.   **4. Cut a piece** of 1-x-2-in (50-x-25-mm) batten to the same width as the cabinet and drill a row of holes using a 1-in (25-mm) spade drill bit.

5. Measure the glass door and make a shallow 3-sided box from plywood, the same width but longer, to fit beneath the dryer, and just deep enough to hold some corrugated iron. Use the drilled wood for the end and 1-x-2-in (50-x-25-mm) wood for the sides.   **6. Paint** white inside.   **7. Tack mesh** across holes to keep insects out.   **8. Add wooden spacers** for the iron to rest on, to let air circulate.   **9. With a hacksaw** cut metal to fit inside the box. Paint it black.

10 11 12 13

10. Screw the glass door to the top of the box.   **11. Hold the box** at the correct height for the optimum angle, as calculated in steps 2 and 3. Use a level to mark a horizontal edge along each side of the box at the open end. Cut along the lines with a saw. These form the edges where the dryer cabinet is attached on top, and determine the size of the stand.   **12. Slide** the black iron inside the collector.   **13. Build a stand**. Use two square frames for the ends, and screw them to two side pieces of 1-x-2-in (50-x-25-mm) wood. The stand should be the same width as the dryer, and the height as calculated in steps 2 and 3 at the back, and the height less the depth of the collector at the front. Attach the collector using lumber side braces.

MAKING THE DRYER

14 15 16 17

14. Mark two staggered rows of holes in the base of the dryer to allow air to enter from the solar collector.   **15. Drill** the holes using a $\frac{1}{3}$-in (8-mm) drill bit. **16. Stand the dryer** on top of the collector, with the air vent at the top, to check the fit, but don't join them together yet.   **17. Cut a door** for the dryer from a piece of plywood and attach it with hinges. Nail equally spaced runners made from thin wooden battens to the sides of the dryer, to hold wire shelves for drying the food.

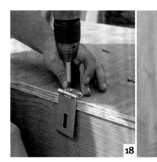

18 19 20

21

18. Add a catch to keep the door securely shut.   **19. Paint the inside** of the dryer white.   **20. Attach a doorknob** to a square piece of wood big enough to cover the vent hole, then screw the wood in one corner so that it can be swiveled open to let air out or closed to keep rain out. Screw collector and dryer together tightly, with no gaps.   **21. Add wire shelves**. For food preparation tips, see pages 242–243.

Curing meat and fish

Preserving food with salt used to be an essential method for storing meat over the winter in pre-refrigeration days. Today it's a traditional skill worth learning for the delicious flavor it gives both meat and fish. By experimenting with spices and herbs, which you can add to a basic salt cure, you can create your own secret recipe for hams, bacon, and fish.

How it works

Salt is an effective preservative because it inhibits the growth of microbes and bacteria. It does this by removing moisture in a process known as "osmosis," where water moves from an area of low salt concentration—the food being preserved—to an area of high salt concentration—the curing mix.

There are two ways to cure food with salt. You can either cover it completely in dry salt, or immerse it in brine. Both methods also create an air-free environment, which prevents the growth of microorganisms. Keep your food in a cool place while curing, as low temperatures inhibit microorganisms. Salting or brining is also the essential first stage when smoking food (see pages 248–249).

Brining

An 80 percent solution of salt is the most effective way to preserve food by brining (see box opposite). This means dissolving a staggering 2½ lb (1.3 kg) of salt in every 1 gallon (4 liters) of water. You can also add extra ingredients for flavor, including brown sugar, cloves, white pepper, molasses, and even rum. Don't rinse after brining: pat with paper towels and then air-dry.

Dry curing

This is a more popular method for beginners, and removes more water from food than brining—worth knowing if you plan to smoke your meat or fish afterward, as you won't need to smoke it for so long. Buy more salt than you think you'll need, as you have to add extra while curing to replace the brine by-product that's drawn out of the food. Table salt is cheap and efficient, but for specialty recipes, such as gravlax (see box below), try coarse sea salt flakes.

When curing for the first time, start with small fish. Lay fillets side by side on a bed of salt and cover them with a ½-in (1-cm) layer of salt. Repeat the layers, finishing with salt, and leave for 1–2 days. Then wash the fish to remove the salt, and hang the fillets to dry for 24 hours.

Air-dried ham (see box opposite) is more of a challenge. When you unwrap it, every bone in your body will be telling you that the meat has spoiled. Trust us: cured properly and air-dried for long enough, the meat inside will be safe and delicious.

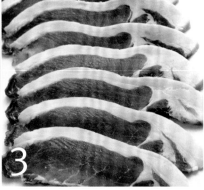

1. Salt and sugar *in roughly equal proportions, plus a teaspoon of ascorbic acid, make an ideal cure for breakfast bacon.* **2. Cured bacon** *is pink all the way through. Soak in cold water for a day if a test slice tastes too salty when fried.* **3. Sliced cured bacon** *can be frozen. Eat within two to three months.*

GRAVLAX

Mix ⅓ cup (75 g) sugar, 2 handfuls of chopped dill, 1 tbsp (15 ml) lemon juice, ¼ cup (50 g) sea salt flakes, 1 tsp (5 ml) black pepper. Lay a fillet of skinless salmon in a dish. Spread with cure and place the other fillet on top. Wrap in plastic wrap and weigh down. Turn after 12 hours, pouring off any brine. Leave for 1–2 days, then rinse, dry, and cover with fresh dill.

Serve gravlax *finely sliced after it has cured for 1–2 days in the fridge.*

RECIPE **Air-dried leg of pork**

This is our version of Parma ham, one of Italy's most famous exports. We like the peppers' kick, but you can vary the mix to your taste. Other ingredients to try are cardamom pods, cumin, coriander seeds, rosemary, star anise, thyme, mustard and caraway seeds, bay, and nutmeg.

YOU WILL NEED
- Leg of pork (10–15 lb/5–8 kg)
- 3 dried chili peppers
- 6 star anise
- handful black peppercorns
- 12 cardamom pods
- 6½ lb (3 kg) salt
- A plastic container large enough to hold the leg of pork, plus a lid
- Spice grinder or mortar and pestle
- Muslin and string
- Stiff brush

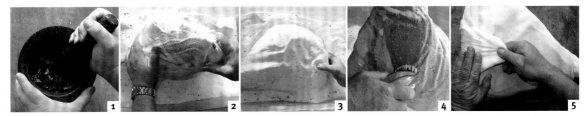

1. Grind the spices into a coarse powder. Pour the salt into a large plastic container and add the spices. **2. Rub the spices and salt** evenly into the meat, working the cure into the skin, especially around the ball joint of the bone. **3. Bury the meat** in the cure, add the lid, and leave in a cold place—ideally in a refrigerator—for 10–14 days, depending on the saltiness you prefer. Every few days, pour out brine that has formed. Add more salt, if required, and rub it in. **4. Lift out the ham**, and remove the cure using a stiff brush. **5. Wrap the ham** in muslin and tie securely with string.

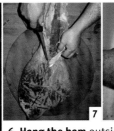
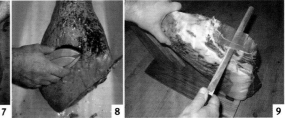

6. Hang the ham outside in a dry but well-ventilated area, such as a lean-to shed, for 18 weeks minimum; we hang for 18–24 months. **7. Unwrap** the meat. **8. Scrub off** any surface mold with cider vinegar. Trim off any yellow (tainted) fat and some of the excess white fat. Pat dry with paper towel. **9. The cured ham** is a pinky-red color in the middle with no gray patches in the flesh.

USING A BRINING AND SALTING TUB

Wooden tubs were originally used for brining and salting, but plastic containers work just as well. Never use metal vessels as these taint food, and always cure fish and meat separately.

For best results
Ensure there is space in the tub between pieces of meat or fish so that the brine can reach every part, and weight the lid. To just flavor meat or fish, rather than preserving it, leave in the brine for 2–3 hours; to cure a ham, leave for 3–4 days. Stir occasionally. After curing, pat with a clean cloth and air-dry. Use fresh brine for new batches of food.

Heavy weight on wooden lid

Cuts of meat or fish

Add a drainer if using the tub for salting instead

Smoking your own food

If you like the taste of smoked food, why pay a premium for it when you can smoke your own at home, for little effort and hardly any cost? So-called smoked food that you buy at a store has often had no contact with real smoke and has been artificially flavored. With these techniques you can smoke everything from a wedge of cheese to a whole chicken just the way you like them.

The principles of smoking

Smoking started out as a way of preserving food in the days before refrigeration. Like brining, it works by drawing moisture out of food so bacteria can't survive. Smoking works by coating food with antibacterial and antioxidant compounds found in the wood smoke, while at the same time adding a delicious, smoky flavor.

Smoking only penetrates the surface of the food—the center won't benefit from the preserving effect— so it is essential to start off by salting or brining food (see pages 246–247). This does most of the preserving; smoking helps and adds more flavor.

Cold smoking

This is our preferred method of smoking food. It's an outdoor activity and to do it successfully you need a slow-burning fuel and an enclosed heatproof container of some sort, with enough space for the smoke to circulate around the food. The fire smolders rather than burns fiercely and produces clouds of aromatic wood smoke. The heat from the fuel doesn't actually reach the food, so the food doesn't cook; instead, it absorbs all of the flavor from the smoke.

Food that has been cold smoked needs to be left for a minimum of 24 hours before eating for the flavor to develop fully. After that, it will normally keep for at least a week in the refrigerator but this all depends on the type of food and the extent to which it has been cured before smoking—if in any doubt, don't eat it! Cold-smoked salmon can be eaten raw, but other smoked foods such as bacon, herring, cod, and haddock will require cooking afterward.

Hot smoking

This method is really more of a cooking technique that gives food a smoky flavor. You can do it in a wok on the stove (see opposite) or in a special stovetop smoker, basically a metal box with racks. Hot smoking uses very hot smoke, and the heat cooks the food while simultaneously smoking it. Hot smoked food doesn't store for long—just a few days in the refrigerator—but, unlike cold smoking, it's ready to eat right away.

Fuel for the smoker

We believe that choosing your own favorite fuel is a journey of personal taste. However, let's start you off by saying that only hardwoods are good for smoking food. Americans swear by hickory; the British adore oak. Other woods to try are beech, maple, birch, chestnut, and apple. We have even heard of dried corncobs used as fuel. We always use shavings or sawdust as they don't flare up, smolder steadily for hours, and generate a consistent column of smoke. Never use kerosene or gasoline to light the fuel as they contaminate food and spoil the taste.

1. Hanging fish *from the bars of a smoker on old coat hangers leaves plenty of room for smoke to circulate.* **2. Cut cheese** *into wedges and blocks to maximize surface area for smoke to penetrate.* **3. Home-smoked cheese** *develops an appealing speckled golden rind; spicy chorizo sausages don't need further cooking after smoking.*

DIY cold smokehouse

In a permanent cold smokehouse, the smoke is produced by a fire in a pit. It passes through a flue and into the smoke chamber, where the food is arranged on shelves or hanging in the space. To build a movable cold smoker see pages 250–251.

The smoke chamber

Almost anything large enough, made of fireproof material, and with no paint or enamel that could burn off and contaminate food, will do—an old refrigerator is ideal. Cold smoking won't damage the plastic lining, which is easy to clean. Do not use galvanized metal, copper, or brass oxides for shelves as they taint the food and are a serious health hazard.

WHAT TO SMOKE

It takes a minimum of five to six hours to smoke small food items. A large ham, on the other hand, can take weeks.

- cheese
- fish
- chicken
- ham
- bacon
- sausages
- hard-boiled eggs

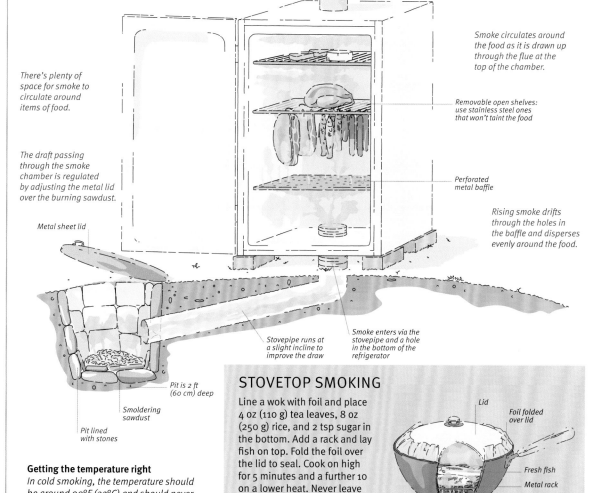

Insect-proof mesh on top of flue

Smoke circulates around the food as it is drawn up through the flue at the top of the chamber.

There's plenty of space for smoke to circulate around items of food.

Removable open shelves: use stainless steel ones that won't taint the food

The draft passing through the smoke chamber is regulated by adjusting the metal lid over the burning sawdust.

Perforated metal baffle

Rising smoke drifts through the holes in the baffle and disperses evenly around the food.

Metal sheet lid

Pit is 2 ft (60 cm) deep

Smoldering sawdust

Stovepipe runs at a slight incline to improve the draw

Smoke enters via the stovepipe and a hole in the bottom of the refrigerator

Pit lined with stones

Getting the temperature right

In cold smoking, the temperature should be around 90°F (32°C) and should never go higher than 122°F (50°C). Use an oven thermometer to check the temperature in the smoke chamber.

STOVETOP SMOKING

Line a wok with foil and place 4 oz (110 g) tea leaves, 8 oz (250 g) rice, and 2 tsp sugar in the bottom. Add a rack and lay fish on top. Fold the foil over the lid to seal. Cook on high for 5 minutes and a further 10 on a lower heat. Never leave unattended and eat the cooked food right away.

Lid

Foil folded over lid

Fresh fish

Metal rack

Rice, tea, and sugar mixture

Make a cold smoker

Building a smoker is surprisingly easy, cheap, and quick—it can be done in an hour. Find a spot for it in the yard on a heatproof base, such as bricks or concrete, but store it under cover when not in use. Experiment with what you put in your smoker. We have tried our own chorizo sausages, eggs, fish, even entire legs of ham. The time it takes to smoke the food to your taste may vary, but the amazing smoky undertones are consistently gorgeous.

YOU WILL NEED

- Empty oil drum
- Flexible metal ruler, pencil, scribe, punch
- Power drill, protective goggles
- Hinges and doorknob
- Electric jigsaw with a metal cutting blade
- Hammer, leather gloves
- Nuts and bolts, threaded metal bars, wire rack, piece of plywood

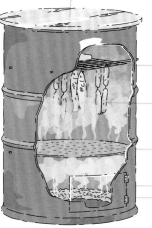

Loose-fitting wooden lid

In a cold smoker, gently smoldering sawdust produces clouds of smoke to flavor and preserve food.

Wire rack to hold food

Space to hang fish or sausages from metal bars

Perforated baffle to distribute smoke evenly

Door for lighting sawdust

Mound of sawdust

CUTTING OUT THE DOOR

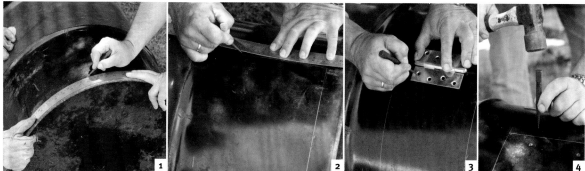

1. Mark the door of the smoker by drawing a small rectangle at the base of the drum using a metal ruler. It should be at least 6 x 10 in (15 x 25 cm). **2. Score the shape** using a metal scribe. **3. Mark the position** of the holes for the hinges on one side of the door using the scribe. **4. Dent the hinge holes** with a punch to stop the drill from sliding around on the metal.

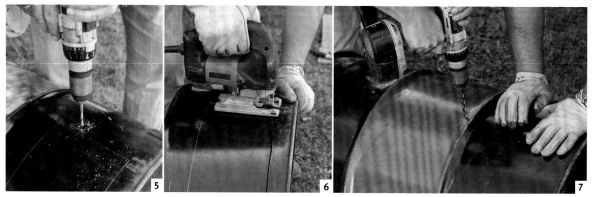

5. Drill holes for the hinge through the drum. The hinge will be fastened in place later but it is good to drill at this stage while the door is still attached to the drum and the surface is solid. Remove any burrs with a small file. Next, drill a hole at each corner of the door that is large enough to fit the jigsaw blade through. **6. Jigsaw out the door** and keep to one side.
7. Drill four holes above the door, two on each side of the barrel, all level with one another. (Use a punch first, as in step 4.) These will hold the two threaded bars that feed through the drum for the baffle to rest on. Make four more holes higher up, which will hold two more threaded bars to rest the grill or wire rack on for cooking—or you can hang food from them.

ASSEMBLING THE SMOKER

8. Perforate the top of the barrel with lots of holes spread evenly around. This will form the baffle, which sits just above the smoldering sawdust and distributes the smoke more evenly around the food.   **9. Cut around the top** of the drum with a jigsaw and place your newly made baffle inside the drum. Throw the door into the drum as well.   **10. Burn off** any unwanted residue or contaminants with a large wood fire. Feed the fire for half an hour or so until the smoke is burning more cleanly. Please be considerate of neighbors and follow local burning regulations.

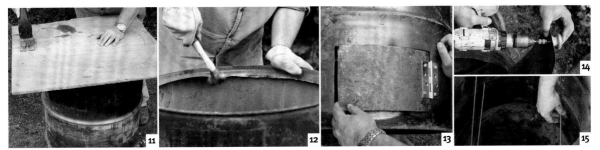

11. Saw a circular plywood lid for your smoker using the jigsaw. This will sit on top of the drum and shouldn't be airtight. **12. Hammer flat** the sharp inside rim of metal on the lid, so you don't cut yourself reaching in and out.   **13. Attach the door** with the set of hinges using nuts and bolts.   **14. Screw a doorknob** onto the door to make opening and closing easier and reduce the chance of injury on sharp metal edges. **15. Feed the metal bars** through the two sets of holes you made earlier.

USING THE SMOKER

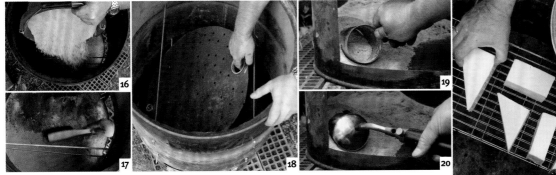

16. Pour the sawdust into the smoker.   **17. Brush it** so that the sawdust curves up and around the edges in a crescent shape, for a slower, more gradual burn.   **18. Position** the baffle.   **19. Use a tin can** with top and bottom cut off, and push it into the sawdust. **20. Light** the sawdust inside the tin can so that the burning starts right within the mound. We use a little butane lighter. Do not use gasoline or other fuels that will affect the taste. **21. Place** food on the wire rack and put the wooden lid on top. Leave to smoke overnight.

PROJECT **Make an earth oven**

Few tastes compare to the stone-baked flavor you get from cooking in a traditional earth oven. They can be used for everything from bread and pizzas to fish pies. On an environmental front, the simple clay structure and use of carbon-neutral wood fuel makes cooking in an earth oven a low-impact option. The cost of building one is next to nothing and the process, while a bit messy, is a lot of fun.

YOU WILL NEED

- Tape measure
- Pen
- Garden sieve
- Rolling pin
- Knife
- Trowel
- Clay—dig your own if possible
- Sand
- Newspaper
- Bricks or cinder blocks
- Stone slabs
- Wood

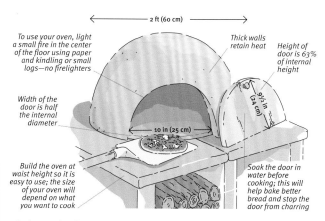

⟵ 2 ft (60 cm) ⟶

To use your oven, light a small fire in the center of the floor using paper and kindling or small logs—no firelighters

Thick walls retain heat

Height of door is 63% of internal height

Width of the door is half the internal diameter

9½ in (24 cm)

10 in (25 cm)

Build the oven at waist height so it is easy to use; the size of your oven will depend on what you want to cook

Soak the door in water before cooking; this will help bake better bread and stop the door from charring

Each oven has its own unique cooking temperature. Light the fire inside the oven, leave the door open, and wait a few hours. When the soot goes from the inside, remove the coals using a shovel and start cooking.

BUILDING THE STAND

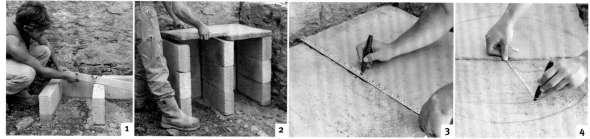

1. Build a firm base. We used some spare cinder blocks. Keep it level and build the structure up to a comfortable working height for cooking. **2. Prepare a solid floor** for your oven. It must have a smooth surface. We used a couple of old paving slabs. **3. Mark the center** of the oven. Make it as large as possible. Ours is about 2 ft (60 cm) in diameter. **4. Draw two circles**, one 3–4 in (7–10 cm) inside the first, to show the thickness of the walls. Note the radius of the inner circle.

PREPARING THE CLAY

5. Sift the clay to remove pebbles and debris if you dug your clay from the ground. **6. Lay a big tarp** on the ground and mix your clay—best done with bare feet. **7. Add sharp sand** (about a bucketful) and some water if the clay is very dry. Mixing takes time and effort. Don't slip!

8. Keep turning and mixing the clay. **9. Test the clay** to see whether it is ready to work with. Make a clay sausage. **10. Hold it** with half in your palm and the other half dangling over your hand. If the clay bends but does not break, it's ready to use.

MAKING THE OVEN BASE AND WALLS

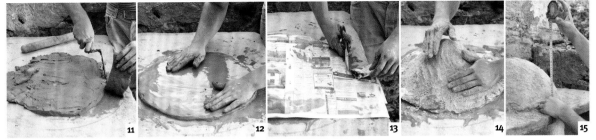

11. Roll out a circular layer ½ in (1 cm) thick on the internal circle of the base. Trim the edges with a trowel.   **12. Wet the clay,** then smooth it with your hands. This will serve as a smooth base for sliding whatever's being cooked in and out of the oven.
13. Cover the circle with a layer of moist newspaper to stop any sand from sticking to it.   **14. Pile on moist sand** and sculpt the shape of the earth oven, making a dome that is a few inches taller than the internal radius of the oven.   **15. Measure the height** of the sand dome, which will be the interior height of your oven. Multiply this by 0.63 to get the height of the door.

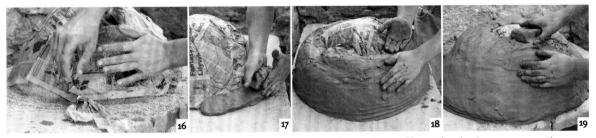

16. Cover the sand dome with wet newspaper to stop the clay from sticking to it.   **17. Shape the clay** into sausages, then flatten and squash them into place. Start at the base and work around and up, to cover the dome.   **18. Use the width** of your hand as a rough measurement: the layer of clay should be around 3–4 in (7–10 cm) thick.   **19. Try to push** the clay against itself, not against the mound of sand, as you add each piece. Cover the entire dome with clay, making sure it is still the same thickness at the top as the bottom. Wet your hands and smooth the surface of the finished dome.

MAKING THE DOOR

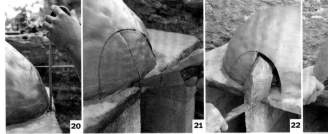

20. Mark out the height of the door using measurements you made earlier. Our sand dome is 15 in (38 cm) tall so the door is just under 9½ in (24 cm) in height. Mark the width of the door. Ours measures 10 in (25 cm)—half the oven's internal diameter and perfectly big enough for a small pizza to slide in and out. **21. Draw the shape** of the door freehand with a pen. Use a sharp knife to cut out the door. Do this in two sections, cutting down the midline of the door.   **22. Slide the knife** under one half of the door. Slide the excess clay out. Repeat for the other half of the door.   **23. Cut away the** excess clay on the inside of the door to enlarge it slightly. Leave the oven for a few days to a week.   **24. Remove the sand** when the walls of the oven resist denting when you poke them.

FINISHING TOUCHES

Repair any cracks that emerge on the oven as it dries, and fit a door.

■ **Wet the surface,** then score it with a cross-hatch pattern (left). Apply more clay to the cracked area (right). Repeat if cracks appear after the oven is used.
■ **Make a wooden door.** Use a paper template to get the shape right. However, it doesn't need to be a perfect fit.

Brewing beer and mead

Over the years we have made and consumed large quantities of our own beer. You can brew beer just about anywhere, and the resulting drink can be strong and delicious. Make your own beer to save money and have fun experimenting, but on the whole we'd recommend brewing more unusual beers or traditional mead—drinks that are not available commercially that test your taste buds.

Beer and ale

Ale was traditionally made with water, malt, and yeast, while beer was produced using a malt brew, with the magic of hops adding bitterness, and over time this became the accepted brewing method.

Brewing kits are probably the simplest way to attempt your own home brew for the first time. Simply mix together sugar, dried yeast, and water, plus other chosen ingredients (see recipes opposite), to enjoy your very own refreshing beer. On the other hand, you may want to go down the traditional route, as follows:

■ **Make "wort"** by using a rolling pin to crush malted grain wrapped in a cloth. Mix the husks with the required amount of hops. Transfer the mix into a muslin bag and place it in a saucepan, cover with water, and simmer for 45 minutes.

■ **Strain the contents** into a vessel for fermenting, such as a demijohn or a clean bucket with a lid. Add cool water to top it off—make it up to 1 gallon (4 liters) in a demijohn.

■ **When the wort cools** to 59°F (15°C), stir 1 tsp yeast into each gallon (4 liters) of liquid. Cover and keep in a warm place for a week.

■ **When fermentation** has ceased (the bubbles are no longer rising to the top), leave the brew for a further day to cool down and for the sediment to settle.

■ **Siphon the beer** into sterilized bottles and add ½ tsp of sugar to each one to give the beer extra fizz when you open it. Label the bottles and start drinking after 2 weeks.

BREWING TIPS

■ **Use brewer's yeast** rather than baking or wine-making varieties for a better-quality beer.
■ **Invest in a bottle capper** to close the caps on the bottles.
■ **Try bottles at intervals** when waiting for your homebrew to mature to ensure you don't get a secondary fermentation. And don't leave them for so long that they explode.
■ **Test your brew** with a hydrometer, which gauges the fermentation progress, showing you when the beer is ready to siphon into bottles. It also indicates the alcohol content.
■ **Most states permit homebrewing** of up to 100 gallons of beer per person age 21 or older. The maximum production allowed is typically 200 gallons, if two or more people of legal drinking age live at the residence. The selling of home-brewed beer is prohibited.

RECIPE Honey mead

Mead is one of the oldest drinks known to man, and was especially popular in northern Europe where grapes didn't grow well. It was drunk after Norse weddings at a celebration known as a "honeymoon." Every year we make our own mead using honey from our beehives, and it's as good a reason as any to become a beekeeper (see pages 212–213).

YOU WILL NEED
■ 4½ lb (2 kg) honey
■ Juice of 2 lemons
■ Juice of 2 oranges
■ 1 heaping tsp yeast

1. Mix the honey with 1 gallon (4 liters) of water in a large pan and warm it until the honey has dissolved. **2. Add the fruit juices** to the honey mixture and leave to cool. **3. Add the yeast** and mix it in. **4. Strain** the golden liquid into a demijohn and leave the mead to ferment with an airlock seal attached to it (see page 257). When fermentation stops, siphon off the mead into sterilized bottles (see page 256) and "lay down" for 6 months to mature.

RECIPE Nettle beer

Nettles make surprisingly delicious beer. Generally we are not too keen on nettle soup or nettle tea, despite the health benefits, but nettle beer is on a whole other level. It is easy to make and tastes great. Use the fresh green tops of the nettles, as they make the best beer, and make sure all your equipment is scrupulously clean (see page 256).

YOU WILL NEED
- 2 lb (1 kg) young nettles
- 2 lemons, rind and juice
- 1 lb (500 g) turbinado sugar
- 2 tbsp (25 g) cream of tartar
- 1 tsp brewer's yeast
- Large pan
- Plastic funnel
- Bottles

1. Cut off the tops of the nettles and throw away any roots. Rinse briefly to get rid of any bugs.   **2. Boil the nettles** in about 1 gallon (4 liters) of water.   **3. Strain the liquid** into a large container and add the lemon rind and juice, sugar, and cream of tartar. Make up to a volume of 1 gallon (4 liters) with water and then stir vigorously.   **4. Transfer** to a demijohn. Then, when the brew is cool, add the yeast. Allow 3–4 days for fermentation to take place and then strain the beer into clean, sterilized bottles (see page 256).

RECIPE Ginger beer

Ginger beer has always been a great favorite of ours, and ever since we discovered that we can grow ginger at Newhouse Farm, the beverage has become a seasonal treat. To grow ginger, in spring plant a sprouting section of root into a pot of good growing mix and wait for the rhizome to develop. Ginger must be brought inside over winter to avoid the cold, and we harvest ours when the tall stalk withers in winter, saving a bit to replant next year.

YOU WILL NEED
- 2 tbsp (25 g) crushed ginger root
- 1½ tbsp (15 g) cream of tartar
- 1 lemon, rind and juice
- 1 lb (450 g) white sugar
- 1 tsp brewer's yeast

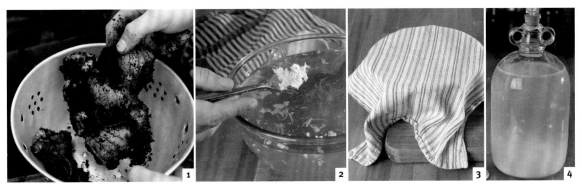

1. Pick your ginger and give it a good scrub before peeling it.   **2. Crush the ginger** in a mortar and pestle and then mix it with the cream of tartar and some grated lemon rind in a bowl. Add to a bowl of boiling water and then mix in the sugar. Stir until the sugar has fully dissolved and allow to cool. Add the yeast and the lemon juice and make the mixture up to 1 gallon (4 liters) with water.   **3. Cover with a dish towel** and leave in a warm place until fermentation starts. Remove the surface scum.   **4. Transfer to a demijohn.** Bottle and cork after 2 days and drink within a few days after that.

Making wine

Pursuing the self-sufficient dream can be a lot of hard work. Indeed, sometimes getting out of bed early in the morning to feed your animals or braving the cold weather to weed the vegetable beds can feel monotonous or deflating. However, on a cold day after laboring outside, what could be better than relaxing in front of a roaring wood fire with a glass of aromatic homemade wine?

Successful winemaking

When you make a good bottle of wine, there's not much in the world that can beat the feeling of satisfaction, pride, and, after a glass or two, relaxation. For a small investment, it's easy to make lots of drinkable wine, and you also get the chance to try some exotic recipes that are not available at any liquor store we know of. To make a fine wine, however, requires good ingredients, overall cleanliness, and loads of patience.

Winemaking can be approached as a scientific experiment with accurate measurements and meticulous preparations, or treated as a vibrant and fun activity, as we do. We are not too bound by a strict regimen and prefer to let the process evolve naturally. Having said that, there are a few basic rules.

Essential tips

All wines consist of water, flavorings, sugar, acid, tannin, and yeast. The quantity of each ingredient varies greatly and the wine improves or degrades accordingly. Time is another key component, and the need to exercise patience during the process cannot be overemphasized.

▓ **Keep bottles** and other apparatus scrupulously clean. Warm bottles in the oven, and then fill with boiling water. Leave for a few minutes, pour out the water, and hang them upside down to dry. Or use a sterilizing solution. Campden tablets clean all types of equipment. Read the instructions and always leave for the full designated time so they can do their job properly.

1. Use scissors to cut bunches of grapes from vines. **2. The traditional way** of making wine is excellent fun. Get your socks off and clean your feet well. Then squish the grapes under your feet and between your toes until they are reduced to pulp and grape juice.

▓ Our quantities of sugar for making wine come from old-fashioned advice. We use 2¼ lb (1 kg) of sugar "in the gallon" (4.5 liters) to make dry table wine ("in the gallon" means you put the sugar in the container and add wine up to the volume of a gallon). Use 2¾ lb (1.25 kg) of sugar for a medium wine; anything over 3 lb (1.35 kg) makes a very sweet wine.

▓ **Use good-quality wine yeast**, granulated or liquid, available from winemaking shops or online. You can use baker's yeast, but it often makes a poorer-quality, frothy wine. For a good, strong wine you can also add yeast nutrients available from most winemaking shops.

▓ **More acid** may be needed for wines made from flowers or grain. Buy citric acid from a wine shop, or use lemon juice, which works well.

▓ **Two stages to fermenting.** The first is the frothy, active stage where the yeasts are multiplying and need some air around them. Leave the jar or demijohn three-quarters full during this stage. For the second stage, top off the jar with water and place a fermentation lock on the top. This allows the gases that have been produced by the wine to escape, while simultaneously keeping the air out. The lock also prevents invasion by the bacteria that turn wine into vinegar, by stopping any fruit flies that carry vinegar bacillus from entering the jar and contaminating your precious wine.

▓ **Temperature** is all-important, and you must try to keep your wine at temperatures favorable to the vital yeasts. During the first fermentation, aim for 75°F (24°C). Do not allow the temperature to rise over 81°F (27°C) or the yeast will start to die; allow it fall beneath 70°F (21°C) and it will be too cold for the yeast to work.

RECIPE **Wine from grapes**

You can make wine out of just about anything! Some of our more unconventional favorites are pea pod, blackberry, nettle, parsnip, and rose hip. We have tried and enjoyed all of them, but in our opinion it's hard to beat the taste of a traditional grape wine. We have struggled to make a heavy-bodied red wine, but have been very successful using our own grapes to make rosé, as shown here. Grape vines can thrive even in our cooler climate (see page 149). Try growing them against south-facing walls, under cover in a greenhouse, or outside on a warm, south-facing slope.

YOU WILL NEED
- Red and white grapes
- Sugar (for quantities, see opposite)
- Wine yeast
- Citric acid
- Wine press
- Mesh cloth
- Campden tablets
- Demijohn, funnel, and fermentation lock
- Sieve
- Bottling and racking equipment

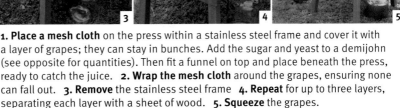

1. Place a mesh cloth on the press within a stainless steel frame and cover it with a layer of grapes; they can stay in bunches. Add the sugar and yeast to a demijohn (see opposite for quantities). Then fit a funnel on top and place beneath the press, ready to catch the juice. **2. Wrap the mesh cloth** around the grapes, ensuring none can fall out. **3. Remove** the stainless steel frame **4. Repeat** for up to three layers, separating each layer with a sheet of wood. **5. Squeeze** the grapes.

6. Don't fill the demijohn right up to the top or it may explode during the first fermentation stage; the yeasts also need air to multiply. Leave it about three-quarters full. **7. When the wine is no longer frothy**, indicating that it is in the second stage of fermentation, top off the jar with water and place a fermentation lock on top. When the wine is six months old, it will be time to rack it and bottle it (see right). **8. The by-product** of the pressing stage of wine-making is a flat, fairly dry cake of grape skins and seeds. We feed this to our pigs as a little treat.

RACKING AND BOTTLING

To "rack" means to siphon your wine off from the yeast (or "lees") that has settled at the bottom, so it doesn't spoil the flavor. We use a short plastic tube to siphon the wine into a clean container. Repeat a month later and, if you have the patience, do it again three weeks after that. Some people leave their wine in a cold place to hasten the settling of any sediment. After six months the wine should be ready to seal in sterilized bottles without risk of exploding. Leave about 1 in (2.5 cm) at the top for the cork. A corking gun is a good investment, or use a wooden mallet. Cork and label the bottles and leave them for a year, stored on their sides in a dark place at about 55°F (13°C).

Flower, vegetable, and fencerow wines

Country wines are fermented drinks made out of all sorts of different ingredients other than grapes. Vegetables also make interesting country wines, but need extra table sugar or honey added to them. Not everyone lives in a location suited to growing grapes, but everyone can make some type of country wine. The only disadvantage is that these wines don't store for long, and are best consumed within a year of bottling.

Flower wines

Flower wines are extremely easy to make, tasty, and beautifully aromatic. Simply pour 1 gallon (4 liters) of boiling water into a large fermenting vessel, preferably made of metal, and add the flowers (see below). Bring the water and the flowers to a boil and simmer on low heat for 15 minutes, stirring occasionally. Let the mixture cool slightly and add 4 lb (2 kg) of superfine sugar and the juice of 3 lemons, and, when it has cooled to about 75°F (24°C), add 1 teaspoon of yeast. Strain and pour the wine into a demijohn, and put a fermentation lock on top. Leave it to ferment and bottle when ready (as described on p257). Leave for a few months and then drink. Some of our traditional flower wine favorites are:

■ **Gorse** Never go and collect gorse flowers in a T-shirt! The fragrant flowers are protected by hundreds of prickly spines, so wear long sleeves and gloves to grab them. It's worth the effort, though, as they make amazing gorse wine, which smells a bit like coconuts and is very sweet. You will need at least 2 quarts (2 liters) of gorse flowers for every gallon (4 liters) of water.

■ **Dandelion** This is a lovely light wine that is fun to make. Collect the dandelion flowers from mid- to late morning and then pick the petals off the flowerheads. You will need 2 pints (1 liter) of petals. Wash them in running water to remove any bugs or unwanted residue. Then leave in 1 gallon (4 liters) of water to infuse overnight. The next day, make the wine as described (see left).

Other traditional favorites

■ **Pea pod** This wine is particularly remarkable because it is made from the part you normally throw into the compost bin. You can use any sort of pea pods, or even bean pods, as long as they are still greenish. Add 4 lb (2 kg) of empty pea pods, plus the rind of an orange and a lemon, to 1 gallon (4 liters) of water. Bring to a boil and simmer for at least 30 minutes, then allow to cool. Strain the liquid over 2 lb (1 kg) of sugar, 1 teaspoon of yeast, and the juice of the lemon and orange, and then stir until everything is dissolved and mixed. Ferment and bottle, and leave for 6 months before indulging in one of the mysteries of the vegetable plot.

■ **Parsnip** These vegetables produce a very pleasant, light white wine. Pick and scrub 4 lb (2 kg) of parsnips. Then slice them, without peeling them, and place in a large pan with 1 gallon (4 liters) of water. Cook until tender and strain the liquid into another vessel. Remove the parsnips and make a warming winter soup with them. For the wine, reheat the infused liquid with 3 lb (1.5 kg) of sugar plus the juice of a lemon, its rind, and 1 teaspoon of yeast. Ferment and bottle, and drink within 6 months.

Pick elderflowers on a hot day while they are in full bloom and strongly scented. It is worth using a ladder to get the best ones, which always seem to be just out of reach. Remember not to strip a tree bare, otherwise there will be no elderberries to use later in the season!

BIRCH SAP WINE

If you like German dry white wine, find some mature birch trees to make a country alternative. Tap the sap in mid-spring from a few trees with trunks at least 12 in (30 cm) in diameter, so that no tree gets overtapped. Use a cordless drill to make a 1-in (2.5-cm) diameter hole in the trunk. Insert a short offcut of pipe into the hole, hang a bucket beneath it, and wait for the rising sap to flow out. Make wine as for pea pods, boiling 1 gallon (4 liters) of sap (adding water if you don't have quite enough) with 2 lb (1 kg) of sugar. Drink after a month.

You can collect *about 1 gallon (4 liters) of sap in a day from a mature tree.*

Elderflower champagne

Elderflower champagne is definitely at the glamorous end of self-sufficiency. It is made simply by fermenting the natural yeasts in the flowers, which then turn into a refreshing bubbly drink that is only mildly alcoholic. The good things about elderflower champagne are that it is cheap, delicious, incredibly fragrant, and quick to make. The main problem with this bubbly stuff, however, is that it if you leave it to ferment for too long, the bottles will start exploding, spraying sticky floral liquid all over the place. Luckily, this can be easily avoided by slowly releasing some of the gases when the plastic bottles start to bulge and look ready to burst.

YOU WILL NEED
- About 2½ cups (600 ml) compressed elderflowers
- 1½ lb (675 g) white sugar
- 2 lemons
- 2 tbsp wine vinegar
- Large metal container that holds 1 gallon (4 liters) water
- Zester
- Pitcher
- Sieve
- Funnel
- Plastic soda bottles

BREWING

1. Once you have collected enough flowers, mix them together with 1 gallon (4 liters) of water and stir thoroughly. **2. Add the sugar** and continue stirring until most of the sugar has dissolved. **3. Remove the zest** from the lemons with a zester. **4. Cut the lemons** in half and squeeze out the juice. **5. Add the zest** to the elderflowers and water and then add the lemon juice and white wine vinegar.

BOTTLING

6. Cover the container and leave in a warm place for 24 hours. **7. The next day**, strain the liquid into a clean pitcher. **8. Then pour** into sterilized bottles. We like to use 2-liter soda bottles, as they allow you to release the explosive gas by turning the screw top a little. Sterilize using Campden tablets rather than boiling water, which could melt the plastic bottles (see page 256). Leave the bottles capped for two weeks and drink before the champagne is a month old.

ELDERBERRY WINE

- **Make elderberry wine** in late summer or early fall. With a fork, strip 4 lb (2 kg) elderberries from their stalks. Crush them in a large bowl using a rolling pin.
- **Add 1 gallon** (4 liters) boiling water, stir and, once it has cooled to 68°F (20°C), add 1 tsp yeast and the juice of 2 lemons. Cover the mixture and leave in a warm place for a few days, stirring daily.
- **Strain the liquid** through a sieve into a pan with 3 lb (1.5 kg) sugar and stir until it has dissolved. Pour from the pan into a large demijohn. After the first ferment has finished, put on a fermentation lock and leave to continue fermenting.
- **Transfer to dark bottles** and wait at least 6 months before opening.

Making hard cider

Cider-making is a really social activity. Every year we collect apples from our orchard, but we also do a bit of "scrumping." This involves making the most of any underutilized fruit trees in the area and going around the village with a trailer attached to a mountain bike—of course, we ask permission first. We then make hard cider from the fermented juice of our apple collection.

Know your apples

Any variety of apple can be used to make hard cider, and even scruffy-looking windfalls can be turned into good "scrumpy," as it's known in the West Country of England. Some varieties of apples store well, but on the whole, apples don't last too long unless they are picked when ripe and are not bruised or damaged in any way. So, the advantage of hard cider is that you can successfully preserve huge quantities of fruit and save lots of money on alcohol by doing so.

Unless you are growing specific cider-making apples, such as Langworthy, Foxwhelp, or Crimson King, which can be brewed on their own, the trick to making a truly tasty cider is to use a mixture of different varieties. Combine about one-third each of bittersweet, sweet, and tart apples for a good brew. Try the following:

■ **Bittersweet apples** are low in acid but high in tannins, such as Dabinett, Somerset Red, and Yarlington Mill.

■ **Sweet dessert apples** that have medium acidity and are low in tannin, such as Cox's Orange Pippin, Golden Delicious, and Worcester Pearmain.

■ **Tart apples** include Royal Russets and Herefordshire Costards.

We have planted all sorts of traditional apple trees for eating, cooking, and for making cider, but until the trees are mature and fruiting well, we tend to use whatever apples we can lay our hands on, and the resulting cider always does the job.

Fermenting

Once you have your fresh apple juice stored in demijohns or a larger fermenting bin, it's time for the natural yeasts to work their magic. We allow the yeasts from the apple skins and surrounding fruit to do the fermenting, but if you want to guarantee success, add a few teaspoons of yeast to the mix.

Many people dislike roughly made scrumpy and add sugar or syrup to their cider to make it taste sweeter.

We don't mind the dryness of pure cider and find that it is also great to use in cooking, particularly with rabbit loin, mustard, and some root vegetables. Yummy...

Once fermentation has ceased (any time from ten days to a month), you can rack off the cider straight into bottles for storage, using a plastic tube to siphon (see page 257). You'll often find a secondary fermentation takes place in the bottle. We once bottled some apple juice after trying to pasteurize it and were surprised to find it had turned into a bubbly cider similar to the fizzy drinks of Normandy. Of course, we didn't reveal the mistake to our guests, who loved it.

There is a stage in the fermentation process of cider when it is described as being "hungry." We have heard countless stories from locals about cider makers throwing in bits of beef and even the odd rat to add strength to the brew. Undoubtedly, most of this will just be hearsay, but it pays to be wary of unknown scrumpy.

Collect windfalls *as soon as possible or they will start to ferment naturally on the ground. Don't worry if they are a little bruised.*

MAKE CIDER VINEGAR

When cider turns into vinegar by mistake, it's a disaster, but when made specially it is great for cooking, and in chutneys and pickles. Soak some wood shavings in a vinegar you like the flavor of, then place them in a large barrel or plastic tub with a spigot at the bottom. Put a wooden or plastic plate, drilled with pin-sized holes, on top of the shavings, and pour on your cider so it drains slowly though the holes. Cover the top of the barrel with muslin. As the cider drips down, it is exposed to air and *Acetobacter* bacteria. Drain off the liquid and leave in an open container; it will turn into vinegar in a week.

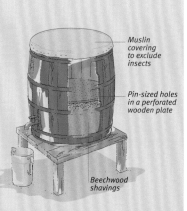

Muslin covering to exclude insects

Pin-sized holes in a perforated wooden plate

Beechwood shavings

RECIPE **Hard cider**

Before you crush your ripe apples, leave them in a heap for 2–3 days to soften, or pick up your windfalls, which will already be very juicy. Try to avoid using apples that have serious pest problems—feed them to the pigs if they are crawling with maggots. Generally, most apples will be usable, and even if they don't look perfect they can still be turned into hard cider. The quantity of juice that apples produce in the press varies greatly, but on average we'd expect 10 lb (4.5 kg) of apples to make just about a gallon (4 liters) of cider. Make sure all of your equipment is cleaned thoroughly. As with many seasonal jobs, it can be almost a whole year since you last used your tools, so a good cleaning is essential. Use this same method for making perry—a sweeter drink than cider, made from pears.

YOU WILL NEED
- Apples (or pears if making perry)
- Apple crusher
- Apple press
- Mesh fabric or muslin
- Sterilized demijohn or fermenting tub

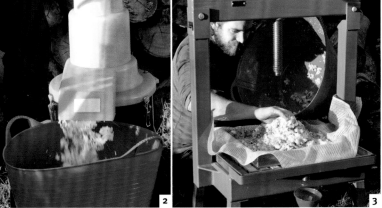

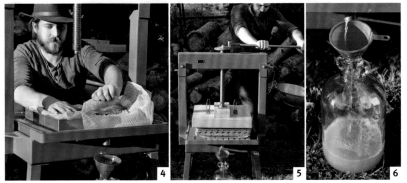

1. Pour your apples into the crusher, keeping your hands away from the rotating blades, having first positioned a container to catch the apples. A lower-tech means is to chop the apples in a wooden box using a spade, described below.
2. The crushed apples will appear, as if by magic, in the container at the foot of the machine. **3. Place the mesh fabric** over the apple press base, leaving plenty of spare fabric around the edges. Spread a layer of crushed apples.

4. Cover the apples with the mesh fabric and place the demijohn under the press.
5. Wind down the pressing mechanism until all the juice has run into the demijohn. Unwrap the leftover pulp and feed it to the pigs or put it in the compost pile. Then refill your press with more crushed apples and repeat the steps until you have pressed them all. **6. The juice looks cloudy** initially, but it clears throughout the fermenting process. Leave to ferment in the demijohn and then bottle.

CRUSHING BY HAND

We have invested in an electric apple crusher that's quick and easy to use, and allows us to make large volumes of cider. But you can crush the apples with just a strong wooden box and a spade. Fill the box almost to the top with apples. Make sure that they are closely packed together so that they can't move easily, but don't overfill the box or the fruit will jump out and spill onto the ground. Use a sharp, clean spade to chop the apples into small pieces before laying them on the fruit press.

NATURAL REMEDIES With an ever-growing awareness of the impact harmful chemicals can have on our bodies, people are returning to more natural ways of treating everyday ailments. We tend to use quite a lot of complementary remedies and have suggested some of our favorites that you might like to try. Our bodies and homes have become battlefields and we are encouraged to use more and more chemical-based products to kill all the germs. We feel that there is a need for balance, and some of the ideas in this chapter may help you think a little differently about the job of cleaning.

Herbal tinctures

Tinctures are an efficient and simple way to preserve herbs. Alcohol, or a mixture of alcohol and water, is used to dissolve and extract the active substances from the herbs at the same time as preserving them. On pressing, fresh herbs yield more tincture than dried herbs, so if you want to make your own at home, consider growing your own medicinal herbs.

The ingredients

Tinctures can be made from all sorts of herbs and flowers. Some plants that make effective tinctures include echinacea for immunity boosting; nettle leaves for arthritis and rheumatism; dandelion to help with indigestion or loss of appetite; and hawthorn to help with high blood pressure. However, we would recommend that you always seek expert advice from a licensed herbalist before making and using your own tinctures, especially for more serious medical complaints.

The simplest way to make a tincture is by maceration (soaking the herbs in a solvent). Clear alcohol such as plain vodka is the most commonly used preserving solvent in tincture making. The minimum alcohol content required to inhibit the growth of unwanted organisms is 50 proof (25 percent). For most homemade tinctures, 80 proof vodka (40 percent alcohol content) works well.

The weight of herbs to volume of alcohol used affects the potency of the tincture: the greater the proportion of herbs, the higher the potency.

Taking a tincture

Consuming your tincture is as easy as making it. All you need to do is add a few drops to a glass of water once a day or as prescribed by an herbalist. Tinctures are stronger than infusions (see pages 266–267), so the required dosage can be much smaller.

RECIPE **Digestive tincture**

This tincture is ideal for those who suffer from burping, bloating, or indigestion. If you have wolfed down a meal too quickly and regretted it, the time spent making this remedy will be more than worthwhile. Take it before or after eating to stimulate your digestive enzymes. Do not use it during pregnancy.

YOU WILL NEED
- 3½ oz (100 g) rosemary
- 3 oz (85 g) bay leaves
- ¼ oz (10 g) wormwood
- 1¾ cups (400 ml) vodka
- Canning jar
- Press
- Muslin
- Dark-colored bottle

1. **Pick your herbs** and remove any insects. Chop the herbs into ¾-in (2-cm) pieces and place in a large jar. Pour the vodka over them, close the lid tightly, and shake the jar well. Continue to shake the jar daily for at least 2 weeks.
2. **Strain the contents** into a cup using muslin or cheesecloth and squeeze as much of the liquid out of the herbs as possible with your hands or with a small press, if you have one.   3. **Transfer the tincture** into a dark glass bottle, label it with the contents and date, and store in a cool, dark place. Take 1 tsp in a small cup of water up to three times a day.

Plant your own medicinal garden

It's easy to create a medicinal bed or border in the smallest garden. At our farm we have a medicinal garden of herbs, which we use in tinctures and infusions to help treat common minor ailments. Medicinal plants not only look attractive, they also tend to attract bees and smell gorgeous. Although many of the plants overlap in their healing properties, together they make a dazzling display.

KEY

Bites and bruises
1 Calendula
2 Comfrey
3 Lavender

Sleep
4 Chamomile
5 Passionflower
6 Valerian
7 Hops

Hangover and fatigue
8 Echinacea
9 Dandelion
10 Mint
11 Chile peppers

Headache
12 Rosemary
13 Feverfew
14 Mint

Coughs and colds
15 Lemon balm
16 Garlic
17 Sage
18 Thyme

Indigestion
19 Senna
20 Mint
21 Fig

QUICK STING RELIEF

If you are plagued by bites and nettle stings in the garden, find the nearest bunch of plantain and pick a handful of leaves. The juice from the leaves is more soothing than the traditional remedy of dock leaves.

Rub the plantain leaves firmly *between your hands until they start to produce some juice. Keep going and then squeeze the cooling green liquid onto the sore area.*

Revitalizing infusions

For a refreshing pick-me-up, cover the leaves and flowers from herbal plants with boiling water to make an infusion. Your choice of herbs will depend on taste and dedication to good health: some are delicious while others are an acquired taste and can be very bitter. Over the years we have tried out various combinations and, as well as those described here, particularly enjoy mint and lemon verbena as an everyday cup of tea. Experiment with different herbs to discover your favorites.

Making an infusion

Infusions are relatively easy to make from leaves and flowers. Place a heaped teaspoon of each herb in a mug of boiling water and allow the leaves and flowers to infuse. Or to be more scientific about it, add 1 oz (30 g) dried herbs or 2 oz (60 g) fresh herbs to 1 pint (500 ml) boiling water. Cover and leave the herbs to infuse for about 10 minutes. We like to use a tea pot with a central strainer. Alternatively, you can use an old-fashioned tea strainer that infuses in the mug and is then removed when the drink isto your taste.

Using infusions

You can drink these herbal teas either hot or cold and also use infusions topically as a wash or in a bath, as a douche or enema, or use them as a mouthwash or gargle; mint is especially effective here.

■ **Drink 1 cup** (250 ml) three times a day if you are under the weather or ⅔ cup (150 ml) every 2 hours to relieve particular symptoms.

■ **Infusions keep** in the refrigerator for 24 hours and can be taken cold, but be aware that cool infusions can stimulate urination.

Great healers

As well as our favorite healing herbs listed to the right, try drinking ginger infusion for travel sickness; feverfew for reducing the intensity of a migraine; elderflowers for helping ease cold symptoms; and nettle leaves—wear your gloves when picking them—to reduce stress.

CALMING HERBS

■ **Chamomile** makes a great lawn and has a reputation for soothing the central nervous system, leaving you super-calm. It also combines well with mint. As well as drinking the flowers as an infusion, place dried chamomile in a muslin bag in the bathtub for extra relaxation. Mix it with any of these calming herbs: comfrey, hyssop, lemon balm, passionflower, and valerian.

■ **Lavender** flowers are highly attractive to bees and as a bedtime drink will encourage a good night's sleep. It is also especially soothing for a headache: use 2 tsp of fresh flowers or 1 tsp dried and infuse.

Beautiful flowers *Chamomile and lavender are, of course, also very attractive additions to the garden, and bees love them, too.*

Take time out to chill *After an afternoon's hard work in the veggie patch, you can't beat a refreshing glass of mint tea, with leaves freshly plucked from the medicinal garden.*

RECIPE **Spiced propolis infusion**

We have been making this drink to soothe sore throats since we first started keeping bees. Propolis is a fantastic bee product used in the hive as a sort of glue, but it has great antiseptic properties. To collect it, install a propolis net above a super or brood box (see pages 212–213). The bees don't like the holes and will fill them with propolis. To harvest it, remove the net and place it in the freezer for a few hours. Scrunch it up and collect the pieces. You will need at least a 120-proof alcohol, such as strong rum or vodka, to dissolve the propolis. For smaller amounts of propolis, use 2 tbsp alcohol to each ¼ oz (10 g).

YOU WILL NEED
- 4 oz (100 g) propolis
- 2 cups (400 ml) 120-proof alcohol
- Fresh ginger root
- 1 lemon
- Cloves
- 1–2 tsp honey
- Glass jar
- Coffee filter

1. Harvest the propolis as described. **2. For the tincture,** put the propolis and alcohol in a jar and shake every day for 6–8 days until the propolis has dissolved. Strain the liquid through a coffee filter to remove bits of bee that may be mixed in with it. **3. To make the drink,** squeeze the juice from half the lemon and slice the rest, studding each slice with cloves. Cut some slices of ginger root. **4. Squirt a few drops** of propolis into a mug and add boiling water with the honey, lemon juice, and slices of ginger root and lemon.

OTHER FAVORITE INFUSIONS

Some of our favorite infusions are (from left to right): lavender and chamomile, the perfect calming drink before bedtime; sage and thyme, for relief from a sore throat; lemon balm, for days when you are feeling stressed out and need to relax; and peppermint and elderflower to ease cold symptoms.

Immunity-boosting syrups

Our mindset with illness is that prevention is considerably better than a cure. Generally, we try to stay healthy by eating plenty of fresh fruit and vegetables full of vitamins and minerals, but sometimes a quick fix is needed when a cold appears on the horizon or if we start to feel under the weather. This is where health-giving syrups come in handy.

Preserving in sugar

Using plenty of sugar in syrups is a common preserving technique that was widely used when refrigeration was not available. Saturating herbs and berries with sugar means there is not enough water for microorganisms to multiply and yeasts to develop.

Some good health-stimulating syrups to make at home are thyme and licorice; rosehip; garlic and honey; and burdock. Always make sure you track down recipes from a trusted source before you start consuming homemade concoctions.

Healing combination

Elderberry syrup, described below, is rich in vitamin C. To make a more intensely soothing concoction, mix equal quantities of the syrup with an elderberry tincture, which is made as the digestive tincture on page 264, mixing together 7 oz (200 g) berries and 14 fl oz (400 ml) vodka. Take 1 tsp of the remedy every few hours.

Elderberries *Elder has been called "the medicine chest of the people," as it provides so many remedies for common complaints. The berries follow the flowers.*

RECIPE **Elderberry syrup**

Elderberry syrup is an excellent remedy for boosting your immune system because it has high levels of vitamin C and antiviral properties, making it effective against colds, sore throats, and even flu. Always use plenty of sugar in syrups, but not so much that the mixture crystallizes when it cools. Elderberry syrup has a high sugar content, so it can be easily stored over the winter months and is pleasant and convenient to take.

YOU WILL NEED
- 1½ cups (200 g) elderberries
- 2 cups (400 g) sugar
- 12 cloves
- 1 in (2.5 cm) sliced ginger root
- Funnel
- Glass bottles

1. Gather ripe stalks of elderberries and strip the berries from the stems with a fork. Put them in a pan and add 1 cup (250 ml) water. Bring to a boil, reduce the heat, and simmer for about 30 minutes, until the berries yield their juice. Remove from the heat and mash the berries. Then strain the contents of the pan through a sieve and return the juice to the pan.   **2. Add the sugar,** cloves, and ginger. Return the pan to the heat and stir until the sugar dissolves. Bring to a boil for a further 5 minutes.   **3. Pour the liquid** into a bottle, seal, and refrigerate. Take 1 tbsp in a mug of boiling water every 2 hours when cold symptoms start and then three times a day until you feel better.

Healing beauty

Working outside on the farm, we suffer from our fair share of scratches, scrapes, bites, and chapped skin—but we still like to look beautiful! We don't spend the day itching and complaining; we just apply some homemade salve. A few years ago we started using dried calendula flowers in oil to soothe rashes and scratches, but now we make a salve using plants from our medicinal garden.

Be kind to your skin

Most skincare items are made with 90 percent water, some petroleum derivatives, and a concoction of chemicals to add fragrance and that bubbly lather. We strongly believe that these products carry much of the blame for exacerbating skin problems, such as eczema, and are not the best beauty option. So try making your own natural beauty products instead; they can save you money and they smell wonderful.

"Natural" products

There are many green and gorgeous skincare products that profess to be natural, but check their ingredients. The words "organic" and "natural" on the label needn't mean they are certified organic. Beware, too, of "green" claims on packaging and in the marketing campaigns of some skin-care giants. They are often misleading and may only mean the contents were derived from nature at some stage in their production.

Calendula *is one of our favorite flowers. It grows easily in a temperate climate, works well for companion planting (see p101), and self-seeds, so it requires very little attention.*

RECIPE **Calendula salve**

Salves are similar to tinctures in that they are made by extracting the active properties of plants and preserving them to be used medicinally. However, salves are made with pure vegetable oil rather than alcohol or vinegar, and combining the oil with wax produces a soothing ointment that can be applied directly to the skin. Calendula has wonderful healing properties and works brilliantly as an antiseptic. It makes a great lip balm, too.

YOU WILL NEED
- Enough dried calendula flowers to fill a tall jar
- Sunflower oil
- Beeswax
- Sieve
- Small glass jars

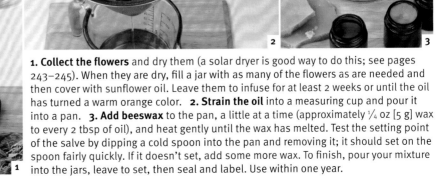

1. Collect the flowers and dry them (a solar dryer is good way to do this; see pages 243–245). When they are dry, fill a jar with as many of the flowers as are needed and then cover with sunflower oil. Leave them to infuse for at least 2 weeks or until the oil has turned a warm orange color.   **2. Strain the oil** into a measuring cup and pour it into a pan.   **3. Add beeswax** to the pan, a little at a time (approximately ¼ oz [5 g] wax to every 2 tbsp of oil), and heat gently until the wax has melted. Test the setting point of the salve by dipping a cold spoon into the pan and removing it; it should set on the spoon fairly quickly. If it doesn't set, add some more wax. To finish, pour your mixture into the jars, leave to set, then seal and label. Use within one year.

Greener cleaners

Surprisingly, the most environmentally damaging substances in our houses tend to be found hiding under the kitchen sink or lurking in the cleaning cabinet. Among all those bottles and cans there are all sorts of harmful combinations of toxic bleaches and chemical-based polishes and disinfectants that can be seriously damaging to us and the environment.

Eco-alternatives

A few years ago we switched from artificially produced cleaning products to eco-alternatives. Many of the cleaners we now use are made from simple homemade recipes and originate from old-fashioned cleaning techniques. As well as being less harmful to humans, animals, and the environment, they are also cheaper. We are reducing packaging waste as well, as we aren't buying new bottles and boxes over and over again.

We also find that, having stopped using conventional products that always seem to promise to "kill 110 percent of all germs," we have become noticeably more sensitive to the noxious smell of commercial cleaners. These days we much prefer the aroma of our natural alternatives, many of which are outlined here for you to make and enjoy yourself.

Baking soda

Also known as sodium bicarbonate, cooking soda, or bicarbonate of soda, this naturally occurring substance is extremely cheap and will not harm you or the environment.

▨ **How to deal with a smelly carpet** Sprinkle baking soda over the carpet. Add dried crushed lavender or basil leaves and leave for 30 minutes. Vacuum thoroughly afterward.

▨ **Cleaning work surfaces** Apply baking soda and scrub with a damp cloth or sponge. For ingrained dirt and stains, use a brush.

▨ **Oven cleaning** Sprinkle the mess with some salt and then mix 2 tbsp of baking soda with water in a cup to make a thin paste and apply to the oven surface. Use an old toothbrush or bristle brush to scrub it off.

▨ **Clogged sinks and shower drains** Conventional drain cleaners are something you should try to avoid having in your home because of their particularly nasty ingredients. If you have a clogged drain, pour in a cup of white vinegar plus one cup of baking soda. Let that sit for a few minutes (don't panic—it's normal for it to bubble like Vesuvius). Then just flush the mixture down with a pot of boiling water.

Distilled vinegar

Also known as clear or white vinegar, this is another great cleaner as well as an effective disinfectant and deodorizer. Any kind of vinegar will do, but we recommend distilled as its smell is less likely to linger than other types. This the only issue that we have with vinegar—the smell reminds us of being in a fish and chip shop. However, mixing in lavender essential oil and/or lemon juice is a very effective way to mask the smell.

If you are using a vinegar cleaner on tiles or marble, always be sure to rinse the cleaned area well because it can continue to react with any lime-based product.

▨ **Window cleaner** Mix ½ cup (120 ml) vinegar with 1 gallon (4 liters) of water and use to wipe down your

1. Baking soda *sprinkled over a surface and then wiped off with a damp cloth makes a very efficient cleaner.*
2. For a clogged drain, *combine baking soda with distilled vinegar in the proportions described above.*
3. To clean windows, *mix equal parts of vinegar and water and put in a spray bottle.* **4. Wipe half a lemon** *over your chopping block to disinfect and deodorize it.*

windows. For extra shine, try rubbing the glass dry with scrunched-up sheets of newspaper.

■ **Replacement for fabric softener** A splash of white vinegar in the final rinse will leave your clothes, sheets, and towels soft and absorbent, and has the added benefit of breaking down the laundry detergent more effectively, thus keeping the washing machine drum clean. It is especially useful for family members who have sensitive skin or allergies. Don't worry—any smell goes away when the clothes are dry.

■ **Basic furniture polish** To bring a shine to wood, mix ¼ cup (60 ml) vinegar with ¾ cup (175 ml) olive oil. Alternatively, mix ¼ cup (60 ml) lemon juice with ½ cup (120 ml) olive oil. Wipe down your furniture with a soft cloth soaked in the solution for excellent eco-cleaning results.

Lemon juice

This everyday liquid is a mild, yet very effective, green cleaner. You can use lemon juice as a nontoxic grease remover and also as an effective antibacterial in many parts of your home.

■ **Disinfectant** Squeeze some pure lemon juice over any tough stains on your chopping board, let the juice sit there for about 10 minutes, then wipe it away.

■ **Freshen and deodorize your microwave** Place a few slices of lemon in a small bowl of water. Heat the bowl on high for 30–45 seconds and then remove it and wipe down all the surfaces.

■ **Everyday toilet cleaning** Sprinkle some lemon juice and baking soda into your toilet and leave it to fizz for a few minutes. Then scrub it clean with a toilet brush.

HERBAL DISINFECTANT

Choose one fresh herb, such as lavender, juniper, or thyme. Simmer a handful of the leaves and stems in a pan of water for about 30 minutes. Add water—the less you add, the stronger the solution and the more useful its disinfectant properties. Strain the liquid and pour it into a bottle with a dash of natural soap. This herbal disinfectant cuts through grease and smells good too.

Sage leaves *steeped in water also work well as a disinfectant. The resulting liquid cleans any surface except glass.*

RECIPE **Natural hand scrub**

Keeping your hands clean can be expensive, especially using liquid hand soaps, so we started making our own scrub to keep next to the sink. Our recipe is basically a salt and oil scrub, which we have found to be excellent at removing garden grime, infused with soothing calendula. Use it regularly and you'll find that it is also a great moisturizer for the skin.

YOU WILL NEED
■ Rock salt
■ Calendula flowers
■ Calendula oil
■ Small jar

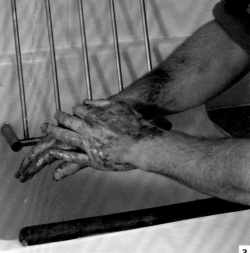

1. To make the scrub, put a 2-in (5-cm) layer of rock salt in the bottom of a small jar. **2. Mix the salt** with some dried calendula flowers and then cover with infused calendula oil (see page 269).
3. To use, scoop a small amount of the scrub, mix it between your fingers, then use like normal hand soap. Wash off with warm water.

CRAFT SKILLS In our consumer-driven society, nearly everything is disposable, probably because we mass-produce things so that objects begin to lose their value. When you make something yourself, from scratch, you will find that you take care of it in a different way because of the effort you have invested in it. We've forgotten many craft skills, and our lifestyles mean that we do not have time to do everything ourselves. Hopefully, this chapter will persuade you to try your hand and, who knows, maybe even end up with a productive new hobby.

Working with wood

You can approach working with wood as science, using a carpenter's discipline. Now that we have learned the basics, we prefer to experiment with this amazing material, for pleasure and to save money. We found that being a perfectionist doesn't always get the job done. Instead, we take a very liberal attitude to woodworking—also known as "near as dammit"!

Choosing wood

Buying wood can be confusing, but it's worth knowing what to look for, as bad wood can lead to all sorts of problems later. Keep an eye open for defects and try to buy wood that is straight. These guidelines will help:

If wood is **warped or bowing** it has probably been badly stacked for some time. This could have introduced stresses into the wood that make it harder to cut.

Look for wood where the **grain runs straight** through the wood, rather than diagonally across it. This reduces the chances of it warping as it shrinks and seasons.

Avoid buying wood with any **"shakes" or splits.** End splits often occur when the wood is dried too quickly, making it difficult to work—

dimensions can shrink and joints may open up. Sealing the ends of lumber with waterproof paint can prevent splitting.

Ingrown bark can ruin the appearance and reduce structural strength. **Knots** in the wrong places make wood harder to work.

Plywood

This is not good-looking wood, but it is cheaper than solid lumber and is less prone to shrinking or warping. It's made from sheets of wood laid so that the grain runs in opposite directions in each sheet, then bonded with adhesive.

Marine plywood is more expensive, but has proved its worth to us in both durability and convenience. It's made with stronger waterproof glue and, as

its name implies, was developed for use with boats, so is ideal for outdoor projects. It's easy to cut and can be varnished or painted.

Hand tools

A properly equipped toolbox or, even better, workshop (see pages 52–53) is essential for woodworking. Here are our recommendations for tools you can't do without and some advice on how to use them.

Saws

You want a hand saw to be straight but flexible—it should spring back into place quickly. A taper-ground blade won't stick in the wood. For greater control, hold a hand saw so that your index finger is extended down toward its "toe." Use the

TYPES OF WOOD

Softwoods come from coniferous trees and hardwoods from deciduous trees—the definition has nothing to do with their relative strength. Each wood has its own particular applications.

Softwoods

Cedar A good, relatively light wood for furniture, and for building greenhouses and sheds.

Larch Tougher than many other conifers, with a straight-grained timber. Ideal for carpentry and fencing.

Pine For light construction work and to make housing for livestock.

Spruce A lovely pale wood for interior carpentry and making boxes.

Cedar   Larch   Pine

Spruce   Ash   Beech

Cherry   Oak   Walnut

Hardwoods

Ash Excellent for replacement handles for tools or for green woodworking (see pages 282–283).

Beech Close-grained, hard, strong; used for cabinet-making and finer indoor furniture, and for chopping boards.

Cherry Our old cherry tree blew down in a gale and we intend to turn its lovely wood to make bowls (see pages 282–283). Often used in furniture-making and for tobacco pipes.

Oak Durable and strong, with a lovely grain—we use it for flooring and furniture. It would be our top choice for an outdoor building project.

Walnut This is a beautiful wood for carving. Its color ranges from golden brown to mud red. Ideal for furniture and, due to its often wavy grain, for making gun stocks.

knuckle of your thumb to align the saw against your mark and gently make a few short strokes, gliding past your thumb until you establish a "kerf." Once the cut is made, use the full length of the blade with slow, steady strokes. Near the end of the cut, support the offcut to avoid splintering the wood.

Planes

Being able to use a plane means you can take salvaged or reclaimed wood and turn it into something attractive enough to make indoor furniture. It takes more effort but saves money on buying expensive prepared lumber.

To use a bench plane, hold the handle with your index finger extended in the direction you are going to plane. Place your other hand on the round knob to provide downward pressure. Stand beside the workbench with your rear foot pointing toward it and your front foot parallel to it. As you start planing, put some pressure on the toe of the plane and, as you finish the length of the stroke, transfer the pressure back to the heel. This avoids rounding off the ends. Plane a flat surface in two different directions, finishing with the grain along its length.

Chisels

Different gouge types suit different jobs. Most chisels have a beveled edge. Respect the sharp edge. We store our chisels in a wall-mounted rack rather than loose in a toolbox as it keeps the tools sharp and our fingers safe.

Using a chisel is a matter of allowing the sharp edge to do the hard work for you. With very little pressure and at the right angle, a chisel can slice through wood like a warm knife through butter. Use your body weight to drive it forward. If you need some extra force, use the ball of your hand on the end of the

1. Use your thumb knuckle *to align a saw as you start to cut.* **2. A bench plane** *smooths rough surfaces. Check your progress by laying the plane on its side to see how flat the wood is.* **3. A sharp chisel** *makes neat work of a tenon (see page 277).* **4. Mark wood accurately** *with a steel ruler.*

handle. For deep cuts, such as a mortise joint, use a wooden mallet. For really delicate work, use the side of the mallet to tap the chisel.

Tape measure and level

A phrase that has stood the test of time with us is, "Measure twice, cut once." Checking your measurements a second time before you cut a piece of wood can save hours of work. Having said that, we are by no means slaves to the level. Often when you are simply throwing something together outside, these tools are just more to put away afterward.

Set squares

These will improve your accuracy and overall carpentry skills. Use one to make sure a joint meets perfectly

at 90°, to mark a right angle on a piece of wood, and even to work out a line at 45° without any fuss. A 45° angle line is also known as a miter.

Hammers

One of our mottos is, "If in doubt, get a bigger hammer!" We have the largest selection of hammers that we know of and we use every single one.

■ **Cross-peen hammers** are worth having for holding nails between your finger and thumb and starting them off. Then swivel and use the striking face to drive them in.

■ **Pin hammers** are for small staples, tacks, and oddly enough, pins.

■ **Claw hammers** come in different shapes and sizes. Our favorite is a steel-shafted claw hammer with a nonslip handgrip. The head is molded onto the shaft. The hammer is unbreakable and comfortable to use.

▪ **Sledgehammer** Good for both fine adjustments and gentle persuasion.

Power drills and screwdrivers

Cordless electric screwdrivers have revolutionized woodwork. However, there are still some basic guidelines. Most important of all is to always match the screwdriver tip to the slot in the screw. If you don't, you will damage your screwdriver or the slot, score the surrounding wood, or get really annoyed. Always screw or unscrew in line with the screw—imagine an invisible line that goes through the screwdriver and aligns with the screw itself. With power tools and cordless drills, use your battery responsibly if you want it to last a long time. We always use ours until they are completely flat and sound like a gramophone playing at slow speed. Then we charge them up for the full amount of time required.

It's worth having more than one battery so that you can use and charge them on a rotational cycle. Some key drill bits worth buying are:

▪ **Dowel bit** with a central lead-point and two spurs on either side prevent the bit from sliding or being deflected by wood grain.

▪ **Countersink tip** cuts a tapered recess into wood so you can hide the head of a screw below or flush with the wood's surface.

▪ **Flat bit** for boring larger holes.

PROJECT **Make a window box**

Making a window box is a great way to practice the basics of woodworking. You can make it out of almost any durable wood and design it to fit even a sloping windowsill exactly. Decorate the front with driftwood for a bit of fun.

YOU WILL NEED
- ▪ Ruler and pencil
- ▪ Saw, hammer
- ▪ Level
- ▪ Drill and bits
- ▪ Durable wood or plywood
- ▪ Brass or galvanized screws, plus glue (optional)
- ▪ Driftwood plus tacks

1. Measure your sill. Deduct twice the thickness of the wood from the length and cut two pieces of wood to this length to form the front and back. Make them around 5 in (13 cm) high, to hide plant pots inside the box without blocking too much light. **2. Lay a level** on the windowsill from the inner to the outer edge. Raise it until it is level, then measure the height from sill to level. **3. Cut each end piece** deeper by this amount at the front, to match the sloping sill. **4. Measure the base** and cut a piece of wood to fit inside the sides, front, and back pieces. **5. Drill ½-in (13-mm) holes** for drainage along the base at intervals of about 4 in (10 cm) before screwing the window box together. **6. Drill pilot holes** and screw all of the joints together. Use wood glue as well if you want to. **7. Tack driftwood** to the front of the box. **8. Secure** window box firmly in place with an angle bracket.

Make the box deep enough to disguise plant pots

Base cut to fit within other pieces of wood

Drainage holes

Driftwood for rustic decoration

Use brass or galvanized screws

Sloping sides match the slope of the windowsill and allow it to support weight of window box.

Window box base line is horizontal to keep plant pots level

276

Screws and nails

Label boxes or keep fasteners in clear jars. Always have a large supply.

■ **Countersunk wood screws** hold tightly and also look good. Make a pilot hole before screwing in, to avoid splitting the wood. Countersink to recess the head.

■ **Roundhead screws** need pilot holes before drilling. We keep a supply of these in stock to replace screws on old household fixtures so that we preserve the original look.

■ **Coach screws** are excellent for outdoors. Galvanized ones last longer. Make small pilot holes and tighten with a wrench.

■ **POZIDRIV screws** are one of the inventions that has most enhanced our ability to build things. They don't need pilot holes. Use for all projects.

■ **Staples** are indispensable if you keep poultry. Use them to attach wire netting to chicken runs.

■ **Roofing nails** are twisted and won't pull out, even in a gale.

■ **Flathead wire nails** are standard nails for fastening wood together. Use galvanized ones for outdoor work.

■ **Masonry nails** are made of toughened steel. Be careful of sparks and splinters when hitting them.

■ **Lost-head nails** are so called because you can bury the head of the nail into the wood. Ideal for floors.

■ **Clout galvanized nails** are for fixing battens and slates to roofing.

■ **Wall bolt** is for when you want a really strong, load-bearing fixing.

PROJECT **Basic joints**

Use these two techniques to make a neat, strong joint between pieces of wood. Dowel kits from hardware stores include the lengths of dowel plus the right size drill bits. Make sure that your pieces of wood are cut exactly with a triangle so that they will fit flush together. The next stage in joinery for beginners is making mortise and tenon joints. The mortise is a slot in one piece of wood and the tenon on the other piece fits neatly into it. Use this joint for more professional-looking projects.

YOU WILL NEED
■ Metal ruler and pencil
■ Clamp
■ Drill and bits
■ Triangle
■ Wood glue
■ Chisel and mallet
■ Saw

DOWEL JOINT

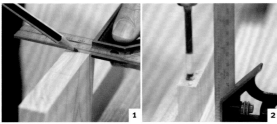

1. Measure and mark the center of the end of the wood with a metal ruler and a pencil. **2. Mark half the depth of the dowel** on the drill bit with tape as a guide. **Drill holes** for the dowels. Insert dowels and marry them up with the end grain of the other piece of wood, marking the centers. Drill holes for the dowels.

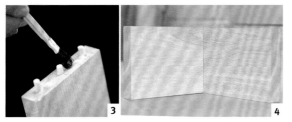

3. Brush dowels and joint with wood glue, and fit the dowels into the holes in the opposite piece of wood. Clamp until the glue sets. **4. The finished joint**.

MORTISE AND TENON JOINT

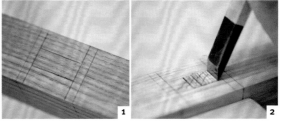

1. Mark out the shape of the mortise. Lay the other piece of wood across and draw on either side. Draw a second set of lines inside: the slot needs to be smaller than the width of the second piece of wood. **2. Chisel out** the mortise using a mallet. Mark out the length of the tenon and run the lines over the end of the wood using a triangle.

3. Cut out the tenon with a sharp saw. Tidy it up with a chisel. **4. Insert the tenon** into the mortise. Adjust the fit with a chisel if necessary. Add glue for extra strength.

Working with willow

Willow is an amazing plant that can grow at a phenomenal rate—more than 1 in (2.5 cm) a day in summer. We harvest its long, straight shoots, or "withies," annually and use them around the farm to make fencing and teepees for climbing plants, as well as weaving them into baskets and hurdles. Nothing is wasted—even the scraps are turned into broom heads.

Growing willow

The roots of willows (*Salix* species) are renowned for absorbing moisture, which is why they are often planted beside streams or rivers to help stabilize banks and keep them intact, or on waterlogged ground where little else will grow. But willow's tendency to draw moisture from the soil also means that you should not grow it, or construct a living willow structure, too close to vegetable plots, sewers, or buildings. We planted our willow in a marshy valley and around the edge of the duck pond.

Different species have different colored stems, from yellow to black. We've mixed in some dogwood (*Cornus* species) too, adding reds and greens to the color spectrum, and we use the cut stems in the same way as willow.

We increase our stocks every year by replanting some of the withies when we pollard (see box opposite). Planting them close together encourages new growth to compete and stretch upward to the light to produce more withies to work with.

When planting willow withies, bury at least a third of the stem in the ground. We made our own "Derby dipper" (an old fork with a 12-in [30-cm] spike welded to the bottom) to make perfectly sized planting holes. Once in the ground, your job is done—the willow will sprout roots, even if you plant it upside down!

Willow crafts

Living willow rods planted into the ground can be shaped and woven into domes, tunnels, and sculptures. We have great fun creating our own structures and weaving baskets (see pages 280–281).

Living boundaries

To make a willow hoop fence, take straight withies and rub off any side shoots. Then push one end in the ground at an angle, bend the willow over into a hoop, and stick the other end into the ground. Overlap them and tie the hoop together at the top with soft twine if you want the stems to graft together. Each winter take the new vertical shoots and bend them down and back into the ground to continue the hoop pattern. This fence needs very little maintenance, but in

1. **A living willow fence** *grows thicker and bushier each year. If you bind stems together, eventually they will fuse.*
2. **Teepees** *are perfect for beans and other climbing plants.* 3. **Weave willow** *into baskets and decorative items, and turn shorter offcuts into brooms.*

PROJECT **Pollard and plant willow**

Pollarding is an agricultural method that has been practiced for centuries. It is a form of pruning that increases a tree's productivity. New shoots grow into straight lengths, known as "withies," which can be used for weaving baskets and hurdles, or to make living structures. Another key reason to pollard willow is to keep it under control and prevent it from growing into a massive tree. Pollard in the winter, between November and March, when the tree is dormant.

YOU WILL NEED
- Pruning saw
- Loppers
- Buckets
- "Derby dipper" for planting
- String

1. Allow the tree to grow and then cut the trunk off at a height of 3 ft (1 m) or 6 ft (2 m) with a pruning saw. This shows the new stems that have sprouted from the cut in one year. **2. Remove any damaged**, diseased, crossing, or dead stems first and put aside for burning. Use loppers to remove any thin withies. **3. Use a sharp pruning saw** to cut thicker branches. Remove all the current year's growth from the pollarding point. Rub off any thin shoots that are sprouting lower down. The finished tree should have a flat top—it could be dangerous to fall onto sharp spikes. **4. Plant some long, straight withies** to make more trees. **5. Soak the withies** in 6 in (15 cm) of water in a bucket and store in a sheltered spot outdoors until you're ready to plant them.

the early stages remove any grass and weeds around the base, as they will compete for water and nutrients. Use the fence to make a decorative edging, as it takes several years before it is livestock-proof.

We have found that planting willow alongside conventional wire fencing is a great overlap system. Eventually, the willow will outgrow and can replace the wire fencing. (See page 174 for making woven willow hurdles.)

Teepees for climbing plants
Push several lengths of tall, dry willow into the ground in a circle and tie the top tightly; you can use willow for this too, but we tend to cheat and use a bit of wire. Weave around the base with flexible withies to bind the uprights together. Once you've woven

to a depth of about 6 in (15 cm) around the bottom, start to spiral upward to strengthen the teepee (see teepees opposite). Lift the structure out of the ground and dry it out before you use it or it will start to sprout roots and turn into a living willow teepee—not ideal for crops.

Using up offcuts
The by-products of working with willow are twiggy little branches and various offcuts. But, you guessed it, all of these have uses too. You can make a useful brush. All you need is a broom handle sharpened into a point at one end and a large hose clamp. Bundle a selection of twiggy offcuts together and use the clamp to fasten them tightly around the broom handle. We've found that dogwood

offcuts make extra-colorful brushes. Alternatively, use your dry willow twigs as bean poles to support your crops (see page 142), and to make charcoal for drawing.

Make a rooting compound
Willow bark contains auxins, a type of plant growth hormone. You can make your own rooting compound from willow offcuts and use it to encourage cuttings of other plants to send out roots. Chop thin stems into 3-in (8-cm) lengths and place in a pan. Pour 1 gallon (4 liters) of warm water over the willow, cover, and leave overnight. In the morning, strain and bottle the rooting extract; seal it and store in a cool place. When you take cuttings (see page 135), dip them in a cup of the extract before potting.

PROJECT **Make a willow basket**

We think everyone should try their hand at making a basket. Sign up for a course, or try this basket made from buff willow, which has been stripped of its outer bark. Soak stems in water for 20 minutes, then wrap in a damp cloth overnight. Keep them pliable by spraying with water as you weave.

YOU WILL NEED
- Willow ring (1)
- Weight (2)
- Block of wood (3)
- Rapping iron (4); bodkin (5)
- Sharp curved knife (6)
- Straight knife (7)
- Pruners (8)
- 4-ft (1.2-m) willow bundle sorted into 6 thick base stakes, 42 thin weavers, 24 thicker rods

MAKING THE BASE

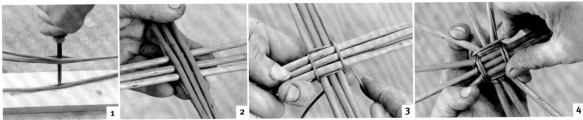

1. Skewer through 3 of the base stakes with a bodkin, protecting your work surface with wood.   **2. Insert the other 3** in the gap.   **3. Weave around the center** of the stakes with 2 thin weavers. Insert the thin tips into the split stakes, then use a pairing weave (see step 5). Weave twice around the center.   **4. Pull the stakes** apart on the third round and weave them.

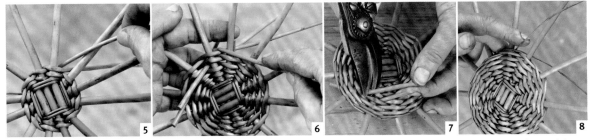

5. Use the pairing weave: take one weaver behind one stake and over the next. Then bring the other weaver in front of the first stake and behind the next, and so on.   **6. Join in 2 more weavers** when the first 2 run out. This time, start with the thick butt ends. Continue pairing.   **7. Trim the butt ends** when the weavers run out. Tuck in the tip ends.   **8. Cut 8 thin weavers** to the same length at the butt end and insert 2 pairs of 2 weavers, tips first, opposite each other on the base. Work with one pair until it reaches the opposite pair; drop them and start weaving with the other pair—the chasing technique.

9. The pairs finish opposite each other.   **10. Add the remaining 2 pairs** of weavers—this time starting with the butt ends. Continue pairing. Tuck in the tip ends.   **11. Cut off the base stakes** using pruners.   **12. The completed base.**

MAKING THE SIDES

13. Select 24 thick rods. Make a sloping cut on the butt ends. **14. Insert the rods,** one beside each of the base stakes. Add a band of waling (see box). **15. Use a heavy weight** to steady the base. Use the back of a knife to kink each rod up at 45°. To do this, bring the rod upward while pressing on the base of the stem with the knife. Let the rod drop back.

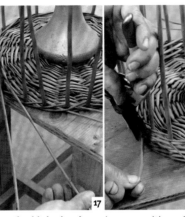

16. Gather the kinked rods and secure with a willow ring. Trim 12 weavers to length. **17. Insert the tip ends** of 3 weavers and work a wale around half of the basket. Insert the tips of another 3 weavers and use the chasing technique (see step 8). **18. Join in** the remaining 2 sets of 3 weavers when the first set runs out. Continue waling. Repeat with another set of 12 weavers.

19. Tap down the sides evenly using a rapping iron. **20. Make a simple border.** Soak the basket in water first. Use a straight knife to kink each upright down to the right. Take it over the next two uprights, weave it behind the third upright, and trim it between the third and fourth upright, so that it lies against the third one. Thread the last few uprights into the first ones. **21. The finished basket.**

WALING

Waling is a strong weave, often used at the bottom and top of the basket to make it sturdy.

◼ Take 3 weavers and insert tips into 3 consecutive spaces.

◼ Take the left-hand weaver in front of 2 uprights and behind the third, working counter-clockwise.

◼ Take the weaver that is now on the left and work in the same way—in front of 2 uprights, behind the next one.

◼ Continue on in this way, always using the weaver on the left.

◼ Using the chasing technique in waling (see step 8) ensures that the basket is an even height.

Waling *is used to strengthen a basket.*

Green woodworking

Using traditional skills that are not a million miles away from modern carpentry, green woodworking produces products with a more rustic feel. As managed woodlands are increasing in number (see pages 182–183), we are seeing a resurgence of the skills needed to turn the freshly felled green timber. Everyone can try their hand at it, and we recommend novices start by carving a spoon.

What is green wood?

Fresh and filled with moisture, green wood is much easier to cut and carve than seasoned lumber, which has an average moisture content of just 20 percent. Our favorite green wood is wild cherry because it is both strong and not too hard to cut, and comes in a surprising range of beautiful colors. Other woods suitable for green woodworking include alder, English pine, elm, and willow. The best introduction to this type of woodworking for a beginner is to make a spoon (see opposite), which allows you to try your hand at the basic techniques before investing in specialty tools.

Using a pole lathe

The real magic of green woodwork lies in the pole lathe, a simple, efficient tool that has a timeless charm. It may be an old technology, but at one point in history it was responsible for the mass production of a whole range of wooden goods, such as tools and kitchenware.

A pole lathe is used for "turning" wood. The wood to be worked on, known as the stock, is held firmly between two points. You then use a foot pedal to rotate the wood while you shape it using a blade resting on a wooden tool rest. Using a pole lathe is like hopping on one leg uphill. It takes skill and practice, but once you've got the knack, you can turn out anything cylindrical.

Preparing the wood

Choose your wood carefully, and check that the shape lends itself to the object you are planning to make. The next stage is to remove the bark using a knife and shave horse, which is essentially a large clamp that holds the wood firmly while you work. You can make one from scrap wood; look up instructions on the internet. Pull a draw knife along the wood to shave off the bark. It will glide through the wood like a knife through cheese. The shavings are great for kindling, and because the wood is so moist, you won't get sawdust in your eyes.

Split green wood with a froe (see opposite), and wiggle it as you ease it down the wood. It will cut with the grain, thereby retaining the inherent strength in the fibers.

Finishing touches

Sand items with some shavings. Dry for a couple of weeks, then coat in a mixture of beeswax and oil warmed together in a pan. Once the mixture has soaked into your items, wash them in warm, soapy water and dry.

1. **A traditional pole lathe** *doesn't need an electrical power supply and can be set up anywhere, even in the woods.* **2. A pine bowl** *and green wood goblet turned on a pole lathe, with a hand-carved cherrywood spoon.* **3. Green woodworking tools,** *including a froe (top left) for splitting wood and various sharp knives.*

PROJECT **Make a spoon**

Michelangelo believed that every stone contained a sculpture, and green woodworkers know that within every length of wood lies a perfect spoon. Making a wooden spoon is a fun way to try out some of the easier green woodworking skills.

YOU WILL NEED
- Short-handled ax
- Shave horse
- Draw knife
- Froe or saw
- Sharp knife and hook knife
- Piece of green wood, e.g., cherry

PREPARING THE WOOD

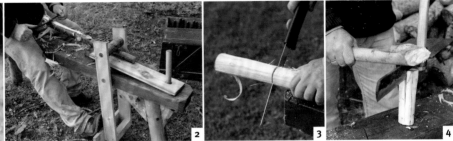

1. Cut off any offshoots from the wood using a short-handled ax.   **2. Remove the bark** by holding the wood in a shave horse and pulling a draw knife along it to shave off the bark.   **3. Saw** the wood roughly to length.   **4. Split** the wood to make a flat block to work with. Use a froe if you have one, and hit it with a lump of wood or a mallet. Otherwise use a saw.

CUTTING AND SHAPING THE SPOON

5. Draw the shape of your spoon onto the wood. We use a template so that our spoons look similar each time we make one—we didn't say identical, only similar.   **6. Make some cuts** from one side of the wood, toward the outline of the spoon. Repeat on the other side. This makes it easier to cut out the shape.

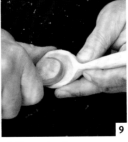

7. Use a small ax or a sharp knife to carve the handle.   **8. Pare shavings** away from the spoon using a sharp straight knife. Be careful not to cut the spoon too thin near the neck. Try to cut over the edges of the grain, not up into them. Leave a bit of a rib on the back of the neck to give it some strength.   **9. Use the hook knife** to shape the bowl. Leave to dry for a couple of days, then use it.

SHARPENING TOOLS

Sharp tools are actually safer, as you don't exert undue pressure when using them, and so they are less likely to slip. Store tools safely when not in use.

Use a mini carbon steel *to sharpen the tip of a knife blade. Draw the steel across the blade a few times.*

Sharpen both cutting edges *of the hook knife with a mini steel. Draw a knife blade back and forth over a large steel to sharpen it.*

Working with metal

Humans have been using metal for millennia, yet to many of us it is a mystery how to fashion it into tools or how to mend it. There are a surprising number of small engineering shops in our area where you can drop in and ask for something to be fixed, but we decided many years ago that it was worth learning a little about metalwork so we could be more self-reliant.

Blacksmithing

To become a competent blacksmith is a long, challenging apprenticeship. It is great to see a significant number of people practicing this skill, though many have become mainly artists to ensure an income.

The basic equipment for setting up a blacksmith shop is not complicated: a forge and bellows, anvil, hammer and tongs, swage and cutter, chisel and punch, and file and drill.

There is no longer the same market for shoes for horses and oxen, or for latches, hinges, farm tools, nails, hammers, axes, chisels, and carving tools. But when you discover that you need some blacksmithing done, you'll discover that the principles have not changed over hundreds of years (see box below).

You don't need to spend a fortune on tools. We have found them in classified ads, on the internet, and at garage sales. Keep your eyes open and you may even find an anvil locally. Your anvil serves as a work bench, as this is where the metal is beaten. The holes in it allow you to punch through your hot metal.

When we're working with small pieces of metal, we just use a gas blowtorch to heat metal up in a vise and bend it with a hammer.

Preparing metal

When you're working with metal, it's important to remove any areas of oxidation—on low-carbon steel, this is otherwise known as rust. You cannot expect your work to survive unless you prepare the metal sufficiently. We use an old leather apron when doing metalwork as metal tends to be quite unforgiving.

Welding

Welding is the process in which two metals are fused together when they are molten. Welding is a very wide subject, but we just think of it as gluing metal together with metal. Using welding equipment requires a basic amount of knowledge so that the tool can be operated safely, correctly, and efficiently. Get expert advice until you are confident and safe. There are four main types of welding that are regularly used:

▪ **Metal inert gas (MIG) welding** is probably the easiest welding to learn (see box opposite).

▪ **Arc (or stick) welding** is similar to MIG welding. A relatively large current is passed through a welding rod (or filler rod) of the appropriate metal and a circuit is completed through it when it comes into contact with the grounded metal being welded. Enough heat is produced to melt the rod. By moving the rod along the piece to be welded, molten metal is laid down and solidifies to create a strong bond between the two items.

To stop oxidation, the filler rod is coated in flux, which produces a shielding gas that protects the metal from the oxygen in the air. The

---

How a forge works

The forge is the heart of the blacksmith's shop. Here, metal is heated up in a hearth to make it malleable enough to work. The hearth is most commonly fired by charcoal or coke. Although forges have become more sophisticated, in essence the way they work is very simple. For example, early hand-operated bellows have been replaced in modern forges by high-power fans or blowers.

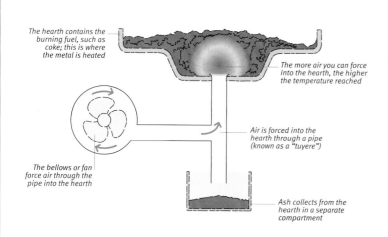

The hearth contains the burning fuel, such as coke; this is where the metal is heated

The more air you can force into the hearth, the higher the temperature reached

Air is forced into the hearth through a pipe (known as a "tuyere")

The bellows or fan force air through the pipe into the hearth

Ash collects from the hearth in a separate compartment

remains of the flux solidify on the metal, which has to be tapped off with a hammer when the work is cool.

■ **Oxy-acetylene welding** uses an oxy-acetylene torch to heat up the work. Usually, a filler rod of the same metal is also heated to its melting point. This is fed into the heated area so it runs onto and fills the area being welded. The metal solidifies and forms a bond of similar strength to the parent metal.

When using oxy-acetylene, make sure the pressure of the oxygen and acetylene are set correctly (around 2 and 5 bar, respectively), and that the valves on the torch are set correctly to give the desired flame. The acetylene is always lit first, and then the oxygen added to turn the sooty flame into the high-temperature blue flame required for welding.

■ **Tungsten inert gas (TIG) welding** uses a fixed tungsten bit, which does not come into contact with the work. It is drawn across the metal at a short distance above the surface, melting the metal below as it does so. A filler rod can be fed into the weld with the user's free hand as with oxy-acetylene welding.

1. The essential MIG welding kit *doesn't require a huge number of items. Above left, there is the shield gas (1), welding gun (2), welder power supply (3), heavyweight welding gloves (4), grinder (5), and welding mask (6).* **2. Learn the basic skills** *of welding and they can be put to use surprisingly frequently. This wheelbarrow has been a trusty friend over the years, so when its bottom fell away, a bit of tender loving care with the welder meant that all was well again.*

SAFETY TIPS

■ **It may sound silly**, but remember that fires are hot. You must also be very aware that metal holds its heat for a long time.

■ **Eye protection**, such as a welding mask, and gloves are essential when grinding and welding. Welding masks protect the eyes from the intense light given off by the arc, but also protect the face from hot sparks and arc burn.

■ **Watch carefully** where your sparks are going because they can easily cause fires and even burn through your clothing.

■ **Do not use galvanized steel** under any circumstances because it gives off poisonous fumes when it's heated up. So do not weld galvanized steel, sheet metal, nails, or rods.

How MIG welding works

Metal inert gas (MIG) welding involves the use of a welding gun, a power supply, and a roll of welding wire. A large current in an electrical circuit melts the wire, which becomes the "glue" that welds the metal pieces you are working. Inert gas, which is expelled from the nozzle of the gun, creates a shield around the area of the weld to keep oxygen away and prevent oxidation of the metal.

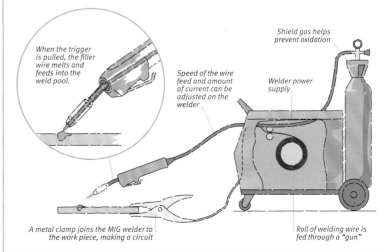

When the trigger is pulled, the filler wire melts and feeds into the weld pool.

Speed of the wire feed and amount of current can be adjusted on the welder

Shield gas helps prevent oxidation

Welder power supply

A metal clamp joins the MIG welder to the work piece, making a circuit

Roll of welding wire is fed through a "gun"

Mending

We firmly believe in the philosophy of "make do and mend" and only throw things away as a last resort. Fixing everyday objects, like clothing and gadgets, will save you lots of money and reduce the polluting waste in landfills. Also remember the old saying, "a stitch in time saves nine," which means that if you repair an item as soon as you notice it's broken, you'll save time mending it later.

Buying goods that can be fixed

Our throwaway culture and high levels of consumption are made worse by small, plastic, breakable components and complicated parts in products that the average person cannot fix. Our advice is to buy good-quality products and then take care of them. If something breaks, attempt to repair it instead of throwing it away, or find clever ways to recycle or reuse it, giving it a new lease on life.

Although not everyone can fix a computer or car, there are still lots of things that anyone can mend.

Reheeling stilettos

Breaking the heel on your favorite pair of shoes doesn't mean the death of them, and most can be repaired in minutes. If you find that the rubber piece of your heel is wearing down, pull it out with a good set of pliers. Stilettos are sometimes provided with spare heel pieces, but if yours aren't, they're really cheap to buy. Place a piece of wood inside the shoe at the heel end to reinforce it while you hammer a replacement rubber piece onto the heel. Wrap your shoe in fabric to prevent it from getting scuffed, and secure it in a vise if you have one, or hold it steady on a table. Then, with the heel pointing upward, hammer the small replacement down into the heel until it is secure.

PROJECT **Basic clothes mending**

Mending a tear and darning a hole are both easy and take no time at all once you get the hang of it. If you have worn through some socks or knitwear, or have a tear in jeans or a shirt, try these techniques.

MENDING A TEAR

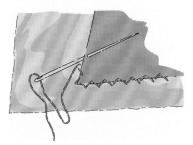

Tack a piece of stiff paper to the underside of the tear with small pins, so that it is temporarily held back together. Using small slanting stitches, push the needle down through one side of the tear and the paper and then bring back up through the paper and material on the other side of the tear. When you have completely sewn the tear neatly back together, remove the paper.

DARNING A SOCK

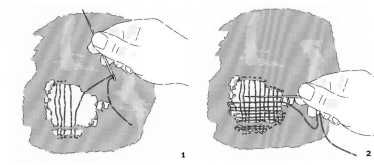

1

2

BASIC SEWING KIT

- **A fine sewing needle** that has a small eye and is sharp.
- **Sewing scissors** are very useful as they are small and perfect for snipping off the ends of thread.
- **Different-sized safety pins.**
- **Soft fabric tape measure.**
- **Pins** to fasten everything in the right place before sewing.
- **Large pair of fabric scissors** that are sharp and cut clean, straight lines. Keep them just for fabric or they will quickly go blunt.
- **A darning mushroom** enables you to stretch a worn sock over the mushroom-shaped wood and gather it tightly at the neck, making it easier to work on a hole in the toe or heel.

1. Use thick thread or thin yarn in a matching color to darn a sock or sweater. First sew around the edge of the hole using a running stitch; the stitches on the back should be equal lengths and half the length of those on the front. Next, sew vertical lines up and down the hole. **2. Fill the hole** in by sewing horizontal lines, weaving the thread from side to side, over and under the vertical lines. Keep darning until the hole is no longer visible.

Saving electronic gadgets

The number of cell phones and small electronic gadgets that are thrown away every year is quite astonishing. Many are difficult to fix, but sometimes quick reactions and common sense can save them. And if not, remember that broken phones and MP3 players can be recycled.

If you drop a gadget in water, fish it out as quickly as possible and remove the battery immediately. Then take out the sim card or other data storage device and allow it to dry. This can often be saved, even if it's too late for the rest of the device.

If any of the components are covered in wine, sugary drinks, or milk, it's important to clean them, as the residue can corrode the circuitry. Carefully clean them with cotton swabs dipped in denatured alcohol, nail polish remover, or some very strong alcohol, and dry with a hair dryer on the cool setting, or a can of compressed air. More moisture can be removed by submerging the phone, battery, or other gadgetry in a bowl of uncooked rice grains. Leave to dry out for 24 hours and with luck you will have saved your gadget from a watery grave.

Remove scratches from DVDs and CDs

It's frustrating when your favorite DVD or music CD gets scratched, but you can remove the problem with some toothpaste or metal polish. First, clean off dirt and dust with a damp cloth and a drop of dishwashing liquid. Then place your scratched disc on a flat, clean surface with the label side facing downward. Rub a little white toothpaste or metal polish along the scratch, from the center of the disc outward. Repeat this a second time and then wash your disc with warm water if you used toothpaste, or a soft, lint-free cloth if you used metal polish.

PROJECT **Fix a flat bicycle tire**

This is a very simple repair and can save you quite a lot of money if you take five minutes to fix a tire yourself rather than take the bike to a repair shop. You will need a tire repair kit and, ideally, a bucket of water, which makes the whole process much easier—a deep puddle at the side of the road will do in an emergency.

1. Remove the inner tube using levers. Then pump it up and listen for any hissing noise, or hold the tube near your face and rotate it until you feel the air escaping.   **2. Alternatively, dunk the tube in a bucket of water** and find the puncture quickly by locating the area from which bubbles are escaping.

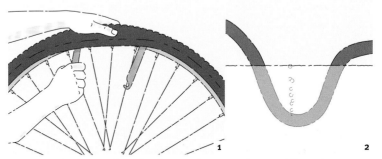

3. Mark the hole with chalk from your repair kit. Sand the area with sand paper, and dry the tube.   **4. Apply a thin layer of glue** and wait until it starts to dry, then place a suitable patch of rubber over the puncture. Press down firmly.   **5. Check the inside rim** of the tire to make sure there are no thorns or glass that will puncture it again. Fit the inner tube when it is slightly inflated.

Resources

We have always found thorough research to be the key to success in any new project. On these pages we list some useful websites, organizations, and books that have helped us achieve a greater degree of self-sufficiency here at Newhouse Farm. Word-of-mouth, the internet, and your local library are vital resources to draw upon to find the information required to live a more sustainable life, and we hope these contacts and suggested reading will give you a head start.

www.bbc.co.uk/lifestyle/tv_and_radio/green
Information and video clips about our television show, *It's Not Easy Being Green*, which was broadcast in the UK.

www.dickstrawbridge.com
More information about Dick and his TV career as well as details of his talking engagements and contact details.

www.jamesstrawbridge.com
Information following James' TV exploits, plus contact details, and workshop opportunities.

HOUSING MATERIALS

Earth Source Wood
www.earthsourcewood.com

The Natural Home Building Source
www.thenaturalhome.com

Building Materials Reuse Association
www.bmra.org

GreenDepot
www.greendepot.com

ENERGY AND WASTE

Battery rechargers:
www.all-battery.com
www.greenbatteries.com
www.batterystuff.com

Calculate your energy costs:
www.energy.gov/energysaver/estimating-appliance-and-home-electronic-energy-use

Energy-saving light bulbs and other eco-friendly products:
www.ecomall.com
www.eartheasy.com
www.ledtronics.com
www.topbulb.com

GREEN ENERGY SUPPLIERS

Renewable Energy Outfitters
www.reosolar.com

AltE Store
www.altestore.com

Infinigi Energy Solutions
www.infinigi.com

GENERAL RENEWABLE ENERGY INFORMATION

Database of State Incentives for Renewable Energy (DSIRE)
www.dsireusa.org

US Department of Energy Efficiency and Renewable Energy
www.eere.energy.gov

Alliance to Save Energy
http://ase.org/

CREST (Centre for Renewable Energy and Sustainable Technologies)
thecrestproject.com

WIND ENERGY

US Department of Energy Efficiency and Renewable Energy—Wind Program
www.energy.gov/eere/renewables/wind

American Wind Energy Trade Association
www.awea.org

Small wind turbines:
www.bergey.com
www.energy.sourceguides.com

BIODIESEL

US Department of Energy: Alternative Fuels Data Center
www.afdc.energy.gov/afdc

COMPOSTING TOILET

Composting Toilet World
www.compostingtoilet.org

www.letsgogreen.com

ENVIRONMENTAL ISSUES

Friends of the Earth
1101 15th Street NW
Washington, DC 20005
P 202-783-7400
F 202-783-0444
www.foe.org

Greenpeace
702 H Street, NW
Washington, D.C. 20001
(202) 462-1177
www.greenpeace.org

RECYCLING

National Recycling Coalition
www.nrc-recycle.org

Earth 911
www.earth911.com

The Freecycle Network
www.freecycle.org

CARPOOLING
www.carpoolworld.com

Association for Commuter Transportation
www.actweb.org

CARBON FOOTPRINT
www.carbonfund.org
www.carbonfootprint.com
www.conservation.org

WILDLIFE & ORGANIC GARDENING

Gardens Alive
www.gardensalive.com

National Pesticide-free Lawn Coalition
www.beyondpesticides.org

National Audubon Society
www.audubon.org

World Wildlife Fund
www.worldwildlife.org

National Wildlife Federation
www.nwf.org

COMPOSTING

US Environmental Protection Agency
http://www.epa.gov/osw/conserve/rrr/composting/
index.htm

www.eartheasy.com/grow_compost.html
www.composting101.com

ORCHARDS

Home Orchard Society
www.homeorchardsociety.org

North American Fruit Explorers
www.nafex.org

Backyard Fruit Growers
www.sas.upenn.edu/~dailey/byfg.html

FORAGING

Foraging with the Wild Man
www.wildmanstevebrill.com

Earthwalk Northwest
www.earthwalknorthwest.com

Foraging Pictures (including mushrooms)
www.foragingpictures.com

LIVESTOCK
Most livestock is subject to a range of federal and state regulations. For more information, contact:

US Department of Agriculture, Animal Welfare Regulations
www.nal.usda.gov/awic

American Veterinary Medical Association
www.avma.org

The Livestock Conservancy
http://livestockconservancy.org

CHICKENS
There are no regulations governing flocks under 250 birds, or on planning permission for small, moveable chicken housing, but contact your local Environmental Health Officer to check local bylaws.

Countryside Network—Backyard Poultry
www.countrysidenetwork.com/category/daily/poultry

BackyardChickens.com
www.backyardchickens.com

American Poultry Association
www.ampltya.com

The American Pastured Poultry Producers Association
www.apppa.org

The City Chicken
www.thecitychicken.com

DUCKS

For information relating to raising ducks in your backyard:
www.countrysidenetwork.com/daily/poultry/poultry-poultry/how-to-raise-ducks-in-your-backyard

PIGS

The Pig Site
www.thepigsite.com

GOATS

South African Boer Goats
www.sa-boergoats.com

The American Goat Society
www.americangoatsociety.com

The American Dairy Goat Society
www.adga.org

CATTLE

The American Association of Bovine Practitioners
www.aabp.org

The American Veterinary Medical Association
www.avma.org

BEES

Beekeeping laws and regulations in the United States vary. For information on your state's laws and other matters related to beekeeping, consult the following organizations and publications:

American Beekeeping Federation (ABF)
www.abfnet.org

Bee Culture
www.beeculture.com

FARMERS' MARKETS

Local Harvest
www.localharvest.org

Farmers Market.com
www.farmersmarket.com

USDA database of farmers' markets
www.ams.usda.gov/farmersmarkets

LOCAL FARMERS' MARKETS

Dane County Farmers' Market
(largest producer-only market in the United States)
P.O. Box 1485
Madison, WI 53701-1485
http://www.dcfm.org
[Madison: Wisconsin]

Cortelyou Greenmarket
Cortelyou Road
Brooklyn, NY 11226
www.grownyc.org/greenmarket/brooklyn/cortelyou
[Brooklyn: New York]

Farmers Market
6333 West 3rd Street
Los Angeles, CA 90036
www.farmersmarketla.com
[Los Angeles: California]

Minneapolis Farmers Market
Attn: Market Manager
PO Box 2006
Inver Grove Heights, MN 55076
www.mplsfarmersmarket.com
[Minneapolis: Minnesota]

Portland Farmers' Market
1001 SE Water Avenue, Suite 455
Portland, OR 97214
www.portlandfarmersmarket.org
[Portland: Oregon]

Union Square Greenmarket
Broadway at 17th Street
New York, NY 10011
www.grownyc.org/greenmarket/manhattan-union-square-m
[Manhattan: New York]

SOLAR COOKING

Solar Oven Society
www.solarovens.org

HOME/CLEANING PRODUCTS

Ecover
us.ecover.com

Seventh Generation
www.seventhgeneration.com

Ecomall
www.ecomall.com

Further reading

BOOKS

Green Building Bible
by Keith Hall,
published by Green Building Press

How to Make Biodiesel
by Jon Hallé and Dan Carter,
published by Low-Impact Living Initiative

**It's a Breeze!: A Guide to
Choosing Windpower**
by Hugh Piggott and Dave Thorpe,
published by The Centre for Alternative
Technology

**Lifting the Lid: An Ecological
Approach to Toilet Systems**
by Peter Harper,
published by The Centre for Alternative
Technology

**The New Complete Book of
Self-Sufficiency**
by John Seymour,
published by Dorling Kindersley

**Saving the Planet Without
Costing the Earth: 500 Simple
Steps to a Greener Lifestyle**
by Donnachadh McCarthy,
published by Fusion Press

**Solar Electricity Basics: A Green
Energy Guide**
by Dan Chiras,
published by New Society Publishers

The Solar House
by Dan Chiras,
published by Chelsea Green Publishing
Company

**Sustainable Energy—Without
the Hot Air**
by David J C MacKay,
published by UIT

The Bee Book
published by Dorling Kindersley

The Complete Gardener
by Monty Don,
published by Dorling Kindersley

Compost
by Ken Thompson,
published by Dorling Kindersley

**The Earth Care Manual:
A Permaculture Handbook**
by Patrick Whitefield,
published by Permanent Publications

Food For Free
by Richard Mabey, published by Collins

The Forager Handbook
by Miles Irving,
published by Ebury Press

Goat Keeping Manual
by Alan Mowlem,
published by The Crowood Press

**Grow All You Can Eat
in Three Square Feet**
published by Dorling Kindersley

Grow Fruit
published by Dorling Kindersley

Grow Organic
published by Dorling Kindersley

Grow Vegetables
published by Dorling Kindersley

A Guide to Traditional Pig Keeping
by Carol Harris,
published by The Good Life Press

How to Make a Wildlife Garden
by Chris Baines,
published by Frances Lincoln

**Keep Chickens! Tending Small
Flocks in Cities, Suburbs, and
Other Small Spaces**
by Barbara Kilarski,
published by Storey Publishing

Keeping Ducks and Geese
by Chris and Mike Ashton,
published by David & Charles

Organic Gardening
by Geoff Hamilton,
published by Dorling Kindersley

Practical Sheep Keeping
by Kim Cardell,
published by The Crowood Press

Craft Cider Making
by Andrew Lea,
published by The Good Life Press

**The Encyclopedia of Green
Woodworking**
by Raymond Tabor,
published by Eco-Logic Books

Encyclopedia of Herbal Medicine
by Andrew Chevallier,
published by Dorling Kindersley

**Hand Mending Made Easy: Save
Time and Money Repairing Your
Own Clothes**
by Nan L. Ides,
published by Palmer-Pletsch

Home Cheese Making
by Ricki Carroll,
published by Storey Publishing

Home Smoking and Curing
by Keith Erlandson,
published by Ebury Press

**Making Country Wines, Ales
and Cordials**
by Brian Tucker,
published by The Good Life Press

Preserve It!
by Lynda Brown,
published by Dorling Kindersley

Step-by-Step Bread
published by Dorling Kindersley

**Woodwork: The Complete
Step-by-step Manual**
published by Dorling Kindersley

MAGAZINES

Mother Earth News
www.motherearthnews.com

Hobby Farms/Urban Farm
www.hobbyfarms.com

Rodale's Organic Life
www.rodalesorganiclife.com

The Ecologist
www.theecologist.org

E/The Environmental Magazine
www.emagazine.com

Index

Acknowledgments

Our thanks
The knowledge we have collected in this book comes from years of experimenting and playing outside. We have to thank everyone who has given their time to teach us, and those who have allowed us to watch and learn. More specifically, this book is dedicated to the ladies—mothers, "loves of our lives," and sisters—who have supported us over the years and allowed us to be the little boys we are.

Dick's personal thanks
I'm not sure that I should be thanking my co-author, but James has been my conscience, personal organizer, and artistic director. While I have been off gallivanting, he has kept the project on schedule and it has been a privilege working with him. It's not often a father gets a chance to spend such quality time with his son; I'm a very lucky man.

James's personal thanks
I would like to thank my Mum for inspiring me and providing useful advice on all things green; my little sister Charlotte for taking so many of the amazing photographs that have been included in this book and for her encouragement; Holly, my fiancée, for her loving support and all her hard work to help make Newhouse Farm so productive—she is a true "Land Girl"; Sophie for introducing us; my Dad for trying to teach me about electricity and allowing me to invite DK down for more and more photo shoots; my Granny in Ireland for teaching me how to pluck turkeys and make pancakes; my Granny in Dorset for instilling in me the ambition to be a writer; my Grandpa for revealing how many beans make five; and Steve, Duncan, Kev, Zoe, Carol, Dave, and Val for helping with their respective areas of expertise. Thanks also to everyone who has ever helped dig the ground, weed, plant, or harvest produce here at NHF over the last few years. Finally, a big thanks to all the editing and design team from Dorling Kindersley who have made creating this book such an enjoyable experience.

Dorling Kindersley would like to thank
James Strawbridge for the artwork concepts; Stephanie Jackson for commissioning; Kat Mead, Adèle Hayward, and Helen Spencer for the set-up; Zia Allaway, Pip Morgan, and Diana Vowles for editorial assistance; Sue Bosanko for indexing; and Lucy Claxton at DK images.

Picture credits
The publisher would like to thank the following for their kind permission to reproduce their photographs:
(key: b-bottom; c-center; l-left; r-right; t-top)
39 Energy Star: (cr). **NAEEEC:** (tr). **Siemens Home Appliances www.siemens-home.co.uk:** (br). **41 Photolibrary:** Johnny Bouchier (tr). **44 Alamy Images:** Paul Glendell (tl). **45 Alamy Images:** Peter Barritt (bl); maurice joseph (tl); Christian Klein (br); Yadid Levy (tr). **46 Photoshot:** David Wimsett (tr). **Science Photo Library:** Alex Bartel (tl). **Still Pictures:** Martin Bond (b). **47 Alamy Images:** The Garden Picture Library (t). **48 Science Photo Library:** David Hay Jones (tl). **49 Corbis:** Dietrich Rose (b). **Still Pictures:** Martin Bond (t). **50 Alamy Images:** Jeff Morgan 05 (t); Steven Poe (b). **51 Alamy Images:** camera lucida environment (b); Steven Poe (t). **54 Marianne Majerus Garden Images:** Caroline Holmes (cl). **68 Science Photo Library:** Martin Bond (l). **80 Science Photo Library:** Simon Fraser (tl). **81 Alamy Images:** Wolfgang Polzer (bl). **88 Photolibrary:** Banana Stock (bl). **89 Alamy Images:** Doug Houghton (tr). **99 GAP Photos:** Jerry Harpur (tr). **121 Getty Images:** Lawrence Lawry (tr); Andrew Parkinson (tl). **122 Getty Images:** Dianna Jazwinski (bl). **123 Getty Images:** Frederic Pacorel (br). **143 Getty Images:** Will Heap (cr). **144 GAP Photos:** Christina Bollen (cr). **145 Getty Images:** Wally Eberhart (cl). **149 Getty Images:** Martyn Chillmaid (r). **150 Getty Images:** Taesam Do (l). **151 Corbis:** Radius Images (r). **Getty Images:** Ina Peters (cr). **152 Getty Images:** Travel Ink (r). **153 Alamy Images:** Goss Images (r). **Getty Images:** De Agostini (cr). **163 Alamy Images:** blickwinkel (cr). **Photolibrary:** Vidal (r). **176 GAP Photos:** Howard Rice (cr). **Garden World Images:** Flowerphotos / Carol Sharp (l); MAP / Alain Guerrier (cl). **Getty Images:** Marc O'Finley (r). **177 Alamy Images:** Nigel Cattlin (l). **GAP Photos:** S&O (cr). **178 GAP Photos:** Howard Rice (r). **Getty Images:** Willard Clay (cr). **179 Corbis:** Mike Grandmaison / AgStock Images (l). **Getty Images:** De Agostini (cl). **Jennifer MacKenzie:** (r). **181 Getty Images:** Thomas Kitchin & Victoria Hurst. **182 Alamy Images:** Christine Whitehead (bl). **211 Alamy Images:** David Page (tr). **248 Getty Images:** Ashok Sinha (bl).

The following images are from the personal archive of Dick and James Strawbridge and are used with permission:
12 (ct); **13** (c, tr); **15** (tl, cl, bl); **16** (c, tr); **17** (r); **19** (cl); **26** (t, bl); **27** (l, tr, cr); **29** (bl, br); **31** (tl); **34** (cl, cr); **37** (tl, bl); **58**; **60** (tl); **65** (l); **78** (tl); **83** (tl); **101**; **108** (tr); **112** (tl, tc, bl, br) **115** (bl, cr); **118**; **123** (cr); **140** (cl); **142** (cr); **145** (cr, r); **147** (r); **152** (l); **157** (cl); **159** (br); **170–171**; **178** (cl); **191** (b); **194** (r); **196** (bl, br); **200** (tl, bl); **202** (bl); **203**; **214** (b); **216** (l, tr); **262** (c); **266** (l).

All other images © Dorling Kindersley. For further information, see www.dkimages.com

The complete guide to a simpler, greener life...

Many of us yearn to live more sustainably, in touch with nature and the seasons, and taking responsibility for what we consume and our impact on the world. This book shows how anyone can live a greener life—whether it's growing your own food in a suburban garden, beekeeping, or living off the land in a country dwelling.

There's something for everyone to try in this practical, easy to follow book. Traditional crafts and cheese- and bread-making sit alongside 21st-century techniques for reducing waste and harnessing wind and solar energy to power your home.

With authoritative advice, step-by-step guidance, and inspiring illustrations, *Self-Sufficiency for the 21st Century* will help you make simple changes that can have a major impact on your life.

Also published by DK

THE BEE BOOK

GROW ALL YOU CAN EAT IN 3 SQUARE FEET
Inventive ideas for growing food in a small space

FSC
www.fsc.org
MIX
Paper from responsible sources
FSC™ C018179

$22.95 USA
$29.95 Canada

ISBN 978-1-4654-5699-1   Printed in China

DK
www.dk.com

9 781465 456991   52295